MERCHANDISE BUYING AND MANAGEMENT

MERCHANDISE BUYING AND MANAGEMENT

John Donnellan

UNIVERSITY OF MASSACHUSETTS—AMHERST

FAIRCHILD PUBLICATIONS

New York

Cover Design: Dutton & Sherman Design
Interior Design: Lloyd Lemna Design

Copyright © 1996
Capital Cities Media, Inc.

Fairchild Publications is a division of Capital Cities Media, Inc.,
a Capital Cities/ABC Inc., company

Library of Congress Catalog Card Number: 95-61983

ISBN: 1-56367-052-6

GST R 133004424

Printed in the United States of America

BRIEF CONTENTS

EXTENDED CONTENTS

APPENDIX

PREFACE

Merchandise Buying and Management has been written for college-level courses covering the topics of retail buying and the management of retail inventories. Though industry restructuring has diminished the number of available retail buying positions, the topics covered in this book are equally important to store-level merchants responsible for space productivity, inventory turnover, and profitability. The topics are presented in the context of a contemporary retail environment where buyers are often responsible for fiscal management and product development, and store management assumes an increasingly active role in planning assortments and presenting merchandise. Advances in retail technology, such as space management, electronic data interchange, and point-of-sale systems, are discussed throughout the book with a focus of their impact on an ever-changing retail environment. A considerable amount of the of the text is dedicated to quantitative procedures for planning and analyzing sales, profit, and inventory. Written in a retail trade vernacular that reflects the perspective of an academician with twenty years experience in department and specialty store merchandising and operations, Merchandise Buying and Management can also serve as a handy reference for retail practitioners.

Sixteen chapters are organized into five parts. Summary points, a list of key terms and concepts, discussion questions, problems in chapters that include quantitative procedures, and suggested readings conclude each chapter. Each chapter is supported by company profiles of "real world" examples of the concepts covered in the chapter. Supplemental information linked to the chapter topics is featured in shaded boxes throughout the text. A glossary of key terms concludes the text.

The five chapters that compose part one explain the structure of the retail industry. *Retail Merchandising* covers the retailer's role in bringing consumer products from their point of production to their point of consumption, and the merchandising functions of a retail enterprise. *Retailing Formats* categorizes retail stores by their merchandising strategies, while *Retail Locations* covers the various settings in which retail stores operate. *Retail Growth and Expansion* is a discussion of the strategies that retailers adopt to grow and remain competitive in the marketplace. *Communicating with Consumers* looks at the various groups of consumers catered to by retail stores, and some of the techniques that retailers use to attract customers to their stores.

The three chapters of part two are product-oriented. *Fashion Merchandising* deals with the merchandising of fashion versus basic goods, while *Brands and Private Labels* deals with merchandising nationally distributed products versus products developed for exclusive distribution by a single retailer. *Resources of Merchandise* describes the wholesale marketplace and the various types of suppliers from which retailers buy merchandise.

Part three includes three chapters that deal with inventory performance and the fiscal aspects of retail merchandising. *Measures of Productivity* covers the critically important concepts of turnover and sales-per-square-foot. *Merchandising Accounting* interprets fundamental accounting concepts from a retail perspective, while determining the value of retail inventories as organizational assets is the topic of *Inventory Valuation*.

The three chapters in part four involve planning, purchasing, and pricing retail inventories. *Pricing* covers the concepts of markup and markdowns, as well as promotional pricing strategies. *Planning* covers several mathematical procedures for determining the amount of inventory that is needed to achieve an organization's sales goals. Price, delivery, and payment negotiations between retail buyers and their suppliers are covered in *Purchase Terms*.

Part five has two sections. *Merchandising Controls* is an explanation of various reports that are used to evaluate sales and inventory performance. *Store Layout and Merchandise Presentation* deals with some fundamental store design and merchandise presentation concepts with which both buyers and store managers should be familiar.

The *Instructor's Guide* for *Merchandise Buying and Management* includes chapter teaching tips, answers to end-of-chapter discussion questions and problems, additional discussion questions, as well as chapter examination questions in the form of multiple choice, fill-in, and true and false. The *Guide* cross-references the material in each chapter with two compatible textbooks published by Fairchild Publications: *Mathematics for Retail Buying, Revised 4th Edition* (1996) by Bette K. Tepper and Newton E. Godnick, and *Merchandising Mathematics* (1994) by Antigone Kotsiopoulos and Jikyeong Kang-Park.

Acknowledgments

I extend a sincere thanks to Gert Lashway of the Department of Consumer Studies at the University of Massachusetts who read the manuscript for this text so many times that she is now qualified to guest lecture on its content, and to Ann-Haggerty Jacobs of the

(Springfield, MA) *Union News*, my *ex-officio* advisor on syntax, semantics, and other linguistic topics. I am deeply indebted to Dr. Judy K. Miler of the University of Tennessee-Chatanooga, who served as a consultant on this project, and who made invaluable recomendations for manuscript improvements.

Readers selected by the Publisher were also very helpful. They included: Lou Canale, Genessee Community College; Sally Fails, University of Utah; Fay Gibson, University of North Carolina - Greensboro; Linda Good, Michigan State University; Cynthia Jasper, University of Wisconsin - Madison; Doris Kincade, Virginia Tech University; Rosetta LaFleur, University of Delaware - Newark; Elizabeth Mariotz, Philadelphia College of Textiles; Grady McClendon, Webber College; Anne Obarski, Art Institute of Pittsburgh; Shiretta Ownbey, Oklahoma State University; Kathleen Rees, University of Nebraska - Lincoln; Teresa Robinson, Middle Tennessee University; Holly Bastow Shoop, North Dakota State University - Fargo.

I am especially grateful for the support of the editorial staff at Fairchild Books and Visuals: for Pam Kirshen Fishman's vision and guidance during the initial stages of this project; for Ilana Scheiner's moral support; for Gabrielle Heitler's work on the visual and graphic components; and for David Jaenisch's artistic direction. I am most indebted to my editor, Olga Kontzias, for her guidance and tolerance throughout this project, and for sharing her unmatched expertise in the art of writing a textbook.

I also wish to thank: Tom Amerman, Parisian, Birmingham, AL; Jeffrey Aronofsky, National Yiddish Book Center, Amherst, MA; John Birt and Joy Purcell, Pier 1 Imports, Fort Worth, TX; Pat Carberry, J.C. Penney, Dallas TX; Dr. Mary Carsky and Dr. Margery Steinberg, University of Hartford, Hartford, CT; Lou Chiera. Sensormatic, Deerfield Beach, FL; Karen Cobb, Fieldrest Cannon, Kannapolis, NC ; Dave Dalieden, Weingarten Realty; Chester Dalzell, Direct Marketing Association, New York, NY; Noel Davidson, BodyTalk, Avon, CT: Joseph Deamarte and Brooke White, Nordstrom, Seattle, WA; Alex Dillard, Dillard's, Little Rock, AR; Elizabeth Doherty, Direct Selling Association, Washington, DC; Justin Dudley, Ingram Merchandising Services, LaVergne, TN; Attorney Edgar Dworsky, Attorney General's Office, Commonwealth of Massachusetts; Anne Eberhardt and Susan Arnot Heany, Elizabeth Arden, New York, NY; Susan Eich and Jacqueline Punch, Dayton Hudson Corporation, Minneapolis, MN; Barbara Firment, Jim Frasso, Sam Gatto, Jim Glime, Daryl Jamison, Dan Lafferty, Bob McAllister, Ray Minton, Dave Schuvie, Kmart, Troy, MI; Tom Grissom, County Seat, Dallas, TX; Rex Halfpenny, RGIS, Rochester, MI; Rebecca Harvey, Champs Sports, Bradenton, FL; Scott

Huston, The Fashion Association, New York; Robert Hutchinson, The Garr Consulting Group, NY; Pat Jackaway, West Hartford, CT; Dr. John Konarski, International Council of Shopping Centers; Attorney David Kirkman, Attorney General's Office, State of North Carolina; Don Klein, The Rouse Company, Columbia, MD; Stephanie Lazar and Valerie Lorzac, Gitano, New York, NY; Alan Loberstein, Merry-Go-Round Enterprises, Joppa, MD; Jayne Lopez, Mall of America, Bloomington, MN; Rick Ludwick, National Association of Wholesaler-Distributors; Mina Lussier, Zanna, Amherst, MA; Donna Magee, Burdines, Miami, FL; Lee Mattson, RCR, New York, NY; Geoff McNally, FRCH Design World, New York, NY; Jim Meisler, Retail Technologies International, Carmichael, CA; Maury Molod, The Pyramid Companies, Syracuse, NY: Jenifer Morton, Polo/Ralph Lauren, New York, NY; Peter Nevengloshy and Paulette Robers, Dun & Bradstreet, New Providence, NJ; Patrick O'Malley, United States Customs Service, Boston, MA; James O'Neill, Clover Stores, Philadelphia PA; Judy Petrucelli, Westfield, MA; Tom Redd, Comshare Retail, Wilmington, DE; Attorney Janet Reis, Attorney General's Office, State of Washington; Jean Reisinger, Federated Department Stores, Cincinatti, OH; Bruce Richardson, Andersen Consulting, New York, NY; Kevin Ryan, Ryan & Ryan Public Relations, Farmingdale, NY; Jeff Saitow, Nielsen Merchandising Solutions Group, Irving, TX; Jane Sanford, Macy's, New York, NY: Pamela Schauffler, Jacobson's, Jackson, MI; Mark Schneider and Stephanie Shern, Ernst & Young, New York, NY; David Shweky, Skaffles, New York, NY; Mary Smith, Linens 'n Things, Chicago, IL; Dr. James Smith, University of Massachusetts, Amherst, MA; Joe Staffieri, Lechmere, Woburn, MA; Ralph & Jean Steiger, Wilbraham, MA; Dr. Marilyn Stephens, Manufacturers' Representatives Educational Foundation; Nancy Strojny, Proctor & Gamble, Cincinnati, OH; Floyd Sullivan, Noritake; Eugenia Ulasawich, Saks Fifth Avenue, New York, NY; Jim van Mannen, DiLeo Hagan, New York, NY; Margaret Walch, CAUS, New York, NY; Gus Whalen, Warren Featherbone, Gainsville, GA; Diane Wilson, Gottschalks, Fresno, CA; Jan Wohlwend, The O'Connor Group, New York, NY.

JOHN DONNELLAN

chapter one

RETAIL MERCHANDISING

The task of assembling assortments that appeal to a retail organization's customers is a challenging proposition. Meeting this challenge requires knowledge of the products available in the marketplace, the incentives that motivate consumers to buy, and the ways in which retailers grow and become profitable. Fundamental to this knowledge is an understanding of the role that retailers play in channeling products from producers to consumers, and the ways in which retail enterprises are structured to perform their function. This chapter covers these two topics, as well as the personal qualifications necessary for individuals who wish to pursue careers in the exciting field of retail merchandising.

After you have read this chapter, you will be able to discuss:

The role of retailing in the marketing channel.

The merchandising functions of a retail enterprise.

The skills needed for success in retail merchandising careers.

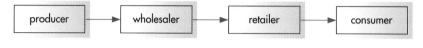

Figure 1.1

The marketing channel represents the flow of goods from producers to consumers.

THE MARKETING CHANNEL

The **marketing channel** represents the flow of goods from point of production to point of consumption. The model traces the distribution of a product from the manufacturer, or producer, to the final consumer, or ultimate user of the product. The marketing channel is sometimes referred to as the *distribution channel* or the *distribution pipeline.*

The marketing channel is composed of *channel members* that are classified according to the function that they perform. A **producer** converts materials (such as fabric) and/or component parts (such as zippers) into products (such as jackets). A **wholesaler** facilitates the distribution process by buying large quantities of goods from producers, and reselling smaller quantities to other channel members, a process called *breaking bulk.*[1] A **retailer** sells products and/or services to the final **consumers** who actually use the product, or derive personal benefit from the service. It is important to note that retailers sell services as well as products. Hairstylists and travel agents are service retailers. A bank that offers financial services to consumers, such as home mortgages, car loans, and checking accounts, performs a *retail* banking function. The same bank may provide similar services to businesses but, in so doing, performs a *commercial* banking function.

Wholesalers and retailers do not physically change the products that they buy and sell. Because they link producers and consumers, wholesalers and retailers are often called *channel intermediaries.* Retailers perform an indispensable function in the distribution of goods to final consumers. A consumer who pays $25 for a blouse is getting far more than fabric, buttons, and workmanship for her money. Inherent in the retail price are the costs associated with assembling a selection of blouses in an assortment of fabrications, styles, colors, brands, and prices at a single location. Without retailers as points of distribution, consumers would need to travel to production sources all over the world to purchase goods. A retail price also covers the cost of amenities, such as attractive facilities, salesperson assistance, and payment options that may include store charges, personal checks, or third-party charges, such as VISA and MasterCard. The channel interactions that occur between retailers of non-food products, such as apparel and home furnishings, and other channel members is the subject matter of this textbook.

Streamlining Distribution

Channel members are sometimes bypassed in the distribution process for the sake of expediency. Because of less handling, goods purchased by a retailer directly from a producer spend less time in the distribution

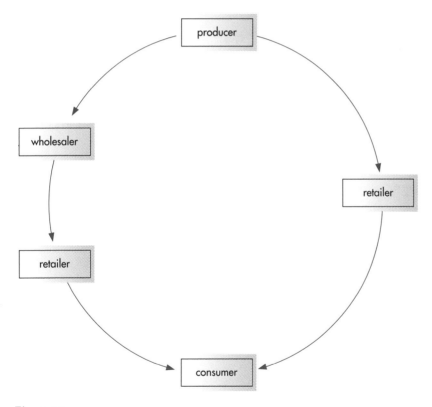

Figure 1.2

Retailers bypass wholesalers in the marketing channel to streamline the distribution process.

pipeline than goods distributed through a wholesaler. Time is a critical factor when dealing with perishable goods, such as food, or goods with short selling cycles, such as fashion apparel.

Cost is another reason why retailers bypass wholesalers. The selling price of a product increases as it passes through the marketing channel, since each channel member's selling price covers that member's operating costs and profit. A retailer circumvents wholesalers' operating costs and profits by buying directly from producers. The retailer then has the option of selling products more profitably, or passing the savings on to the consumers in the form of lower, more competitive prices. Wal-Mart, the world's largest retailer, is a model of streamlined distribution. By bypassing intermediaries, Wal-Mart profitably prices its offerings lower than many of its competitors.[2,3] Though buying directly from producers is advantageous for many retailers, wholesalers play an important role in the distribution of certain categories of merchandise to certain types of retailers, a topic covered in Chapter 8.[4]

Vertical Integration

Performing more than one channel function is called **vertical integration.** Companies vertically integrate for increased channel control, and for the fiscal advantages associated with performing multiple channel functions. Producers that sell their product lines directly to consumers through **manufacturer-sponsored specialty stores,** or *signature stores,* are vertically integrated. These stores facilitate direct contact between producers and consumers and permit producers to retain control over the presentation and sale of their product lines. Some producers also use signature stores as laboratories to test new items. Coach produces a line of fine handbags and small leather goods distributed through prestige department and specialty stores.[5] Coach also operates an international retail division of more than 100 stores. Laura Ashley and Liz Claiborne are other examples of signature stores.

Retailers vertically integrate when they develop their own product lines for exclusive distribution in their stores, a merchandising concept called *private labeling* covered in Chapter 7. The Limited is a vertically integrated retailer. Mast Industries is an operating division of The Limited, Inc. that develops and sources many of the products sold at stores owned by The Limited, Inc., including Abercrombie & Fitch and Structure.

Figure 1.3

Liz Claiborne and Laura Ashley are vertically integrated producers that operate their own specialty stores.

Companies that vertically integrate risk alienating other channel members. Producers that operate manufacturer-sponsored specialty stores compete directly with the retailers that sell their products through conventional distribution channels. Similarly, producers resent retailers that develop private label goods that are often imitations of products that they have painstakingly developed.[6,7]

RETAIL ORGANIZATIONAL STRUCTURES

A **table of organization,** or *organizational chart,* is a diagram that depicts a company's corporate structure. An organizational chart reflects the various functions performed by an organization, and the way in which organizational activities are *departmentalized,* or grouped into organizational units. A table of organization defines the hierarchy, or *chain of command,* in an organization, as well as lines of communication and responsibility. A table of organization is sometimes called an *organizational pyramid.* Chairman of the board, president, chief executive officer (CEO), chief fiscal officer (CFO), chief operating officer (COO), and vice-president are some of the *top management* titles that appear at the top of a table of organization. These functions have a broader scope of authority, responsibility, and salary than lower-level functions.

As organizations grow, functions with a broad range of responsibility are often split into more specialized functions. An apparel retailer may split the function of *buyer of junior sportswear* into two specialized functions, *buyer of tops* and *buyer of bottoms,* when business reaches the point that it requires, and can support, two distinct positions. In general, tables of organization of large retail organizations have many specialized functions, while the tables of organization of small retail organizations have fewer, more general functions.

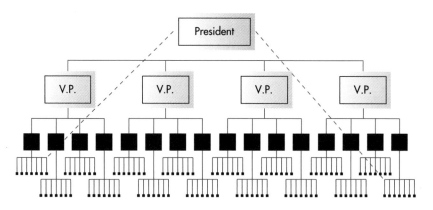

Figure 1.4

A table of organization depicts a company's corporate structure and chain of command.

In 1927, Paul Mazur, an investment banker, was commissioned by the National Retail Dry Goods Association, now the National Retail Federation, to develop a model organizational structure for retail stores. Mazur proposed a table of organization with four major functions:

- *Merchandising* Responsible for procuring, or buying, merchandise and reselling it. These duties were performed primarily by *buyers.*
- *Publicity* Responsible for stimulating sales through advertising and display.
- *Control* Responsible for the fiscal functions that are typical of most organizations, such as accounts payable, accounts receivable, and payroll.
- *Store management* Responsible for the sales support functions, facilities management, and the merchandise processing functions of receiving, checking, and marking merchandise upon delivery.[8]

Though formulated decades ago, Mazur's structure is still the core of most contemporary retail tables of organization. However, the growth of retail enterprises, and the need for a higher degree of specialization have necessitated several enhancements to Mazur's original plan. The territorial expanse of multiunit operations spurred the creation of geographically defined hierarchies of store *regions* and *districts.* As retailers began to recognize employees as an important organizational resource, *personnel*, originally a store management function, evolved into a separate organizational function called *human resources.* Computer technology fostered the development of *Information Systems* (IS) as a distinct organizational function.[9]

The Separation of Buying and Selling

In Mazur's day, most retail organizations were single-store operations where buying and selling occurred under one roof. Because Mazur identified *buying* and *selling* as related activities, he proposed a merchandising function that included responsibility for merchandise procurement, as well as selling-floor activities, such as customer service and stock keeping.

As single-unit retail operations evolved into multiunit chains, buying became a centralized, corporate-level function performed remotely from stores. The corporate merchandising division's interaction with

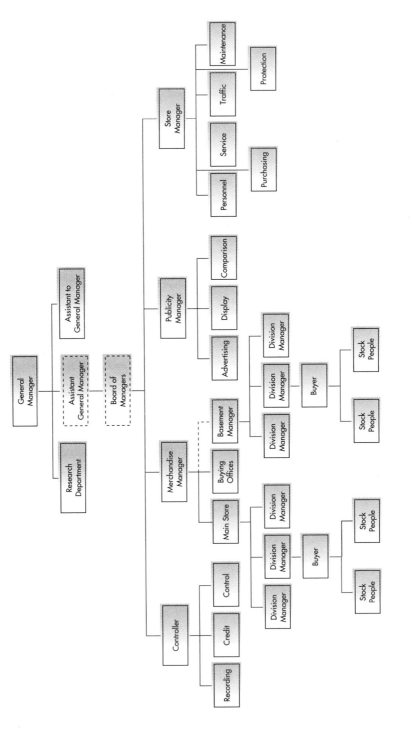

Figure 1.5

The table of organization developed for retail stores by Paul Mazur in 1927.

stores diminished, and the store-level merchandising activities once orchestrated by buyers became the responsibility of store management. Today, the **store operations,** or *store administration,* function in a retail organization is a descendent of Mazur's store management function, but a far cry from the facilities management function that Mazur originally proposed. The contemporary store operations function is likely to include considerable merchandise-related responsibilities, such as assortment planning, merchandise presentation, and inventory management.

Line and Staff Functions

Organizational functions can be grouped into two categories based on the type of activities performed. A **line function** performs mainstream activities fundamental to an organization's mission. Buying and selling merchandise are a retailer's mainstream activities. Thus, merchandising and store operations are a retailer's line functions. These functions are sometimes referred to as the *store line* and the *buying line.* A **staff function** supports or advises line functions and/or other staff functions. A retail organization's legal department is a staff function that supports both line and staff functions by performing activities such as negotiating store leases, and interpreting legislation concerning the use of the term *sale* in advertising.

Authority is clearly defined through a chain of command in a line function. Within the store operations function, an assistant store manager reports to a store manager, who reports to a district manager, who reports to a regional manager, who reports to a director of stores. Staff authority is not as clearly defined as line authority. Though the managers of staff functions have authority within their departments, staff managers merely "advise" the managers of other functions without having formal decision-making authority over them. Staff managers sometimes have *functional authority* over other managers in matters that involve their areas of expertise.

The day-to-day operation of a retail organization requires frequent interaction between staff and line functions. Incongruous strategies of managers responsible for those functions can be the source of organizational conflict. Though the ultimate goal of every retail organization is to make a profit, line and staff managers sometimes adopt different strategies to attain this goal. A store manager maximizes profit by employing a competent selling staff. A corporate attorney maximizes profit by avoiding lawsuits. The attorney may contest a store manager's decision to terminate a sixty-year-old sales associate for incompetence, recognizing the potential for an age-discrimination suit.

Organizational conflict can also occur between line functions in a retail organization. Unrealized sales objectives are a frequent source of conflict, as the following scenario portrays:

> The dress department of a store within a chain of stores fell short of its monthly sales goal. When asked to explain the shortfall, the store manager listed the following reasons:
>
> - Selections are inappropriate for the store's customers. The store caters to career women, yet casual looks dominate the assortment.
> - Selections are too high-priced. A soft regional economy and the arrival of off-price competition in the area necessitate lower-priced assortments.
> - Size assortments are skewed. There is an overabundance of larger sizes (12s and 14s), and too few smaller sizes (4s and 6s).
>
> Based on observations made during periodic visits to the store, the buyer retorted with the following reasons for the sales shortfall:
>
> - The goods are poorly presented. Looks are not pulled together by color, fabric, or vendor. Goods wrinkled in shipment are not steamed. Customers are frustrated by racks of sale goods that are not sized.
> - Staffing is inadequate. In an effort to conserve expenses, the store manager reduced the selling staff, thus hampering customer service. Also, newly hired sales associates are poorly trained and unmotivated.
>
> In essence, the buyer and the store manager have each assumed a "not my fault" stance, and blamed each other for the sales shortfall.

Conflict between the store line and the buying line has become legendary in many retail organizations. Some organizations promote empathy between store operations and merchandising by recruiting candidates for corporate positions from stores, hoping that common roots will yield greater cooperation. Similarly, many department store executive training programs include apprenticeships within both store operations and merchandising, regardless of ultimate career objective.

RETAIL MERCHANDISING

The term *merchandising* has many connotations. In the apparel industry, merchandising involves the planning, development, and presentation of a product line suitable for a firm's intended customers.[10] Mazur cited a classic definition of merchandising for the retail industry: "to have the right goods, at the right time, in the right quantities, and at the right prices."[11] In a broad context, *retail merchandising* includes all of the activities directly or indirectly associated with procuring and reselling merchandise. In a narrow context, retail merchandising embraces only the merchandise procurement function. In this textbook, **retail merchandising** will be defined in the broader context to include all of the activities associated with buying, pricing, presenting, and promoting merchandise. Though some merchandising functions are common to all retailers, the job titles associated with these functions differ from one organization to another. Though job titles cannot be defined consistently for all retailers, the following titles and responsibilities are common to many retailers.[12]

Corporate-Level Merchandising Functions

Corporate-level merchandising functions are performed within a central organization, or corporate office, for all stores. Buying is the main function of a corporate merchandising division. Traditionally buyers were responsible for a diverse group of activities that included inventory planning, selection, and allocation. However, the growth of large retail chains has fostered greater specialization in executing the buying function. Many retailers have split buying into four specialized functions: buying, planning, distribution, and product development.

A **buyer** buys and prices merchandise for resale. A buyer's challenge is to compose assortments that are appealing to the organization's intended customers, and to obtain the best possible goods at the lowest possible prices. Buyers explore the offerings of the wholesale marketplace by visiting domestic and foreign markets, and through frequent interaction with producers' sales agents. Buyers are also responsible for pricing goods low enough to be competitive with other retailers, yet high enough to meet the organization's profit objectives.

The magnitude of a buyer's responsibility is defined by annual sales volume, and, as might be expected, the buyer of a $100 million department is paid a higher salary than the buyer of a $1 million department. The importance of a buying position may also be linked to the complexity of the wholesale market or the risk associated with purchase decisions. A purchase decision for fashion goods, such as dresses, involves higher risk than a purchase decision for basic goods, such as

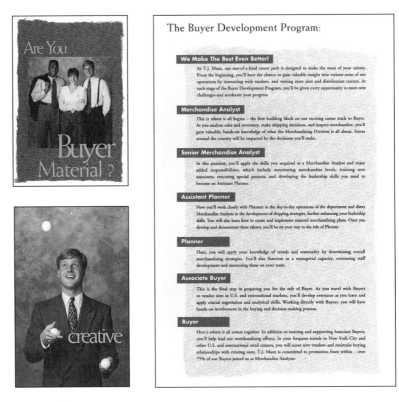

Figure 1.6

Corporate-level merchandising responsibilities at T.J. Maxx include distribution, planning, and buying functions.

hosiery. Buying decisions for fashion goods are based on uncertain predictions of consumer acceptance of new styles. An inaccurate prediction will result in poor sales, and the need to sell off the inventory at profit-threatening prices. Buying decisions for basics are often just reorders of historically best-selling brands, styles, colors, and sizes.

A **planner** projects sales and inventories based on an analysis of sales history, current market trends, and the organization's performance objectives. Planning is a statistical function that requires astute analytical aptitude and the ability to make multidimensional decisions. A **distributor** allocates arriving shipments of merchandise to individual stores based on each store's capacity, current sales trends, and inventory levels. Often called *allocators*, distributors are a critical link between the corporate merchandising division and stores. A **product developer** determines which products can be developed internally

Company Profile 1.1

Since 1902, Macy's at Herald Square has been as much a symbol of New York as the Empire State Building, Yankee Stadium, or the Brooklyn Bridge. The "largest store in the world" is the cornerstone of the 187-store chain that became a division of Federated Department Stores in 1995.

For many years, Macy's grouped its stores into geographic regions each operated independently of each other. The buying function in each region was performed in a manner that was typical of most department stores in that buyers were responsible for buying and allocating goods to stores. Frequent store visits and telephone conversations reinforced communication between Macy's buying line and store line.

Additional stores and the consolidation of regions weakened this communication, however. As buyers became responsible for more stores, their visits to stores became less frequent. Ultimately, they began to rely on sales volume as the major criterion for allocating goods. In essence, low-volume stores received the same assortments as high-volume stores, but in smaller quantities. Though a seemingly sound concept, the strategy erroneously assumed that similar sales volume is indicative of similar customer profiles. The result was that store line merchandisers spent considerable time on the phone with buyers attempting to fine tune their assortments to suit their customers' needs. Buyers spent considerable time redistributing goods from one store to another though costly inter-store transfers.

Macy's resolved the shortcomings of this system with an organizational strategy called buyer-planner-store merchandising, or BPS. The concept involved the creation of a planning function as an organizational link between Macy's buying line and store line. In essence, planners serve as advocates for stores, working with store-line merchandisers to plan assortments on a store-by-store basis. Planners react to local trends by adjusting on-orders, editing slow-sellers, and building inventories for businesses that demonstrate growth potential.

BPS is also advantageous to buyers. Planners provide information to facilitate buying decisions, such as the minimum number of units needed to make an adequate presentation of an assortment in a store, and the timing of deliveries relative to climate differences by store. Because buyers spend less time allocating merchandise, they spend more time in the market planning assortments and negotiating lucrative deals with their suppliers. In essence, BPS ensures that the "right" merchandise, is in the "right" store, at the "right" time.

with the store's private label. Product developers establish specifications for the design, production, and packaging of these goods. They are also responsible for contracting producers to manufacture the goods according to the specifications.

The interdependence of the activities of buyers, planners, distributors, and product developers requires harmonious interaction in the performance of all four functions. In some retail organizations, the planning and distribution functions are combined. In small, conventionally structured organizations, the buyer is responsible for planning and distribution, as well as buying. The product development function exists only in stores that engage in private labeling. Many organizations use titles such as *senior* planner or *lead* analyst to indicate seniority or level of responsibility. As the title suggests, an *assistant buyer* assists a buyer and is often being groomed for a buying position. An *associate buyer* is one step closer to the goal of buyer, and often assumes responsibility for buying a category of goods within the buyer's total area of responsibility.

Related merchandising responsibilities are grouped into organizational units called *departments*. Related departments are grouped into *divisions*. Divisions and departments are identified by product line. A *men's division* is composed of several *men's departments*, such as men's outerwear, men's suits and sport coats, men's designer collections, and men's accessories. A **divisional merchandise manager** (DMM) is responsible for a merchandise division. The DMM monitors the sales, inventories, and assortments of the departments within the division to ensure consistency with the organization's merchandising and profit objectives. DMMs report to a **general merchandise manager** (GMM) who manages a group of related merchandise divisions. A GMM is typically at the vice-president, senior management level. Organizational hierarchies for planning and distribution often parallel organizational hierarchies for buying.

Visual merchandising and fashion direction are two other corporate-level merchandising functions. **Visual merchandising** is responsible for store decor, signage, display, fixturing, and standards for presenting merchandise. Visual merchandising works with buyers to develop *planograms*, or floor layouts, as well as with store planning to design new stores or renovate existing ones. A **fashion director** is responsible for researching dominant color, style, and design trends in apparel, accessories, and home furnishings markets. The fashion direc-

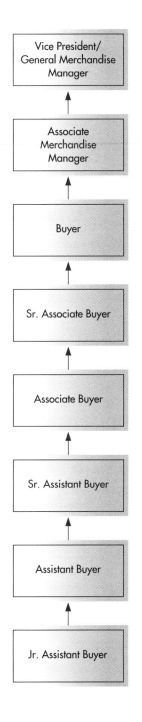

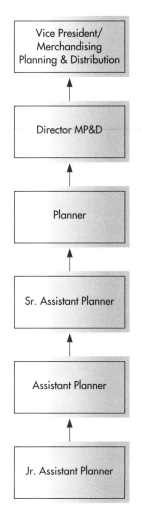

Figure 1.7

Organizational hierarchies for planning and distribution often parallel organizational hierarchies for buying. *County Seat Stores, Dallas, TX.*

tor communicates this information to buyers so that they can strategically select assortments consistent with current trends.

Store-Level Merchandising Functions

In general, store-level merchandising ensures that merchandise is presented on the selling floor in a manner that is consistent with a company's visual standards, and that inventory levels and assortments are appropriate for the store's merchandising sales objectives. Store merchandising functions sometimes include responsibility for operational activities as well. A considerable amount of communication occurs between store and corporate merchandising functions.

A **general manager,** or *store manager,* is ultimately responsible for the merchandising and operation of a store. A general manager is sometimes assisted by an operations manager, a human resource manager, and/or a **store merchandise manager.** Large stores sometimes have more than one store merchandise manager, each responsible for

Figure 1.8

Store-level merchandising responsibilities at Lord & Taylor.

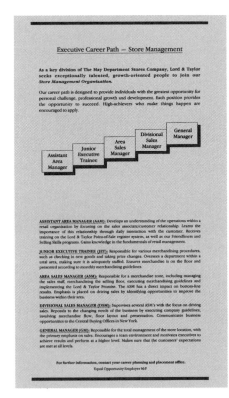

specific merchandise divisions. There is little consistency among the titles for this function. Titles synonymous with store merchandise manager include *divisional sales manager* and *assistant store manager of merchandising.* A **department manager,** or *sales manager,* usually reports to a store merchandise manager, and is responsible for an area defined by department or division. This position usually includes both merchandising and operational responsibilities.

The store merchandising hierarchy just described is typical of large stores: a department store, such as Macy's, or a full-line discounter, such as Kmart. The management structure of a specialty store, such as The Gap, is much simpler, composed of a store manager, and one or more assistant managers. The responsibilities associated with these positions are general in nature, encompassing both merchandising and operational duties.

Multistore retailers have a geographically defined organizational hierarchy that links the stores to the corporate office. A **district manager** is responsible for a group of stores located within a defined geographic area. The number of stores in a district varies from one retail organization to another, and even within the same organization depending on the distance between stores. In the densely stored areas of the Northeast, a district may include twelve stores within a fifty mile radius. A district in the Southwest may have eight stores within a 100 mile radius. The amount of time required to travel to the stores in the Southwest is compensated for by responsibility for fewer stores. A **regional manager** supervises a group of district managers and reports to a corporate level person, such as a vice-president or director of stores. Some organizations link stores to the corporate office with only one managerial level, typically the regional level.

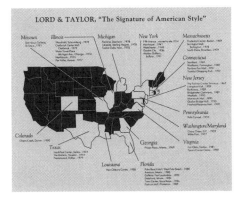

Figure 1.9

Geographically dispersed stores are grouped into hierarchies of regions and districts to link stores to the corporate office.

Since merchandising activities occur at both store and corporate levels, the topics covered in this textbook are relevant to students wishing to pursue either corporate merchandising or store administration careers. Though industry restructuring has diminished the number of corporate merchandising career opportunities, considerable opportunities remain for store management executives with merchandising savvy. Knowledge of retail merchandising is also important for students interested in retail sales promotion, shopping center administration, or any phase of the distribution of consumer goods.

Qualifications for Merchandising Positions

There is rigorous competition for the highest paid and most gratifying retail merchandising positions. Merchandising functions at all levels of an organization require dynamic, productive individuals, challenged by aggressive goals, and committed to standards of excellence. Specific

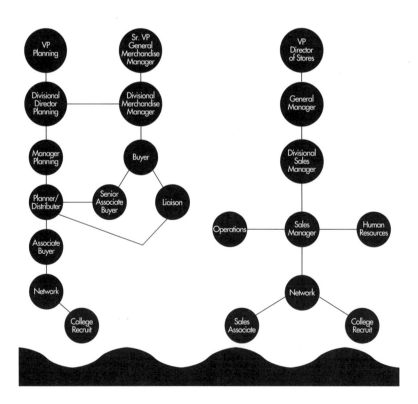

Figure 1.10

The store line and buying line at Burdines.

We only hire one kind of person. THE BEST

At Venture Stores, everyone we hire is a minority. They're an elite member of a small group; the very best in retailing. As one of the Midwest's and Southwest's fastest-growing retail chains, we see people for only one thing, their talent for keeping us on the leading edge of retailing. We're looking for talented people who want to make a big difference with a retail leader for the following opportunities:

Buyers
Assistant Buyers
Merchandise Planners
Merchandise Distributors
Co-Managers
Assistant Store Managers

Send or fax your resume to: **VENTURE STORES;**

Attn: Executive Recruitment; 2001 E. Terra Lane;

P.O. Box 110; Dept: DSN; O'Fallon, MO 63366-0110.

Fax: (314) 281-6049. Or call 1-800-876-7786.

EOE/Venture is committed to a diverse work culture.

//Venture

share our SUCCESS

It's hard not to get excited about Talbots impressive growth and the dynamic people who make Talbots such a great place to work. Consider the following positions:

Product Development

Talbots New York based product office is currently seeking experienced Product Development professionals to share the success and excitement of Talbots private label brand development. Qualified candidates will have proven background in interpreting trends and developing product. Ability to create and implement product strategies, knowledge of fabrications and color, and negotiating skills are also required.

Candidates must be available for travel. Current opportunities include entry-level Assistants up to Product Managers. Preferred categories include Accessories and Petites.

Sourcing

Our Hingham, Massachusetts Corporate Headquarters is currently seeking experienced sourcing professionals. Responsibilities include placement of private label import purchases with established manufacturers as well as price negotiation and follow-through of all product to final delivery. Thorough knowledge of the Far East and its markets in addition to experience in children's apparel production (wovens, cut and sewn knits, sweaters) required. Accessories experience a plus.

Please forward resume to: **Talbots, Department SW, 175 Beal Street, Hingham, MA 02043.** Talbots is an equal opportunity employer committed to diversifying its organization.

Talbots

We support cultural diversity in our workplace.

STORE MANAGERS
ESCADA

ESCADA is a leading designer of upscale women's fashion. If you're a strong leader with excellent interpersonal skills and 4 years of upscale retail management experience, we offer exciting opportunities at our ESCADA stores in CHESTNUT HILL, MASSACHUSETTS and HONOLULU, HAWAII.

We will look to you to expand our clientele base and manage all aspects of store operations, including expense controls, merchandising, marketing, sales volume and tracking, visual presentation and customer relations.

ESCADA provides a generous compensation package, excellent benefits and a team-spirited environment. If you are qualified, please mail/fax your resume, indicating location of interest, to:

ESCADA (USA) INC.
Att: Human Resources
10 Mulholland Drive
Hasbrouck Heights, NJ 07604
FAX: 201-462-6091

Equal Opportunity Employer

WE'RE LOOKING FOR STYLE AND SUBSTANCE

The Florida Store needs a Home Fashion Director to join the team!

We're Burdines, a division of Federated Department Stores and we cover the state with 42 stores. As the fashion leader of our home division, you'll have direct impact on merchandising and marketing. Responsibilities include:

- Fashion trends/color direction
- Market coverage with merchant organization
- Product/theme development
- Floor presentation & visual concepts
- Import & decorative accessory buying
- Buying responsibility for Furniture floor accessories

We offer competitive salary, a comprehensive benefits package, growth potential based on proven performance. And, we're pleased to provide a drug-free, smoke-free working environment for every associate.

Send us a resume or-- if yours isn't yet updated-- a brief letter of inquiry. Only prospective candidates will be contacted for an interview. Submit to:

Executive Recruitment--BW
22 East Flagler Street
Miami, Florida 33131
Fax: (305) 577-2372, EOE

Burdines
THE FLORIDA STORE

Accessories Buyer

The right accessories add polish and finish to any style. A wide black leather belt...Patterned stockings... A knockout pair of earrings -- It's the one or two accessories that turn a simple outfit into a fashion statement.

As an Accessories Buyer with Montgomery Ward, your ability to spot item, design and color trends and your strong analytical and financial skills will be important as you help us create a winning accessories mix.

Your background should include 5 years retail buying experience with at least three years in accessories. Bachelor's degree preferred.

If you're eager to play an important role in one of retailing's most impressive success stories, mail or FAX your resume, including salary history, to: Montgomery Ward, Attn: D. Spaulding, B-3, One Montgomery Ward Plaza, Chicago, IL 60671. FAX: (312) 467-3828.

Montgomery Ward
THE BRAND NAME SAVINGS STORE
Equal Opportunity Employer M/F

Figure 1.11

Employment ads for retail merchandising positions that have appeared in retail trade publications.

Figure 1.12

Jacobson's job description and performance appraisal for a buyer.

JACOBSON'S

JOB DESCRIPTION
Buyer

Responsibilities:

To achieve established gross margin goals by effective inventory management and careful monitoring of sales, pricing, turnover, and markdowns.

To develop a constant awareness of current market trends and offerings.

To cultivate positive relationships with vendors.

To seek opportunities for new business.

To monitor our competitive position through careful observation of our competitors' pricing, advertising, and assortments.

To offer merchandise assortments consistent with our customers' quest for value, quality, and fashion.

To work cohesively with

Visual Merchandising in developing planograms.

Store Planning in determining fixture requirements for new or renovated stores.

Advertising in executing a multimedia marketing strategy.

To act as mentor to subordinates, helping them to grow by regular counseling and coaching.

To communicate effectively within the buying organization and with stores.

To implement practices to improve productivity and efficiency.

Organizational Relationships:

Reports to a Divisional Merchandise Manager. Works closely with Advertising, Finance, Logistics, MIS, and Stores.

Cultural Requirements:

Ability to function as a team player and to focus on the success of the total organization.

Position Requirement:

Fundamental knowledge of marketing and retail management generally acquired by the completion of a related four-year degree college program, plus 3–4 years of experience in merchandising. Multiple category experience preferred. Store experience a plus. Demonstrated competence in profit and loss management.

Job Demands:

Work environment is a typical office setting. Heavy travel required.

---

qualifications for merchandising positions differ from one retail organization to another depending on factors such as a company's size, culture, merchandise mix, and operational strategy. Though there is no set of qualifications universally required by all retailers, the following summarizes a few skills that major retailers have cited as fundamental to success in their organizations.[12]

JACOBSON'S

JOB PERFORMANCE APPRAISAL
Buyer

Merchandise Selection and Distribution

Selects merchandise consistent with Jacobson's standards for quality, taste level, and pricing structure.

Maintains appropriate breadth and depth of assortments.

Distributes merchandise to reflect each store's current selling trend and inventory status.

Researches and tests new vendors.

Develops new products.

Market Relations

Represents and promotes Jacobson's effectively in the market.

Maintains relationships with vendors that are conducive to Jacobson's long-term trade advantage.

Negotiates effectively to maintain the most desirable terms and concessions.

Works effectively with U.S. and overseas buying offices.

Planning and Analysis

Effectively uses the tools of the Merchandise Information Office to identify inventory imbalances among stores.

Reacts to positive selling trends.

Monitors and updates open-to-buy.

Advertising and Sales Promotion

Selects appropriate merchandise for advertised events.
Purchases to cover advertised merchandise.
Develops creative special events, including shows of collections, personal appearances.

Communication

Visits stores regularly.

Keeps stores informed of new merchandise, fashion trends, and presentation techniques through buyer's bulletins and videotapes.

Communicates well with stores and responds quickly to their needs.

Accepts constructive criticism well.

Procedural Detail

Prioritizes work well.

Responds in a timely manner when merchandise is ready to disposition in the Distribution Center.

Accurately executes purchase orders, key recs, returns-to-vendors, markdowns, and other merchandise control documents.

Other

Assists the Divisional Merchandise Manager in training and developing assistant buyers and executive trainees.

Relates effectively to subordinates and peers.

Performs the duties assigned by the Merchandise Manager necessary to assure Jacobson's continued growth.

Decision-Making Skills Retail merchandising requires the ability to evaluate information from multiple sources, as a basis for making decisions with far-reaching implications. Planners determine the weighted importance and interaction of market trends, the economy, competition, and consumer behavior to project the amount of inventory that a buyer should purchase. An understated projection will yield inventories that are too low to meet the organization's sales potential. An overstated projection will result in excessive inventories, a poor investment of the company's fiscal resources.

Communication Skills The ability to communicate effectively, both orally and in writing, with people inside and out of the organization is fundamental to the success of a merchandising executive. Conveying ideas to superiors, directives to subordinates, and negotiating price, payment arrangements, and advertising allowances with suppliers are just a few of the instances in which carefully honed communication skills are a necessity.

Analytical Skills Computers have reduced the amount of computational and clerical activities associated with merchandising functions, allowing merchandising executives to devote more time to analyzing reports of sales, inventory, and profit. Physical remoteness from stores has increased reliance on these reports. A single store merchant can "eyeball" inventory and see that "mediums are low," and that it's time to reorder. In large multiunit operations, this type of stock replenishment decision is based on reports that define inventory status quantitatively.[13]

Computer Skills Merchandising executives use computers to generate orders, retrieve sales and inventory information, and communicate by electronic mail. Though it is impossible to be exposed to all of the available hardware and software with merchandising applications, a fundamental understanding of computer capabilities, the keyboard, and basic computer terminology is highly useful to the aspiring merchandising executive.

Organizational Skills Merchandising positions require careful orchestration of the human and fiscal resources of the organization. The administrative skills used to manage time, develop procedures, and prioritize tasks are critical to the success of a merchandising executive.

BLOOMINGDALE'S

E X E C U T I V E T R A I N I N G

Merchandise Math:

Learn the formulas for calculating markup, markdown, and the components of profit.

Purchase Order Management:

Follow an order from the moment the buyer writes it to the moment the vendor receives payment for the goods.

Consumer Buying Habits:

Learn how different merchandise appeals to different customers and how factors such as climate and the economy affect spending.

Forecasting:

Learn how to identify sales opportunities and how to profile a customer by lifestyle.

Buying Decisions:

Learn the buying decision process and how a buyer decides what's hot and what's not. Learn how advertising and visual presentation drive sales.

Merchandise Presentation:

learn how the placement of merchandise in a department affects sales and how to use various types of fixtures to maximize sales.

Supervisory Skills:

Develop effective communication skills, time management skills and how to coach and motivate others.

Figure 1.13

Many retail organizations, such as Bloomingdale's, have training programs to groom aspiring young executives.

BUYERS: ENDANGERED SPECIES?

Acrystal ball has always been a key piece of equipment for buyers. The job has involved predicting the future in fine detail and then committing millions of dollars to those prognostications. In recent years, however, computer-based inventory management systems capable of planning sales, analyzing trends, reacting to business opportunities, and replenishing inventory levels are replacing the crystal ball as the buyer's abacus, and rewriting the buyer's job description. The decisions buyers once made by using instinct, taste, business acumen, and knowledge of the marketplace are now dictated by rows of neatly arranged numbers in a computer printout making the buyer's job less intuitive and more precise. Technology has enabled a buyer to make better decisions with less reliance on the crystal ball.

However, like so many of life's pleasures, inventory management technology represents the proverbial "double-edge sword" for many buyers. An increased stress level is associated with the buyer's position in that constant knowledge of inventory levels at every store location requires buyers to react quickly to balance inventory inequities and to replenish inventories that are low. Some go so far as to say that automatic order replenishment systems make the buyer's job redundant, foreseeing that the buying function will eventually be eliminated in some stores.

The news is not all bad for buyers. Some organizations have extracted the quantitative aspects from the buying function and have created merchandise analysts who perform the "number crunching" functions involved with planning and distributing inventory. This frees the buyer to concentrate on the qualitative aspects of the job and to devote exclusive attention to what most buyers do best: buy. The buyer is still responsible for getting the best merchandise, at the best price, and at the best delivery terms. There are some judgmental decisions that buyers make that a computer can't perform, such as making the maximum use of fixture and floor space, developing merchandise assortments, tailoring those assortments to individual markets, and determining the best items for advertising and promotions.

Inventory management systems have fostered the development of strong partnerships between retailers and their suppliers, with suppliers assuming greater responsibility for maintaining favorable inventory positions in stores and eliminating the need for buyers to place orders for replenishment merchandise. However, it is the buyers who are

continued

*Adapted from:
Hartnett, Michael.
(September 1993).
Buyers: Endangered
Species?* Stores.
pp. 53–54.

Buyers: Endangered Species? *continued*
responsible for cultivating these relationships. The responsibility associated with this task is significant, since poorly chosen or poorly executed alliances can lead to a disastrous selling season plagued by poor sales and gross margin.

Without question, technology has forced many retailers to restructure their merchandising function, and to redefine the jobs that buyers do, but realizing that, once in a while, buyers still need to pull out a crystal ball.

Mobility is a requirement for some merchandising positions. Large multistore organizations sometimes require store executives to relocate and buyers must be willing to travel to domestic and foreign markets. Though company-paid travel adds to the attractiveness of a buying position, the travel is often not as glamorous as it seems. Buying trips allow little time for sightseeing and other recreational activities, since there is typically much to accomplish in a short time period. Some feel that good taste is a qualification for merchandising positions, especially in the area of fashion goods. However, the ability to translate customers' tastes into merchandise assortments is more important than personal taste. Upon reviewing a fashion jewelry line, a buyer of impeccable taste once declared to the sales representative: "This is the ugliest, most ostentatious line that I've seen this season! I'll take it. My customers will love it!"

Many organizations have structured training programs to groom aspiring merchandising executives to fill projected employment needs. Trainees are promoted from entry-level positions to more advanced levels of responsibility upon successful completion of various levels of training. Because of the desirability of these programs, competition for entrance into them is fierce, and the result of an intense screening process. Large retail organizations are more likely than smaller companies to have training programs than smaller ones.

SUMMARY POINTS

- The marketing channel represents the flow of goods from point of production to point of consumption.

- Marketing channel members are sometimes bypassed in the distribution process in the interest of time or cost.
- Performing more than one function in the marketing channel is called vertical integration.
- A table of organization depicts a company's corporate structure and defines an organization's lines of communication and responsibility.
- Paul Mazur proposed a table of organization for retailers that included four major functions: merchandising, publicity, control, and store management.
- Line functions are fundamental to an organization's mission. Staff functions are support functions. Merchandising and store operations are a retailer's line functions.
- Retail merchandising includes all of the activities associated with buying, pricing, presenting, and promoting merchandise at both store and corporate level.
- Merchandise procurement responsibilities are defined by four functions: planning, buying, distribution, and product development.
- Store-level merchandising ensures that merchandise is presented in a manner consistent with a company's visual merchandising standards and that inventory levels and assortments are appropriate for the store's customers and sales objectives.
- Decision-making skills, communication skills, analytical skills, computer skills, and organizational skills are necessary for those pursuing merchandising careers.

KEY TERMS AND CONCEPTS

buyer	line function	store operations
consumer	manufacturer-sponsored	store merchandise
department manager	specialty store	manager
divisional merchandise	marketing channel	table of organization
manager	planner	vertical integration
distributor	producer	visual merchandising
district manager	product developer	wholesaler
fashion director	regional manager	
general manager	retailer	
general merchandise	retail merchandising	
manager	staff function	

FOR DISCUSSION

1. Discuss some of the disadvantages of separating the buying and selling functions in a retail store.
2. If you have ever held a position in a retail store, discuss the interactions that you may have observed between line and staff managers, or between store operations and corporate merchandising.
3. Which corporate merchandising position most entices you? Which store merchandising position most entices you? Why?
4. Match your aptitudes to the qualifications for success in retail merchandising. How can you cultivate yourself in the area(s) in which you have assessed yourself as weak?

SUGGESTED READINGS

Evans, Joel R. & Barman, Barry. (1994). *Marketing.* New York: Macmillan.

Kinnear, Thomas C. & Bernhardt, Kenneth L. (1990). *Principles of Marketing.* New York: HarperCollins.

Lamb, Charles W., Hair, Joseph F. & McDaniel, Carl. (1992). *Principles of Marketing.* Cincinnati:South-Western.

Levy, Micahel & Weitz, Barton. (1995). *Retailing Management.* Chicago: Irwin.

Pride, William M. & Ferrell, O.C. (1993). *Marketing Concepts and Strategies.* Boston: Houghton Mifflin.

Stoner, James & Freeman, R. Edward. (1994). *Management.* Englewood Cliffs, NJ: Prentice Hall.

ENDNOTES

1. Levy, Michael & Weitz, Barton. (1995). *Retailing Management.* Chicago: Irwin. p. 8.
2. Dentzer, Susan. (1995, May 22). Death of a middleman. *U.S. News & World Report.* p. 56.
3. Stalk, George, Evans, Philip & Shulman, Lawrence. (March–April 1992). Competing capabilities: The new rules of corporate strategy. *Harvard Business Review.* pp. 57–69.
4. Dolan, Patrick & Samek, Steve. (1992). *Facing the forces of change 2000: The new realities in wholesale distribution.* Distribution Research and Education Foundation, Washington D.C.
5. Lisanti, Tony. (February 7, 1994). Time is right for supplier as retailer. *Discount Store News.* p. 9.

6. Reda, Susan. (June 1995). When vendors become retailers. *Stores.* pp. 18–21.

7. Monget, Karyn. (1995, April 3). Sara Lee stores get retailers' OK. *Women's Wear Daily.* p. 10.

8. Mazur, Paul. (1927). *Principles of Organization Applied to Modern Retailing.* New York: Harper & Brothers.

9. In many retail organizations, the responsibility for computers was originally a control function, since the first computer applications were typically fiscal in nature (e.g., payroll).

10. Glock, Ruth & Kunz, Grace. (1995). *Apparel Manufacturing.* New York: Macmillan. p. 602.

11. Mazur, Paul. (1927). *Principles of Organization Applied to Modern Retailing.* New York: Harper & Brothers. p. 66.

12. Donnellan, John. (1996). Educational requirements for management level positions in major retail organizations. *Clothing and Textiles Research Journal.* Vol. 14, #1. pp.16-21.

13. Moin, David. (1995, June 28). Buried by paperwork, buyers lament loss of creative juices. *Women's Wear Daily.* pp. 1, 8–9.

chapter two

RETAILING FORMATS

By definition, all retailers sell goods and/or services to final consumers. However, retailers differentiate themselves from each other by factors such as the type of merchandise offered, pricing strategies, and the size and location of facilities. Though every retail organization struggles for uniqueness in the marketplace, many adopt similar merchandising and operational strategies. This chapter classifies retailers according to those similarities.

After you have read this chapter, you will be able to discuss:

The distinctions among various retailing formats.

Discounting as a significant retailing sector.

Nonstore retailing.

DEPARTMENT STORES

A **department store** caters to multiple needs of several groups of customers. Department-store offerings include **softlines,** such as apparel and household textile products, as well as accessories for the home. *Full-line* department stores offer a more extensive selection of **hardlines,** or non-textile products, such as furniture and consumer electronics. A department store satisfies the shopping needs of a diverse group of consumers including men, women, and children, often at more than one price level. Department stores carry well-known, nationally distributed, brand-name merchandise, such as Estée Lauder cosmetics, Arrow shirts, and Braun countertop kitchen appliances. Department stores complement their selections of brands with private label merchandise made exclusively for their distribution. A department store's prices are based on conventional pricing for the products and/or manufacturers' suggested retail prices.[1] Some highly recognized department store names include Bloomingdale's, Dillard's, Dayton's, Lord & Taylor, and Macy's.

Figure 2.1

Miami-based Burdines, Little Rock-based Dillard's, Dallas-based JCPenney, and Atlanta-based Rich's, are some familiar department store chains.

The origins of most department stores can be traced to the nine-teenth century and major cities. Many evolved with multifloor urban emporiums that catered to *many* needs of *many* customers with hundreds of categories of merchandise, including toys, sporting goods, and major appliances. Apparel was departmentalized by price, ranging from *bargain basement* and *main floor,* to the higher priced goods located on upper floors. Primary services, such as hair salons, restaurants, and travel agencies, were once typical department store offerings.[2] Today, department stores are smaller versions of their urban ancestors that no longer carry hardlines, such as furniture and toys or low-end apparel

Figure 2.2

Marshall Field's State Street store in Chicago is among the few remaining department store "emporiums".

price points. Most are **anchors,** or major tenants, of enclosed suburban shopping centers. Some department store chains have closed their urban flagships, including J.L. Hudson's of Detroit, and Rich's of Atlanta. Other urban department stores have been considerably downsized. Once independently owned, most department stores are now part of publicly-owned corporations that operate many stores. The Dayton Hudson Corporation is the owner of Marshall Field's of Chicago, Dayton's of Minneapolis, and Hudson's of Detroit.[3]

There is considerable speculation relative to the viability of the department store and its likelihood of survival. The list of department stores that have failed within recent decades includes Gimbels of New York, a cornerstone of U.S. retailing, as well as Bonwit Teller and B. Altman, also of New York, Garfinkel's of Washington, D.C., Frederick & Nelson of Seattle, and Joske's of San Antonio, to name but a few. The July 1986 edition of *Stores* magazine, an authoritative retail industry trade publication published by the National Retail Federation, listed nearly 100 department stores with annual sales of $100 million or more.[4] Within ten years, over half of the department stores listed had either:

- ceased operation,
- been acquired by another company,
- been consolidated with another operating division within a conglomerate, or
- filed bankruptcy.

Several reasons have been attributed to the department store's decline. Some observers feel that department stores lack uniqueness, and that consumers are bored with the sameness of selection among competing stores. Also a department store's intricate organizational structure often inhibits quick reaction to the marketplace. Less complex organizations can respond more rapidly to changes in consumer expectations, fashion trends, and competition. By virtue of its size, a department store's operating expenses are higher than those of retailers that operate smaller facilities and more streamlined organizations. Perhaps the most often cited reason for the alleged encroaching demise of the department store is the intense competition from other retailing formats.[5,6]

In spite of dismal prognostications, the department store remains an important sector of the retail industry. Many customers appreciate the convenience of one-stop shopping, and many producers rely on the prestige of department stores to give credibility to their brand names.

As symbols of fashion leadership, department stores are often the distribution point at which producers introduce new products or innovative styles to consumers. Department stores still account for approximately 25 percent of all sales in the shopping centers in which they are located, and it is estimated that two-thirds of the traffic in a shopping center is generated by the department store anchors.[7] Thriving department store conglomerates, such as the May Department Stores Company and Federated Department Stores, attest to the viability of the department store format. Both organizations have enhanced their profitability by investing in state-of-the-art technology, reducing operating expenses, streamlining organizational structures, improving customer service, and building strong supportive partnerships with their suppliers.[8,9,10,11]

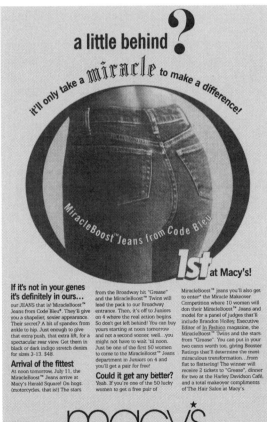

Figure 2.3

Department stores are often the distribution point at which innovative products are introduced to consumers.

Company Profile 2.1

In 1901, a Seattle shoemaker offered John W. Nordstrom, a Swedish immigrant, a partnership in a shoe store. By 1960, the single store had grown into the

largest independent shoe chain in the United States with locations throughout the Pacific Northwest. In 1963, John Nordstrom's descendants diversified the company's offerings through the acquisition of Best's Apparel of Seattle. In 1975, Nordstrom purchased three stores in Alaska from Northern Commercial Company. By 1978, Nordstrom had entered the highly competitive market of California's Orange County with the opening of a store at South Coast Plaza, thereby laying the groundwork for rapid expansion throughout the state.

The year 1988 marked Nordstrom's East Coast foray with the opening of a store at Tysons Corner in McLean, Virginia. Mid-west expansion began in 1991 with the opening of a store at Oakbrook Center in suburban Chicago. In 1992, Nordstrom opened a store at the Mall of America in Bloomington, Minnesota, the nation's largest retail and entertainment center. Today, Nordstrom's portfolio of stores includes fifty-seven specialty department stores with fashion apparel and accessories for men, women, and children, seventeen clearance stores called Nordstrom Rack, and eleven lease shoe departments that are operated in Hawaii's Liberty House Department Stores.

Since 1901, Nord-strom has been guided by its founder's philosophy of offering customers the best in selection, service, quality, and value. John Nord-strom carried large shoe sizes to accommodate his lumbering Swe-dish customers unable to find large sizes elsewhere. A commitment to deep assortments still prevails at Nordstrom. Women's shoes range in size from 4 to 13. Men's dress shirts are available in fifty-seven sizes, from 14 1/2 by 30 inches to 19 by 38 inches.

Customer service has become legendary at Nordstrom. As a gesture of goodwill, sales associates are encouraged to write thank you notes to customers. In Alaska, employees have been known to warm up cars while the drivers spent a few extra minutes shopping. According to company lore, a salesperson once accepted the return of a tire from a customer, even though Nordstrom has never sold tires.[1,2,3]

1. Jones, Dori. *(June 15, 1992). Nordstrom's gang of four.* Business Week. *pp. 122–123.*
2. Yang, Dori. *(September 3, 1990). Will the "Nordstrom Way" travel well?* Business Week. *pp. 82–83.*
3. Lassen, Tina. *(August 1995). Have a ball at America's largest mall.* World Traveler. *pp. 51–58.*

Company Profile 2.2

In 1969, Donald G. Fisher, a San Francisco real estate developer, attempted to exchange a pair of Levi's jeans at a local department store for a pair with a longer inseam. The simple exchange became a frustrating experience because of the store's poor size assortment. Deciding that San Francisco needed a store with a complete selection of Levi's in every style and size, Fisher opened a store on Ocean Avenue in San Francisco with a $63,000 investment. He called the store The Gap, a derivation of "generation gap," a popular term of the era that referred to the ideological rift between parents and their children. The original Gap boasted of "four tons of Levi's," a slogan that remained The Gap's advertising theme until 1974, the year that the company added private-label clothing to its offerings. By 1970, there were twenty-five Gap stores in six states. By 1981, there were 500 Gap stores in forty-eight states.

In 1983, Millard S. Drexler joined The Gap as president and CEO of The Gap stores. The former president of Ann Taylor implemented a product development program that gave the company

complete control over the design, quality, and sizing of its private label goods. Drexler also introduced The Gap's trademark "pocket-T" and fleece activewear—both in twenty-one colors. The Gap began to upscale its image and to target a more mature market age twenty to forty-five. Good style, good quality, and good value was Drexler's mantra.

Drexler recognized an unmet need for well-designed, good quality garments for children. His solution was GapKids, a store with comfortable, fashionable children's wear, much like grown-up Gap, established in 1986. In 1990, babyGap was born, making its appearance in twenty-five GapKids stores, and providing customers with a refreshing alternative to traditional pastel-colored baby clothes. Today, The Gap operates more than 900 Gap Stores and 400 GapKids in the United States, Canada, England, and France. The Gap organization also caters to an upscale market with its 200 Banana Republic stores, as well as to price-conscious customers with more than 100 Old Navy stores.[1,2]

1. *Mitchell, Russell. (March 9, 1992). The Gap.* Business Week. *pp. 58–64.*

2. *Mitchell, Russell. (November 30, 1992). A bit of a rut at The Gap.* Business Week. *p. 100.*

Figure 2.4

Ann Taylor and Banana Republic are apparel specialty stores.

SPECIALTY STORES

A **specialty store** caters to specific needs of a narrowly defined group of customers, with a single or limited number of merchandise categories, such as dresses, jewelry, or books. A specialty store's customers are defined by characteristics such as gender, income bracket, interests, or taste level. Career women, gourmet cooks, avid readers, trend-conscious teens, and chocolate lovers are some of the customers to whom specialty stores cater.[12,13] Many specialty stores ensure their exclusivity with private-label merchandise. Private labeling allows tremendous pricing flexibility, since customers have no basis for price comparison. These specialty stores have a profit advantage over department stores that must price their branded assortments competitively with other retailers.[14] Specialty stores can be a single unit, privately owned operation, or a group of several hundred stores, such as Ann Taylor, Sharper Image, and Banana Republic.

HARD-TO-CLASSIFY STORES

Some stores fit neither the department store nor the specialty store mold, catering to too few customers and too few needs to be a department store, or to too many customers and too many needs to be a specialty store. These stores are hybrids that fall somewhere in the middle

Figure 2.5

Nordstrom and Sears are among those "hard-to-classify" stores.

of a continuum defined at one end by department stores, and the other end by specialty stores. Examples include Saks Fifth Avenue, Neiman Marcus, and Nordstrom. Like department stores, all three are large and multidepartmental, offering several categories of merchandise. However, by only offering apparel, they fall short of the department store paradigm that includes at least a limited selection of home fashions. Stores such as these are often dubbed *departmentalized specialty stores* or *specialty department stores.*[15]

Though JCPenney, Sears, and Montgomery Ward are technically department stores, the three are sometimes referred to as *general merchandise chains* or *national department stores* in that they offer such a broad range of merchandise and/or are geographically dispersed throughout the United States.[16]

DEPTH AND BREADTH

Merchandise assortment can be characterized by their depth and breadth. **Breadth** refers to the number of unique items, categories, styles, brands, sizes, colors, or prices in an assortment. **Depth** refers to the selection within the elements of an assortment that define its breadth. An assortment with extensive breadth is described as a *wide assortment;* an assortment with limited breadth is described as a *narrow assortment.* An assortment with extensive depth is described as a *deep* *assortment;* an assortment with limited depth is described as a *shallow assortment.* There is typically a trade-off between depth and breadth for the obvious reason that to offer extensive depth *and* extensive breadth would require a mammoth store. A retailer who increases a store's breadth by adding categories of merchandise, restricts the depth of selection within the categories carried. A retailer who decreases a store's breadth by eliminating categories of merchandise, frees space to deepen the selection within the remaining categories.

In general, specialty store assortments are characterized as narrow and deep. Assortments are limited to one or a few categories of merchandise, but the selection within those categories is usually extensive. Department stores offer greater breadth than specialty stores. By carrying fewer merchandise categories today than many years ago, department stores have increased the depth of the softline categories that they've retained. The depth/breadth gap that once separated department stores and specialty stores has narrowed so that many department stores rival the deep assortments of their specialty store competitors.

DISCOUNTING

A **discounter** is a retailer that sells goods at prices that are lower than the conventional prices of other retailers. Low wholesale prices and low operating expenses are fundamental to a discounter's low pricing strategy. Discounters procure goods at favorable prices by buying large quantities of first quality goods, or by buying manufacturers' closeouts, end of season merchandise, and overruns. Discounters maintain low operating expenses with "no-frills" facilities that are plain, operationally efficient and economical to construct. Discount stores transact customer purchases at a centralized checkout area, or *front end.* This self-service approach to customer service is more economical than the decentralized customer service of department stores. Labor-intensive supplementary services, such as gift wrap and alterations, are also absent at discounters.

The emergence of discounting as a significant and diversified retailing sector did not occur until after World War II. However, discounters can be traced back to the turn of the century when "under-sellers," such as S. Klein of Manhattan and J.W. May of Brooklyn, sold apparel at prices that undercut department stores.[17]

Figure 2.6

Wal-Mart and Kmart are the two largest full-line discounters. Venture is a St. Louis-based regional discounter.

Types of Discounters

There are several types of discounters, each unique in terms of merchandising strategy:

Full-Line Discounter   A **full-line discounter,** or *general merchandise discounter,* offers a wide assortment of merchandise that most often incudes apparel, home accessories, consumer electronics, housewares, health and beauty care products, and toys. Offerings sometimes include automotive and hardware. Full-line discounters feature lower-priced brands not offered by department stores, such as Fruit of the Loom underwear, Wrangler jeans, and Maybelline cosmetics. Like department stores, full-line discounters complement their branded offerings with private label merchandise. Many full-line discounters have upscaled their image by offering higher-priced brands and emulating the decor, fixturing, and merchandise presentation strategies of department and specialty stores.[18]

The *Big Three* discounters are Wal-Mart, Kmart, and Target. Collectively, the three operate nearly 5000 stores spanning every state. A *regional discounter* operates approximately 100–200 stores in a specific region of the country. Bradlees in the Northeast, Rose's in the Southeast, and ShopKo in the Midwest and Pacific Northwest are

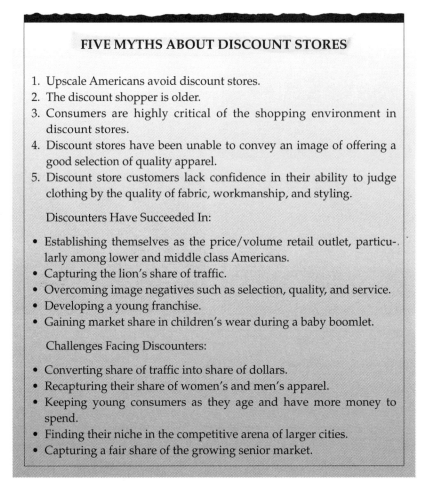

FIVE MYTHS ABOUT DISCOUNT STORES

1. Upscale Americans avoid discount stores.
2. The discount shopper is older.
3. Consumers are highly critical of the shopping environment in discount stores.
4. Discount stores have been unable to convey an image of offering a good selection of quality apparel.
5. Discount store customers lack confidence in their ability to judge clothing by the quality of fabric, workmanship, and styling.

Discounters Have Succeeded In:

- Establishing themselves as the price/volume retail outlet, particularly among lower and middle class Americans.
- Capturing the lion's share of traffic.
- Overcoming image negatives such as selection, quality, and service.
- Developing a young franchise.
- Gaining market share in children's wear during a baby boomlet.

Challenges Facing Discounters:

- Converting share of traffic into share of dollars.
- Recapturing their share of women's and men's apparel.
- Keeping young consumers as they age and have more money to spend.
- Finding their niche in the competitive arena of larger cities.
- Capturing a fair share of the growing senior market.

regional discounters. Regional discounters face strong competition from the *Big Three* and for some, survival is a struggle.[19,20,21]

Category Killer A **category killer,** or *specialty discounter,* offers a deep assortment of branded merchandise in a single merchandise category. Category killers "kill" the category of business for more generalized retail formats, such as department stores and full-line discounters, whose assortments are shallow by comparison. Toys "R" Us is one of the largest and best-known category killers, capturing well over 20 percent of all retail toy sales in the United States.[22] Other category killers include Circuit City (consumer electronics) and Sports Authority, the nation's largest sporting goods retailer.

Figure 2.7

Based in Moorestown, NJ, Today's Man is a men's wear category killer that offers unbeatable selections of men's suits, ties, accessories, and sportswear. *Photography ©ELLIOTT KAUFMAN.*

A category killer's success is often rooted in identifying an unsatisfied need in the marketplace. Staples, an office supply category killer, capitalizes on the needs of a growing number of small businesses, and people who conduct some or all of their business at home.[23] The founders of Home Depot determined that consumers bought do-it-yourself (DIY) merchandise at either full-line discounter stores, where prices were low but service was poor, or at small, privately owned "mom and pop" hardware stores, where service was good but prices were high. They developed a 100,000-square-foot home improvement store serviced by professional carpenters, electricians, and plumbers, to satisfy consumer demand for extensive selections, low prices, and good service.[24]

Off-Price Discounter An **off-price discounter,** or *off-pricer,* buys manufacturers' irregulars, seconds, closeouts, canceled orders, overruns, and goods returned by other retailers, as well as end-of-season closeout merchandise from department and specialty stores.[25] Though off-pricers have the reputation of carrying damaged goods and last year's styles, many now offer first quality merchandise bought early in the

A NEW BREED OF CATEGORY KILLERS

Though the category killer concept is often associated with hard-lines, several of the more recent entrants to the category killer arena are focused on apparel and related fashion products:

- Presently operating more than 150 stores, Goody's is a Knoxville, Tennessee-based category killer of moderately priced casual apparel for men, women, and children. Goody's aspires to become the Toys "R" Us of apparel retailing by opening more than 250 new stores by the year 2000.[1]
- Today's Man is a thirty-four unit men's wear superstore based in Moorestown, New Jersey, that offers selections of men's suits, ties, furnishings, and sportswear in 25,000- to 30,000-square foot stores. Operating more than sixty stores, The Cosmetic Center promotes itself as a one-stop beauty shop featuring no fewer than 25,000 items including cosmetics, fragrances, personal care appliances, and bath and hair care products.[2,3]
- The Duncan, South Carolina-based Baby Superstore operates more than sixty stores in fifteen states featuring 25,000 items of furniture, apparel, and toys for newborns and toddlers up to age three. Assortments include selections from 500 suppliers, including Fisher Price, Baby Dior, Carter's, and OshKosh.
- KidSource of Boca Raton, Florida, operates three 40,000-square-foot children's megastores featuring vast selections of branded apparel, shoes, toys, juvenile furniture, bedding, party supplies and a portrait photography studio.
- Sterling Inc. operates several mall-based jewelry chains, including Kay Jewelers, J.B. Robinson, and Black Starr & Frost. Sterling is also experimenting with a 10,000-square-foot category killer concept called Jared Galleria of Jewelry. The stores offer selections of more than 10,000 pieces of value-priced gold, diamonds, colored gemstones, men's jewelry, and watches, covering a price range of $20 to $20,000. Customers can design their own jewelry on a computer screen by adjusting stones, mountings, and other design elements on images of basic pieces of jewelry. Shoppers can also examine gemstone quality through a video system that magnifies the image of a stone by ten times on a 19-inch television screen. Other on-site services include custom mounting, cleaning, and repairing.[4]

1. *Lee, Georgia. (July 22, 1994). Goody's goal: Category killer.* Women's Wear Daily. *p. 14.*
2. *Brookman, Faye. (February 1993). The Cosmetic Center. Having it all.* Women's Wear Daily. *p. 10.*
3. *Lettich, Jill. (April 19, 1993). A Cosmetics "R" Us for women.* Discount Store News. *pp. 12, 14.*
4. *Staff. (September 13, 1993). Sterling to launch "category killer" in October.* Women's Wear Daily. *p. 11.*

Figure 2.8

Off-pricers are positioned as department store competitors.

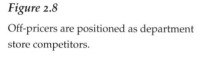

season. Positioned as department store competitors, off-pricers sell many department store brands at prices 20 to 60 percent less than regular retails. Leading off-pricers include Marshalls, T.J. Maxx, Burlington Coat Factory, Kids "R" Us, and Loehmann's.[26,27]

Frieda Loehmann gave birth to off-price discounting in the 1920s as she stalked designer showrooms on New York's Seventh Avenue to buy samples and canceled shipments to sell off-price at her namesake store in Brooklyn.

Closeout Store   A **closeout store** is operated by a retailer to clear slow-selling or end-of-season merchandise from its regular price stores. Department stores have taken the lead in developing this format. Nordstrom Rack, Off 5th-Saks Fifth Avenue, and Last Call, operated by Neiman Marcus, are examples of the closeout format.[28] The closeout

What the Shoppers Say

	Nat'l Chains	Discount Stores	Off Price	Specialty Chains	Upscale Specialty	Dept. Stores
I know they carry styles I like	B	B	C	B	C	A
Is the only place to find real bargain	D	A	B	F	F	D
Has believable every day low prices	D	A	C	F	F	F
I know I can find clothes that fit me	B	C	C	C	C	A
I know I can find good values in fashion apparel	B	C	B	D	D	C
Provides best discounts off regular/full prices	D	A	B	F	F	D
Carries all the clothing items I need	B	B	D	D	D	B
Pleasant shopping environment	B	B	D	C	C	B
Carries the best quality apparel	C	F	D	D	B	B
Appealing presentation and display of apparel	B	C	D	B	B	A
Provides excellent service	B	C	D	C	C	C
My favorite type of store for clothing	C	C	C	C	C	B
Good place to shop for casual but not career clothes	D	A	D	C	F	F
I shop at this type of store more than I used to	C	A	C	D	D	D

60%+ = **A**; 45%-59% = **B**; 30%-44% = **C**; 15%-29% = **D**; 0-14% = **F**.

This **"report card"** uses letter grades to reflect the percentages of store shoppers agreeing with the statement. For example, 60 percent of department store shoppers say they know the store carries styles they like, rating "A." However, only 45 to 59 percent of discount store shoppers feel these stores carry styles they like, hence a grade of "B."

Figure 2.9

Survey conducted by *Women's Wear Daily.*

store is not a new concept. In 1908, Edward Filene of Boston established Filene's Automatic Bargain Basement to clear goods from the upper floors of his family's namesake department store. Today, Filene's Basement is an off-price retailer operated independently of the "upstairs" Filene's, a division of May Department Stores.[29,30]

Manufacturer's Outlet A **manufacturer's outlet** was originally conceived as a "no-frills" break-even operation for unloading a producer's overruns, irregulars, and goods returned by department and specialty stores. However, producers that were operating at less than full production capacity found that they could increase their production capacity to 100 percent and profitably sell the additional merchandise in their outlet stores. Today, most manufacturers' outlets are profitable operations that feature first quality merchandise in attractive settings.[31,32,33]

ADVENTUROUS SHOPPERS

The emergence of less traditional kinds of retailing, such as warehouse clubs and home shopping networks, has made consumers more adventurous in their shopping habits, according to a survey of consumer attitudes commissioned by MasterCard and the National Retail Federation. Though affluent customers are the most adventuresome, most consumers shop four or five different types of retail formats. Seventy percent of all consumers shop at moderate department stores, such as Sears and JCPenney, and full-line discounters, such as Wal-Mart and Kmart; 51 percent are regulars at department stores, and 37 percent frequent apparel specialty stores, such as The Gap and The Limited. The report was based on information obtained from the NPD Consumer Purchase Panel Group, which includes data from 16,000 households that report their monthly apparel purchases.

Solomon, Barbara. (January 27, 1993). Shoppers experiment more, says survey. Women's Wear Daily. *p. 6.*

As in the case of manufacturer-sponsored specialty stores, producers that operate outlet stores run the risk of channel conflict by competing with the conventional retail channel members that they supply. The National Shoe Retailers' Association, a trade group of independent shoe retailers, once adopted a resolution criticized shoe manufacturers who channel first-run merchandise to factory outlet stores in direct competition with their retail accounts, giving the impression that independent shoe retailers are overpriced.

Warehouse Club A **warehouse club**, or *membership club*, is a wholesale/retail hybrid that offers deep discounts on a limited number of food and general merchandise items. About two thirds of a warehouse club's business is generated from small businesses; the other one third is generated from consumers. Between 50 percent and 60 percent of a warehouse club's sales are food items; less than 5 percent are apparel; the remaining sales are hardlines.[34] Consumers pay a membership fee to shop in a warehouse club so that a warehouse club generates income before customers make a single purchase.

Operating at the lowest profit margin of any retailer, warehouse clubs epitomize the "no frills" concept with cement floors and steel rack fixtures. Though supermarkets are most vulnerable to the compe-

Figure 2.10

Warehouse clubs and supercenters are food and general merchandise discounters. Sam's Club is a division of Wal-Mart. Kmart's combination stores are called Super Kmart Centers.

tition from warehouse clubs, warehouse clubs also compete with general merchandise discounters and category killers.

The warehouse club concept was pioneered in 1978 by Sol Price who opened the first Price Club in San Diego. The format grew quickly and has already matured, leaving little growth opportunity for existing clubs or new entrants. The two largest warehouse club retailers are PriceCostco and Sam's Club, a division of Wal-Mart.[35,36]

Supercenter A **supercenter,** or *combination store,* is a combined supermarket and full-line discount store links the frequency of visits of the food shopper with the higher profit margins of the full-line discounter. The concept was inspired by *les hypers,* an enormous 200,000-square-foot format featuring assortments ranging from food to fashion that were introduced in France in 1960 to respond to a lack of American-style supermarkets, discount stores, or enclosed shopping centers. The supercenter is actually a scaled-down version of the *hypermarket.* The full-line discount store/supermarket combination. Though a relatively new concept in most areas, Meijer of Grand Rapids has been operating in this format for many years, as has Fred Meyer of Portland, Oregon. Both Kmart and Wal-Mart are planning to add a significant number of supercenters to their portfolios of stores by the year 2000.[37,38,39,40,41,42]

A NEW CHAPTER IN RETAILING

The free-standing book superstore attracts serious book buyers with a high level of service and a selection of more than 100,000 attractively presented titles in a space about four times the size of a mall-based bookstore. The superstore combines the ambiance of a library and an old-fashioned bookstore with carpeted seating areas, over-stuffed arm chairs, oak tables, and piped-in classical music. Espresso bars in some superstores encourage customers to linger, based on the theory that browsers are likely to become buyers. Deep discounts on best sellers, frequent buyer programs, and high-tech tracking systems for title searches are other customer attractions.

Book superstores have become tough competition for independent bookstores, mall-based chains, and, to a lesser degree, discount stores, supermarkets, and warehouse clubs. However, book superstores purport that they are merely capitalizing on an under-penetrated category of business with untapped buying potential. Some observers feel that book superstores will reach a point of saturation quickly in that they are intimidating to the casual reader and that the serious reader targeted by the superstore represents too narrow a market segment to perpetuate the concept.

The leader in the book superstore concept is Barnes & Noble which opened its first superstore in 1990, and now operates more than 200 stores. The Barnes & Noble flagship store in New York is a tri-level shop with a cafe, that features 150,000 book titles and 1000 newspapers from around the world. Barnes & Noble also operates more than 700 mall stores under the names B. Dalton, Doubleday, and Scribners. Borders is the number two book superstore operator with more than 100 superstores, along with about 1000 mall-based Waldenbooks and Waldenkids stores.[1,2,3,4]

1. *Fitzgerald, Kate. (April 12, 1993). Bookstores in competitive thriller.* Advertising Age. *p. 12.*
2. *Friday, Carolyn; Rosado, Lourdes & Riebstein, Larry. (May 18, 1992). The book on marketing.* Newsweek. *pp. 55–56.*
3. *Liebeck, Laura. (May 3, 1993). Superstores write new chapter in retailing.* Discount Store News. *pp. 27–28.*
4. *Grimes, William. (August 3, 1995). Book war: Shops vs. superstores.* New York Times. *pp. B1, B2.*

Catalog Showroom A **catalog showroom** uses a retail showroom and a catalog to sell jewelry, consumer electronics, home accessories, sporting goods, and juvenile products. Catalog showrooms offer a higher level of service than other discounters, including gift registries, jeweler services, and telephone shopping.

Catalog showrooms flourished during the post World War II decades by selling department store brands at discounted prices at a time when full-line discounters sold only lower quality *off-brands.*

Catalog showrooms have been threatened by competition from category killers and full-line discounters that now offer major brands. A catalog showroom's merchandising flexibility is encumbered by the production of its catalog, which involves several months of advance planning.[43,44] The major catalog showroom retailers are Service Merchandise and Best Products.

Variety Store   A long-enduring but disappearing member of the retail circle is the **variety store,** commonly referred to as the *5&10* or *dime store.* The variety store dates back to the nineteenth century when merchants such as Sebastian S. Kresge and Frank W. Woolworth founded chains of stores that sold goods at five cent and ten cent retails. Inflation and expanded assortments that included housewares, linens, fashion jewelry, and cosmetics, eventually made "5&10" a misnomer. However, variety stores remained a dominant retailing format for many decades, dotting virtually every downtown shopping area and the earliest suburban shopping centers.

Variety stores had difficulty withstanding the competition from a growing number of full-line discounters that carried many of the same merchandise categories in greater depth. Recognizing the dismal future of this format, some of the major variety store chains diversified

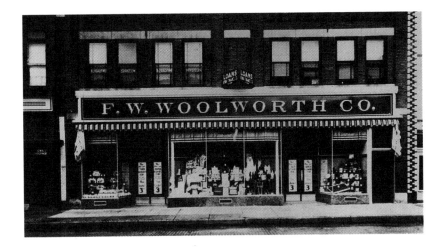

Figure 2.11

Variety stores once dotted virtually every downtown shopping area.   *BETTMANN Archives.*

Company Profile 2.3

Incredible Universe is a consumer electronics megastore conceived by The Tandy Corporation, parent organization of Radio Shack. The prototype features an exhaustive selection of consumer electronics and appliances in a four-acre facility, including more than 77 VCRs, 181 refrigerators, 340 video games, 292 car stereos, and 45,000 music and video titles.

Incredible Universe has put the fun back in shopping with an interactive shopping environment in which customers can play video games, operate a camcorder, and pick up a microphone in a karaoke studio and appear on the 315 television screens on the display floor. A large rotunda is the site of big-screen displays, entertainment, educational programs, and product presentations by manufacturers' representatives. At Incredible Universe piped in music is replaced by live disc jockeys.

Exceptional customer service is provided by a staff of sales associates who spend 10 percent of their workday in the Incredible Universe Training Center learning about new products and the latest technological developments. Customer services include product repair, installation, delivery and training, a kids play area, a restaurant, and an automatic teller machine to facilitate impulse buying.

Silverthorne, Sean. (October 2, 1992). Tandy store will try anything to lure shoppers. Investor's Business Daily. *p. 5.*

into areas with greater growth potential. In 1962, the S.S. Kresge Company opened the first Kmart in a Detroit suburb, and eventually abandoned its variety store format to become one of the nation's largest retailers. Likewise, F.W. Woolworth has evolved into a diversified conglomerate of specialty stores that includes Kinney Shoes, Foot Locker, Champs Sports, After Thoughts, and Northern Reflections. McCrory is the largest chain of variety stores, operating stores under the name of McCrory, J.J. Newberry, H.L. Green, and S.H. Kress.[45,46]

Some see *dollar stores* as the contemporary equivalent of the 5&10. Dollar stores, or *closeout stores*, are off-pricers that offer discontinued health and beauty care products, housewares, inexpensive fashion jewelry, books, food, and seasonal goods at a single retail price of $1. Dollar stores attract impulse shoppers intrigued by the ever-changing and unpredictable assortments. At least part of the dollar store's popularity may be attributable to the principle of making customers feel like they're getting a lot for their money, a concept fundamental to the success of the pioneers of the 5&10.[47]

OTHER RETAILING FORMATS

The aforementioned formats encompass the vast majority of retail stores in the United States. However, the list is in no way exhaustive. Other formats that are not as prominent. Some are unique to a product category. Levitz Furniture, the nation's largest furniture retailer, pioneered the *warehouse showroom* concept, a showroom of accessorized room settings with an attached warehouse of inventory of the merchandise displayed. Warehouse showroom customers can drive away with their purchases instead of waiting six to eight weeks for special orders to arrive from manufacturers, a scenario often typical of furniture retailing.

Other terms are used to refer to various types of retailers. The terms *megastore* and *superstore* are sometimes used to refer to especially large category killers or specialty stores. Nike Town is a superstore that

Figure 2.12
NIKE TOWN, Orange County superstore, Costa Mesa, CA.

features Nike's entire line of athletic footwear in a high-tech multimedia setting with sports memorabilia displays and a basketball court to "test-drive" a new pair of shoes. The term *destination store* refers to a store with a unique or extensive assortment of merchandise. Destination stores are attractive as shopping center tenants because of their ability to lure customers.

The franchise and the lease department are two other retailing formats worthy of mention. A **franchise** is a contractual agreement between a *franchisor* and *franchisee* that gives the franchisee the right to sell a franchisor's product line or service. The franchisor often provides a source of supply, a set of operating procedures, and a national advertising program. The franchise is purchased by the franchisee for a price based on the franchise's success record and growth potential. The terms of the franchise agreement are often very rigid, specifying hours of operation, facility design, and so on. This insures consistency among all franchised operations, a goal fundamental to maintaining the integrity of the franchise. Profits generated from operating the franchise are shared by the franchisor and the franchisee.

The most commonly known franchises are in the fast food industry, including McDonald's and Burger King. Consumer goods franchises include Benetton, Radio Shack, Athlete's Foot, and i-natural Cosmetics. Though a franchisee is most often an independent operator,

Figure 2.13

Some Benetton stores are franchised operations.

Figure 2.14

Kleinfeld of Brooklyn operates bridal boutiques at Saks Fifth Avenue stores in New York and Atlanta. *The Wedding Dress at Saks Fifth Avenue.*

the franchisee may be another retailer. Kmart is the largest franchisee of Little Caesar's restaurants.[48]

An *authorized dealership* is a strategic partnership between a producer and a retailer to sell a product line. The producer provides the retailer with product training and marketing incentives. The retailer, in turn, agrees to maintain specified levels of inventory, sales staffing, and promotional activity. This type of arrangement occurs between many major appliance producers, such as RCA and Whirlpool, and consumer electronics retailers, such as Circuit City and Montgomery Ward. An authorized dealership is sometimes referred to as a franchise.

A **lease department** is a retailer that operates as a department within another retail store. Rent is paid to the store in which the lease department is operated based on the lease department's sales and the amount of space occupied. The most common type of lease departments are:

- Traffic-generating services, such as restaurants and photography studios;

- Departments with large, difficult-to-manage inventories, such as shoes;
- Departments that require specialized selling, such as fine jewelry.

Some lease departments operate anonymously, blending in like any other department in the store and adopting the store's policies, operating procedures, and promotional calendar.

Examples of lease operations include Revillon Furs of New York which operates fur salons at thirty Saks Fifth Avenue locations around the country. Kleinfeld which operates bridal boutiques at Saks Fifth Avenue in New York and Atlanta. The Shoe Corporation of America operates approximately 500 department store shoe departments, including those of Carson Pirie Scott and Younker's, and more than 1200 departments in discount stores including Ames, Bradlees, and ShopKo.

NONSTORE RETAILERS

Not all retailers have storefronts. **Direct marketing** is a direct relationship between a retailer and a customer without the use of a retail facility. **Direct-response marketing** is a type of direct marketing that uses a nonpersonal print or electronic medium to communicate with consumers. There are three forms of direct-response marketing: catalog retailing, electronic retailing, and direct selling.

Catalog, or *mail-order,* retailing was originally conceived for customers who lacked convenient access to retail stores. The proliferation of shopping centers and automobiles has increased customers' accessibility to stores, so that today's catalog shopper is more likely to be a time-pressed consumer who appreciates the convenience of shopping at home. The Direct Marketing Association reports the existence of over 10,000 catalogs of consumer goods. Some of the largest catalog merchants include Lands' End, Spiegel, J. Crew, and L.L. Bean. Some catalog retailers rely on their catalog as their only vehicle of distribution, while others operate stores as well. J.Crew operates over forty stores nationwide. Spiegel operates twenty Spiegel Outlet clearance stores. Talbots uses catalog sales to identify potential locations for new stores. When catalog sales reach $150,000 in an area, Talbots begins to explore possible store sites.[49]

Catalog retailing has essentially become a specialty business. Most successful catalogs are targeted to customers defined by characteristics

Figure 2.15

William-Sonoma, Lands' End, J. Crew,
Spiegel and L.L. Bean are among the most
successful catalog retailers.

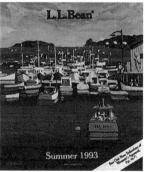

cathy®   **by Cathy Guisewite**

Figure 2.16

such as income, interests, and lifestyle. In 1993, Sears abandoned publication of its 1500-page *Big Book* of general merchandise in favor of several smaller catalogs, including *Great Kitchens* and *Leather Connections*. Some catalog retailers publish multiple catalogs. The Williams-Sonoma family of catalogs includes, *Williams-Sonoma* (food and housewares), *Gardener's Eden* (gardening supplies), *The Pottery Barn* (home accessories), *Hold Everything* (storage containers), and *Chambers* (bed and bath linens and accessories).

Several factors have contributed to the growth of catalog retailing in recent decades, including toll free "800" numbers, third-party charge cards, and efficient delivery alternatives to the U.S. Postal Service, such as United Parcel Service. In spite of their tremendous growth, catalog retailers are not without challenges. Market saturation, printing and mailing costs, and the problems of collecting and paying sales taxes in many states, are among some of the problems facing catalog retailers.[50,51,52,53,54]

Often referred to as *home shopping*, **electronic retailing** has three formats: infomercials, on-line computer shopping services, and television shopping channels. *Infomercials* are program-length product demonstrations, sometimes hosted by a celebrity. *On-line computer shopping services*, such as America Online, CompuServe, and Prodigy, allow subscribers to make purchases via their home computers.

Television shopping channels represent the largest electronic retailing segment. The major shopping channels are QVC and HSN. Once

Company Profile 2.4

In 1963, an entrepreneurial Gary Comer left his position as a copywriter at the prestigious advertising agency of Young & Rubicam to establish a mail-order company that sold sailboat hardware. Gradually, Comer broadened his selections to include duffel bags, luggage, and apparel for the sailing set, and eventually, a more general line of casual clothing. In 1976, the company discontinued its sailing gear to focus on the more profitable apparel and luggage lines, though retaining its original nautically inspired name, Lands' End.

The Lands' End catalog is a combination marketing and literary piece that sometimes includes short stories by mystery writers, and biographical sketches of famous people. Instructional guides periodically appear, such as how to carve a pumpkin and roast the seeds. Products are described in understandable and unpretentious prose with detailed descriptions of product construction and fabrication. Real people are used as models, displaying all of the imperfections of the average customer.

Lands' End stresses quality of production. Its classic rugby shirt was tested over a four-year period on the University of Chicago rugby team, and then on the USA Eagles, America's national team. One of the company's most popular specialty products is a multipocketed canvas attache bag, a more relaxed version of the cumbersome hard-sided briefcase. From its inception, Lands' End has made a strong commitment to customer service. Order takers are noted for their willingness to answer questions regarding fit, send color swatches, or simply talk about the weather.

Lands' End is located amid the rolling cornfields of Dodgeville, Wisconsin (pop. 4000), a site consistent with the company's image as a nice, honest, and folksy retailer. Besides its flagship catalog, the Lands' End family of publications includes *Coming Home*, a bed and bath catalog, and *Beyond Buttondowns*, a men's apparel catalog, *Kids*, for sizes infant to 18 months, and *Corporate Sales*, a business-to-business catalog. In a highly competitive lineup of apparel specialty catalogs, Lands' End vies for first place with L.L. Bean, the long established leader of the pack.[1,2,3,4]

1. *Both, R.T. (December 1991/January 1992). Winning through sincerity.* Midwest Ex-press Magazine. *pp. 10-12.*
2. *Rudolph, Barbara. (July 17, 1989). The chic is in the mail.* Time. *pp. 74-75.*
3. *Sloane, Leonard. (December 12, 1994). In a Lands' End ad, the sweater is usually not as important as the company's catalogue image.* New York Times. *p. D8.*
4. *Staff. (January 9, 1989). Big Picture Strategy.* Forbes. *pp. 70-72.*

plagued by the tawdry image of the high pressure selling of cubic zirconia[55] and nonstick frying pans, the perception of home shopping has changed dramatically since 1992 when designer Diane von Furstenberg sold $1.2 millon of merchandise in a ninety-minute segment on QVC.[56] Electronic retailing will assume a new dimension with interactive technology that will allow consumers to take electronic "shopping trips" by choosing a store or catalog from a menu at the touch of a button. Shoppers will be able to browse on their TV screens, place an order, charge it to a credit card, and choose a delivery option. Even services like grocery shopping will be offered through interactive systems. Some observers predict that home shopping will increase a hundred fold by the turn of the century. Others feel that these projections are exaggerated. Many see catalog retailers as being most threatened by electronic retailing.[57,58,59,60,61,62,63]

Direct selling is a form of direct marketing that uses personal explanation or demonstration to sell a product. There are two types of direct selling: person-to-person selling and the party plan. *Person-to-person selling* involves one-to-one interaction with a customer. Door-to-door selling, the practice of canvasing customers at home, was an early form of person-to-person selling. A declining number of people at home during the day and a reluctance to open the door to strangers has all but eradicated door-to-door sales.[64] Avon, remembered for its famous "Avon calling" door-to-door campaign, now targets women in the workplace as both sales representatives and customers.

The *party plan* uses a festive atmosphere in the home of a host/hostess to demonstrate a product line to a group of customers. Tupperware, a producer of high quality plastic storage containers, is one of the best-known party plans. In response to the changes in the lifestyle of today's homemaker, Tupperware has taken the party out of the home and into the workplace with the "rush-hour party" held at the end of the work day. Tupperware also targets an increasing number of single households by including men in their market.[65,66,67]

Network marketing, or *multilevel marketing,* is a strategy used by some direct selling organizations to reward sales representatives for recruiting other sales representatives. Commissions are based on personal sales as well as the sales of a "downline" of recruits. The two largest network marketers are Amway household products and Nu Skin skin care products.

SHOPPING IN 2010

Let's turn our looking glass around and peer through the eyes of the consumer. Say you want to buy new curtains for your living room. You don't have to drive to the shopping center if you don't want to. You can pick up your phone, with its built-in computer and TV screen, and browse through a video selection of your options.

But you want to see and touch some samples, and you want a second opinion from an expert. So you carry your personal preference card to a department store, and hand it to a design consultant. The consultant slips the card into a computer and lets you enter your personal identification number to access the data on the card. The card calls up a three-dimensional image of your living room.

Next, the consultant shows you different colors and styles of curtains and draperies exactly as they will appear in your living room. You look at some samples and make a selection. The curtains will arrive at your home within the next 24 hours.

Now, while you're at the store, you decide to look around. Like most consumers, you're busy and don't get out to the mall very often. You're thinking you might buy a new suit, so you check into the department store's custom-made suit department. You're surprised by how low the prices are, thanks to the advances in manufacturing technology.

And rather than spending hours in front of the tailor's mirror, you step into a holographic imaging device that takes your measurements and lets you "see" yourself in the suit of your choice. You can order the suit in any color or fabric—your personal preference card, with its record of your past shirt and tie purchases, helps coordinate the suit with your existing wardrobe.

Then the sales associate offers you another new option that sounds appealing. Thanks to your unreliable weather forecaster (after all, some things never change), you're always sweating in a suit that's too warm, or shivering in one that's too cool. Now you can choose climate-controlled fabrics! Materials researchers in Japan and the United States have developed fibers that change color and adjust their insulation for changes in temperature. You make your selection, pay with your personal preference card, and 48 hours later, the custom-made suit is at your doorstep.

I've just made a few predictions. However, no matter how clear our crystal ball is, uncertainty will always be with us, even more so as things change more rapidly in the next two decades.

Reprinted by permission. DIMENSIONS, published by DECA (Distributive Education Clubs of America), Fall/Winter 1992.

SUMMARY POINTS

- A department store caters to multiple needs of several groups of customers. A specialty store caters to the specific needs of a narrowly defined group of customers.
- Breadth refers to the number of unique items in an assortment. Depth refers to the selection within an assortment.
- Discounters offer low prices in a "no-frills" setting. There are several distinct types of discounters: full-line discounters, category killers, off-pricers, closeout stores, manufacturers' outlets, warehouse clubs, supercenters, catalog showrooms, and variety stores.
- Other retailing formats include franchises and lease departments.
- Direct marketing is nonstore retailing; direct response marketing employs a nonpersonal medium to communicate with customers; direct selling involves personal selling.

KEY TERMS AND CONCEPTS

anchor	direct-response	manufacturer's outlet
breadth	marketing	off-price discounter
catalog retailing	direct selling	softlines
catalog showroom	discounter	specialty store
category killer	electronic retailing	supercenter
closeout store	franchise	variety store
department store	full-line discounter	warehouse club
depth	hardlines	
direct marketing	lease department	

FOR DISCUSSION

1. Make a list of specialty stores that operate locally. Define each store's customer in terms of gender, age, income, and interests.
2. Make a list of stores that operate locally. Classify each by format. Are some stores difficult to classify? Why?
3. Identify some categories of merchandise not sold by category killers. Do any represent opportunities for an entrepreneurial retailer? Explain.
4. Identify a regional full-line discounter that operates stores locally. Compare it to a *Big Three* discounter in terms of assortments, prices, and facilities. Is the regional discounter effectively competing with the *Big Three* discounter? What are your predictions for the regional discounter's future?

5. Discuss the future of home shopping. Do you feel that home shopping will grow as predicted? What are some of the factors that will contribute to or hinder its success?

SUGGESTED READINGS

Berman, Joel & Evans, Barry. (1995). *Retail Management.* Englewood Cliffs, NJ: Prentice Hall.

Dunne, Patrick; Lusch, Robert; Gable, Myron & Gebhardt, Randall. (1992). *Retailing.* Cincinnati: South-Western.

Ferry, William. (1960). *A History of the Department Store.* New York: Macmillan.

Levy, Michael & Weitz, Barton. (1995). *Retailing Management.* Chicago: Irwin.

Mayfield, Frank. (1949). *The Department Store.* New York: Fairchild.

Wendt, Lloyd & Kogan, Herman. (1952). *Give the Lady What She Wants.* South Bend, IN: and books

ENDNOTES

1. This description of a department store is consistent with the National Retail Federation's definition of a department store as a multidepartmental soft-lines store with a fashion orientation, full markup policy, carrying national branded merchandise and operating stores large enough to be shopping center anchors. By contrast, the U.S. Department of Commerce defines a department store as an establishment normally employing 25 people or more, having sales of apparel and softlines that amount to 20 percent or more of total sales, and selling each of the following lines of merchandise: furniture, appliances, radios, and TV sets; a general line of apparel for the family; household lines and dry goods. To qualify as a department store, sales of each of these lines must be less than 80 percent of total store sales. An establishment with total sales of $10 million or more is classified as a department store even if sales in one of the merchandise lines exceed the maximum percent of total sales, provided that the combined sales of the other two groups are $1 million or more. The U.S. Department of Commerce is a dated definition that was composed when "radios and television sets" were standard department store offerings, and when $10 million was a considerable amount of business.

2. Cohen, Daniel. (March 1993). Grand emporiums peddle their wares in a new market. *Smithsonian.* pp 122–133.

3. Sternlieb, George & Hughes, James. (August 1987). The demise of the department store. *American Demographics.* pp. 31–33, 59.

4. Schultz, David. (July 1986). Top 100 stores. *Stores.* pp. 13–24.

5. Barnett, Todd; Nelson, Margaret; King, Patricia & McCormick, John. (December 11, 1989). Shop till they drop. *Newsweek.* pp. 76–78.

6. Strom, Stephanie. (January 11, 1994). Retailers' drive to consolidate. *New York Times.* pp. D1, D2.

7. Strom, Stephanie. (1992, February 3). Department stores remain a strong franchise. *New York Times.* pp. D1, D4.

8. Berry, Kathleen. (April 22, 1994). Are department stores up to the task? *Investor's Business Daily.* p. A3.

9. Crites, Jennifer. (August 1992). The next chapter in department store retailing. *Chain Store Age Executive.* pp. 24A–26A.

10. Forsyth, Julie. (August 1993). Department store industry restructures for the 90s. *Chain Store Age.* pp. 29A–30A.

11. Lagnado, Isaac. (April 10, 1994). The department store, revitalized. *New York Times.* p. C17.

12. Adler, Sam. (September 12, 1994). Specialty stores do the right thing. *Home Furnishings Daily.* pp. 20A–21A.

13. Staff. (November 1994). Rating the stores. *Consumer Reports.* pp. 712–722.

14. Schultz, David. (August 1991). Expansion: Specialty retailers tinker with revamped formats and larger stores to lure customers back. *Stores.* pp. 43–45.

15. Gill, Penny. (February 1990). What's a department store? *Stores.* pp. 8–17.

16. As a multiunit retailer, Sears is a department store. However, Sears' value-oriented prices have led many to classify the retailer as a discounter. Others argue that decentralized service disqualifies Sears as a discounter. Though Sears, JCPenney, and Montgomery Ward are often mentioned in the same breath, most concur that, as a retailer of moderately-priced, nationally branded apparel and home accessories, JCPenney is, in fact, a department store.

17. Staff. (September 21, 1992). Discounting: Chronicles of its evolution. *Discount Store News.* pp. 49, 104.

18. Staff. (August 16, 1993). Regionals succeed as innovative Davids among retailing's Goliaths. *Discount Store News.* p. 58.

19. Pogoda, Diane. (October 6, 1994). Jousting with Wal-Mart. Better clothes, better trappings. *Women's Wear Daily.* p. 24.

20. Swisher, Kara. (August 11, 1991). Attention, shoppers! Here come the big, flashy discount stores. *Washington Post.* pp. H1, H6.

21. Robaton, Anna. (August 1995). *Shopping Centers Today.* pp. 1, 8, 12.

22. Stephanie Strom. (December 19, 1994). Toys "R" Us still titan of toyland. (Springfield, MA) *Union News.* pp. G1, G2.

23. Staff. (December 11, 1989). Staples, Inc. *The Wall Street Transcript.* p. 95685.

24. Thompson, Roger. (February 1992). There's no place like Home Depot. *Nation's Business.* pp. 30–32.

25. The term *off-price* is sometimes used to refer to any retailer that sells goods at discounted prices.

26. Staff. (December 7, 1986). Racking up competition. *Los Angeles Business Journal.*

27. Barmash, Isadore. (March 1981). How they're selling name brands off-price. *Stores.* pp. 9–14, 55.

28. Pogoda, Diane. (May 12, 1993). Closeout stores: Retailing's last stop. *Women's Wear Daily.* pp. 8–9.

29. Book, Esther. (April 10, 1995). On the edge. *Forbes.* p. 65.

30. Reid, Natalie. (June 1991). Edward A. Filene. *New England Business.* p. 64.

31. Edelson, Sharon. (April 4, 1995). Once a poor relation, outlets go legit-and trouble looms. *Women's Wear Daily.* pp. 1, 8, 9.

32. Hartlein, Robert. (September 30, 1992). Manufacturers' outlets: Retailing's hot numbers. *Women's Wear Daily.* pp. 18–19.

33. Orgel, David. (December 14, 1992). The outlet game: New players face new rules. *Women's Wear Daily.* p. 13.

34. Staff. (March 1, 1993). Warehouse club closeup. Evolution key to continued club success. *Discount Store News.* pp. 17–24.

35. D'Innocenzio, Anne. (April 14, 1993). Warehouse clubs: Is the novelty wearing off? *Women's Wear Daily.* p. 14.

36. Zellner, Wendy. (April 19, 1993). Warehouse clubs butt heads—and reach for the ice pack. *Business Week.* p. 30.

37. Deeny, Godfrey. (April 28, 1993). Hypermarkets: A real French bargain. *Women's Wear Daily.* p. 17.

38. Lawson, Skippy & Lee, Georgia. (May 13, 1992). American Fare: Is bigger better? *Women's Wear Daily.* p. 8.

39. Lieback, Laura & Longo, Don. (May 3, 1993). Discounters spearhead super-centers' decade. *Discount Store News.* pp. 1, 18.

40. Staff. (September 20, 1993). Carefour makes plans to bid *adieu* to U.S. market. *Discount Store News.* pp. 4, 84.

41. Staff. (August 1, 1994). Supercenters: Anatomy of a hybrid. A supplement of *Women's Wear Daily* Fairchild Publications.

42. Tosh, Mark. (June 7, 1995). Supercenters: The race is on. *Women's Wear Daily.* p. 14.

43. The catalog showroom is sometimes referred to as a *hardlines specialty store* since so little business is derived from catalog orders today.

44. Staff. (December 7, 1992). Retailing for the new millennium. *Discount Store News.* pp. 53–63.

45. Miller, Annetta. (January 4, 1993). A dinosaur no more. *Time.* pp. 54–55.

46. Pogoda, Diane. (October 20, 1993). Woolworth's closings: What went wrong? *Women's Wear Daily.* p. 16.

47. Fields-Meyer, Thomas. (April 21, 1993). Five-and-dimes for the 90s. *Wall Street Journal.* p. A12.

48. Feder, Barnaby. (August 16, 1993). Dining out at the discount store. *New York Times.* pp. D1, D2.

49. Reda, Susan. (July 1995). Talbots thrives with innovative synergies, consumer research. *Stores.* pp. 34–35.

50. Fisher, Christy. (October 10, 1994). Last rush to fuel double digit catalog jump. *Advertising Age.* pp. S2–S12.

51. Gill, Penny. (July 1990). Targeting direct mail. *Stores.* pp. 42–47.

52. Staff. (October 1991). Mail order companies. *Consumer Reports.* pp. 643–647.

53. Staff. (September 12, 1994). Direct-mail channel proves fast growing. *Home Furnishings Daily.* p. 16A.

54. Staff. (October 1994). Mail-order shopping: Which catalogs are best? *Consumer Reports.* pp. 621–626.

55. Imitation diamonds.

56. McGraw, Dan & Fischer, David. (November 14, 1994). Designing for dollars. *U.S. News & World Report.* pp. 103–106.

57. Carlin, Peter. (February 28, 1993). The jackpot in television's future? *New York Times Magazine.* pp. 36–41.

58. Donaton, Scott. (April 19, 1993). Home shopping networks bring retailers on board. *Advertising Age.* S8.

59. Morgenson, Gretchen. (May 24, 1993). The fall of the mall. *Forbes.* pp. 106–112.

60. Zinn, Laura. (July 26, 1993). Retailing will never be the same. *Business Week.* pp. 54–60.

61. Robichaux, Mark. (November 22, 1994). Home shopping loses its shine for retailers. *Wall Street Journal.* pp. B1, B10.

62. Reilly, Patrick. (November 16, 1993). TV shopping hooks high toned viewers. *Wall Street Journal.* pp. B1, B10.

63. Turnage, Neal. (August 12, 1991). HSN's uphill battle. *Women's Wear Daily.* p. 11.

64. Underwood, Elaine. (September 9, 1991). The modern trials of the Fuller Brush Man. *Adweek's Marketing Week.* pp. 16–17.

65. Klebnikov, Paul. (December 9, 1991). The power of positive inspiration. *Forbes.* pp. 245–249.

66. Roha, Ronaleen. (November 1991). The ups and downs of downlines. *Kiplinger's Personal Finance Magazine.* pp. 63–70.

67. Staff. (December 1992). Door-to-door selling grows up. *Black Enterprise.* pp. 76–90.

chapter three

RETAIL LOCATIONS

An age old cliche asserts that the three factors that contribute most to a retailer's success are *location, location,* and *location.* Proponents of nonstore retailing might disagree with this posture. However, in spite of the success of many nonstore formats, most retail industry observers concur that location can make or break a storefront retailer. Chapter 3 considers the synergy between retailing format and retail location, and the various location options available for retail stores.

After you have read this chapter, you will be able to discuss:

The various shopping environments in which retailers operate stores.

The important role that location plays in a retailer's success.

UNPLANNED SHOPPING DISTRICTS

The earliest retail shopping districts were unplanned clusters of stores that evolved in the centers of cities. Known to many as *downtown,* **central business districts** (*CBDs*), or *urban cores,* were vital hubs of commerce and transportation. The great department store emporiums were founded in CBDs. Many cities had two or more department stores that rivaled each other for market dominance by distinguishing themselves in terms of size or prestige. Specialty stores were also an important part of the CBD's retail mix. Though many were single-unit independents. CBDs were the original home of national specialty chains, including Kay Jewelers, Lerner Shops,[1] and Thom McAn Shoes.[2] In spite of the fact that there was no strategic master plan for locating stores within a CBD, districts defined by certain categories of goods, such as jewelry, men's wear, women's apparel, or furniture, often evolved in large CBDs.

CBDs are no longer major retail shopping districts, except in the case of some large urban metropolises. Several factors have contributed to the decline of the popularity of CBDs as retail locations. The proliferation of the automobile meant that public transportation was no longer an important factor in drawing shoppers to a shopping district. Traffic congestion and the expense and inconvenience of parking a car diminished a city's attractiveness. Urban decay compounded the problems of the CBD, leading many shoppers to perceive cities as unattractive and unsafe places to shop. The migration of customer populations to the suburbs is perhaps the factor that has contributed most to the demise of downtown retail districts.[3]

Secondary business districts (*SBDs*), or *subshopping districts,* sprouted in outlying areas of cities as populations migrated toward these areas. Likewise, **town centers** evolved in towns and suburbs peripheral to cities. SBDs and town centers remain important locations for independently owned specialty stores and service retailers. Chain specialty stores and small branches of department stores occasionally appear in SBDs or town centers.

Unplanned commercial districts that evolve on busy thoroughfares are home to many *free-standing* retailers, each with its own parking area, such as car dealerships, furniture stores, supermarkets, movie theaters, fast-food restaurants, and various types of discounters. Traffic congestion is a frequent problem along these thoroughfares.

Figure 3.1

Secondary business districts and town centers are home to many independently owned specialty stores and service retailers.

PLANNED SHOPPING CENTERS

A **shopping center** is a commercial complex with on-site parking that is developed, owned, and managed as a unit. The trading area from which a shopping center draws its customers is a function of its size. Large shopping centers draw from a wider trading area than small centers, in that consumers will travel a greater distance for an extensive selection of stores. The value of space in a shopping center is a function of the number of shoppers that the center attracts. Rent in large, heavily trafficked centers is higher than rent in small centers. Shopping centers blossomed on the retail landscape during the years following World War II as real estate developers responded to the needs of rapidly growing numbers of consuming suburbanites.[4]

The International Council of Shopping Centers has identified several distinct types of shopping centers. The most common are the:

- neighborhood center
- regional center
- community center
- superregional center

Table 3.1 ICSC SHOPPING CENTER DEFINITIONS

Type	Concept	Sq. Ft. (Inc. Anchors)	Acreage	Typical Anchor (s)		Anchor Ratio*	Primary Trade Area**
				Number	Type		
Neighborhood Center	Convenience	30,000–150,000	3–15	1 or more	Supermarket	30–50%	3 miles
Community Center	General Merchandise; Convenience	100,000–350,000	10–40	2 or more	Discount dept. store; super-market; drug; home improve.; large specialty/disc. apparel	40–60%	3–6 miles
Regional Center	General Merchandise; Fashion (Mall, typically enclosed)	400,000–800,000	40–100	2 or more	Full-line dept. store; jr. dept. store; mass merchant; disc. dept. store; fashion apparel	50–70%	5–15 miles
Superregional Center	Similar to Regional Center but has more variety and assortment	800,000+	60–120	3 or more	Full-line dept. store; jr. dept. store; mass merchant; fashion apparel	50–70%	5–25 miles
Fashion/Specialty Center	Higher end, fashion oriented	80,000–250,000	5–25	N/A	Fashion	N/A	5–15 miles
Power Center	Category-dominant anchors; few small tenants	250,000–600,000	25–80	3 or more	Category killer; home improve.; disc. dept. store; warehouse club; off-price	75–90%	5–10 miles
Theme/Festival Center	Leisure; tourist-oriented; retail and service	80,000–250,000	5–20	N/A	Restaurants; entertainment	N/A	N/A
Outlet Center	Manufacturers' outlet stores	50,000–400,000	10–50	N/A	Manufacturers' outlet stores	N/A	25–75 miles

* The share of a center's total square footage that is attributable to its anchors.
**The area from which 60–80% of the center's sales originate.

Reprinted with permission of the International Council of Shopping Centers Research Quarterly, Volume 1, Number 1, May 1994. © 1994 by the International Council of Shopping Centers, Inc., New York, New York.

Neighborhood Center A **neighborhood center** has approximately 30,000–150,000 square feet of retail space, often with a supermarket or a large drug store as major tenants, complemented by service retailers, such as dry cleaning establishments and shoe repair shops.

Community Center A **community center** has approximately 100,000–350,000 square feet of retail space, often with a supermarket and a full-line discounter as major tenants, complemented by other specialty and service retailers. Category killers and off-pricers are sometimes major tenants in community centers.

Regional Center A **regional center** has approximately 400,000–800,000 square feet of retail space with two or more department stores as major tenants, complemented by general merchandise specialty retailers of apparel and home furnishings.

Figure 3.2

The typical community center tenant mix includes a supermarket, a full-line discounter, and several specialty and service retailers.

Superregional Center   A **superregional center** has over 800,000 square feet of retail space with three or more department stores as major tenants, complemented by general merchandise retailers collectively offering broad and deep selections of apparel and home furnishings. Food courts are a common feature of superregional centers, as are forms of entertainment, such as movie theaters and miniature golf.[5] Many regional centers have become superregionals by adding new anchors and additional space for more specialty stores.[6,7]

Strips and Malls

Most neighborhood and community centers are *strip centers*, linear arrangement of stores with off-street parking in front of the stores. An open-air canopy often connects the stores in a strip center. J.C. Nichols built the first strip center, Country Club Plaza, in Kansas City, Missouri in 1922. Department store **branches,** microcosms of large urban flagships that offered the same categories of merchandise but in limited selections, were often tenants in the early strip centers.[8] Since the 1960s, most department stores have abandoned strip centers for larger units at regional or superregional centers.

Strip centers are attractive to many types of retail tenants, especially discounters, because of their heavily trafficked locations and relatively low rent structures. Many strip centers have strengthened their market position as value-oriented destination centers with an

Figure 3.3

Strip centers are attractive to retailers because of their heavily trafficked locations and relatively low rent structures. *Photography by Terry Vine, Weingarten Realty Investors, Houston, TX.*

expanded mix of stores that includes off-pricers and category killers. Some have added office space to attract the professional services of physicians and dentists, while others have added *out-parcel* units for free-standing *big box* tenants such as warehouse clubs. Landscaping, better signage, and improved ingress and egress have made many strip centers pleasant shopping destinations.[9] Strip center proponents claim that strip centers attract time-pressed destination shoppers more likely to make a purchase than the browser who shops the regional or super-regional center.[10,11,12]

Regional and superregional centers are typically enclosed and climate controlled with an inward orientation of stores connected by pedestrian walkways. Open air and/or decked parking surrounds most regional and superregional centers. Commonly referred to as *malls*,[13] the first enclosed shopping center, Southdale, opened in a Minneapolis suburb in 1956. The development of the interstate highway system spurred the growth of regional and superregional centers. Sites at highway interchanges became desirable mall locations because of their high visibility and easy accessibility.

Since the late 1970s, regional centers have been faced with fierce competition from larger superregional centers. Though department stores have traditionally been the preferred anchors in enclosed shopping centers, many smaller centers have repositioned themselves as value-oriented centers by replacing shuttered department stores with category killers, off-pricers, and full-line discounters.[14,15] Having lost Sears to an abutting superregional center, South Hills Mall in Poughkeepsie, New York leased its prime space to Burlington Coat Factory, Service Merchandise, and a supermarket.[16] Some centers adopt an eclectic merchandising approach to broaden their customer base.[17] The Tallahassee Mall in Florida is anchored by an upscale Parisian at one end, and a value-oriented Montgomery Ward at the other. Gayfer's, a moderate-price department store, and Service Merchandise complete the tenant mix.

Other Types of Shopping Centers

Other types of shopping centers incorporate the characteristics of both strips and malls, but are distinct in terms of location and retail composition. They are:

- mixed-use center
- festival marketplace
- power center
- pedestrian mall
- outlet center

Figure 3.4

The Scottsdale Mall is a superregional center in South Bend, Indiana, with three anchors more than 75 specialty stores. *FRCH Worldwide, New York, NY.*

Mixed-Use Center   A **mixed-use center,** or MXD, is a retail, office, parking, and hotel complex that sometimes includes a convention center, and/or high-rise condominium or apartment complex in one sprawling development. MXDs were often part of revitalization projects to salvage decaying cities. The MXD's retail component was an effort to maintain the CBD as a viable shopping district. Airwalks often connected the MXD to local department stores and other retail complexes. Though many urban MXDs have been successful as office and hotel facilities, most never realized their developers' expectations as retail centers.

MXDs have been catalysts for development in suburban areas, as integral parts of planned suburban communities in a high growth, densely populated area. *Washington Post* reporter, Joel Garreau, has dubbed these areas *edge cities*, mini-metropolises that have sprung up along interstate highways within the shadows of major urban cores.[18,19]

Pedestrian Mall   Attempting to emulate the freedom and safety that customers enjoy walking from store to store in enclosed shopping centers, urban planners developed the **pedestrian mall** to recapture the business that CBDs were losing to suburban centers by closing off streets within a group of city blocks and creating a park-like ambiance of trees and benches. Examples include Fresno's Fulton Mall, the Mid-America Mall in Memphis, and Miami Beach's Lincoln Road Mall.

Unfortunately, pedestrian malls were not the answer to the declining retail business of the CBD. Critics of the concept claim that pedestrian malls hamper retail business because of the confusing traffic patterns created by rerouting the traffic. Some pedestrian malls have been converted back to conventional paved roadways with sidewalks.

A close kin of the pedestrian mall is the *transit mall*, which is a pedestrian mall closed to traffic except public transportation. Minneapolis' Nicollet Mall and Chicago's State Street Mall are examples of this concept.[20,21]

Festival Marketplace   A **festival marketplace,** or *urban specialty center,* is a shopping center composed of specialty stores, pushcart peddlers, and walkaway food merchants, that is often a tourist attraction within a city's cultural and entertainment center. Sometimes a creative reuse of abandoned warehouses or factories, urban specialty centers include

Figure 3.5

The Rouse Company is the leading developer of festival marketplaces. Their properties include New York's South Street Seaport, and Bayside in Miami.   *Courtesy of The Rouse Corporation.*

Company Profiles 3.1

The Mall of America has stretched the concept of the superregional shopping center to mammoth dimensions. Located in Bloomington, Minnesota, in suburban Minneapolis-St. Paul, the mall spans 4.2 million square feet, an area equivalent to ninety city blocks. The mall is anchored by Macy's, Nordstrom, Bloomingdale's, and Sears, joined by more than 400 specialty stores and more than 50 restaurants.

An extensive mix of stores is not the Mall of America's only draw. Designed as the largest retail and entertainment complex in the country, the Mall of America offers fourteen movie theaters, an eighteen-hole bi-level miniature golf course, Knott's Camp Snoopy, and the nation's largest enclosed theme park with indoor roller coaster. Unquestionably, the Mall of America is the quintessential shopping destination. Skeptics question the long-range future of the center, claiming that the Twin Cities are already overstored as home to more than a dozen shopping centers. However, the Mall of America does not rely soley on the Twin Cities market for its success. The mall competes with Disney World and the Grand Canyon as a major tourist attraction, drawing more than forty million domestic and foreign travelers each year.[1,2,3,4,5]

1. *Moin, David. (August 10, 1992). Mega-gamble in Minnesota.* Women's Wear Daily. *pp. 1, 6–7.*

2. *Kanner, Bernice. (March 29, 1993). Mall madness.* New York. *pp. 18–19.*

3. *Russell, David. (November 1990). Mega-gamble in Minneapolis.* American Demographics. *pp. 45–47.*

4. *Trachtenberg, Jeffrey. (October 30, 1990). Largest of all malls in U.S. is a gamble in Bloomington, Minn.* Wall Street Journal. *pp. A1, A14.*

5. *Waldrop, Judith. (August 1992). The biggest mall of all.* American Demographics. *p. 4.*

Roosevelt Field was constructed as an open-air shopping center in Garden City on New York's Long Island in 1956. The original Roosevelt Field had a Macy's and approximately twenty specialty stores, as well as an outparcel supermarket. The design of the center was unique in that it incorporated a central ice skating rink and cobblestone walks between stores. The time and place were right. Nassau County was one of the most densely populated and fastest growing areas of the country. Its roster of townships includes Levittown, the prototypical U.S. suburb.

As years passed, upscale and value-oriented centers emerged within short distances of Roosevelt Field, creating a fiercely competi-

continued

Company Profiles 3.1 continued

McQuiston, John. (April 23, 1993). Mall that helped start it all remakes itself to stay ahead. New York Times.

tive trading area. However, Roosevelt Field kept pace with the times and responded to increasing competition with a massive tenant mix and all the amenities of a shopping mecca. In 1968, the center was enclosed. When department store anchors went out of business, many were quickly replaced. Stern's replaced Gimbels, and Abraham & Straus replaced Alexander's. A JCPenney store eventually replaced the skating rink, and in 1995, Bloomingdale's replaced A&S. Renovations and/or expansions have occurred every

five to seven years at Roosevelt Field, a rate more than twice the shopping center in-dustry standard. In 1993, Roosevelt Field underwent a $150 million expansion and renovation that re-sulted in the addition of ninety stores bringing the total to more than 200 stores on three levels. A $12.5 million expansion begun in 1996 will add sixty stores, two parking decks, and Nordstrom as a fifth anchor, making Roosevelt Field one of the nation's most desirable retail locations.

1. *Doocey, Paul. (January 1992). When retailing's not enough, there's always densification. Shopping Centers Today.*
2. *Flanagan, Barbara. (March 14, 1991). A suburban mall is now "downtown". New York Times.*
3. *Swan, Marc. (February/March 1989). A tradition begins. . . Mashpee Commons brings community to a center. Cape Cod Life. pp. 28–37.*

Clapboard buildings, cast iron lampposts, a church with a towering steeple, and a village green with a bandstand come to mind when envisioning a traditional New England town. These images are especially descriptive of Mashpee Commons, the town center of Mashpee, Massachusetts, located on picturesque Cape Cod. However, unlike most New England town centers that can trace their roots to pre-Revolutionary days, Mashpee Commons began as the New Seabury Shopping Center, a strip center constructed in 1962.

Incorporated long after its neighboring townships, Mashpee's development was atypical of other

Cape Cod towns. Though Mashpee grew into a fully developed residential community, its commercial development was stifled by a protracted land ownership suit filed by the Wampanoag Indian Council that took many years to resolve. The result: a town without a town center, requiring the residents of Mashpee to travel to other communities for retail purchases, as well as for professional services and entertainment.

The owner of the New Seabury Shopping Center, Arnold Chace, recognized the need for a town center with convenient shopping and services. Along with Douglas Storrs, Chace conceived Mashpee

continued

Commons, a mixed use center of retail stores, a church, a library, a post office, and a housing complex for the elderly. Carved out of the New Seabury Shopping Center's parking lot, Mashpee Commons was designed as a replica of an old New England town with tree-lined streets, narrow sidewalks, granite curbs, benches, and rounded brick front federal-style buildings that reflect the architecture indigenous to the area.

Mashpee Commons reverses the original concept of the MXD, which converted a downtown into a mall, by converting a mall into a downtown. As one of the developers of Mashpee Commons observed: The concept is over 200 years old. Its just been ignored for the past forty years.[1,2,3]

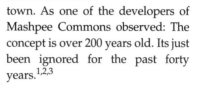

Boston's Quincy Market and Faneuil Hall Marketplace, New York's South Street Seaport, Baltimore's Harborplace, and Miami's Bayside. The Rouse Company of Columbia, Maryland, is the reputed innovator and leading developer of festival marketplaces.

Outlet Center   An **outlet center** is a strip or enclosed center with a tenant mix composed of factory outlet stores. Originally attracting retailers of moderately priced goods, such as Van Heusen shirts and Hanes underwear, an increasing number of producers of upscale merchandise now operate outlet stores. The tenants of Woodbury Common in Central Valley, New York include Adrienne Vittadini, Dansk, Charles Jourdan, Anne Klein, Donna Karan, Mark Cross, Waterford Crystal, and Gucci.

Outlet centers experienced significant growth in the 1980s as manufacturers began to recognize the advantages of vertical integration. Though manufacturers' outlets represent the majority in an outlet center's tenant mix, off-pricers are also becoming more common in these centers, leading some to refer to an outlet center as an *off-price center* or a *value-oriented center.*

To avoid conflict between manufacturers and their conventional retail channels, outlet centers are often located in excess of sixty miles from traditional distribution channels, though some recently developed centers fall within this geographic boundary. Outlet centers are destination centers to which customers drive an average of 125 miles and where tour buses are the mainstay of marketing programs. The

Figure 3.6

Slidell Factory Outlets, Slidell, Louisiana, managed by Company Store Development Corporation, Brentwood, Tennessee.

Lake Erie Outlet Center is located fifty miles from Cleveland and Toledo, and 100 miles from Columbus. The center benefits from its proximity to the Lake Erie vacation area, which annually attracts 7.5 million tourists.[22,23,24]

Power Center   A **power center** is typically an open air center with a tenant mix of big box discounters such as category killers, warehouse clubs, off-pricers, full-line discounters, and supercenters. The mix is sometimes supplemented by a strip of smaller stores with a food supermarket and/or full-line discounter. Becoming popular in the mid 1980s, the power center is a growing shopping center category. Like strip centers, power centers operate on a low cost structure. They are often located near a superregional shopping center in an effort to feed off its traffic.

Power centers rely on the consumer's interest in value shopping versus recreational or fashion shopping. Because each store in a power center is a destination store, there is little browsing, cross shopping, or comparison shopping from store to store as there is in a mall. As a destination center, power centers claim that 85 percent of power center shoppers buy something upon each visit, versus only 50 percent of mall shoppers.[25,26]

Figure 3.7

Anaheim Plaza in Southern California was an enclosed regional shopping center that was converted to an open-air power center.   *The O'Connor Group, New York, NY.*

The growth of the shopping center industry in the United States has been explosive. There were 4500 shopping centers in the country in 1960. By 1990, the number had increased to 36,650, a growth rate higher than the growth rate of the population or retail sales or any other economic indicator.[27] Most observers concur that the marketplace is saturated with shopping centers and that future shopping center development will be the renovation, expansion, and new use of existing centers, and not ground-up construction of new centers.

THE MIX OF STORES IN A SHOPPING CENTER

An ideal mix of shopping center tenants offers a range of merchandise categories, brands, services, and prices, while avoiding redundancies. Often the mix is designed to attract a specific type of customer, or to satisfy a particular shopping need. *Convenience, discount, fashion,* and *upscale* are all words that are used to characterize shopping centers. Anchors strongly influence a shopping center's image. A center anchored by JCPenney and Sears conveys a moderate-price image. A

Table 3.2   **REAL ESTATE—WINNERS AND LOSERS**

Winners	Losers
Dominant superregionals	Two-anchor regional malls
Specialty discount superstores	Warehouse clubs
Neighborhood centers with strong supermarkets	Unanchored strips
Surviving department stores	Hypermarkets
Home Depot	Regional home improvement chains
Power centers with premier category killers	Power centers with third-string category killers
Lifestyle clustering of store types	Scattering children's wear or shoe stores throughout the mall
Market-sensitive store mix	Cookie-cutter malls

Reprinted with permission. M. Leanne Lachman and Deborah L. Brett, Retail Trends: Consumers, Goods, and Real Estate, *Schroder Real Estate Associates "Commentary," New York, New York (Summer 1994), p. 28.*

center anchored by Nordstrom and Bloomingdale's conveys an upscale image.

Though anchors establish a center's image, specialty tenants contribute to a center's breadth. To ensure compatibility with other stores in a center, specialty stores often state specific **cotenancy requirements.** An upscale store, such as Ann Taylor, may require the presence of other prestigious stores such as Abercrombie & Fitch, Eddie Bauer, and at least one fashion department store before signing on with a center.

The strategy for composing a tenant mix is based on the type of competition between stores. **Directly competing** stores offer the same merchandise. **Indirectly competing** stores offer the same type of merchandise, but different assortments of prices and brands. **Complementary stores** stimulate each other's sales. An apparel store and a shoe store are complementary. Leasing agents maximize the number of customers drawn to a shopping center by creating a synergistic mix of indirectly competing and complementary stores. As indirect competitors, JCPenney and Lord & Taylor contribute to a center's breadth and attractiveness to a diverse group of customers. Complementary stores enhance customer convenience and one-stop shopping. Direct competition in a shopping center cannibalizes the sales of competing stores. The presence of PriceCostco and Sam's Club in the same power center makes no sense competitively.

MARKETING MYOPIA

Francesca Turchiano, president of In-Fact, a New York-based consulting firm, predicts that many of the regional shopping centers now operating in the United States will close by the 21st century. She cites several factors that are causing shrinking profits in the shopping center industry, including the fragmentation of consumer markets, the high cost of removing asbestos from older malls, the shopping preferences of working women, and the proliferation of catalogs. However, Turchiano cites the four main causes of the coming contraction as "marketing myopia", the department store debacle, an aging population, and shopping fatigue.

Marketing myopia is a term that characterizes the behavior of shopping center owners who allow return on investment, operating efficiencies, and profit margins to take precedence over satisfying customers. Physical evidence of marketing myopia is poor housekeeping, an inconsistent tenant mix, outdated mall directories, and too many redundant clothing stores. To survive and prosper in the 21st century, shopping center managers must manage centers as integrated entities that connect with all other channels of distribution. Each center needs to be designed, leased, and marketed in such a way that its target market will find it compelling, and its competitors will find it hard to duplicate.

The Department Store Debacle: The foundations of many department stores have weakened in recent years. In an effort to bolster profits, many have reduced sales help and store maintenance. Many shoppers see department stores as stale and unexciting. The shakeout among department stores will continue, causing a falling domino effect across the shopping center industry.

An Aging Population: People aged fifty and older control half of the nation's discretionary income. Yet few shopping centers know how to respond to an aging population. Five sure selling points to attract mature customers to a shopping center include: security, quality, comfort, and convenience, socialization, and recognition. With the exception of security, these qualities are not easily found in most shopping centers. Restrooms are difficult to find; mall seating is sparse to deter teens from loitering; mall directories are often out of date and printed in small type; and salespeople are underpaid, undertrained, unfriendly, and impersonal. If regional shopping centers do not develop programs to attract and retain older shoppers, they can expect many more customers to defect to armchair shopping.

continued

Marketing Myopia   *continued*

Shopping fatigue: "Shop Till You Drop" was the motto of the 1980s, however, a published report of *The Wall Street Journal* indicates that many Americans are curtailing their acquisitiveness. Some have indicated that they have fulfilled most, if not all, of their material needs. The majority of Americans may now want to clear their closets and shop for new experiences, not new merchandise. They're frustrated with high prices, mediocre quality, and lack of customer service. Poor service may have been tolerated in the past, however, today's consumers now have many shopping options. They will bypass poorly run centers in favor of less stressful shopping alternatives.

In general, shopping center owners and managers must target specific market segments within their trading areas to capture a significant share of the expenditures of that market. Tomorrow's survivors will renovate, lease, and market the mall to be one irresistible product.

Adapted from Turchiano, Francesca. (April 1990). The Malling of America. American Demographics. pp. 37–39.

SUMMARY POINTS

- Unplanned shopping areas include central business districts, secondary business districts, and town centers.
- Planned shopping centers include open air neighborhood and community centers, called strips, and enclosed regional and superregional centers called malls.
- Other types of planned centers include mixed use centers, pedestrian malls, outlet centers, and power centers.
- Competition among stores in shopping areas can be direct, indirect, or complementary.

KEY TERMS AND CONCEPTS

branch	festival marketplace	regional center
central business	indirect competition	shopping center
district	mixed-use center	strip center
community center	neighborhood center	superregional center
complementary store	outlet center	town center
cotenancy requirement	pedestrian mall	
direct competition	power center	

FOR DISCUSSION

1. Identify the following types of shopping areas/centers in the local area and the stores that are in each:

    town center   community center
    neighborhood center   power center

2. Identify a regional and superregional center. How do they compare in terms of the number of anchors and the types of stores? The number of stores? At which center do you prefer to shop? Why?

3. Identify an MXD in a familiar city. Assess its retail component. Assess the retail environment of the CBD in which the MXD is located.

SUGGESTED READINGS

Kowinski, William. (1985). *The Malling of America.* New York: William Morrow.

Lebhar, Godfrey. (1963). *Chain Stores in America.* New York: Chain Store Publishing.

ENDNOTES

1. The predecessor of Lerner New York, now a division of The Limited.
2. Lebhar, Godfrey. (1963). *Chain Stores in America.* New York: Chain Store Publishing.
3. Ghosh, Avijit & McLafferty, Sara. (Fall 1991). The shopping center: A restructuring of post-war retailing. *Journal of Retailing,* 67, 3. pp. 253–267.
4. Staff. (1987). The evolution of regional shopping centers. Equitable Real Estate Investment Management.
5. Reynolds, Mike. (August 1990). Food courts: Tasty! *Stores.* p. 52–54.
6. Doocey, Paul. (February 1992). Northeast rally. *Stores.* pp. 67–69.
7. Pearson, Bill. (August 1993). The times, they are a changing. *Stores.* p. 73.
8. Many branches were in fact *twigs,* stores that offered only a limited number of merchandise categories available in the flagship.
9. Peterson, Eric. (March 1990). Strip centers: Changing? *Stores.* pp. 53–54.
10. Walker, Chip. (October 1991). Strip malls: plain but powerful. *American Demographics.* pp. 48–51.
11. Barmash, Isadore. (September 27, 1992). For shopping centers, less is becoming more. *New York Times.* p. 5.
12. Edelson, Sharon. (August 9, 1995). Strip centers: The chain reaction. *Women's Wear Daily.* p. 9.
13. Webster defines a mall as a "shaded walk or public promenade" and a "shop-lined street for pedestrians only." Thus, a mall is not necessarily

enclosed. Bal Harbour Shops is an upscale, open-air shopping center located north of Miami Beach, Florida. The open-air pedestrian walkways that connect the stores at Bal Harbor Shops are closed to vehicular traffic.

14. Peterson, Eric. (February 1990). The 1990s: What's ahead. *Stores.* pp. 73–76.
15. Edelson, Sharon. (August 9, 1995). A new hybrid: The category killer moves in. *Women's Wear Daily.* p. 8.
16. Rudnitsky, Howard. (March 30, 1992). Battle of the malls. *Forbes.* p. 46–47.
17. Solomon, Barbara. (March 17, 1993). Malls mix it up. *Women's Wear Daily.* pp. 1, 6–7.
18. Garreau, Joel. (1991). *Edge City: Life on the New Frontier.* New York: Doubleday.
19. Peterson, Eric. (January 1986). MXD-mall excitement. *Stores.* pp. 144–146, 151–152, 187.
20. Houstoun, Lawrence. (June 1990). From street to mall and back again. *Planning.* pp. 4–10.
21. Robertson, Kent. (December 1990). The status of the pedestrian mall in American downtowns. *Urban Affairs Quarterly,* 26, 2. pp. 250–273.
22. Bredin, Alice. (March 1992). Outlet centers prosper. *Stores.* pp. 63–65.
23. Morgenson, Gretchen. (May 27, 1991). Cheapie Gucci. *Forbes.* pp. 43–44.
24. Staff. (April 1990). Factory outlet centers keep their distance. *Chain Store Age Executive.* pp. 39–42.
25. Staff. (September 1986). Power centers: Everybody wins. *Chain Store Age Executive.* pp. 35–40.
26. Staff. (November 18, 1992). Power centers fast and focused. *Women's Wear Daily.* pp. 14, 18.
27. Ghosh, Avijit & McLafferty, Sara. (Fall 1991). The shopping center: A restructuring of post-war retailing. *Journal of Retailing,* 67, 3. pp. 253–267.

chapter four

RETAIL GROWTH AND EXPANSION

Bigger is often better in today's retail environment. Large retail organizations have distinct competitive advantages over smaller retailers because of their dominance of the marketplace and the clout that they exert with suppliers.[1,2] To remain competitive, aggressive retail organizations continually pursue growth opportunities by opening stores in new markets, buying existing retail enterprises, and developing new formats or merchandising concepts.[3] Chapter 4 covers some of the strategies used by retailers to position themselves for continued growth.

After you have read this chapter, you will be able to discuss:

The impact of centralization on operational and fiscal efficiency.

Retail expansion strategies.

The importance of international retailing.

Opportunities for independent retailers.

CENTRALIZATION

Centralization involves performing functions for an organization's remote facilities from a single location, usually a corporate office, for the sake of fiscal and operational efficiency. In a retail organization, *centralized buying* means that merchandise is bought corporately for all stores. Decentralization is the opposite of centralization. *Decentralized buying* means that individual stores are responsible for buying their own merchandise.

Centralization is an organizational concept that is fundamental to the success of many retailers. To understand the impact of centralization, consider the following scenario:

Marie Taylor is the owner of five children's specialty stores in Florida called Monkeys and Pumpkins. Marie opened her first store on Fort Lauderdale's Los Olas Boulevard in 1985. The store's immediate success spurred the opening of a second store in Palm Beach, and subsequent stores in South Miami Beach, Key West, and St. Augustine. Though the stores have a common identity, they function independently of each another. A buyer/manager at each location is responsible for merchandising/operating the store with the assistance of office and selling staffs.

The strategy that Marie has adopted for operating her stores is rare. In multistore retail organizations, functions that do not require cus-

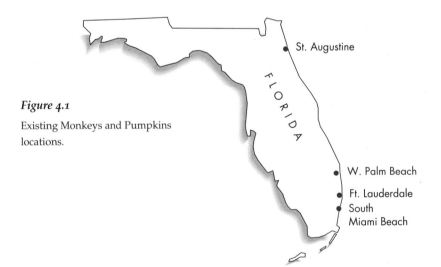

Figure 4.1

Existing Monkeys and Pumpkins locations.

tomer proximity are likely to be centralized for the sake of operational efficiency. Stores perform only those activities that are directly related to selling, and the operational activities of maintaining the store and inventory. Functions, such as buying, accounting, and sales promotion, are executed centrally.

To understand the advantages of centralization, consider the positive results of Marie Taylor's decision to centralize the buying functions in an office facility in Orlando.

- Redundancies are reduced. Prior to centralization *five* buyer/managers shopped the same wholesale children's wear markets and processed *five* sets of orders for merchandise. By centralizing, *one* buyer can cover the market, and processes one set of orders for all stores.
- Specialization is fostered. Prior to centralization, five buyer/managers performed a mix of merchandising and operational functions. The centralized buyer can devote undivided attention to buying. As the organization grows and additional buyers are hired, each can concentrate on specific children's market segments, such as boys, girls, and infants and toddlers, resulting in more intense market coverage.
- Expenses are reduced. Though operating a central organization is costly, the expenses are more than offset by eliminating the non-selling functions in stores.
- Quantity discounts are realized. The buyer/managers wrote orders for *hundreds* of items. The central buyer can write orders for *thousands* of items, thus qualifying for price incentives from suppliers for placing large orders.
- Merchandise offerings are consistent in every store. Image was inconsistent among the stores when assortments reflected the choices of five different buyer/managers.
- The groundwork for expansion is laid. The inventory needs of the new stores that Marie is planning in Savannah, Naples, and Charleston, can be served by the existing central buying structure without having to add additional staff.

Advancements in transportation and communication have facilitated centralization. The Interstate Highway Act of 1955 enabled the construction of an infrastructure to transport merchandise from national and regional distribution centers to a network of stores. Computer systems that track sales and inventory activity at hundreds

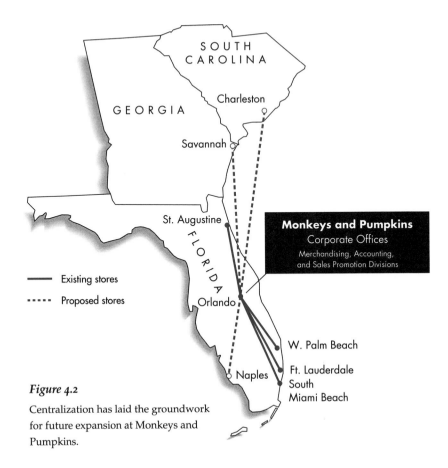

Figure 4.2

Centralization has laid the groundwork for future expansion at Monkeys and Pumpkins.

of retail locations, triggering immediate replenishment of goods from vendors as the merchandise is sold, have made it possible to buy for a vast complex of stores from a single location.[4]

In spite of the many positive outcomes that result from centralization, there are some who decry it, claiming that centralization strips stores of their ability to respond to local market conditions. In response to this dilemma, some retailers adopt a decentralized or regional merchandising approach. Dillard's and Nordstrom are two highly successful department store chains that group stores by geographic regions defined by climate and customer profile. Each region has a buying organization to serve that region. Both companies feel that regional differences require different merchandise assortments and that customers' needs are best met when buyers are close to the point of sale.

The warehouse and requisition plan and the price agreement plan are modified versions of central buying whereby some degree of purchase decision is retained at store-level. In the **warehouse and requisition plan,** a central buyer determines the assortments that are carried in stores, however, store level merchandisers choose specific quantities by size, color, and style. The system is used for the replenishment of basic goods that are centrally warehoused and carried from one season to another. In the **price agreement plan,** or *listing plan,* a central buyer provides stores with a list of preferred merchandise resources from which stores can directly order goods. At JCPenney, store-level merchandisers compose individual store assortments based on demographics and climate. Corporate buyers use an electronic satellite system to show the products available, ranking each from high to low in terms of sales potential. The buyers also communicate information on planned promotional events and the key factors that will drive business. The process is supported by print and electronic price lists of product images with specifications of fabric content and color availability.

Centralization is not a new concept nor is it peculiar to retailing. The early variety store chains were centralized operations. The strategy is applied in every industry with multifacility operations, including financial services, manufacturing, and service franchising.

RETAIL OWNERSHIP

An understanding of a retail organizations' ownership structure is fundamental to understanding its competitive position in the marketplace and potential for growth. Type of ownership is often tied to the manner in which a retail organization carries out its merchandising function, and the way in which the organization is managed.

A **public,** or *publicly held,* retail organization has many owners, or shareholders. A public company's stock is available to the general public and is sold, or traded, on a public stock exchange, such as the New York Stock Exchange (NYSE), or the American Stock Exchange (AMEX). The stock of a **private,** or *privately held,* retail organization is not traded on a public exchange. A private company has fewer owners than a public company, sometimes only one. The owners are sometimes a family or a management group within the organization. When a public organization is bought by private investors, the organization is said to be *taken private.*

Dillard's believes that buyers should be close to the point of sale. To achieve this objective, the 250 Dillard's stores are grouped into seven geographically defined regions of between seven and fifty stores. Each region has a merchandising structure of general merchandise managers, divisional merchandise managers, and buyers. The regional structures allow each region to respond to the geographic distinctions among Dillards' customers, insuring that the down coat inventories in the Cleveland region are peaking at about the same time that the swimwear is beginning to arrive in the Florida region. The merchandising function is further refined for stores that do not fit into the profile of a region. Because the Dillard's store in McAllen, Texas, on the border of the Rio Grande, is distinct from the other stores in the San Antonio region, McAllen has its own group of four buyers who respond to the needs of a large number of Mexican shoppers. Individual stores are responsible for replenishing reorderable merchandise, such as cosmetics and hosiery. The system fosters faster response to stockouts of certain sizes or colors that may sell more rapidly in one store than another.

Consistency among stores and a merchandise mix that is distinctly Dillard's is ensured through a strong interplay among the seven regional merchandising structures. Merchandise resources for each department are determined by a committee of buyers representing the various regions. However, regional buyers determine the actual committments to each vendor for the stores in their region. A vendor structure for better sportswear might include Liz Claiborne, Jones New York, and Calvin Klein, however, each regional buyer determines how much to buy from each resource.

Dillard's acknowledges that the heart of its business is on the selling floor and encourages intense interaction between its merchandising divisions and stores through frequent buyer visits. Buyers also play an active role in product training for salespeople, using satellite communication to convey vendors' product information and the product characteristics that stimulated their purchase decisions.

Though a decentralized buying structure is more costly to administer than a single centralized structure, the investment has paid off for Dillard's. In just over sixty years, Dillard's has grown from a single Little Rock, Arkansas store to one of this country's most highly reputed and profitable department store groups.

Public companies often begin as private companies. Private companies *go public* with an **initial public offering** (IPO) of stock to obtain capital to expand the organization. By going public, the original owners relinquish some of their control over the organization in that, as owners, the new shareholders acquire voting power that can be exercised in the organization's decision making. The original owners of a public company can retain voting control in the organization by retaining ownership of more than 50 percent of the company's stock. The Dillard family owns a majority of the stock of Dillard Department Stores.

The term *independent* is often used to refer to a single, privately owned store. However, privately held, multistore retailers are also "independent." Though small retail organizations are likely to be private, and large organizations are likely to be public, size is not an absolute indication of public or private ownership. Saks Fifth Avenue, a group of more than fifty specialty department and resort specialty stores, is privately held.

A **chain** of retail stores is two or more stores with the same ownership and identity. The word chain is often used to refer to a large group of value-oriented stores, such as Sears or Kmart. However, a chain can be as few as two stores and the use of the term is irrelevant to type of retail format. Chains are classified as local, regional, or national, relative to the geographic span of stores:

- A local chain operates stores within a narrow geographic area, usually defined by a city and its outlying areas.
- A regional chain operates stores within a region or regions of the country, such as the Southwest, or Northeast.
- A national chain operates stores in virtually every region of the country.

A **conglomerate** is an organization that unites the ownership of independently operated **subsidiaries,** or *operating divisions*. A conglomerate is often referred to as a *parent company,* or *parent organization.* One of the oldest retail conglomerates is the Cincinnati-based Federated Department Stores. Founded in 1929, Federated united the ownership of New York's Abraham & Strauss and Bloomingdale's, Cincinnati's Lazarus Department Stores, and Boston's Filene's. Today, Federated's portfolio of stores includes more than 400 department stores in six operating divisions that still includes Bloomingdale's, as well as New York-based Macy's, Miami-based Burdines, Atlanta-based Rich's,

Figure 4.3

Federated Department Stores is one of the oldest existing retail conglomerates.

Seattle-based The Bon Marche, and Paramus, New Jersey-based Stern's.

A conglomerate is often organized to perform centralized functions for its operating divisions. Federated Merchandising is a division of Federated Department Stores that is responsible for developing merchandising strategies for the Federated operating divisions. FM provides leadership in the areas of merchandise systems, visual presentation, inventory management, and merchandise distribution. FM is also responsible for coordinating private label programs for all Federated divisions.

Though the parent organization performs certain centralized functions, operating divisions in a conglomerate remain autonomous. This level of autonomy varies from one organization to another. Federated Department Stores was once a highly decentralized conglomerate. Each division was operated as a distinct retail entity with little control by Federated's Cincinnati headquarters. However, Federated's failure to eliminate organizational redundancies with a higher degree of centralization led to a decline in profitability during the early 1980s. Federated's depressed stock value made it ripe for a takeover by the Campeau Corporation, which ultimately led the organization into bankruptcy.[5]

May Department Stores is a highly centralized conglomerate. Though May's operating divisions have different banners, including Foley's of Houston, Filene's of Boston, and Hecht's of Washington, D.C., many functions are coordinated centrally for all divisions at May's St. Louis headquarters, including store design, customer service programs, and operating systems.

A retail organization can be decentralized at conglomerate level, but centralized at division level. The operating divisions of The Limited, Inc. have complete merchandising and operational autonomy. Though financial controls are administered centrally, each division develops its own merchandising strategy independent of the parent company.[6] Though The Limited is a decentralized conglomerate, the operating divisions of The Limited are highly centralized. Store operations are rigidly orchestrated through manuals, floor plans, and other forms of communication disseminated from each division's Columbus, Ohio headquarters.

Diversification

Diversification is an organizational growth strategy that involves entering a line business that differs from present businesses. Retail organizations diversify when they perceive limited growth within their existing formats or merchandising concepts. Diversified retailers insulate themselves against changes in the marketplace that may affect one of its operations. The Dayton Hudson Corporation is a diversified conglomerate with a portfolio of stores that includes three formats:

- an upscale department store division that includes Dayton's, Hudson's, and Marshall Field's,
- a value-oriented specialty department store division called Mervyn's; and
- a fashion-oriented full-line discounter called Target.

Table 4.1 DILLARD'S GROWTH THROUGH ACQUISITION

Year	Store, Owner	Number of Stores and Their Locations	Price
1984	Stix Baer & Fuller Associated Dry Goods	12 stores in Kansas and Missouri	$90 million
	John A. Brown Dayton Hudson Corporation	6 stores in Oklahoma	$140 million together
	Diamond's Dayton Hudson Corporation	12 stores in Arizona and Nevada	
1986	Macy's R.H. Macy & Company	12 stores in Kansas and Missouri	Not available
1987	Joske's/Cain-Sloan Allied stores	31 stores in Arizona, Tennessee, and Texas	$255 million
1988	50% of Higbee Independent	14 stores in Ohio	$82.5 million
1989	D.H. Holmes Independent	18 stores in Alabama, Arizona, Florida, Louisiana, and Mississippi	$40 million
1990	J.B. Ivey & Company B.A.T.U.S.	23 stores in Florida, North Carolina, and South Carolina	$110 million
1991	Maison Blanche Independent	8 stores in Florida	$68 million
1992	Remaining 50% of Higbee Edward J. DeBartolo	14 stores in Ohio	Not available

Copyright © 1994 by the New York Times Company. Reprinted by permission.

Retailers diversify by developing, or *spinning off*, new retail formats or merchandising concepts. A steady emergence of new specialty store concepts transformed the Woolworth Corporation from a retailing dinosaur to a progressive specialty retailer. Woolworth's diversified portfolio of over forty different merchandising concepts includes Champs Sports, After Thoughts (accessories), and the San Francisco Music Box Company (gifts). Woolworth strongly encourages its management to develop new merchandising concepts which, when approved, are tested in five test market shopping centers for a year. Though some concepts, such as Foot Locker, have been instant success

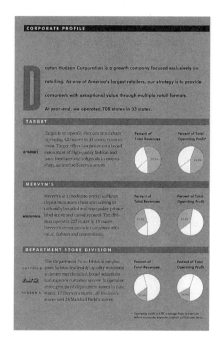

Figure 4.4

The Dayton Hudson Corporation is a diversified retail conglomerate.

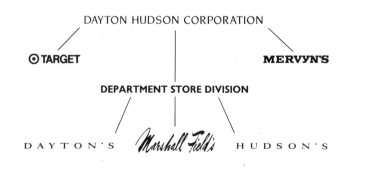

stories, other merchandising experiments have fizzled. Face Fantasies, a value-priced cosmetics outlet; Frame Scenes, a retailer of prints and frames; and J. Brannam, a discount apparel chain, are among Woolworth's infant fatalities. However, Woolworth's one year trial period ensures that poor performers do not drain company profits for very long.[7,8]

Spinning off new merchandising concepts too closely related to existing businesses results in **cannibalization.** Woolworth's Foot Locker gave birth to Kids' Foot Locker, Lady Foot Locker, and World Foot Locker. Though each new offspring evolved into a viable merchandising concept, each cannibalized some of the parent division's business.[9,10] Cannibalization also occurs when a chain opens new stores too close to existing stores.

MERGERS AND ACQUISITIONS

Retail organizations grow through mergers and acquisitions. A **merger** occurs when two or more companies are combined to form a new organization. When two retail organizations are merged, or *consolidated*, the corporate structure of one company, typically the weaker or smaller, is dissolved, leaving a single corporate structure to support both groups of stores. In 1969, The Dayton Company of Minneapolis merged with J.L. Hudson's of Detroit to form the Dayton Hudson Corporation.

Not every merger is a perfect union. In 1988, Ames Department Stores acquired Zayre, another full-line discounter, making Ames the nation's fourth largest full-line discounter after the Big Three. The incompatibility between Ames and Zayre became evident quickly. Ames' nonpromotional pricing strategy targeted to small-town consumers in secondary markets alienated Zayre's urban customers who were accustomed to a barrage of sale events. Ames filed bankruptcy in 1990, and closed most of the Zayre stores before emerging from bankruptcy in 1993.

Operating divisions within a conglomerate are sometimes merged for operational efficiency and expense savings. In 1995, Federated Department Stores merged Lazarus with Rich's. In 1993, May Department Stores merged G.Fox with Filene's. The Lazarus/Rich's merger resulted in a $27 million annual savings for Federated.[11] The G.Fox/Filene's merger resulted in annual savings of more than $30

WHAT CONSTITUTES A MONOPOLY?

The Lord & Taylor division of May Department Stores operates stores in shopping centers anchored by other May Company department stores. Why does the Federal Trade Commission permit this? For two reasons: Since Lord & Taylor is more upscale than May's other divisions, Lord & Taylor customers are perceived as a different market than the customers of other May Company stores. Secondly, the shopping centers in which May operates both a Lord & Taylor and another May Company store are typically superregional centers with other anchor stores that dilute the potential of a May monopoly.

---

million for May.[12] May Department Stores has taken advantage of the geographic proximity of several of its operating divisions by merging them into eight streamlined groups of stores.

An *acquisition*, or *takeover*, is the purchase of another organization. An acquisition that is welcomed by the organization being acquired is called a *friendly takeover*. In a friendly takeover, the acquired organization often recognizes management compatibility, or that the acquiring organization, or *friendly suitor*, is in a position to provide financing to an otherwise poorly capitalized or fiscally troubled company.[13] An acquisition that is resisted by the organization being acquired is called a *hostile takeover*. In a hostile takeover, the organization being acquired fears incompatibility of merchandising or management philosophies, or loss of jobs.

A **bidding war** sometimes ensues between two or more parties interested in acquiring the same organization. The parties attempt to outbid each other by a series of counter-offers, often resulting in the sale of an organization's stock for a price greater than its worth. In 1988, the Campeau Corporation offered the shareholders of Federated Department Stores $4.2 billion for the company. As a result of a two-month bidding war with Macy's, Campeau paid $6.6 billion for Federated, a price far greater than the value of the company.

An acquisition that is financed through debt is called a **leveraged buyout** (LBO). An *internal buyout* is the acquisition of an organization by its employees. In 1986, 348 Macy's executives acquired Macy's from its shareholders in the largest internal buyout of any retail organization in history. Unable to meet the bond and interest payments associated

---

MARRYING FOR MONEY

When real-estate values skyrocketed in the 1980s, many retailers became the takeover targets of real-estate developers covetous of valuable store sites. Department stores were especially vulnerable to takeover in that other retailers, such as specialty stores and discounters, were more likely to lease rather than own sites. The acquisition of a department store also ensured developers of a captive anchor for future shopping center developments.[1]

Though a seemingly compatible match, many shopping center/department store marriages were of short duration. Crown American once owned Hess's Department Stores of Allentown, Pennsylvania. Australia-based L.J. Hooker owned New York's Bonwit Teller and B. Altman, and Sakowitz of Houston. Donohoe, O'Brien & Company owned Miller & Rhoads of Richmond. Vyzis Development was the owner of Frederick & Nelson in Seattle. The Taubman Investment Company was once the largest shareholder of Woodward & Lothrop of Washington, D.C., and John Wanamaker of Philadelphia. None of these department stores are in business today.[2]

1. Gilman, Alan. (May 1990). Who was minding the store? Retailing Issues Letter. *pp. 5, 6.*
2. Bivins, Jacquelyn. (May 1988). Campeau in control at Federated. Chain Store Age. *pp. 39–42.*

with the highly leveraged buyout, Macy's filed bankruptcy in 1992. The ailing Macy's was acquired by Federated Department Stores in 1994.

Acquired organizations are either operated as subsidiaries, or merged with another corporate entity. Acquisitions are typical of a department store's growth strategy, since department stores have reached a saturation point in most markets with few opportunities for building new stores. The Federal Trade Commission, a regulatory agency that monitors unfair competition, reviews all proposals for acquisitions and mergers to determine if the resulting organization will restrict competition by its dominance in the marketplace. When Federated Department Stores acquired Macy's in 1994, Federated agreed to sell off several stores in shopping centers where the company already operated stores.[14,15]

Divestiture is the sale of an organization's assets. Retail organizations divest of stores or entire operating divisions to generate capital and/or to concentrate on other areas of business. Unprofitable units or divisions are the most likely candidates for divestiture. At one point in its history, the portfolio of Federated Department Stores included sixteen groups of stores including three discounters, Main Street, Gold Circle, and Richway. May Department Stores once owned two full-line discount chains, Venture and Caldor. Both companies sold their discount chains to concentrate on their core department store businesses. Kmart divested of three specialty businesses, Sports Authority, Office Max, and Borders/Waldenbooks, to devote more attention to its full-line discount stores.

BANKRUPTCY

Unfortunately, a discussion of the growth and expansion of retail organizations is incomplete without a discussion of bankruptcy. **Bankruptcy** occurs when an organization becomes insolvent or incapable of paying its debts. An organization is bankrupt when its liabilities exceed its assets.

Many retail bankruptcies were rooted in leveraged buyouts of the prosperous 1980s. The financing for these pricey acquisitions was often obtained by using the assets of the organization as collateral to borrow from lending institutions, and the issue of high-yield, high-risk **junk bonds**[16] The interest payments on these large debts put an added expense burden on the retailers. When the retail business went into a slump at the end of the decade, sales could no longer support the interest payments. The Campeau Corporation paid over $11 billion for the acquisitions of Allied Stores and Federated Department Stores in 1986 and 1988, respectively. Much of the funding for these acquisitions was through junk bonds that carried an annual interest debt of $600 million. Two years later, the merged Allied/Federated was unable to meet its interest payments and filed bankruptcy, owing more than $8 billion to more than 40,000 creditors.[17]

The Federal Bankruptcy Act was enacted in 1898 to establish guidelines for insolvent debtors to pay their creditors. The act was written in sections or chapters; the most often cited is Chapter 11. In 1978, the laws were rewritten to "protect" companies from their creditors by prohibiting their petitioning a court for liquidation of a debtor's assets to pay its debts. Chapter 11 freezes a debtor's indebtedness to lending institutions, suppliers, and the holders of junk bonds. The debtor organization retains its assets for use in a **plan of reorganization** (*POR*) designed to help the debtor regain profitability.[18]

Company Profile 4.2

When Allen Questrom left Federated Department Stores for Dallas-based Neiman Marcus in 1988, he had no idea that he would return to Federated two years later to rescue the prestigious department store conglomerate from the ravages of high debt and eroding market share that forced it into bankruptcy. As Chairman and Chief Executive Officer, Questrom embarked upon a plan of reorganization that included a highly focused merchandising strategy. His *11 Commandments of Retailing* placed a stronger emphasis on private label merchandise. He developed more efficient buying practices by centralizing many of the buying functions of the conglomerate's operating divisions. He deemed high markdowns and slow-turning merchandise as deadly sins. Questrom's plan encouraged a more intense focus on the home furnishings and accessories business. Since much of this business had been abandoned by department stores, Questrom felt that the limited amount of competition would ensure Federated an exclusive niche in the marketplace.

Questrom's strategy was highly successful. Federated emerged from bankruptcy in 1992. Two years later Federated surpassed May Department Stores as the nation's largest department store conglomerate when it acquired the bankrupt R.H. Macy. Federated's 1995 acquisition of The Broadway created a portfolio of stores that span the country from the east to west coasts, recapturing Federated's distinction as a preeminent department store conglomerate, well poised for future growth.[1,2]

1. *Phillips, Stephen & Zinn, Laura. (July 16, 1990). Can Allen Questrom get the up escalator moving?* Business Week. *pp. 66–67.*
2. *Einhorn, Cheryl. (February 13, 1995). Miracle worker.* Barrons.

Some of the actions typical of a POR include:

- Terminating the organization's leadership, and hiring a "turn-around" leader with a track record of rescuing ailing retailers.
- Closing unprofitable units.
- Implementing expense-saving measures.
- Selling unprofitable units or divisions. The sell-off infuses the company with cash to reduce debt, and generally results in a smaller but better focused organization.[19]

Because its pre-Chapter 11 debts are frozen, a bankrupt retailer starts with a clean slate and can obtain a new line of credit from lending institutions to continue shipments from suppliers. Creditors are

Figure 4.5

Carson Pirie Scott emerged from bankruptcy as a stronger, more clearly focused retailer.

willing to extend credit to the retailer, since Chapter 11 guarantees that indebtedness incurred after the Chapter 11 filing will receive priority payment, taking precedence over the payment of any old debt. Emergence from bankruptcy occurs when the company becomes profitable. Pre-Chapter 11 debts are settled by offering creditors equity in the company as partial debt payment. Thus, the creditors become the owners of the company.[20]

Critics of the Federal Bankruptcy Laws claim that the 1978 revisions to Chapter 11 encourages organizations to take reckless risks, knowing that the government will shield them from their creditors. Why does the federal government "protect" organizations that have been haphazard in their fiscal management at the expense of creditors who, in good faith, financed and supplied the debtor? Consider the tragic alternative to Chapter 11: lost jobs, vacant storefronts, fewer points of distribution for suppliers, and fewer shopping alternatives for consumers.[21]

INTERNATIONAL RETAILING

Throughout the 1980s, retail space in the United States grew by 58 percent, rising from 13 square feet per capita to a staggering 18 square feet.[22] As the United States marketplace becomes saturated with retail stores, expansion in less competitive foreign markets has become a viable alternative to domestic growth. The assortments, convenience, and value that United States retailers offer consumers is unmatched in many other countries, making retailing a very exportable concept.

Several factors have made the global marketplace ripe for retail expansion. The North American Free Trade Agreement (NAFTA) has created the world's largest free trade zone between the United States, Canada, and Mexico. Mexico has become an area of promising opportunity since the passage of NAFTA. Foreign manufacturers have stimulated Mexico's economy by creating jobs which, in turn, has stimulated

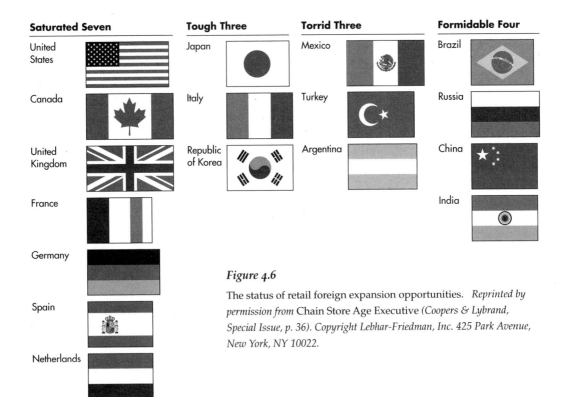

Figure 4.6

The status of retail foreign expansion opportunities. *Reprinted by permission from* Chain Store Age Executive *(Coopers & Lybrand, Special Issue, p. 36). Copyright Lebhar-Friedman, Inc. 425 Park Avenue, New York, NY 10022.*

a greater demand for consumer products. Kmart, Wal-Mart, and Sears have identified Mexico's growth potential with plans for future store openings.

The consolidation of the European marketplace has paved the way for retail opportunities there. Pier 1 Imports, The Gap, T.J. Maxx, and Staples have a strong presence in The United Kingdom. The Gap has a 3100-square-foot boutique in Galeries Lafayette, France's premier department store.[23] The Woolworth Corporation conducts 40 percent of its business in foreign markets with stores in England, Germany, Belgium, Luxembourg, the Netherlands, France, Spain, and Italy. Recognizing the pent-up consumer demand in countries freed from Communism, Kmart has opened stores in the Czech Republic and Slovakia.

Revisions of the General Agreement on Tariffs and Trade (GATT) have lowered tariffs worldwide and have opened doors to other foreign markets. A growing demand for Western goods has presented opportunities for retailers in Asian countries. The stable economies of Thailand, Hong Kong, and Singapore have attracted Kmart, Talbots, and Toys "R" Us. China, with one quarter of the world's population, is yet another growth opportunity.[24,25]

Joint ventures with foreign partners are a common foreign expansion strategy. Kmart operates stores in Singapore through a joint ven-

Figure 4.7

A Wal-Mart in Mexico (above). The Gap (right) operates a boutique in Galeries Lafayette, France's premier department store.

Company Profile 4.3

Toys "R" Us has become an icon of international retailing with more than 200 foreign operations in Canada, Australia, and twenty Asian and European countries.

Not every country greets a Toys "R" Us invasion with enthusiasm, however. The first Toys "R" Us in Germany encountered open hostility from native toy sellers who feared the competitive pricing strategy of Toys "R" Us. A nasty anti-Toys "R" Us campaign was launched, warning consumers about the "dangerous" self-service concept. News releases cautioned parents about buying a jungle gym or other potentially hazardous items at Toys "R" Us because "toy experts" were not on hand to advise about possible injury.

Tougher barriers to entry existed in Japan. The greatest obstacle for Toys "R" Us to overcome was the Large Store Law, designed to protect Japan's independent retailers from large retailers. To protest the regulation that saddled companies with a cumbersome review process, Toys "R" Us joined forces with McDonald's. Together they appealed to the Ministry of International Trade & Industry, Japan's gatekeeper of foreign trade. The final approval required Toys "R" Us to close their doors for thirty days a year to be on a competitive par with other Japanese stores that are closed that number of days annually.

Once trade barriers have been overcome, Toys "R" Us identifies cultural idiosyncrasies that necessitate adapting its domestic operational and merchandising strategies. In London, store mangers had to reconsider the typically American practice of standing cashiers at their registers when they discovered that it was a common European practice for cashiers to sit at their work stations. Local preferences are evaluated to plan assortments. Porcelain dolls are popular items in Japan. Wooden toys are German favorites. A Hong Kong version of Monopoly replaces *Boardwalk* and *Park Pace* with the names of two affluent Hong Kong suburbs, *Heko* and *Repulse Bay*. In France, Toys "R" Us offers a scale model of France's technological success story, the TGV high speed train.[1,2]

1. *Miller, Annette, Rosado, Lourdes; McKillop, Peter & Kirk, Don (March 23, 1992). The World "S" Ours. Time. pp. 46–47.*

2. *Staff. (August 26, 1991). Toys "R" Us' open passport. World Toy News.*

ture with Metro Private Ltd., a company that owns retail operations in Singapore and Malaysia.[26] Licensing agreements are another foreign expansion option. JCPenney licenses the Liwa Trading Co., a retail, shipping, and oil conglomerate in the United Arab Emirates, to sell goods with JCPenney labels in JCPenney Collection shops in the Middle East.[27]

Global expansion is not without obstacles. Laws designed to constrain foreign competition, the lack of advanced technology and transportation systems, and differing consumer values can make global expansion difficult. Retailers must be sensitive to each foreign market's unique sociological and economic characteristics.

INDEPENDENT RETAILERS

The dominance of the marketplace by a handful of large retail corporations is obvious even to the casual observer. These *power retailers* have definite competitive advantages over small independently owned retailers in that the depth of their assortments and their competitive prices are difficult to match.

In spite of the formidable presence of large-scale retailers, there remains considerable opportunity for independent retailers. Because power retailers cater to the mass market, they fail to satisfy consumers dissatisfied with mass market offerings. These voids in the marketplace are opportunities for independent retailers to differentiate themselves from power retailers with unique items not available in large stores.[28,29] The highly centralized organizational structures of power retailers allow for little decision making at store level. Independents can respond to local events, regional tastes, and weather conditions in a way that power retailers cannot.[30]

Power retailers are often constrained by their size. Home Depot discontinued its $80 million per year ready-to-assemble (RTA) furniture category because, as a power retailer, it needed to dedicate as much space to the category as its major RTA competitor, IKEA. Home Depot's average of 4000 square feet was a paltry comparison to IKEA's 200,000 square foot stores dedicated to RTA furniture. This $80 million of abandoned business presented opportunities for independent retailers not compelled to compete with IKEA.

Company Profile 4.4

When Mina Lussier arrived at the University of Massachusetts in the late 1950s, she had no idea that her intended four-year stay as a student in Western Massachusetts would be extended to no less that four decades. While at UMass, Mina met and married Sam Lussier. The couple settled in the picturesque New England town of Amherst, and eventually became the proud parents of Jana and Adam.

As their child-rearing responsibilities lightened, Sam and Mina began to seek other outlets for their energies and, as more of a pastime than serious business venture, they opened a shoe store in downtown Amherst where pizza parlors and bookstores are the dominant retail formats. Zanna (a contrived name chosen for its intrigue) flourished. Its success spurred the opening of an adjacent women's apparel store. Sam left his position as assistant admissions director at UMass to become Zanna's full-time fiscal manager. Adam joined the burgeoning enterprise upon graduation from Bowdoin College. Two more stores were added to the Zanna portfolio in Williamstown, Massachusetts, and Brattleboro, Vermont.

The Lussiers attribute their success as entrepreneurial retailing to factors such as a state-of-the-art inventory management system that provides a wealth of sophisticated decision-making tools. Naturally, the Lussiers' business acumen, merchandising skills, and innate sense of fashion have also contributed to Zanna's growth. However, the Lussiers credit much of their success to a customer-centered culture where assortment decisions are based on team discussions with salespeople of what Zanna customers like and don't like.

Customers return to Zanna because they find what they often don't find at chain retailers: assortments that seem as if they were chosen just for them.

Women's Shoes, Clothing & Accessories
Amherst   Brattleboro
413.253.2563   802.254.4421

SUMMARY POINTS

- In a centralized retail organization, functions that do not require proximity to customers are performed collectively for all stores in a central location for efficiency and cost effectiveness.
- Retail ownership can be public or private. Retail organizations can be structured as conglomerates, chains, or single-unit operations.
- Retail organizations expand by developing new merchandising concepts and through, acquisitions, and mergers. They downsize through divestiture.
- Bankruptcy occurs when an organization's liabilities exceed its assets. Chapter 11 protects a bankrupt retailer from its creditors while it reorganizes to become a profitable organization.
- As the U.S. marketplace becomes saturated with retail stores, retailers are extending their boundaries beyond domestic borders into locations in Asia, Europe, and South America.
- Though today's retail marketplace is dominated by power retailers, opportunities still exist for small independent retailers to fill the gaps in selection and service left open by large retailers.

KEY TERMS AND CONCEPTS

acquisition	diversification	plan-of-reorganization
bankruptcy	divestiture	price agreement plan
bidding war	initial public offering	private company
cannibalization	joint venture	public company
centralization	junk bond	subsidiary
chain	leveraged buyout	warehouse and
conglomerate	merger	requisition plan

FOR DISCUSSION

1. A high degree of centralization ensures consistency among stores in a retail organization. What are the positive aspects of this "consistency?" What are the negative aspects?
2. Research the media coverage of a retail organization that has recently gone public and discuss the financial analysts' views on the value of the stock.
3. Obtain information on a large retail conglomerate such as May Department Stores, Federated Department Stores, the Dayton Hudson Corporation, the

Melville Corporation, or Woolworth. Discuss its history of acquisitions, mergers, and divestitures.

4. Research a retail organization currently in Chapter 11. What factors contributed to its bankruptcy? Discuss elements of its POR. When is emergence from Chapter 11 expected?

5. Choose a retailing format and a merchandise mix that you feel is very exportable. Research information in an encyclopedia or a world geography book on the economy, culture, climate, and so on, of several countries as potential locations.

6. Assume that a financial backer has agreed to finance a retail store for you. What format would you choose? Why? Describe the depth and breadth of the store's merchandise mix.

ENDNOTES

1. Collins, Glen. (July 15, 1994). All eyes on Federated's chief, again. *New York Times.* p. D4.

2. Schiller, Zachary; Zellner, Wendy & Stodghill, Ron. (December 21, 1992). Clout! More and more, retail giants rule the marketplace. *Business Week.* pp. 66–73.

3. Sidney Rutberg. (August 9, 1993). The Bottom Line: Financial adviser Gilbert Harrison thinks mergers are a matter of survival. *Women's Wear Daily.* p. 10.

4. Loeb, Walter. (May 1992). Unbundle or centralize: What is the answer? *Retailing Issues Letter.* pp. 1–4.

5. Gilman, Alan. (May 1990). Who was minding the store? *Retailing Issues Letter.* p. 5.

6. Loeb, Walter. (May 1992). Unbundle or centralize: What is the answer? *Retailing Issues Letter.* pp. 1–4.

7. Miller, Annetta. (January 4, 1993). A dinosaur no more. *Time.* pp. 54–55.

8. Rickard, Leah. (May 15, 1995). Woolworth walking down a new path. *Advertising Age.* p. 4.

9. Silverman, Edward. (February 11, 1990). Woolworth's new tactics belie image, buoy profits. (Springfield, MO.) *Sunday Republican.* p. G5.

10. Caminiti, Susan. (October 17, 1994). Can The Limited fix itself? *Fortune.* pp. 161–172.

11. Moin, David. (January 23, 1995). Federated merges Rich's, Lazarus into $2.2B unit. *Women's Wear Daily.* pp. 2, 4.

12. Blanton, Kimberly & Rosenberg, Ronald. (September 12, 1992). May merges N.E. operation in Boston. *Boston Globe.* pp. 1, 9.

13. Reda, Susan (February 1994). Changing landscape. *Stores.* pp. 16, 17.

14. Siegel, Jeff. (August 24, 1994). Macy merger hits a snag named Koppell. *Women's Wear Daily.* pp. 1, 20.

15. Solomon, Peter. (September 4, 1994). Marketplace should decide stores' fate. *New York Times.*

16. Stone, Donald. (May 1990). Mergers and acquisitions in retailing. *Retailing Issues Letter.* pp. 1–4.

17. Byczkowski, John. (February 2, 1992). Bouncing back from bankruptcy. *Cincinnati Enquirer.* p. I2, I1.

18. Rutberg, Sidney. (January 27, 1992). The Macy Watch. *Women's Wear Daily.* pp. 4, 5.

19. Fields, Gregg. (February 2, 1992). Back from the brink. *Miami Herald.* pp. 1K, 4k.

20. Norris, Floyd. (July 15, 1994). Bondholders' triumph, shareholders's distress. *New York Times.* p. D4.

21. Passell, Peter. (April 12, 1993). Critics of bankruptcy law see inefficiency and waste. *New York Times.* pp. A1, A6.

22. Katzen, Larry. (September 1993). Retailing—The global mandate. *Retailing Issues Letter.* pp. 1–5.

23. Weisman, Katherine. (September 20, 1993). Paris gets a Gap. *Women's Wear Daily.* p. 3.

24. Bermingham, Geoffrey. (October 18, 1993). What's up at retail? *Home Furnishings Daily.* pp. 68, 139.

25. Staff. (August 1995). Asia is the hottest market, report says. *Shopping Centers Today.* p. 1.

26. Liebeck, Laura. (September 6, 1993). Kmart's Singapore venture test for expansion in the Pacific Rim. *Discount Store News.* pp. 1, 57.

27. Haber, Holly. (September 13, 1993). Penney's goes globetrotting for growth. *Women's Wear Daily.* p. 26.

28. Barmash, Isadore. (August 5, 1995). Restructurings create retail niches. *Shopping Centers Today.* pp. 4, 27.

29. Logan, Stanley. (January 1995). The small store—a struggle to survive. *Retail Issues Letter.*

30. Staff. (June 21, 1995). A 12-step program to revive fashion. *Women's Wear Daily.* pp. 1, 6–9.

chapter five

COMMUNICATING WITH CONSUMERS

Customers' needs, tastes, and spending power differ relative to factors such as gender, age, income, and pastimes. To develop a strategy for selecting specific merchandise categories, brands, sizes, styles, items, and colors, buyers need a clear profile of a store's intended customers. Chapter 5 deals with some of the ways in which a retailer defines its customer base, and some of the strategies used by retailers to draw customers into their stores.

After you have read this chapter, you will be able to discuss:

The consumer segments to whom retailers cater.

The concept of store image.

The retail sales promotion function.

MARKETS

A **market** is a group of customers with the potential to buy. Claiming that there is "a market" for a product or service implies that there is a group of customers with the desire or need for it, and the financial resources to purchase it. A **mass market** is a large group of customers with similar characteristics and wants. A **niche market** is a smaller group of customers with characteristics or wants that differ from the mass market. **Market segmentation** is the process of identifying niche markets that are undersatisfied or dissatisfied with current marketplace offerings. A niche market must be large enough to yield enough sales to suggest the costs of designing, processing, promoting, and distributing a product. Marketers respond to the wants and needs of niche markets with a constant flow of new goods and services.

Retailers cater to the wants and needs of various markets. However, even the largest retailer lacks the physical capacity to satisfy every market. Attempting to be "everything to everyone" and catering to too many markets can result in shallow, disjointed assortments. Most retailers tailor their assortments to clearly defined market segments.

Markets can be segmented in several ways. **Geographic segmentation** involves profiling customers by geographic region of the country. Climate is an obvious reason for this segmentation. Ski parkas are an important apparel category in Minnesota, but not in Louisiana. Swimwear has a longer selling season in southern Florida than in northern Maine. Consumer tastes are also linked to geography. Noritake, a producer of fine china and dinnerware, identifies their most popular selling patterns by region of the country. Floral clusters and lace looks are favorites in the Midwest; tailored looks inspired by English bone china are popular in New England. The Southeast prefers colorful selections, tartan plaids, and realistically rendered fruit patterns. In the Southwest and Florida, stoneware, stylized flowers, and primary color bands are popular. Type of geographic area, such as urban, suburban, or rural, is an important segmentation consideration. Lawn mowers are an appropriate offering for a suburban full-line discounter, but not for an urban store.

The geographic regions defined by the U.S. Census Bureau are not necessarily ideal for segmenting markets. Though Wheeling, West Virginia, and Miami, Florida, fall within the Southern Atlantic region, they differ vastly as markets. In *The Nine Nations of North America*, Joe Garreau splits the country into nine economic areas based on market-

Table 5.1 **CUSTOMERS DIFFER BY WANTS AND NEEDS**

The Bridal Customer

- Pattern, price, and accessory pieces, respectively, determine a couple's choice in selecting tabletop merchandise.
- The upstairs tabletop market is driven by bridal sales and has been battling the moderate decline in marriages in recent years. The return to tradition and the increasing popularity of formal weddings has boosted sales in the upstairs market.
- An increase in at-home entertaining and the influence of the once-elusive groom, have also expanded bridal registries. The retailer's ability to prolong registries by marketing them for bridal showers and anniversaries as well as weddings, has contributed to the expansion of sales.

The Self-Purchase Customer

- In order of importance, pattern, price, and longevity of a pattern influence the decision-making process of a self-purchase consumer.
- Yet price has more influence on the self-purchase customer than the bride. Promotions are particularly effective in capturing self-purchase sales—this customer is educated and value conscious.
- According to the Cooper Marketing Group, there are three distinct consumers when it comes to pattern selection: The color-forward consumer, representing 20 percent of the buyers, is the one who takes the most risk and who mainly purchases casual tabletop products which are trend-oriented; the color-prudent consumer, representing 50 percent of buyers, purchases and follows trends one year later when the trend is translated into a more livable design; and the color-loyal group, representing 30 percent of the population, prefers tried-and-true selections.

The Gift Buyer

- Packaging, advertising, and competitive price points are used to create perceived value. Although vendors say it is difficult to come up with a conclusive figure on giftware sales, they estimate that giftware represents up to 50 percent of total sales.
- It is price and perceived value that drive giftware sales. The under-$100 price point in giftware categories that include crystal, porcelain and alternative metals are the most active. When it comes specifically to glassware, porcelain and ceramic serveware, the under $50 range is the most popular.

DIFFERENCES
West Coast

Experimental/Trendy
Broad Suburban Area
University System in CA
Ethnic: Mexican, Asian
Informal Dress - Sport Coat
Outdoor Entertaining
Individual Auto Travel
"Work to Live" Mentality

DIFFERENCES
East Coast

Traditional
Central Urban City
Ivy League
Ethnic: Jewish, Puerto Rican
European Travel
Formal Dress - Suit
Indoor Entertaining
Train Travel - Mass Transit
"Live to Work" Mentality

SIMILARITIES

High Degree of Travel
Sophistication
Entertainment for Business/Pleasure
Entertainment Industry - Broadway/Hollywood
International Contacts for Commerce & Tourism
Strong Support for Sports Teams
High Cost of Living
Japanese Cars

Figure 5.1

One interpretation of regional distinctions among consumers.

ing characteristics, ignoring the political boundaries established as far back as the eighteenth century.[1]

Demographic segmentation involves identifying markets by measurable characteristics such as gender, age, education, and income. The Baby Boom generation born between 1946 and 1964 attracts significant attention as a demographic group. Comprising one-third of the population, marketers cater to the whims of Baby Boomers because of the great demand for products and services that Boomers create at every stage of life through which they pass. Several product lines are targeted to aging Baby Boomers, including Dockers by Levi Strauss, a line of casual trousers with roomy thighs, and Eterna 27 by Revlon, a cosmetics line for women over fifty.[2] Though fewer in number than their Baby Boom parents, the ranks of Baby Busters[3] will reach 2.2 million by 2000.

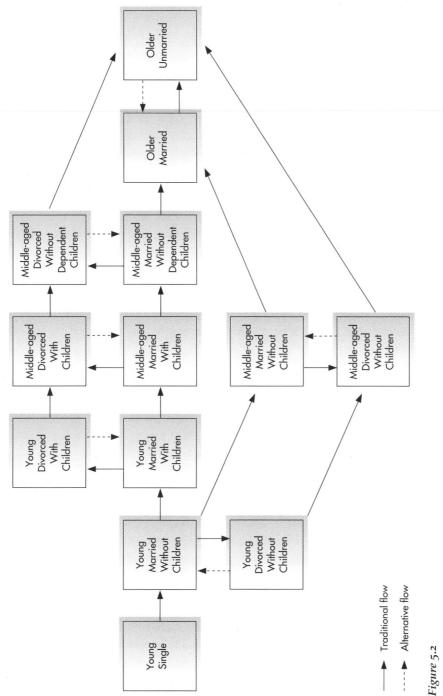

Figure 5.2

The Modernized Family Life Cycle.

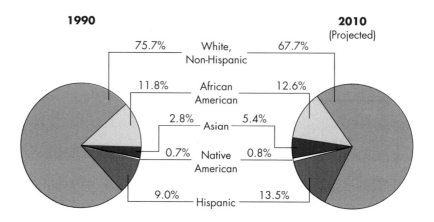

Figure 5.3

By 2010, one-third of the U.S. population will be nonwhite.

Sometimes referred to as the bitter, disenchanted *Generation X,*[4] Baby Busters are important consumers of music, fashion, and consumer electronics.[5,6]

The demographic characteristics of a market are important to retailers. A children's retailer will seek markets with a high percentage of families with children under twelve. The amount of space that a department store dedicates to Esprit, a pricey junior apparel line, will vary from one store to another relative to the number and spending power of teenagers in each store's market. Off-pricers seek markets with well-educated consumers discerning enough to appreciate the value of low-price branded offerings. Older consumers are an attractive market because of their high discretionary income.[7,8] Levitz created its Classic House Furniture Galleries of high-end upholstered and occasional furniture targeted to the affluent 45- to 65-year-old customer.

Family-life-cycle segmentation is based on marital status and the presence or absence of dependent children in a family. Murphy and Staples have identified thirteen life cycle stages in the *Modernized Family Life Cycle* shown in Figure 5.2.[9] Purchasing power and spending habits differ at each stage of the family life cycle relative to the number of dependent children. A *middle-aged married without dependent children* has more spending potential than a *young married with children,*[10] however the latter is a more lucrative target for retailers of juvenile furniture. The Murphy and Staples family life cycle reflects a more contemporary perspective than previous versions of the family life cycle that did not consider the effect of divorce on families. Divorce is an important economic consideration, since divorce breaks families into smaller, less affluent units. Recognizing that furniture purchases are tied to the family life cycle, IKEA developed an ad campaign targeted to customers experiencing significant life changes, such as marriage, the birth of a child, and divorce. One ad in the series portrayed a newly divorced woman who wanted new furniture so "that I can have guys over maybe in, like, ten years."

Ethnic segmentation has become an important market distinction because of the rapid growth of populations of African, Asian, and Latino descent.[11] Several producers have responded to the increasing demand for ethnic-specific products. Maybelline's Shades of You, Revlon's ColorStyle, and Pavion's Black Radiance and *Solo Para Ti* are complete cosmetics lines formulated for the complexions of people of color. Essence is a hosiery line shaded for the skin tones of African American women. Lovable is an innerwear line with a bilingual labeling option.

Figure 5.4

Producers and retailers have identified the growing importance of ethnic markets.

Figure 5.5

Lifestyles and values can influence a customer's shopping needs.   *CATHY © Cathy Guisewite. Reprinted with permission of UNIVERSAL PRESS SYNDICATE. All rights reserved.*

Retailers have also responded to the transition of the United States from a homogeneous "melting pot" to an ethnically diverse "salad bowl." Kmart has experimented with Afrocentric apparel in stores where African-Americans represent more than 50 percent of the market. Selections include caftans and kuffi hats made in Gambia and Dakar. JCPenney produces *Fashion Influences,* a catalog of authentic African fashions and contemporary African art. Developed jointly with *Ebony* magazine, Spiegel has a fashion catalog for African-American women called *E Style.*[12]

A market can be segmented by **psychographic** characteristics such as lifestyle, values, and attitudes. The yuppies, or young urban professionals, were a lifestyle market segment that symbolized the conspicuous consumption of the 1980s. Yuppies thrived on aspirations of glory, prestige, recognition, and power. Their status symbols included Armani suits, Burberry rainwear, Gucci shoes, Cuisinart food processors, and Perrier. Trendy retailers, such as Bloomingdale's and Crate and Barrel, were among the yuppies' favorite shopping haunts. The economic downturn of the late 1980s dramatically altered the lifestyle of many yuppies. Some became altruistic *frumpies* (frugal, urban, mature professionals), placing a higher value on satisfaction with life than designer clothing. Suddenly, it became chic to shop at off-pricers for '80s brands at '90s prices.[13,14,15] Lifestyles influence customers' attitudes toward shopping. A steady decline in leisure time and a continu-

Company Profile 5.1

Service Merchandise identifies its core customer as anyone between the ages of fifteen and ninety with an emphasis on those forming new households, such as college students,  first apartment dwellers, engaged couples, newlyweds, and first home buyers. Service Merchandise is also the largest retailer of wedding bands and engagement rings in the United States, and has the largest on-line wedding gift registry. *Now and Forever: A Guide for Selecting the Right Gifts for Your New Life* is a thirty-five page, full-color guide distributed to customers shopping for diamond engagement rings. The guide offers tips important to young couples setting up new homes, such as how to match various items of tableware, and how to choose a vacuum cleaner. The guide contains generic product information on the selection and care of diamonds, crystal, dinnerware, silverware, cutlery, and housewares, and explains the advantages of Service Merchandise's on-line bridal registry which is updated instantly through satellite communication as gifts are purchased.

Andreoli, Teresa. (May 15, 1995). Marketing your strengths, knowing your customer. Discount Store News. *pp. 67, 69.*

ing increase in the number of 25- to 44-year-old women in the workforce have led to the virtual extinction of "recreational shoppers." Today's busy, time-pressed customers shop through necessity, espousing convenience and service as they never have before.[16]

Geodemographic segmentation involves segmenting markets by neighborhoods typified by lifestyle. This microcosmic segmentation is based on information from various synthesized sources, including the U.S. census, mailing lists, and marketing surveys. PRIZM is the original and most widely used neighborhood target marketing system. PRIZM defines every neighborhood in the United States based on forty demographically and psychographically distinct neighborhood types called "clusters."

Geodemographic information is used by retailers to determine new store sites, plan product assortments, and target customer mailings. The Bon Marche use PRIZM clusters to typify the shopper most likely to shop its monthly *Day-O-Sale*. By targeting only the clusters with inhabitants likely to shop *Day-O-Sale*, The Bon edited its mailing list of 750,000 customers to 500,000, and saved $1.5 million annually on mailing costs.[17]

A SIZABLE MARKET

Until the mid-1980s, women in the 14 to 26 size range were ignored by a fashion industry that assumed an inverse relationship between a woman's size and her interest in clothing. Though one-third of the women in the United States wore large sizes, they represented only 15 percent of total apparel sales. A dismal selection of frumpy merchandise, not lack of spending power, was the reason for their conservative spending.

Recognizing that Baby Boomers grow larger as they grow older, several prestigious designers now create large size collections that speak of fashion first and size second, including Givenchy's *En Plus*, Harvé Benard's *Pour la Femme* and Gianni Versace's *Versatile*. Retailers likewise responded. In 1992, Saks Fifth Avenue opened a 6000 square foot shop in its flagship Manhattan store called *Salon Z*. Large size apparel sales have exceeded the $3 billion level, and are growing at a faster rate than other female apparel market segments.[1,2]

1. *Barrier, Michael. (March 1989). Woman with a large idea.* Nation's Business. *p. 71.*
2. *Feldman, Amy. (March 16, 1992). Hello, Oprah, goodbye, Iman.* Forbes. *pp. 116–117.*

Retailers define their markets by various other characteristics. Some retailers target markets by body type with *big and tall* assortments for men, and *special size* assortments of petites for women 5'4" and under, and *women's* and *half sizes* for full-figured women. Because big and tall and special size customers have fewer shopping options than average-size customers, they become dedicated to the stores that cater to them.

Markets can be segmented by multiple characteristics. Ethnic markets can be targeted geographically in cites with large ethnic populations such as Memphis and New Orleans (African American), and Miami, San Antonio, and Los Angeles (Latino).[18] Some markets are targeted seasonally. Men are an important market segment for retailers of women's fragrances and intimate apparel at gift-giving holidays, such as Valentine's Day and Christmas.

Some retailers target multiple markets. The Gap owns three casual apparel specialty groups, Banana Republic, The Gap, and Old Navy. Each is targeted to a different market segment based on price. Banana Republic is positioned at the high end of the market, The Gap in the middle, and Old Navy at the low end. The Gap's signature one-pocket T-shirt sells at a price 50 percent higher at Banana Republic, and 30 percent lower at Old Navy. The products are differentiated by fabrication and quality of construction.

Department stores target several market segments with diverse groups of product categories and brands. Macy's *Sudden Impulse* department is targeted to the contemporary customer with labels such as Leon Max, Laundry, Parallel, and Nouveau. Macy's *New Signatures* department features cutting edge designer labels, such as Vivienne Tam, Anna Sui, and Todd Oldham.[19]

Some chains tailor their assortments to the markets of individual stores. Caldor carries broader assortments of dresses and career apparel in urban markets. Target offers broader assortments of apparel in small communities than large communities because there are usually fewer apparel shopping options for consumers in small communities. Target carries more robes, intimate apparel, and women's hosiery in markets with older demographics. Kmart tailors its apparel assortments based on store location type, such as retirement area, beach resort area, and ski area.[20]

Figure 5.6

Some retailers target customers by body type.

POSITIONING AND STORE IMAGE

A store's **image** is the way in which it is perceived by the public. An image positions a store in the marketplace by distinguishing the store from its competitors. A store's image is the product of a multifaceted marketing strategy. References to a store's image include terms such as *value-oriented, fashion forward,* and *prestigious.* Though negative images are never intended, some stores are perceived as *stodgy, over-priced,* or *boring.*

A store's name can reflect its image. Long-established retail enterprises often bear the family name(s) of their founder(s). However, more contemporary names often identify a store's offerings or target market. The word *mart* in Wal-Mart and Kmart conveys a discount image. The word *club* in Charter Club conveys an image of exclusivity. A French name, such as *Cacique,* conveys an image of fashion. Store names such as *Petite Sophisticate, 5-7-9, Kids "R" Us,* and *Casual Male,* convey clear images of product line and target markets.

Location and physical facilities are other store image components. Though the lines of demarcation are blurring, mall and strip center tenants are distinct in terms of service, price, and fashion. A store's archi-

WHAT'S IN A NAME?

Frederick's of Hollywood, Victoria's Secret, and Lady Grace are all innerwear/sleepwear specialists that target vastly different markets. Frederick's of Hollywood is known for its alluring sensual styles, such as leopard G-strings, fishnet pantyhose, and wet-look catsuits. The traditional selections at Lady Grace are targeted to older customers and include flannel robes, cotton pajamas, and conventional innerwear brands. The feminine, luxurious, and colorful selections at Victoria's Secret fall between Frederick's of Hollywood and Lady Grace on a continuum that runs from risque to traditional.

Note how each retailer's name subtly hints at the store's image. As the seat of the motion picture industry, *Hollywood* has become synonymous with *taboo.* As a person's name, *Grace* is most often associated with older women. *Grace* also has liturgical connotations, while the word *lady* connotes propriety. *Victoria* connotes the romanticism of the Victorian era, while the word *secret* hints at the softness of a whisper.

tecture, interior decor, fixturing, signage, and merchandise presentation can deliver messages of prestige, service, or price. Marble floors and scenic elevators convey an image distinctly different from vinyl tile and shopping carts. Talbots is an upscale specialty retailer of classic female and children's apparel that uses architectural elements, such as entry foyers, maple flooring, and wainscoting, as well as antiques and equestrian-theme prints to convey a gracious, residential ambiance in their stores.

The merchandise division of a retail organization plays a critical role in creating and maintaining a store's image. Buyers' choices of brands, styles, fabrics, and colors reflect a store's image. To reinforce an image of fashion, a buyer searches the market for the latest styles and trends. To maintain an image of value, a buyer seeks opportunistic buys of goods that can be retailed at prices lower than competitors'. Buyers are arduous in their efforts to convey a consistent image throughout an entire store or department. When The Limited attempted to appeal to young trend-conscious customers while following the tastes of its customers as they grew older, the result was a confusing image of sophisticated jackets and pants for career-oriented women, adjacent to blue jeans, T-shirts, and halter tops.[21]

A store can reposition itself by donning a new image. Unable to compete with the *Big Three* as a low price full-line discounter, Green Bay, Wisconsin-based ShopKo repositioned itself as a retailer of moderately priced national brands. Beginning in 1983, JCPenney transformed

A CHANGE IN IDENTITY

The Lillian Vernon Corporation repositioned its *Welcome to Your New Home* renaming it *Welcome to an Organized Home*. The original catalog featured finishing touches and decorative accessories for new homes and was targeted to people who had recently moved. The mailing list for *Welcome to Your New Home* was derived from change of address information obtained from the U.S. Postal Service. When the Post Office ceased providing change-of-address information to direct marketers because of a privacy issue, Lillian Vernon transformed *Welcome to Your New Home* to *Welcome to an Organized Home*, a catalog of storage and organization products targeted to a more general niche of those seeking control of their space and their lives.

Hill, Dawn. (April 10, 1995). Lillian Vernon catalog gets organized. Home Furnishings Daily. *p. 109.*

itself from a dowdy "chain" store to a fashion-oriented national soft-lines department store by eliminating hardlines, such as sporting goods and appliances, and carrying department store brands such as Levi's, OshKosh, and Ultima II.[22,23] In 1993, Sears began a *Come See the Softer Side of Sears* marketing effort to reposition itself from a hardlines retailer to a fashion-oriented store.

SALES PROMOTION

In a retail organization, the **sales promotion** function is responsible for inducing customer traffic and sales by communicating information to customers pertaining to assortments, prices, services, and other sales incentives. An effective sales promotion strategy positions a store in the minds of consumers and is thus an important factor in defining a store's image. Sales promotion encourages repeat business and customer loyalty. To establish shopping habits at an early age, Rose's issues an Official Kid Card, a "credit card" for kids that awards prizes, such as whistles, yo-yos, play money, water guns, and key chains, each time a child visits a Rose's store with a parent.[24]

Sales promotion functions include advertising, publicity, and special events. **Advertising** conveys a message to a large group of people through a mass medium, such as newspapers, magazines, radio, and television. The cost of delivering the message is paid for by an advertiser, or sponsor. Newspapers are a local advertising medium appropriate for retailers with trading areas that parallel a newspaper's circulation. Regional and national retailers reach their customers by advertising in many newspapers. Because newspapers attract a diversely demographic readership, retailers that target a diverse group of customers are appropriate newspaper advertisers. An age-old alliance between department stores and newspapers dates back to their historical growth alongside each other in cities populous enough to support both. Department stores and full-line discounters continue to be major newspaper advertisers, though newspapers now share retail advertising budgets with newer forms of advertising, such as television.[25]

The preprinted insert has become a popular newspaper advertising vehicle. Often called *circulars*. The most common type of insert is the multipage ten-by-fifteen-inch tabloid. The piece is prepared by the retailer's advertising department, printed, and then sent to various newspapers for insertion into the folds of a specific edition, often a Sunday paper. Newspapers charge retailers an insertion fee of approximately twenty-five cents per insert for inserting the piece, and for using the newspaper to carry the advertising message.

Preprinted inserts are an alternative to the conventional practice of placing ads within the paper. Retailers prefer preprinted inserts for two major reasons:

1. Preprinted inserts can be printed on paper that reproduces color with greater clarity than newsprint.
2. The cost of producing and inserting an insert is less than buying the same amount of space within the paper.

Figure 5.7

The preprinted insert has become a popular newspaper advertising vehicle.

Figure 5.8

A store's charge customers are the likely recipients of direct-mail pieces.

Magazines are a national advertising medium whose major advertisers are producers of nationally distributed consumer products and services. As a national medium, magazines are a popular advertising vehicle among national retailers, but not common for local or regional retailers. Unlike newspapers, magazines are targeted to readers with clearly defined interests, such as sports, fashion, and health. The products and services advertised in magazines reflect their readership. Priscilla of Boston, the prestigious wedding gown design house, advertises in *Modern Bride, Weddings and Brides,* and *Bride's* magazine. Producer-sponsored magazine advertising sometimes includes the names of retailers at which the product line is available.

Like newspapers, radio is a local advertising medium. Radio's inability to convey a visual message limits its desirability as an advertising medium for retailers who need to convey the physical attributes of their assortments. However, radio is an effective advertising medium for events, such as a *One Day Sale.*

As a national advertising medium, television is most appealing to national retailers. JCPenney, Sears, and Kmart conduct extensive prime-time advertising on major television networks and cable stations. Small independent retailers, and the regional divisions of department store conglomerates, buy television time though local network affiliates and cable companies. The high cost of producing quality television advertising makes it a prohibitive advertising vehicle for many independent retailers.

Direct-response advertising, such as catalogs, bill enclosures, and flyers, is another form of retail advertising. Commonly called direct mail, a store's charge customers are the likely recipients of direct response advertising. Retailers occasionally use **out-of-home advertising,** such as billboards and transit advertising that appears on various forms of public transportation.

Publicity is "free advertising" through a mass medium in the form of news coverage. A retailer's newsworthy events include the announcement of plans for new stores, the appointment of new executives, or the latest quarterly report of earnings. The news media often rely on buyers as news sources for timely comments on fashion, hot items, and consumer purchasing.

Special events are promotional attractions, such as informal modeling, "how-to" seminars, and appearances of television and sports

Figure 5.9

Cooking demonstrations are popular special events.

celebrities, that create an exciting shopping atmosphere in stores. Though special events are often considered the domain of department stores, other types of retailers, including discounters, include special events in their promotional strategy. The concept of the "store as the-ater" was popularized at Bloomingdale's flagship at Lexington and 59th in New York where "sprizting" by fragrance company models, book signings by famous authors, and cooking demonstrations are everyday occurrences.

The merchandise division is often the source of special events. Suppliers frequently offer retailers special events opportunities, such as product demonstrators, appearances by designers, or the use of vin-tage collections of their product line. Cole of California, a division of Authentic Fitness Corporation, offers a collection of swimsuits that documents swimwear styles from the Roman "bathing suit" worn around 395 A.D. to Cole's 1964 *Scandal Suit* collection. The collection is loaned to retail stores for displays or runway shows and has been dis-played at Nordstrom, Bloomingdale's, and Macy's.

CLASSIFICATIONS OF RETAIL ADVERTISING

Retailer advertising is classified according to the type of goods adver-tised and/or the message conveyed.

Regular Price Advertising   **Regular price advertising** features premier assortments at conventional prices. Brand, quality, styling, and assort-ment are emphasized in regular price advertising; price is typically downplayed. Regular price advertising reinforces an image of fashion or prestige and is common among department and specialty stores.

Promotional Advertising   Commonly called "sale" advertising, **promo-tional advertising** features a retailer's regular offerings at discounted prices. Value is emphasized in promotional advertising with compar-isons of the promotional price to the regular price. The discounted price is typically offered for a specified period stated in the ad.

Clearance Advertising   Like promotional advertising, **clearance adver-tising** features goods at discounted prices. However, clearance goods are residual assortments of end-of-season, slow-selling, or discontinued merchandise.

Institutional Advertising   Often called image advertising, **institutional advertising** reinforces a store's position as a leader in value, service, fashion, or prestige. Institutional advertising often characterizes the lifestyle of the store's targeted customers, without reference specific merchandise or prices.

Retail advertising is often tied to a promotional theme or event, such as a *Men's Wardrobe Sale,* an *After Inventory Clearance,* or a *Fall Fashion* catalog. Events are categorized by their scope.

- A store-wide event includes virtually all categories of merchandise in a store, such as an *Anniversary Sale* or *Summer Clearance.*
- A divisional event includes a single merchandise division, such as *Great Gift Ideas for Dad* ad, or a *Back-to-School Sale.*
- A departmental event includes a single department or category of merchandise, such as a *Fragrance Festival* or a *Dress Bonanza.*
- A vendor event includes a single vendor, such as *Vanity Fair Week.* The advertising expense for vendor events is usually shared with the supplier, a topic to be discussed in Chapter 14.

Though events typically encompass multiple items, some retailers choose to advertise single items. Regular prices ads for single items are often semi-institutional in nature, symbolizing a store's image of prestige. The products featured in single-item promotional ads are usually exceptional values and powerful traffic inducers.

The sales promotion and merchandising functions are closely allied in a retail organization, sometimes falling within the same organizational pyramid. The two work in tandem to develop promotional strategies, budgets, and event schedules. Advertising is responsible for the creative development and production of advertising pieces, and for coordinating the purchase of media space and time. The merchandising division is responsible for choosing the merchandise that appears in ads, ascertaining that the goods are consistent with the theme or event. Buyers often obtain photographs or art from their supplier for ads, or they provide samples to be photographed or sketched. Buyers furnish product information for the copy or wording of ads. They then proofread the copy to ensure that product descriptions and prices are correct. Buyers are also responsible for support from suppliers to share

Figure 5.10

Classifications of advertisements:

a. storewide promotional event.

b. an institutional ad.

c. a vendor ad.

d. a single-item, regular-price ad.

e. a divisional promotion with a theme.

f. a promotional event for a single category of merchandise.

g. a vendor promotion.

h. a storewide clearance event.

i. a divisional event.

the cost of advertising their goods, a topic to be discussed in Chapter 14. A merchandising division is responsible for insuring the arrival of goods in stores by the time an ad breaks and for ascertaining adequate levels of inventory. There is hardly a more frustrating shopping experience than to travel to a store in response to an ad and find a paltry selection of advertised goods or, worse yet, none at all.

PERSONAL SELLING

Personal selling is one-to-one communication between a salesperson and a customer. In manufacturing organizations personal selling is a sales marketing function. However, in a retail organization, the human resource division is typically responsible for personal selling programs and personal selling training. As a store level function, the supervision of personal selling falls within the realm of store administration. Though the merchandising division is not directly responsible for personal selling, buyers are often the source of the product information that is used to train salespeople on the features and benefits of the goods that they are selling in stores.

Retailers have historically attached more importance to procuring goods than to selling goods, a distinction that is obvious when salaries for the two functions are compared. Low wages coupled with the erratic work schedules contribute to a high turnover rate among retail salespeople, who are often not committed to selling as a profession. Customer service in retail stores is often inhibited by sales force reductions to cut operating expenses.[26]

Many retailers recognize that good customer service is a competitive advantage and that good service can influence a consumer's choice of retail outlet. These retailers have developed customer service programs to foster good customer relations and to reward star sellers.

> **A**cknowledge the Customer
> **S**eek Out What They Are Looking For
> **S**uggest Specific Merchandise
> **E**nsure Timely and Efficient Transaction
> **T**hank the Customer By Name

Figure 5.11

An example of a canned sales approach.

Some retailers use a "canned" sales approach, a step-by-step selling technique. The following steps are typical of many canned approaches:

- *Greet the customer.* Avoid closed ended questions or cliches that will yield a reflexive "no" such as, "May I help you?" "Hi! A little muggy out there today!" is a better ice breaker.
- *Determine the customer's wants and needs.* "Looking for a Mother's Day gift?" or "What's her favorite color?"
- *Explain product features and benefits.* "This blend of polyester and cotton is perfect for a busy person with little time for ironing."
- *Suggest additional merchandise.* "How about a moisturizer to go with the cleanser?"
- *Close the sale.* "Thanks so much, Ms. Jones. No problem with returning the scarf if the match isn't perfect."

The pitch is typical of those used in department and specialty stores. Though discount stores are essentially self-service, discounters convey an image of service through "greeters" at the store entrances, efficient front-end operations, liberal return policies, and various customer services. IKEA provides customers with free tapemeasures, pencils, and paper. Strollers, free diapers, and child care are offered to shopping parents.

RELATIONSHIP MARKETING

Relationship marketing is an individualized mass marketing strategy of tracking customer purchases to anticipate their future needs. The concept involves identifying customers at point-of-sale by their credit cards or other identification vehicles, such as frequent shopper cards, gift registries, or signups for drawings, and maintaining a database of their brand, style, and price preferences.

The database of customer purchase histories has many useful applications. A store can reduce mailing costs by targeting promotional mailings only to customers who have made prior purchases. Coach uses its customer purchase histories to develop mailing lists by price category. Relationship marketing also has cross selling applications. A customer who purchases an expensive brass bed may be interested in luxurious satin sheets or a designer bed linen ensemble.[27,28]

Frequent shopper programs are relationship marketing concepts that reward shoppers for dedicated patronage with perks, such as advance notice of promotional events, free gift wrapping, and discounts. The criteria for determining preferred customers is spending over a period of time, typically a year. JCPenney issues *Privilege* cards to customers who spend $800 or more over a two-year period. Perks include a free JCPenney catalog, a free gift wrap, and a coupon for 25 percent off anything in the store. Saks Fifth Avenue credited its *Saks First* frequent shopper program with $56 million in additional sales during its inaugural year. Macy's Frequent Shopper program increased spending among members by 14 percent, thanks to enticements such as free alterations, delivery, and gift wrap, and points redeemable for dollars off purchased merchandise every time customers use their Macy's charge.[29]

Sears uses its purchase history of more than 70 million households to support a full range of direct marketing applications. Members of

Figure 5.12

Relationship marketing has been facilitated by sophisticated computer systems such as the STS Customer Profile System.

C o m p a n y   P r o f i l e   5 . 2

Proffitt's, an fifty-four unit department store chain based in Alcoa, Tennessee, tracks customer purchases for a rolling twenty-four months to develop mailing lists for promotional events. The histories are used to identify customers who have purchased merchandise, or merchandise similar to that featured in forthcoming events. For instance, a direct mail piece for a Haggar slacks promotion will be sent to all customers who have purchased Haggar slacks in the past twenty-four months. Haggar slacks customers are also profiled to determine consistent purchases of other product categories or brands. For instance, assume that 20 percent of all Haggar customers also buy Arrow

shirts. The figure is benchmarked against the total database of Proffitt's customers to determine if Haggar customers are more likely to buy Arrow shirts than the average Proffitt's customer. The analysis generally yields a handful of categories or brands that are shopped more often by the targeted customers. The cross brands or categories are then searched for customers who have purchase histories similar to Haggar customers, but have not purchased the brand yet. Their names are added to the Haggar mailing list as customers likely to try the Haggar brand. The end result is highly targeted mailing lists and a considerable reduction in advertising expense.

Staff. (June 1994). Proffitt's solution. Stores. p. 37.

Sears' *Hosiery Club* receive a free pair of Sears private label hosiery free after purchasing twelve pair. Sears' *Best Customers* are identified by frequency of visit and amount purchased over a time period. Best Customers are entitled to periodic discounts, advance notice of promotions, and priority appointments for service. As a token of appreciation for their patronage throughout the year, Best Customers receive a box of chocolates embossed with the letters SBC at Christmas.[30]

Relationship marketing has been facilitated by sophisticated database systems such as the STS Customer Profile System that tracks the department, category of merchandise, style number, and brand of a purchase, as well as customer characteristics such as size, occupation, hobbies, and birthday. Targeted mailing lists can be derived from the data base on any combination of criteria. STS can also evaluate the effectiveness of promotional mailings by tracking customer purchases of the goods featured in the mailing.

Using databases to reinforce relationships with consumers is widely used in direct marketing. The concept is gaining greater acceptance among store-front retailers in an effort to personalize their customer transactions, enhance service, foster long-term customer loyalty, and to tap more revenue from core customers.[31,32]

SUMMARY POINTS

- A market is a group of customers with the desire and ability to buy. Retailers develop merchandising strategies to satisfy the wants and needs of markets that are undersatisfied or dissatisfied with current retail offerings.
- Large markets are segmented into smaller markets on the basis of similar geographic, demographic, ethnic, psychographic, family life cycle, or geodemographic characteristics.
- A store's image is the way that it is perceived by the public. Retailers develop an image to position themselves in the marketplace and to distinguish themselves from their competitors.
- Sales promotion is an organizational function responsible for advertising, special events, and publicity.
- Personal selling involves one-to-one communication with customers.
- Relationship marketing uses historical customer purchase data to anticipate future purchases.

KEY TERMS AND CONCEPTS

advertising

clearance advertising

demographic
  segmentation

direct-response
  advertising

ethnic segmentation

family life cycle
  segmentation

geodemographic
  segmentation

geographic segmentation

institutional advertising

market

market segmentation

mass market

niche market

out-of-home advertising

personal selling

promotional advertising

psychographic
  segmentation

publicity

regular price advertising

relationship marketing

sales promotion

special events

store image

target market

FOR DISCUSSION

1. Obtain a list of specialty stores at a local enclosed shopping center. Profile the target market(s) of each store by demographic, psychographic, and other segmentation characteristics.
2. Compare the target markets of several pairs of stores that sell the same categories of merchandise within the same type of retailing format. Do the target markets differ? Do the stores compete directly or indirectly? Explain.
3. Refer to the list of specialty stores used in #1. Characterize each store's image based on its name, physical facilities, and merchandise assortments.
4. Collect various forms of print advertising from newspapers, magazines, and direct mail pieces from a variety of retail stores. Classify each ad as regular price, promotional, clearance, or institutional. Can any be classified in two categories?
5. Make a list of product categories or brands carried by a department store. Identify some cross selling opportunities for each of the items. Explain your rationale for making these associations.

SUGGESTED READINGS

Garreau, Joel. (1981). *The Nine Nations of North America.* New York: Avon Books.

Mitchell, Arnold. (1983). *The Nine American Lifestyles.* New York: Macmillan.

Pepper, Don & Rogers, Martha. (1993). *The One to One Future.* New York: Doubleday.

ENDNOTES

1. Garreau, Joel. (1981). *The Nine Nations of North America.* New York: Avon Books.
2. Braus, Patricia. (February 1995). Boomers Against Gravity. *American Demographics.* pp. 50–57.
3. *American Demographics* (May 1993) defines Baby Busters as those born between 1965 and 1976.
4. The resentful 18- to 29-year-olds who grew up as latchkey children in broken homes. The term *Generation X* was popularized by a novel of the same name by Douglas Coupland.
5. Zinn, Laura; Power, Christopher; Yang, Dori; Cuneo, Alice; Ross, David. (December 14, 1992). Move over, boomers. *Business Week.* pp. 74–82.
6. Cobb, Nathan. (September 28, 1994). Agent X. *Boston Globe.* pp. 35, 40.
7. Cook, Stephanie. (September 1989). Riding the silver streak. *Retailing Issues Letter.* pp. 1–4.

8. Haller, Terrence. (August 14, 1995). Older consumers don't believe you. *Advertising Age.* p. 14.

9. Murphy, Patrick & Staples, William. (June 1979). A modernized family life cycle. *Journal of Consumer Research.* pp. 16–17.

10. Freeman, Laurie. (November 7, 1994). Completing the span of "bridge" to boomers. *Advertising Age.* p. S8.

11. Staff. (June 6, 1994). Experts map markets by ethnic factor. *Home Furnishings Daily.* p. 10.

12. Erlick, June. (May 16, 1994). Spiegel: Africa-look home lines. *Home Furnishings Daily.* p. 12.

13. Deveny, Kathleen. (December 20, 1990). Reality of the '90s hits yuppie brands. *Wall Street Journal.* pp. B1, B5.

14. Dunkin, Amy. (July 20, 1992). It's chic to be cheap: A penny-pincher's primer. *Business Week.* pp. 94–95.

15. Lachman, Leanne & Brett, Deborah. (1994). Retail trends: consumers, goods, and real estate. *Commentary,* a special supplement to *Shopping Center World,* p. 6.

16. Selbert, Roger. (March 1991). Retailing's five most important trends. *Retailing Issues Letter.* Vol. 3, No. 2.

17. Mitchell, Susan. (February 1995). Birds of a feather. *American Demographics.* pp. 40–48.

18. Kahn, Robert. (March 1994). Minority populations are not evenly spread. *Retailing Today.* p. 3.

19. Moin, David. (June 29, 1995). Macy's Herald Square readies sudden impulse. *Women's Wear Daily.* p. 2.

20. Solomon, Barbara. (June 18, 1994). Mass chains tuning stock store by store. *Women's Wear Daily.* pp. 1, 17.

21. Caminiti, Susan. (October 17, 1994). Can The Limited fix itself? *Fortune.* pp. 161–172.

22. Zellner, Wendy. (April 5, 1993). Penney's rediscovers its calling. *Business Week.* pp. 51–52.

23. Staff. (May 15, 1995). JCPenney reaping the rewards of soft lines transition. *Discount Store News.* p. 45.

24. Staff. (February 7, 1994). Rose's Stores gives kids credit. *Discount Store News.* p. 41.

25. Drake, Mary; Spoone, Janice & Greenwald, Herbert. (1992). *Retail Fashion Promotion and Advertising.* New York: Macmillan. p. 151.

26. Glen, Peter. (1990). *It's Not My Department.* New York: William Morrow.

27. Erlick, June. (October 10, 1994). Carson Pirie Scott gets personal. *Home Furnishings Daily.* p. 10.

28. Fitzgerald, Kate. (October 31, 1994). Hallmark alters focus as lifestyles change. *Advertising Age.*

29. Underwood, Elaine. (April 11, 1994). Big retailers focus on frequent buyers. *Brandweek.* p. 5.

30. Erlick, June. (October 10, 1994). Inspiring loyalty by filling needs. *Home Furnishings Daily.* p. 11.

31. Staff. (May 15, 1995). Talbots' database pampers customers. *Discount Store News.* pp. 55–56.

32. Moin, David. (August 22, 1995). Mitchells of Westport wields the computer as a service booster. *Women's Wear Daily.* pp. 18–19.

chapter six

FASHION MERCHANDISING

Predicated on a continuous change of product line, the world of fashion is a dynamic and highly competitive arena that provides challenging and rewarding careers to millions. Though the word *fashion* is often associated with women's apparel and accessories, the concept is far more pervasive. Fashion is inherent in men's, women's and children's apparel, home furnishings, food, entertainment, and virtually every facet of culture. Fashion is an integral part of our economic system that embraces a host of industries including manufacturing, advertising, and retailing. Entire textbooks and courses are dedicated to a comprehensive study of fashion. The following is an abbreviated discussion of some fashion concepts and their relevance to retail merchandising.

After you have read this chapter, you will be able to discuss:

The pervasiveness of fashion.

Basic fashion terms.

The relevance of fashion to retail merchandising.

THE CONCEPT OF FASHION

Fashion theorists, designers, and retailers have proposed innumerable definitions of fashion that differ based on the theoretical or occupational biases of the originators. However, it is generally agreed that **fashion** is an expression that is widely accepted by a group of people over time. The group that accepts a fashion is usually defined by demographic and/or psychographic characteristics. Young marrieds, senior citizens, and urbanites are groups associated with certain fashions. The acceptance of a fashion by one group is independent of its acceptance by another. Apparel that is fashionable to 18- to 22-year-old college students may not be fashionable to 25- to 40-year-old professionals. The time period that defines the duration of a fashion cannot be generalized. Something may be fashionable for a short time, such as a month, or remain fashionable for decades.

TRENDS

A **trend** implies the direction or movement of a fashion. The word *trend* is often used synonymously with fashion.[1] Thus, something that is *trendy* is also *fashionable*. Trends are described in ways that imply degree of acceptance (a *strong* or *key* trend), direction (an *emerging* or *dying*

STYLE VS. FASHION

Style refers to an item's distinctive characteristics or design features. *Turtleneck, mock turtleneck,* and *crew neck* are collar treatments that define the style of a garment, just as *cocktail-, ballerina-,* and *tea-length* indicate skirt lengths. The word *style* is not synonymous with fashion, though popular use of the word sometimes implies that it is. Something that is dated is said to be *out-of-style* when, in fact, it is *out-of-fashion.* Something said to be *stylish,* is really *in fashion.* Only when a style is popular, is it a fashion. All fashions have at least one style, but not all styles are fashions. Fashions change, styles do not. Safari jackets may be fashionable one season and not the next, however a safari jacket is always a style whether or not it is fashionable.

Figure 6.1

Fashion acceptance by one group is independent of its acceptance by another group.

trend), duration (a *seasonal* trend), or relationship to other trends (a *secondary* or *background* trend). Trends are identified in a multitude of areas, including apparel, home furnishings, and lifestyles.

Retailers follow trends because of their impact on customer purchases. The *fitness craze* is a lifestyle trend associated with an interest in health and fitness. The trend has fueled the popularity of fleece, thermal, and jersey activewear, and the sale of major activewear lines such as Champion, Danskin, Russell Athletic. The fitness trend has also stimulated athletic footwear sales, a category that has grown from a few "sneaker" styles, such as tennis and basketball, to an overwhelming assortment of styles, such as walking, running, cross-training, fitness, casual, high performance, high-tech. Keds and Converse are the mainstay athletic shoe brands. Relatively recent but highly successful newcomers are Nike and Reebok.[2]

A casual dressing trend has also fueled the sale of activewear and athletic footwear and the popularity of *Casual Friday*. The relaxation of office dress codes has been instrumental in the success of soft-look apparel lines produced by Giorgio Armani, Donna Karan, and Hugo

Figure 6.2

The fitness trend has fueled the sale of fleece activewear and the popularity of activewear lines such as Champion.

Figure 6.3

Brooks Brothers' Soft Classics is a line of casual attire for today's relaxed office environment.

Boss.[3,4] Other apparel producers have responded specifically to the wardrobe needs of workers in relaxed office environments. Bagir International produces a line of menswear called Easy Friday. Wolverine Worldwide, maker of Hush Puppies, has produced an instructional video on casual dressing tips for office workers. Retailers have also reacted to the corporate casual trend. Brooks Brothers, a long-established retailer of traditional men's wear, introduced Soft Classics, a line of relaxed sport coats, trousers, shirts, and ties for young men between the ages of twenty-five and forty. Marshall Field's has conducted Workday Casual seminars to offer guidelines for casual office dressing, and suggestions for the casual office wardrobe.[5,6,7]

Some trends have negative impact on sales. London Fog, best known for its traditional dressy rainwear, lost a considerable amount of business to retailers of casual outerwear, such as Lands' End and Eddie Bauer, because of the trend toward casual dressing. To regain some of its market share, London Fog acquired Pacific Trail, a line of skiwear and rugged coats and jackets. The women's hosiery industry is a victim of Casual Friday. In 1994, the Sara Lee Corporation, the producer of Hanes and L'eggs sheer hosiery, cut 9000 jobs from its worldwide organization to respond to declining sheer hosiery sales.[8,9]

The impact of multiple trends can impact the sale of certain lines. *Home and hearth* is a lifestyle trend reflected by an increase in the amount of time that people spend at home. The fitness trend coupled with the home trend have spurred the sale of exercise equipment for home fitness centers, such as NordicTrack. The casual lifestyle trend coupled with the home trend has stimulated the sale of furniture and consumer electronics for leisure spaces, such as dens and playrooms. The home trend has also triggered the sale of products for home enter-

Figure 6.4

The casual lifestyle trend coupled with the home trend has stimulated the sale of furnishings for leisure spaces.

Table 6.1 **MERCHANDISING TRENDS**

What's Hot	What's Not
Bookstores with coffee bars	Tobacco shops
Highly targeted specialty stores	Unfocused mom and pop operators
"Career casual" apparel	Men's suits
Home fashions and furnishings	Conspicuous consumption
Flannels	Furs
Everyday low prices	Sales hype
Knowing your market	Offering everything to everybody
Ethnic-sensitive retailers	Undifferentiated mass merchants
Customer service	Buyer beware
Regular soda (with sugar)	Hard liquor
Self-service access	Locked-up display cases
Weekend delivery	8 to 5 mentality
Family fun at the mall	Shop 'til you drop
Computerized product information	Untrained sales staff
Roasted chicken	Fried chicken
"Vintage" clothing	Designer chic

Reprinted with permission. M. Leanne Lachman and Deborah L. Brett, Retail Trends: Consumers, Goods, and Real Estate, *Schroder Real Estate Associates. "Commentary," New York, New York (Summer 1994), p. 19.*

taining, such as gourmet cookware and casual glassware and dinnerware. *Telecommuting* is also associated with the home trend. The more than forty million people who conduct their business at home are major consumers of home office furniture and equipment. Crate & Barrel, IKEA, Pier 1 Imports, Levitz Furniture, Pottery Barn, and Williams-Sonoma are among the many retailers of home furnishings and accessories that are major benefactors of the trends toward entertaining, exercising, and conducting business at home.[10,11]

Brands, items, colors, styles, and fabrications are often associated with trends. In the early 1980s, Izod Lacoste sportswear was identified with the popular *preppy* trend. Food dehydrators, juice extractors, and bread makers are countertop appliances akin to the fitness trend. *Pastels, brights, naturals,* and *darks* are color shades that have been identified with a season's fashion trends. Hemp, an inexpensive fiber that had become nearly obsolete due to legislation that prohibited its production in the United States, was resurrected as a fashion fabric in 1995. In an era of increasing ecological awareness, hemp was touted as being environmentally correct in that it can be grown with limited fertilizing and no pesticides.[12,13]

THE FASHION LIFE CYCLE

The **fashion life cycle** depicts the evolution, culmination, and decline of fashion acceptance over time. The fashion life cycle is a function of sales, an indication of fashion acceptance, and time. The cycle has three major phases: growth, peak, and decline.[14]

　　Fashion leaders, or *trend setters,* adopt a fashion during the introductory stages of the cycle's growth phase. Fashion apparel during this

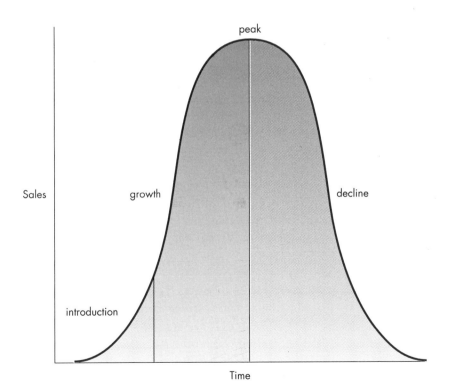

Figure 6.5

The fashion life cycle.

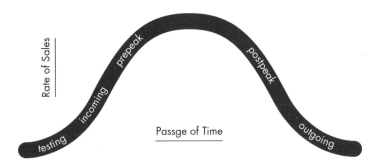

Figure 6.6

Dayton Hudson's interpretation of the fashion life cycle.

stage is called **high fashion,** available only through designers or exclusive stores. Prices during this stage are high, but fashion leaders are willing to pay the price for the sake of exclusivity and novelty.

Knockoffs, copies of the most successful fashions but in less expensive fabrications, are characteristic of the later stages of the growth phase. The fashion becomes **mass fashion,** produced in large quantities for a broad customer base with distribution through many retailers, including discounters. The fashion is adopted by trend setter emulators called **fashion followers** during this stage. Trend setters abandon a fashion at this point. Their commitment to exclusivity motivates them to explore the latest fashion innovations.

Mature fashions reach a peak when they have realized their sales potential. A plateau, or period of stabilization where sales neither increase nor decrease, is sometimes characteristic of a fashion's culmination. Fashion decline is characterized by diminishing sales and distribution. Retailers that carry the fashion are likely to have it marked down for clearance in order to make room for fashions in earlier cycle phases. The slow adopters who purchase fashion during this phase are called **fashion laggards.** *Non-fashion* customers who purchase based on the functional aspects of a product versus its fashion attributes, are also decline-phase customers. Difficulty in finding a producer who makes a fashion or a store that sells it are good indications that a fashion has died.

Though all fashions pass through the various life cycle phases, the duration of the cycle or any of its phases varies from one fashion to another. Something may be fashionable for a single season or for many years. The durability and replacement rate of a product are often determinants of the length of a fashion life cycle. Goods with limited durability, such as apparel, have shorter fashion life cycles than durable goods, such as home furnishings. Fashions targeted for the young evolve and die so quickly that they are often referred to as *disposable*. The fashion life cycle reinforces the notion that consumer purchases define fashion. Many of the "fashions" that appear on fashion show runways are styles that never become fashion.

FADS AND CLASSICS

Fads and classics are two types of fashions that represent extremes of the fashion life cycle. A **fad** has a short fashion life cycle. Fads rise and fall in popularity quickly, enduring for as little time as a few weeks. Some call fads *miniature* or *minor* fashions, hesitant to classify fads as true fashions because of their brief acceptance. Fads are especially popular among the young. Fads that have attained historical significance in the annals of American pop culture include hula hoops (c.1958), mood rings (c.1975), and hot pants (c.1971).

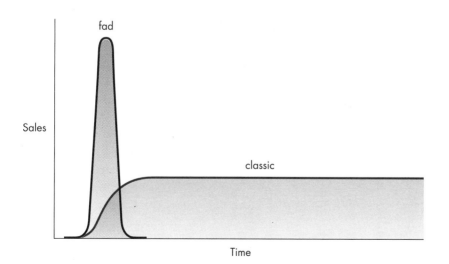

Figure 6.7

The fashion life cycles of fads and classics.

Fads generate generous revenues for retailers who identify their emergence early. Fads represent a high risk, however. When they die, they die quickly. Fads purchased late in the fashion life cycle must be sold off at drastic price reductions.

A **classic** has a long fashion life cycle. Some are reluctant to classify a classic as a fashion, since the term *fashion* implies change and classics seldom change. When classics do change, the changes are very subtle. Classics remain popular indefinitely, which is why the word *timeless* is frequently associated with classics. Classic apparel is often promoted as *investment dressing,* accentuating the enduring acceptance of classics season after season. Often referred to as *traditional,* classics appeal to customers with conservative taste. Classics include navy blue wool blazers, strings of pearls, and the color black. Unlike fads, classics are low risk with stable rates of sale season after season.

Sometimes a fashion is dubbed a fad when its duration is expected to be short. Denim blue jeans became popular on college campuses in the 1960s. History suggested that blue jeans would go the way of the poodle skirt and khaki pants that were fashionable on campuses a

Figure 6.8

Classics are often promoted
as enduring fashions that
remain popular season after
season.

cathy®　　　　　　　　　　　　　　**by Cathy Guisewite**

Figure 6.9

decade earlier. Though the college students of the 1960s eventually turned in their fringed vests and tie-dyed shirts for three-piece suits, blue jeans found a permanent place in their closets as a casual apparel staple. The five-pocket denim jean has, in fact, become a classic.

THE TRICKLE THEORIES

The trickle theories explain the transmission of fashion acceptance from one socioeconomic group to another. The **trickle-down theory** traces the origins of fashion to upper socioeconomic classes. The theory proposes that lower socioeconomic groups imitate the fashions of the upper socioeconomic classes, and that the wealthy abandon a fashion when it is mimicked as mass fashion, unwilling to share their high fashion symbols of superiority. The trickle down theory supports the long-held notion that a year or more passes before the high fashions that appear on the runways of the fashion centers of Milan, Paris, and New York are reinterpreted as mass fashion.[15]

The **trickle-across,** or *diffusion, theory* suggests simultaneous adoption across all socioeconomic groups. Proponents of the trickle-across thoery claim that the trickle-down theory is dated in that it does not consider the impact of mass communication and computerized design and production capabilities on accelerating the availability of high fashion knockoffs in mass markets. The trickle-across theory accounts for the fact that similar fashions appear concurrently at stores that cater to diverse socioeconomic groups. A knockoff of a Neiman Marcus fashion may appear concurrently at Wal-Mart. The Neiman Marcus fashion may be 100 percent wool with finished seams and a folded hem. The Wal-Mart fashion may be a polyester blend with unfinished seams and a taped hem. Though fabric and construction are different, the same fashion is available simultaneously at both stores.[16]

Still other fashion theorists find evidence of a **trickle-up theory,** or *status float phenomenon.* The theory proposes that fashions float up from lower socioeconomic groups to higher socioeconomic groups. The street born *grunge* look of used jeans and flannel shirts was inspired by rock groups, such as Pearl Jam and Nirvana. Eventually high-priced versions of the look appeared in the collections of prestigious designers, such as Perry Ellis and Anna Sui.[17]

Though evidence of one trickle theory may be more prevalent at one time than another, each theory can be supported by examples of

Figure 6.10

The status-float phenomenon proposes that street-born looks can inspire high-priced fashions.

fashions that have traveled up, down, or across socioeconomic groups. The challenge to retailers is to identify fashion trends in all groups, realizing that they can travel in any direction, or that they can stagnate and not travel at all.

FASHION/BASIC CONTINUUM

Merchandise is often classified as either basic or fashion. **Basic goods** are functional goods that change infrequently and are generally considered necessities.[18] **Fashion goods** are aesthetically appealing goods that change frequently and are generally considered nonnecessities.

Basic goods and fashion goods can be represented at the opposite ends of a continuum that represents frequency of change, degree of necessity, and functional versus aesthetic qualities. Goods at the far left of the continuum are purely basic. Men's white cotton T-shirts are at this end. Their fabrication, styling, and color do not change from one season to another. A T-shirt is a functional garment worn for warmth and to protect outer garments from body oils and perspiration. Goods at the far right of the continuum are purely fashion. Fashion jewelry[19] is at this end. The coloration, composition, and styling of fashion jewelry changes each season. Fashion jewelry is used for adornment and is purchased for its aesthetic value and not as a necessity.

Basics are purchased on a replacement basis and out of necessity. A mattress pad is purchased when an old one wears out. Customers do not typically walk by a display of mattress pads and expound: "What a great looking mattress pad! I think I'll buy one!" Price coupled with

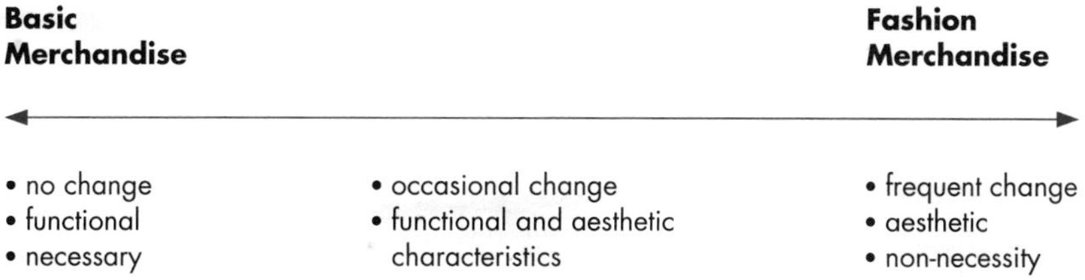

Basic Merchandise		**Fashion Merchandise**
←		→
• no change	• occasional change	• frequent change
• functional	• functional and aesthetic characteristics	• aesthetic
• necessary		• non-necessity

Figure 6.11

Fashion / Basic continuum.

Company Profile 6.1

The Color Association of the United States (CAUS) has been predicting consumer color preferences since 1915 when it published the first edition of *The Standard Color Reference of America,* a compilation of 192 color shades illustrated with silk ribbon samples. The colors were named by their likeness to college colors (Yale blue), gems (garnet and topaz), foods (apricot and eggplant), wines (burgundy and champagne), birds (cardinal and peacock), flowers (lavender, lilac, and rose), and precious metals (gold and silver).

CAUS is sponsored by dues-paying members, including fiber producers, apparel manufacturers, designers, and auto makers, that rely on CAUS for guidance in determining popular colors for their products. Experts in the field of color, styling, marketing, and merchandising come together to project the shades that will be popular two years in advance of a selling season. Decisions are based on the prevailing "color climate" that embraces everything from politics and the economy, to cultural and environmental movements. Forecasts are made twice annually for the women's wear, men's wear, and children's wear industries to ensure the availability of coordinated shoes, scarves, and other accessories. Forecasts for the interior design industry are made once a year to ensure the coordination of upholstered furniture, draperies, carpeting, and home accessories.

need is more likely to be the purchase incentive. Fashion purchases are based on consumer desire for novelty and change. Uniqueness of styling, color, or texture entice consumers to buy fashion goods, as does the way in which the goods are packaged or displayed. A consumer purchases a $350 Coogi sweater because of its interesting coloration and texture. A less expensive sweater could fulfill a functional need for warm clothing.

Goods that fall between these extremes on the continuum have both basic and fashion characteristics. A coat is an apparel necessity in many climates in that it insulates the body from the cold. The functional characteristics of a coat do not change from season to season.

However, fashion elements, such as color, styling and fabrication, change seasonally. Merchandise on the left half of the continuum is primarily basic with limited fashion qualities. This includes goods, such as pastel-colored bath towel ensembles, flannel pajamas, and pumps in basic colors, such as black, brown, beige. These goods are most often purchased as replacements, but uniqueness of color or some minute variation in style will sometimes induce the consumer to buy more frequently than necessary or to buy multiple quantities. Merchandise on the right half of the continuum is primarily fashion with some basic characteristics. These goods have functional uses, however their purchase is based primarily on characteristics of styling, prestige, or color.

TRANSFORMING BASICS INTO FASHION

Producers entice consumers to buy other than on a replacement basis by transforming basic goods into fashion goods with new product features or interesting styles, colors, or fabrications. In the 1980s, the women's legwear industry transformed a replacement business into a fashion business by introducing colored and textured hosiery, encouraging the purchase of a pair of hosiery to coordinate with every outfit. Similarly, the women's innerwear industry has transformed basic

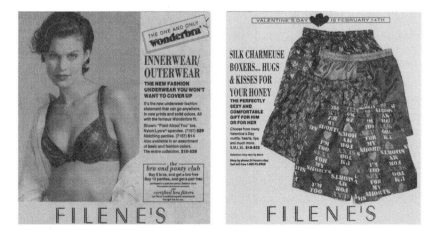

Figure 6.12

Customers buy more frequently than on a replacement basis when basic goods are transformed into fashion goods.

assortments of white and beige, spandex, nylon, rayon, and cotton goods into fashion assortments of coordinated slips, bras, and panties in an array of colors and prints in luxury fabrications such as silk and satin. The introduction of color and sexy styles, such as the bikini, have added a fashion dimension to men's underwear, a merchandise category that was once dominated by white cotton and cotton blend T-shirts and jockey shorts. Men's underwear sales have been further augmented by the transformation of the boxer short, long considered a vestige of the past worn only by older men, into a fashion item available in assortments of solid and patterned silks.

Producers retain consumer interest in their products with a continuous flow of product changes. Color is the simplest and least costly change to implement in that changing color does not require new designs, fabrics or materials, production patterns, or manufacturing setups. In a survey of catalog retailers conducted by *Consumer Reports*, respondents claimed that only one out of five items in a new edition of a catalog had not appeared in previous editions. The others four out of five items were new colors or textures of previously appearing styles.[20] The Gap offers many of the same basic styles in new color palettes and

Figure 6.13

New fashions are sometimes reinterpretations of fashions of the past.

fabric designs each season, enticing many customers to purchase the same item in a different color in successive seasons. Periodic color changes are also important to the home furnishings industry. Major appliances appeared in pastel colorations in the 1950s; *harvest gold* and *avocado green* in the 1970s; and *almond* in subsequent decades. The periodic change of color dates appliances that otherwise don't change very much, and encourages consumers to buy a complete set of coordinated new appliances when one wears out.

Fashion changes are often reinterpretations of successful fashions of the past.[21] The 1990s have been dotted with attempts to revive the *hippie* looks of the 1960s with tie dyes, bell bottoms, hip belts, head wraps, and beads.[22] The *1928* fashion jewelry line consists of antique reproductions from the Victorian era and the *Roaring '20s.* Jessica McClintock's successful dress line features large lace collars, dropped waists, and peplums reminiscent of the 1920s and 1930s. Kitsch 'n Couture is a line of coordinated kitchen linens that includes check and gingham designs reminiscent of the 1940s and 1950s.[23]

Not every attempt to resurrect a popular fashion of the past is successful. In 1991, Generra Sportswear created Hypercolor, an apparel

Figure 6.14

The Nehru suit was an unsuccessful attempt to transform a basic business into a fashion business.

1. *Lauer, Robert &
Lauer, Jeanelle.
(1981).* Fashion
Power. *Englewood
Cliffs, NJ:
Prentice Hall.*
2. *Hollander, Anne.
(November 16, 1978).
The fabric of life.*
New York Times.

VILLAINOUS FASHION

The topic of fashion is sometimes a controversial one. Fashion has been proclaimed as "inconsequential" and the "tyrant of humanity" associated with "mindless vanity" and "obsessive narcissism." Critics base their condemnation on two factors: inefficient production and wasteful consumption. From the production standpoint, it is argued that new fashions are seldom improvements of a product, but merely an effort to stimulate the consumer's desire to purchase it. Critics claim that producers ignore quality to limit product durability.

From the consumption standpoint, critics assert that fashion is wasteful because it encourages the replacement of goods, not because they are no longer useful, but because they are no longer fashionable. They decry the media hype used to promote fashion especially that which is targeted at the impressionable young or the less-educated poor. Critics object to the images that are portrayed in fashion advertising, asserting that they are often sexist or misrepresentations of reality. They argue that promoting fashion encourages consumers to purchase frivolously when their dollars might be better spent on more functional items.[1,2]

line that reacted to changes in atmospheric heat by changing color. The concept was reminiscent of the 1970s mood ring fad that enjoyed phenomenal success. The ring changed color according to fluctuations in body heat, allegedly an indicator of the wearer's mood. Unfortunately, Hypercolor was not as popular as mood rings. The colors changed inconsistently on the garment because of higher body temperature in areas such as underarms.[24,25]

Not every attempt to transform a basic business into a fashion business is successful. In the mid-1960s, the men's wear industry launched a casual lapelless suit with a mandarin collar called the Nehru, confident that the style would be a success as traditional dress standards began to ease. However, men were not ready to replace their dark suits and herringbone sport coats with this revolutionary new fashion. The Nehru was an abysmal failure and became the proverbial Edsel[26] of the men's wear industry. Today, men's apparel undergoes far more fashion change than three decades ago. However, the core of the men's suit business remains in traditional grey, brown, and navy suits in wool and wool blends. Occasionally vests appear, lapel and pant widths change, as do the treatment of vents, pleating, and cuffs. However, the Nehru taught the men's wear industry a lesson that fashion change in suits should be gradual and minute.

Though consumers reject drastic change, they will not buy unless they perceive an appreciable difference between current and previous offerings. The fashion change that draws the line between consumer acceptance and consumer rejection is a fine one contingent upon many factors such as the target market, economic conditions, and the type of merchandise. There is no universal answer to the question of how much change is too little and when is it too much. Perhaps the best response is "to make something familiar look new."

FASHION INFLUENCE

Fashion change is rooted in the changes that occur in technology, the economy, and society. Producers react to these environmental changes by designing or developing products consistent with these changes.

The technological advances that have contributed to the growth of the fashion industry date back to the Industrial Revolution and the invention of the sewing machine (c. 1850) which enabled the production of mass-produced *ready-to-wear* garments that could be purchased from racks in stores. (Previously, garments were tailor made.) More recent advances in computer-aided design (CAD) and computer-aided manufacturing (CAM) have maximized production efficiency, making fashion affordable to a greater number of consumers.[27]

Fashion is linked to economic conditions. Reflecting the economic uncertainty of the late 1980s and early 1990s, many fashion designers developed less expensive *bridge* lines (also called *diffusion* or *secondary* lines) priced at about 60 percent less than the designer's top-of-the-line creations. Though designers use less expensive fabrics and fewer details in bridge lines, the garments still carry the cachet of a designer line. *DKNY* and *Anne Klein II* are two bridge lines targeted to this level of business.[28,29]

The mood of the times and the values of the era are expressed through fashion. A legendary fashion theory claims a correlation between the rise and fall of the stock market and the rise and fall of women's hemlines. In 1925, a time of economic prosperity, hemlines

1. *Staff. (December 30, 1979). Decoding the styles of the 70's.* New York Times Magazine. *pp. 24–27.*
2. *Morris, Bernardine. (February 27, 1990). The directions of the innovators.* New York Times Magazine. *pp. 132–133, 166.*

FASHION AND THE 1960s

The 1960s was truly an era when fashion mirrored the times. At first glance, vinyl go-go boots and *Courreges* miniskirts had little in common with the tattered garb of the fashion-rejecting hippies. However, both symbolized the anti-establishment attitude of a decade. Standards for socially acceptable behavior were rejected as were traditionally held dress standards. Miniskirts became common for formal occasions, while long flowing floor lengths were worn for daytime attire. Women wore their hemlines shorter than they had at any time in the history of the Western world, baring more leg than in the 1920s, another period of social upheaval.[1]

The 1960s was an era of personal freedom and liberation. The topless bathing suit of 1965 was a profound declaration of the sexual revolution that was taking place.[2] The seeds of the Women's Movement were sowed in the early 1960s, and it was during this period that the definition of *appropriate* apparel for women was redefined. Pants became popular in career, casual, and social occasion apparel, allowing women the same comfort and freedom of movement that men had been privileged to enjoy for centuries.

rose for the first time in history. Following the 1929 stock market crash, hems plunged to just eleven inches off the floor. During the economically prosperous World War II years, the 1960s, and the 1980s shorter skirt lengths, including the mini, become popular. Periods of economic recession during the 1950s and the 1970s were characterized by longer skirts including the *midi* and *maxi*.[30]

Famous people often inspire fashion. The wedding dress that Princess Di wore at her internationally televised 1981 storybook wedding to Prince Charles spurred the design of dresses with sleeves was mimicked worldwide by the dress industry. The Halston pillbox hat that Jacqueline Kennedy wore to her husband's 1961 inauguration as president of the United States became the fashion symbol of the day.[31] First Lady Nancy Reagan's favorite color, red, was a popular fashion color in the early 1980s. Later in the decade, triple strands of pearls, a wardrobe staple of First Lady Barbara Bush, were in demand. First Ladyship does not always guarantee fashion leadership, however. The broad-brimmed hat that Hillary Rodham Clinton wore to her husband's

Company Profile 6.2

An amalgamation of Cannon Mills and Fieldcrest Mills, Fieldcrest Cannon, Inc. has achieved worldwide status as a leading producer of household textile products. Throughout the years, Cannon specialized in large volume production and mass market distribution. Fieldcrest pinned its reputation on goods for upscale department stores. The 1986 merger of the two companies has led to the distribution of labels, such as Fieldcrest, Royal Velvet, Charisma, Touch of Class, St. Mary's, Cannon Royal Family, Cannon Monticello, Caldwell, and Sure Fit, across diverse retail channels, that include Macy's, Bloomingdale's, Rich's, Bon Marche, Burdines, Wal-Mart, Kmart, and Target.

Product innovation has been an integral part of Fieldcrest Cannon's history. Cannon Mills was a leader in the development of

FIELDCREST CANNON, INC.

hemmed ready-to-use bedsheets and specialized textile products for the kitchen, such as potholders and countertop appliance covers. In the early 1920s, Cannon Mills added colored borders to its flat weave "huck" towels at a time when white linens were standard fare. Spurred by consumer interest in the fashionable homes of Hollywood's glamorous motion picture sets, Cannon introduced its classic reversible woven towel pattern in the late 1920s. In 1956, Fieldcrest introduced a line of color coordinated fashion sheets, towels, and bedspreads called *One Look*. In recent years, computer-aided-design (CAD) and development of new technologies in production, dyeing, finishing, fabric printing, and sewing techniques have kept Fieldcrest Cannon on the cutting edge of home fashion for over a century.

1993 inauguration received unrelenting criticism by fashion aficionados, being called a "cross between Padding-ton Bear's . . . headgear and a Bowery Boy . . . mashed-brim fedora. . ."[32].

Since the advent of motion pictures, actors, actresses, and entertainers have replaced the aristocracy as models of fashion. In the early 1960s, *Bonnie and Clyde* revived many fashions of the 1930s. The menswear-inspired designs in women's wear of the mid-1970s were influenced by the costumes worn by Diane Keaton in the movie *Annie Hall*. The film *Saturday Night Fever* gave birth to *discomania* and the *disco*

Figure 6.15

Jacqueline Kennedy's pillbox
hat became a fashion symbol
of the day.

shirt, a polyester pointed open-collar shirt worn by the film's star John
Travolta.[33] When Tom Cruise wore Ray-Ban's *Wayfarer* sunglasses in
Risky Business, Ray-Ban was forced to revive production of the discontinued style.[34] In 1980, the magnificent wardrobe worn by Richard's
Gere in *American Gigolo* popularized the fashions of Giorgio Armani.
Television is also an important fashion medium. *Dynasty* stimulated
knockoffs of the elegant creations of Nolan Miller, designer for the
show's fashions. The characters of *Beverly Hills 90210* and *Melrose Place*
became later fashion icons.[35]

   The U.S. fashion industry grew rapidly after World War II when
Seventh Avenue apparel manufacturers began to visit European fashion centers to "steal from the rich to give to the poor" by mass producing copies of European couture. The *rag* business evolved into the
fashion business, and the rapid expansion of the national economy was
paralleled by an equally rapid growth in the fashion industry.[36]

THE NAME GAME

The image of a product can be enhanced by attaching a celebrity's name to it. A Nordstrom private-label sportswear line is named for the late motion-picture star, Greta Garbo. Since 1984, more than thirty million shoppers have purchased apparel at Kmart that bears the name of former *Charlie's Angels* star, Jaclyn Smith. Other celebrity names associated with apparel lines include Ivana Trump, Kathie Lee Gifford, and Marla Maples. Celebrity accessory lines include Joan Rivers (jewelry), Cheryl Tiegs (eyewear, hosiery, and jewelry), and Sophia Loren (eyewear).[1]

Men also lend their names to product lines. Filmmaker Spike Lee is identified with 40 Acres & A Mule, a line of streetsmart styles for men and women; Country singer Kenny Rogers is identified with a line of western wear; exercise guru Richard Simmons' name is on a clothing line for full-figured women.

Though celebrities sometimes offer input relative to the styling of their namesake lines, they do not actually *design* them. Celebrities are paid a fee or royalty for the use of their name to promote the product.[2]

1. *Ozzard, Janet. (June 29, 1995). "I want to be a line": Nordstrom get Garbo name for designer apparel.* Women's Wear Daily. *p. 9.*
2. *Daria, Irene. (February 1994). Celebrities as fashion designers.* Glamour. *pp. 123–124.*

Fashion has become an integral part of our economic system and is so much a part of our culture that it is difficult to find a product that does not have some inherent element of fashion.

RETAILERS AND FASHION

Retailers communicate fashion to their customers through advertising, sales promotion, product presentation, and direct selling. Though fashion stimulates sales, fashion adds to the complexity of a retailer's job. When bed linens were white, buying decisions were often just reorders of the most popular selling sizes and fabrications. Today, a household textile buying decision involves a vast number of purchase options that includes many merchandise resources each offering myriad colors, patterns, and styles. A sheet department is as fashionable as an apparel department, boasting of designer names that include Ellen Tracy and

HOW BARBARA TURF CHOOSES
THE HOT PLACE MATS OF 1997

Barbara Turf, merchandising chief for Crate & Barrel stores, is a betting woman. When blues and greens with a yellow tone are all the rage in Europe, she figures that color scheme will spread to households across the United States in eighteen months. By traveling, reading magazines, and astutely observing everything around her, Ms. Turf is Crate's secret weapon in the battle to anticipate and provide for consumers' changing tastes. The housewares and furnishing chain "may just be the best fashion retailer in the country," says retail consulting firm McMillan/Doolittle.

Ms. Turf joined the Crate & Barrel as a part-time sales clerk. The mother of three worked her way up, and since 1978 she has been overseeing the buying of everything from frying pans to four-poster beds. Ms. Turf considers what we eat, drive, and wear before deciding what we'll want for our homes. She always has an eye on Europe, where she says trends often begin about eighteen months before they reach our shores. But she's watching what's happening here as well. When people started driving Jeep Cherokees instead of Cadillacs, she moved to more casual dinnerware. Changes in eating habits led her to stock pasta and fajita makers and ease up on waffle irons. A resurgence of linen in clothes, she says, will translate to linen in the home. "You've got to be a visionary and see and feel what's coming." she says. "A lot of people make the mistake of letting the consumer lead them."

Ms. Turf's ability to choose appealing merchandise and sometimes, like all good buyers, put her own preferences aside—has made Crate the envy of buyers in the much bigger apparel industry. Privately held Crate says its sales are nearly three times the housewares industry average of $200 to $300 a square foot.

Started in 1962 by Gordon Segal and his wife, Carole, Chicago-based Crate reaches out to both a trendy crowd and a clientele that has been coming back year after year for products mostly ignored by mass merchandisers and department stores. In Crate's bright, homey floor space, each product is meticulously displayed in artful, colorful arrangements—a touch that competitors watch closely and try to imitate. Clerks bustling around in aprons answer questions on the latest products. Industry experts say Crate is more consistently upscale than Pier 1 Imports, Inc. and more affordable than Williams-Sonoma, Inc. and its Pottery Barn unit.

continued

How Barbara Turf Chooses the Hot Place Mats of 1997 *continued*

Whether copying a successful European competitor or following a hunch, this is a tricky, unscientific business. If Ms. Turf guesses wrong, Crate is stuck with excess merchandise that will have to be sharply discounted. She gambled on a pinkish plaid place mat. Not a single one sold over the entire first weekend. But even when she gets it very, very right, she doesn't necessarily buy more of the hit item. The company updates its products and colors at least three times a year to stay ahead of imitators—an industry rule of thumb, but one some of their competitors have a tough time following. It takes stamina, says Mr. Segal, the company's president, for a buyer to discontinue popular items and buy other things for next year.

In choosing merchandise for the '90s, Ms. Turf says people are entertaining more at home, so they'll want versatile tableware. Time-pressed, harried consumers also want "less messy, less complicated" home decor, so styles should be simple and clean, she adds. In retailing these days, most buyers are more accountant than merchant. Ms. Turf is the exception. Amid all the haggling, she rarely pushes a vendor for the rock-bottom price. She admits that Mr. Segal would like her to pay a bit more attention to the bottom line.

Adrienne Vittadini. Fashion adds risk to retail buying decisions. Large retailers commit to hundreds of thousands of dollars for a single fashion item or a group of related fashion items. Faulty fashion predictions impact sales and profit.

SUMMARY POINTS

- Fashion is an expression that is widely accepted by a group of people over time.
- A trend implies the direction or movement of a fashion. The word *trend* is often used synonymously with fashion.
- The fashion life cycle depicts the growth, culmination, and demise of a fashion.
- Fads are short-lived fashions. Classics are long enduring fashions.
- Fashion goods have aesthetic qualities, change frequently, and are generally considered nonnecessities. Basic goods have functional

qualities, change infrequently, and are generally considered necessities.

- Fashion acceptance can be explained by the trickle-down, the trickle-across, and the trickle-up theories.
- Sales are stimulated by the transformation of basic goods into fashion goods.
- Fashion is influenced by technological, economic, and societal change. Famous people and popular entertainment also influence fashion.

KEY TERMS AND CONCEPTS

basic goods	fashion laggard	trend
classic	fashion leader	trickle-across theory
fad	fashion life cycle	trickle-down theory
fashion	high fashion	trickle-up theory
fashion follower	knockoff	
fashion goods	mass fashion	

FOR DISCUSSION

1. Trace the transformation of several products from a basic business to a fashion business.
2. Identify some emerging trends. What impact will these trends have on fashion and the products that consumers will buy?
3. Identify some fashions of the past that have recently reappeared. How do the recent fashions differ from their predecessors? Have the recent fashions been as successful?

SUGGESTED READINGS

Frings, Gini. (1992). *Fashion: From Concept to Consumer.* Englewood Cliffs, NJ: Prentice Hall.

Jarnow, Jeannette; Guerreiro, Miriam & Judelle, Beatrice. (1990). *Inside the Fashion Business.* Englewood Cliffs, NJ: Prentice Hall.

Jernigan, Marian & Easterling, Cynthia. (1990). *Fashion Merchandising and Marketing.* New York: Macmillan.

Sproles, George & Burns, Leslie. (1994). *Changing Appearances.* New York: Fairchild.

ENDNOTES

1. Fraser, Kennedy. (1981). *The Fashionable Mind: Reflections on Fashions, 1970–1981.* New York: Knopf. p. 145.

2. Monget, Karen. (January 26, 1995). Opportunity's knocking. *Women's Wear Daily.* pp. 12, 16.

3. McGraw, Dan & Fischer, David. (November 14, 1994). Designing for dollars. *U.S. News & World Report.* pp. 103–106.

4. Weir, June. (November 7, 1994). Casual look "defining" character of the '90s. *Advertising Age.* pp. S2, S12.

5. Reynolds, Pamela. (1995, May 30). How fashion stole dress-down day. *Boston Globe.* pp. 57, 60.

6. Berger, Joseph. (February 6, 1995). Black jeans invade Big Blue. *New York Times.* pp. B1, B8.

7. Reynolds, Pamela. (May 30, 1995). How fashion stole dress-down day. *Boston Globe.* pp. 57, 60.

8. Zinn, Laura. (August 21, 1991). The suit market is coming apart at the seams. *Business Week.* pp. 42–43.

9. Strom, Stephanie. (November 20, 1994). London Fog: Out of the drizzle and into the rain. *New York Times.* p. F5.

10. Burke, Martin. (December 1991). The psychology of the home: Why am I thinking about sofas more than skirts? *Retail Control.* pp. 15–21.

11. Reda, Susan. (August 1994). Home and hearth motivate shoppers. *Stores.* pp. 46–49.

12. Young, Tracy. (September 1990). Frock around the clock. *Vogue.* p. 658.

13. Chun, Rene. (July 11, 1995). Hemp fashion: World's oldest fabric now its newest. (Springfield, MA) *Union-News.* pp. C2–3.

14. Nystrom, Paul. (1928). *Economics of Fashion.* New York: Ronald Press. p. 18.

15. Meadus, Amanda. (October 24, 1994). From runways to mass: A slow trickle. *Women's Wear Daily.* p. 8.

16. King, Charles. (1963). Fashion adoption: A rebuttal to the "trickle down" theory. Proceedings of the Winter Conference of the American Marketing Association. December 27, 28. Boston. edited by Stephen Greyser.

17. Howard, Rebecca. (January 31, 1993). "Grunge" is in—primp is out. (Springfield MA) *Sunday Republican.* p. E7.

18. The term *staple* is often used synonymously with basic. Technically, staples are goods with year-round demand, as opposed to seasonal goods that are only in demand at certain times of the year. The term *basic* is not associated with seasonal or year-round demand.

19. The preferred industry term for costume jewelry.

20. Staff. (October 1994). Mail-order shopping: Which catalogs are best? *Consumer Reports.* pp. 621–626.

21. Muschamp, Herbert. (January 1991). Now and then. *Vogue.* 99, 186–190, 219.

22. Morris, Bernadine. (October 9, 1992). Recalling the love-bead era. *New York Times.* p. B6.

23. Gustke, Constance. (May 29, 1995). Courting the upscale market. *Home Furnishings Daily.* p. 2A.

24. Losee, Stephanie. (July 29, 1991). Products to Watch. *Fortune.* p. 128.

25. Staff. Hypercolor is hopping at Generra. *Apparel Industry Magazine.* p. 6.

26. In 1958, the Ford Motor Company developed a car of revolutionary styling called the *Edsel.* Though supported by an aggressive marketing campaign, the car was vehemently rejected by U.S. car buyers and has become a classic example of a marketing disaster.

27. Isaacs, McAllister. (August 1994). Race is on to find new uses for microfibers. *Textile World.* pp. 45–48, 73–74.

28. Caminiti, Susan. (February 24, 1992). The pretty payoff in cheaper chic. *Fortune.* pp. 71–72.

29. Riemer, Blanca & Zinn, Laura. Haute couture that's not so haute. *Business Week.* p. 108.

30. Buckley, Christopher. (July 1991). High & low. *Vogue.* pp. 180–183, 205.

31. Reed, Julia. (October 1990). Fashion and society. *Vogue.* pp. 388–393, 439–440.

32. McEnroe, Colin. (January 25, 1993). The hat people among us. *Hartford Courant.* pp. B1, B2.

33. Lord, Shirley, (February 1994). Striking poses. *Vogue.* pp. 173, 176, 178, 180.

34. Schleier, Curt. (February 1994). Manipulated by the movies. *A&E Monthly.* pp. 41–43.

35. Lefton, Terry. (December 14, 1992). No body part is spared a 90210 hits lips, hair. *Brandweek.*

36. Staff. (December 15, 1970). Man of the year. *Clothes.* pp. 26–32.

chapter seven

BRANDS AND PRIVATE LABELS

Producer-sponsored marketing campaigns targeted to consumers create demand for products in retail stores. The strategy works well for both producers and retailers. Product sales to retailers are enhanced in that retailers will buy goods for which there is consumer demand. Retail promotional costs are minimized, since the goods are "pre-sold" by the time they arrive in the store. In spite of this dual advantage, some retailers choose to carry products that are not marketed by a producer to reap advantages of another type. Chapter 7 deals with the advantages and disadvantages associated with two types of products: branded goods which are marketed by their producers, and private label goods which are not.

After you have read this chapter, you will be able to discuss:

Branding and licensing.

Private labeling.

The synergy of brands, licensed products, and private labels in a merchandise assortment.

BRANDED MERCHANDISE

Brand-name, or **branded merchandise,** is identified by a name and/or symbol associated with certain product characteristics, such as price, quality, fit, styling, and prestige. These characteristics position a product in the marketplace by distinguishing the branded item from its competitors. Packaging and/or labeling are often important elements of brand identification. Recognizable brand names include Lee jeans, Giorgio fragrances, and Fruit of the Loom underwear.

A **designer brand,** or *signature brand,* bears the name of a designer, such as Christian Dior or Tommy Hilfiger. A *power brand* is a term used to refer to a brand that represents a significant segment of business.[1] Wilson sporting goods, Black & Decker countertop appliances, Maybelline cosmetics, and Mattel toys are power brands at full-line discount stores. A brand is sometimes referred to as a *manufacturer's brand* or a *national brand.* Many "national brands" are in fact "interna-

Figure 7.1

Intense competition for market dominance leads to a continuous emergence of innovative branded products.

tional brands." Levi Strauss, the largest apparel manufacturer in the world, has production facilities in more than forty countries, and has sold more than 2.5 billion pair of jeans worldwide since its founding in 1853. Other brands have existed for many years. Waterford (crystal) dates back to the mid-1700s.[2] Jantzen (swimwear) was founded in 1910, Bulova (watches) in 1875. Some brands have gained worldwide prominence in relatively short time. DKNY was established in 1984, Reebok in 1981.[3]

Intense competition for market dominance leads to a continuous emergence of innovative branded products. In 1911, John E. Barbey revolutionized the fabrication of women's lingerie by using silk tricot, a glove lining fabric, in a line called Vanity Fair. In 1951, Hanes developed the seamless stocking.[4] Later Hanes product developments included Underalls, the all-in-one pantyhose, and an opaque microfiber for Hanes Soft Touch hosiery. In 1960, Corning Ware developed a material for oven-to-table cookware that has become an American kitchen classic. Totes was the innovator of the compact umbrella. More recently, Levi Strauss developed a mass customization program called *Pair* that uses store-based computers to create specifications for custom-fitted jeans, the delivery of which is guaranteed in three weeks.[5,6,7]

Positioning a Brand in a Store

Producers of branded products use advertising and sales promotion to position their products in the marketplace and to generate consumer demand for them. This strategy of *pulling* products through the marketing channel encourages retailers to carry branded products in reaction to consumer demand.[8]

Various advertising media are used to promote brands. Calvin Klein's marketing strategy includes a mix of television and out-of-home advertising, as well as countless fashion-oriented consumer magazines. Other brands concentrate on a single advertising medium. Vanity Fair (innerwear) advertises almost exclusively in fashion and lifestyle magazines. Bugle Boy (jeanswear) has an aggressive bus shelter advertising program.

Along with emphasizing product characteristics, advertising for brands is often image oriented, portraying the lifestyle of the targeted consumer. The advertising for Polo/Ralph Lauren appeals to the adventurous and well-bred. Calvin Klein's advertising appeals to the

Figure 7.2

Advertising for brands is often image-oriented, portraying the lifestyle of the targeted customer, such as Chic's "Life's an open road" campaign.

young and sensuous. Endorsements by celebrities can reinforce a brand's image. Celebrity/brand partnerships have included sports figures Joe Montana for L.A. Gear, and Michael Jordan for Nike. Innovative advertising has been instrumental in increasing brand recognition. In 1955, Playtex shocked viewers by the unprecedented advertisement of bras and girdles on television. In 1980, fifteen-year-old Brooke Shields caused a similar reaction when she cooed that nothing came between her and her Calvin Klein jeans.

Advertising expenditures are often linked to a brand's success. Calvin Klein's annual advertising budget is estimated at more than $10 million.[9] The advertising budget for L'eggs hosiery exceeds the advertising expenditures for competitive brands. However, L'eggs accounts for over half of the hosiery sales in the retail outlets in which the brand is distributed.[10] Event sponsorships, publicity, and other forms of sales promotion also enhance brand recognition. Sponsorship of the Miss USA, Miss Universe, and Miss Teen pageants have built brand recognition for Catalina swimwear. Swatch, noted for its trendy inexpensive plastic watches, commanded media attention by introducing its platinum edition watch on the floor of the New York Commodities Exchange.

The retail channels through which brands are distributed play an important role in positioning a brand. As a bridge sportswear line, Ellen Tracy is distributed through upscale specialty department stores, such as Nordstrom and Bergdorf Goodman. Gitano value-oriented apparel and accessories are distributed through full-line discount stores. Chanel, Germaine Monteil, and Elizabeth Arden are *prestige* cosmetics lines sold in department stores. Maybelline, Max Factor, and Cover Girl are *mass market* cosmetics lines packaged for self-selection and sold in discount stores and drug stores. Producers protect their brand image by ensuring that their products are not sold to unintended retail channels by third-party wholesalers called **diverters.**[11] After Florida's 1992 Hurricane Andrew and California's 1994 Northridge Quake, Estée Lauder bought back its own product from the insurance companies that acquired damaged stock from department stores, fearing that the product would be diverted to discount stores.

Many brands owe their initial success to an introduction by a reputed retailer. The men's designer label movement began in December 1965 when Lord & Taylor opened the first John Weitz shop at its Fifth Avenue store.[12] The successful debut of Guess? occurred in 1981 when Bloomingdale's sold out thirty pair of the line's form-fitting jeans in three hours.[13] Bloomingdale's was also the first to open its doors to Liz Claiborne, destined to become the fastest growing women's apparel lines in Seventh Avenue history.[14] Just as brands use retailers as a market positioning tool, retailers use brands to define their image. Wal-Mart enhanced its low fashion profile by adding labels such as White Stag sportswear, Catalina activewear, and Puritan men's wear to its assortments.[15,16]

The apparel industry uses a price/quality hierarchy to position lines. **Designer lines** are exclusive creations of a reputed designer. **Bridge,** or *diffusion,* lines are the lower-priced designer creations with limited distribution through prestigious stores, such as Saks Fifth Avenue and Bloomingdale's. **Better lines** and **moderate lines** are broadly distributed through less prestigious department store conglomerates, such as May and Dillard's. Moderate lines have broader distribution than better lines, and may also appear at JCPenney or

Figure 7.3

Retailers use brands to define their image and position themselves in the marketplace.

Sears. **Budget lines** are carried by full-line discounters. The following breakdown of designer, bridge, better, moderate, and budget lines in the misses sportswear industry best exemplifies the system:

- Designer—Donna Karan, Calvin Klein
- Bridge—DKNY, Adrienne Vittadini, Anne Klein II, Ellen Tracy
- Better—Liz Claiborne, Jones New York, Carole Little, Susan Bristol
- Moderate—Alfred Dunner, Chaus, Koret, Norton McNaughton, Cricket Lane
- Budget—Most budget lines are private labels sold exclusively by full-line discount stores.

The system has been adopted by other industry segments in modified form. The terms *better* and *moderate* are often used to describe the price and quality of other types of apparel, accessories, and other consumer products.

Producers sometimes alter their distribution strategies when greater potential is identified in alternative channels. Evan Picone was a better misses sportswear line that was repositioned by new owners as

Figure 7.4

Producers of branded products often support the sale of their product line at the retail level with fixtures and various services.

a moderate line. Originally a department store hosiery line, Underalls was repositioned as a mass market line. Recognizing the need for a moderately priced jeanswear brand for department and specialty stores, the VF Corporation rechanneled its Lee brand from full-line discounters to department and specialty stores. Unwilling to give up its healthy discount store business, VF created a line called Riders as a replacement for Lee at discount stores.

Sometimes producers attempt to increase their sales by distributing their brands through multiple retail channels. The distribution of a prestigious brand through value-oriented retailers is especially upsetting to upscale retailers who feel that a brand's image is sullied by such a distribution policy. OshKosh B'Gosh, a producer of trendy children's wear, irked many of its upscale department store accounts, such as Dayton's, Bloomingdale's, and Macy's, when it began to distribute through JCPenney and Sears.[17,18]

Multichannel distribution often leads to abandonment by upscale stores. Both May Department Stores and Federated Department Stores discontinued Revlon's Ultima II line because of broadened distribution through JCPenney.[19,20] Being snubbed by an upscale retailer is not always devastating to a brand. Macy's discontinued Levi's jeans when Levi Strauss began to distribute the line through JCPenney and Sears. JCPenney eventually became one of Levi Strauss' largest accounts. Several years later, Macy's resumed carrying the line.

Producers of branded products often support the sale of their products at the retail level by providing product training, promotional aids, and funds for store-sponsored advertising. Producers sometimes provide fixtures and signage especially designed for their product to enhance consistent and prominent presentation in all stores. Branded product producers sometimes share the risk of carrying a line by allowing retailers to return slow-selling goods for credit after an agreed-upon selling period.

Brand Extension

Brand extension involves adding related products to an existing line of branded products, or developing a new product line with the same brand identity. By extending a brand, a producer capitalizes on a

Figure 7.5

Jockey For Her is a brand extension of Jockey's men's line.

brand's reputation, as well as the company's production expertise, and the channel relationships established with existing products.

Jockey International's reputation for quality men's underwear prompted the development of Jockey For Her, a line that now generates sales nearly equivalent to the sales of Jockey's long-established men's line. Relying on its reputation for sturdy men's jeans, Levi Strauss extended its brand name to jeans for women and children, and other forms of men's casual apparel, such as knit and woven shirts. Dockers is a Levi Strauss brand extension that began as a line of casual cotton men's wear. Dockers now includes a line of cotton women's wear and a boy's line. Multiple extensions result in a *megabrand*, a brand that encompasses several related merchandise categories, such as dresses, accessories, shoes, and sportswear. Some companies produce a portfolio of branded product lines, each targeted to different markets. Jessica McClintock has three "McClintock lines": Scott McClintock, a dress and sportswear line; Jessica McClintock Bridal, and the Jessica McClintock designer collection.[21] The company also produces Gunne Sax, a junior line, and Gunne Sax for Girls, a dressy

Figure 7.6

Brown Shoe Company owns a portfolio of shoe brands each targeted to different customers.

Figure 7.7

The Warnaco Group's innerwear brands are distributed through various types of retail channels.

apparel line for infant through preteen girls. Jantzen has a junior line called Electric Beach, a contemporary line called Bolero, Coastal Zone for the woman over thirty-five, and Classics for the more mature customer. When its department store business began to stabilize, Liz Claiborne acquired several moderate labels, among them The Villager, a megabrand of dresses, accessories, and shoes, distributed through Montgomery Ward and Sears.[22] Estée Lauder commands over a third of the prestige cosmetics sales with a portfolio of four product lines each targeted to different customers that includes Estée Lauder, Prescriptives, Origins, and Clinique.[23] Portfolios of brands are sometimes highly diversified. Along with its signature food products, the Sara Lee Corporation produces L'eggs and Hanes hosiery, Playtex and Bali innerwear, and Totes umbrellas. The VF Corporation's portfolio of branded products includes Vanity Fair and Vassarette innerwear, Wrangler and Lee jeans, and Jantzen swimwear.

The various brands within a portfolio are often intended for distribution through a specific retail channel. Munsingwear, a men's sportswear line identified by its trademark penguin, created a mass market line called Stix to reserve its flagship line for department stores. The

Company Profile 7.1

At the turn of the century, gloves were essential to the wardrobes of properly attired fashionable women. It was during this gloved hand era that the Stanton brothers created Aris of Paris, a line of fine-quality leather gloves.

«ARIS»

ISOTONER

As styles and times changed, glove wearers became less concerned with propriety, and more concerned with fit, comfort, and function. Aris of Paris responded to the change with the Isotoner glove, a brand name reflecting the glove's *isometric* and *toning* fit. The one-size-fits-all glove made of nylon and spandex trimmed in leather was an immediate success, leading to renaming Aris of Paris to Aris Isotoner, the same year that the organization became a subsidiary of Consolidated Foods, now the Sara Lee Corporation.

The Isotoner line has been extended to include gloves for men, and athletic and fashion hosiery for men and women. Aris Isotoner entered the slipper market in 1983 and now offers slipper lines for men, women, and children in an array of silhouettes, such as ballerinas, moccasins, boots, and espadrilles in fabrications that include satin, terry, velour, and fleece.

Recognizing the importance of gloves as holiday gifts, Aris Isotoner developed the concept of boxed gloves. Responding to the emergence of more casual lifestyles, Aris Isotoner developed the Country Collection of gloves, slippers, and socks made of comfortable fabrications. A more recent product innovation includes the raindrop-resistant, Teflon-coated *Stay-Dri* umbrella that can be closed without drying even after being subjected to a downpour.

Department stores are Isotoner's primary channel of distribution, representing 60 percent of Isotoner's business. Aris Isotoner is equally important to department stores, representing seventy percent of department stores' cold weather accessory business. Strategically developed point-of-purchase displays are instrumental in Aris Isotoner's success. A traveling team of merchandisers guides stores in creating Isotoner "shops within a shop" that maximize the impact of Aris Isotoner products with banners, three-dimensional logos, and plastic-embedded posters.

Figure 7.8

Purchases of denim blue jeans are brand-driven because of each brand's unique fit.

Warnaco Group produces several innerwear brands, including Warner's, Olga, Valentino Intimo, and Calvin Klein for department stores; Fruit of the Loom label for discounters, such as Kmart and Wal-Mart; and the Van Raalte label for Sears.[24] The Authentic Fitness Corporation has several swimwear brands, including Speedo, a performance line for specialty stores; White Stag, a mass market line for discount stores; and Jantzen, Cole, and Catalina for department stores.

Brand-Driven Purchases

Consumer choices that are based primarily on brand preference are called **brand-driven** purchases. Purchases are brand-driven when clear distinctions differentiate brands. When clear distinctions do not differentiate brands, consumers adopt a "one brand is as good as the next" attitude basing their purchases on factors such as price or color, with minimal consideration of brand. Fragrances purchases are brand driven because of each brand's distinctive scent. Purchases of denim blue jeans are brand driven because of each brand's unique fit.[25] The pur-

---

WHO BUYS BRANDS?

In a study of fifty-nine apparel brands, Management Horizons found that consumers recognized designer brands 70 percent of the time, manufacturers' brands 60 percent of the time, and private labels 50 percent of the time. The private labels that were correctly identified most often were those related to a store's name.

The study linked demographic characteristics to brand popularity and showed that:

- Designer brands are popular among urbanites, blacks, the young, and the affluent.
- National brands are popular among older and middle-to-upper-middle class customers.
- Private labels are popular among the less affluent and the middle aged, though the profile varied significantly according to the type of store.
- Profiles of private label buyers are similar to the profiles of the store's customers in general.

The study also showed that:

- Discount store private labels appeal to utilitarian consumers.
- National brands appeal to the conventionally oriented and to the risk averse.
- Designer brands fulfill the desire for adventure and uniqueness and the needs to be fashionable, to display symbols of wealth or power, and to fit in with one's peers.

Staff. (May 1990). Battle of brands: Who's winning? Stores. pp. 77–79.

chases of designer label apparel, cosmetics, and toys are also brand-driven. Consumers are reluctant to accept substitutes for purchases that are brand driven. Customers who consistently purchase the same brand are called *brand loyal.*

To understand the concept of brand-driven purchases, consider the male customer who consistently purchases Levi's 501 blue jeans. Three product characteristics are important to him: a comfortable, consistent fit, easy care, and durability. The customer is not enticed by lower-priced competitive brands that he has found are not as comfortable, nor as durable. The same customer may make a necktie purchase irrelevant to brand. His selection of a tie is based solely on color, pattern, and the feel of the fabric. The product features relevant to fit, care, and durability that influenced his jeans purchase are irrelevant to his necktie purchase in that neckties are a standard size, they typically require dry cleaning, and they do not have points of stress to cause concern for durability. The jeans purchase is brand driven. The necktie purchase is not. When approached by a salesperson in a retail store, the customer states his needs as "a pair of Levi's 501", and a "tie to go with a navy blue suit."

LICENSING

Licensing involves the use of a merchandising property in the design of a product or a product line. Merchandising properties have many forms, including brand names (Totes), designer names (Oscar de la Renta), trademarks (Coca-Cola), designs (a polo player on a horse), characters (Mickey Mouse), celebrity names (Kathie Lee Gifford), sports teams (the Dallas Cowboys), and various forms of entertainment, such as movies (*The Lion King*), television shows (*Beverly Hills 90210*), and special events (the Olympics™). In a licensing agreement, the owner of the merchandising property (the licensor) permits (licenses) a producer (the licensee) to use the property for a fee, or royalty. The licensee is responsible for the design, production, and distribution of the product. *Cross licensing* involves the use of two licensed properties, such as a necktie depicting Bugs Bunny wearing a New York Giants sweatshirt.

Licensing provides the licensor with an opportunity to extend a brand without having to develop, produce, or market a new product. A property becomes licensable after a reputation for prestige, quality, style, or popularity has been established in the marketplace. Bill Blass's reputation as an apparel designer spurred licensing agreements for dresses, swimwear, outerwear, activewear, jeans, loungewear, hosiery, fragrances, menswear, and bedding. The licensee reaps the marketing advantage of the established reputation or popularity of the merchandising property.[26] In order to protect the reputation of the merchandising property, licensors most often reserve the right to approve the material, color, quality, and design of the licensed product.

Licensed products are often related to product lines from which they are descended. The names of apparel designers appear on lines of

Table 7.1a **SHARES OF ALL LICENSED PRODUCT RETAIL SALES BY PRODUCT CATEGORY — 1993**

Product Category	1993 Retail Sales
Accessories	$ 6.20
Apparel	11.60
Domestics	4.20
Electronics	1.06
Food/Beverage	5.24
Footwear	2.03
Furniture/Home Furnishings	0.75
Gifts/Novelties	6.00
Health and Beauty	3.70
Housewares	2.18
Infant Products	2.16
Music/Video	1.18
Publishing	4.23
Sporting Goods	2.25
Stationery/Paper	3.10
Toys/Games	7.26
Video games/Software	3.26
Other—small size category	0.20
TOTAL	$66.60

Dollar Figures in Billions;
United States and Canada only

Table 7.1b **SHARES OF ALL LICENSEND PRODUCT RETAIL SALES BY PROPERTY TYPE—1993**

Product Category	1993 Retail Sales
Art	$ 4.74
Celebrities/Estates	2.55
Entertainment/Character	15.80
Fashion	11.80
Music	0.97
Non-Profit	0.65
Publishing	1.50
Sports	13.14
Trademarks/Brands	12.64
Toys/Games	2.55
Other—small size category	0.26
TOTAL	$66.60

Dollar Figures in Billions;
United States and Canada only

accessories; dinnerware companies license designs to producers of table linens and glassware. The London Fog moniker appears on licensed hats, umbrellas, and children's outerwear. General Mills licensed the Betty Crocker name for a line of cookware and small electrical appliances.

Licensees often have considerable expertise in the design, production, and distribution of licensed products. Hanes produces licensed hosiery lines for Donna Karan and Liz Claiborne. Timex makes Guess and Monet watches; Bulova makes Benneton, Sportime, and Harley Davidson watches. Licensor and licensee relationships are sometimes intricately woven. Jantzen licenses its name to Phillips-Van Heusen to produce a line of Jantzen men's knit shirts. Jantzen is the licensee for Nike swimwear and related activewear.[27]

Licensing agreements are significant sources of revenue for many companies. With the exception of its image-setting women's sportswear collection, Calvin Klein is essentially a licensing operation. Rio Sportswear produces Calvin Klein jeans, as well as Bill Blass jeans. Calvin Klein underwear is produced by the Warnaco Group. Calvin Klein fragrances are produced by Unilever. Calvin Klein hosiery is produced by Kayser-Roth, the producer of No-Nonsense pantyhose.[28]

Licensing has grown into a $60 billion industry in the United States. Apparel and accessories represent the largest category of licensed products. Popular licensed apparel items include T-shirts, sweatshirts, and sleepwear.[29] Other commonly licensed categories include novelties, toys, and stationery. Even chocolates (Bill Blass) and car interiors (Ralph Lauren) are licensed. Licensed products represent a significant amount of sales volume for many retailers. Some have assigned a buyer to be solely responsible for identifying hot properties and for merchandising shops and coordinating promotions tied to the licensed properties.[30]

The licensing of designer names began in 1924 when the famous French designer Coco Chanel permitted the use of her name on a newly developed fragrance. The association was a controversial one at a time when designer names appeared only on high fashion couture. Chanel No. 5 was an immediate success and remains so today.[31] With over 900 licensees, Pierre Cardin is the uncrowned king of designer-name licensing. However, extensive licensing can diminish the exclusivity of a designer's cachet. The high fashion image of Halston was severely tainted in 1984 when the company licensed a line of female apparel for distribution at JCPenney.

PRIVATE LABELS

Private label merchandise bears the name of the retail store in which it is sold, or a name used exclusively by the retailer. Products with a Brooks Brothers or The Gap label are private label goods, as are products with the Erika Taylor or Claybrooke labels used exclusively by May Department Stores. Unlike branded goods that are "presold" by producer-sponsored advertising and sales promotion, the retailer relies on its own reputation to validate the quality, style, or value of private label merchandise.[32] A Nordstrom label conveys an image of fashion to a consumer, while a Kmart label conveys an image of value. Private label goods are produced according to retailers' specifications for color, styling, and fabrication. The goods are then packaged and labeled with a retailer's name or logo, or name unique to the retailer.

Some stores, such as Ann Taylor and The Gap, offer only private labels. Other retailers, such as department stores and full-line discounters, balance a mix of both branded and private-label merchandise, hoping to draw brand-conscious customers, and also to reap the generous profit margins of private labels. These retailers offer consumers brand/price alternatives by strategically locating private label goods adjacent to branded goods.

Some producers specialize in the design and production of private label goods. Cygne Designs is a New York-based private label resource of male and female sportswear. Cygne's customers include Ann Taylor, The Limited, Dillard's, Federated, Dayton Hudson, and JCPenney.[33] The Evergreen Group of South Easton, Massachusetts specializes in female sportswear, dresses, and suits. Evergreen's clients include Neiman Marcus, Saks Fifth Avenue, and Talbots.[34] Some producers

Figure 7.9

Some of Federated Department Store's most popular private labels.

Figure 7.10

Some producers manufacture both
branded and private label goods.

manufacture both branded and private label goods. Botany 500 produces private label men's suits, as well as the Bert Pulitzer, Bernhard Altmann, and Gladiator Athletic Fit labels. Scotch Maid, a bodywear maker, produces Instant Replay for Target, Modern Motion for Wal-Mart, and its own Cool Moves brand.[35]

Retailers that conduct considerable private label business often have product development functions within their merchandising organizations responsible for designing private label goods and contracting their production. MAST Industries is a division of The Limited that designs products for the various Limited divisions according to buyers' specifications. MAST then sources fabric and production. Within an eight-week period, the item is distributed throughout hundreds of Limited stores.

Private-label goods are frequently the opening, or lowest, price point in a basic category of merchandise. However, some private labels are upscale fashions targeted to customer segments not satisfied by branded offerings.[36] Saks Fifth Avenue's private label collections include:

- The Works—a career line in the lower bridge price points
- Real Clothes—a casual line of silks and linens
- SFA Collections—knitwear and sportswear in the higher bridge price points[37]

Private-label goods are often knockoffs of successful branded products or product lines.[38] The best-selling department store brands of robes and sleepwear appear as private labels at full-line discounters, including Honors at Target, Upstart at Wal-Mart, Ashley Taylor at Kmart, and Sarah Morgan at Caldor.[39] JCPenney's Jacqueline Ferrar emulates the bridge sportswear collections of Ellen Tracy and Adrienne Vittadini. Macy's Charter Club and JCPenney's Hunt Club apparel lines bear a striking resemblance to Polo/Ralph Lauren. Tastefully designed in-store shops for private label collections further contribute to the designer illusion.

Though the producers of branded goods are frustrated by the value-oriented imitations of their lines, consumers benefit from the rivalry. The competition between the innovators and the imitators ensures a continual flow of distinctive merchandise.[40]

Advantages Private labels are advantageous to retailers for several reasons:

- Private label goods are less expensive than branded goods of comparable quality. The cost of developing and marketing branded prod-

Figure 7.11

Tastefully designed in-store shops create a designer illusion for some private label lines.

ucts is inherent in the price of branded goods. Product development and marketing costs are minimal for private label goods.

- Because of lower costs, a retailer can price private label goods more competitively and more profitably than branded goods.[41]
- Private label goods are exclusive to a store. This exclusivity allows the retailer considerable pricing latitude since consumers have no basis for price comparison.[42]
- Retailers can develop private-label goods targeted specifically to their customers without being restricted to the offerings of the marketplace.[43]

Disadvantages   In spite of the advantages listed above, there are several disadvantages associated with private label merchandise:

- There is no national advertising or any type of vendor support to promote the sale of private label goods.
- Consumers reject private label substitutes for brand driven purchases and sometimes associate the low price of private labels with low quality.[44]
- Private labeling is often a capital intensive proposition. Goods contracted overseas are paid for months in advance of their arrival. This precludes many small or undercapitalized retailers.[45,46]

Lines created exclusively for a retailer with a brand or designer name should not be confused with private labeling. *Only at Bloomingdale's* is a collection of apparel and home furnishings with noted designer names such as Calvin Klein, Anne Klein II, and Isaac Mizrahi, created exclusively for Bloomingdale's. The annual assemblage of exclusives is promoted with a catalog, extensive publicity, and special events that include guest appearances by the designers.

Private labeling is not a new concept. Once the cornerstone of the merchandising strategies of JCPenney and Sears, there are countless satisfied customers who can attest to the quality and value of their Kenmore washing machines, Toughskins jeans, DieHard automotive batteries, and Craftsman tools that they purchased at Sears.[47] Since the 1940s, Macy's has had one of the most successful private label programs in the department store industry.[48]

INNERWEAR
By Outlet

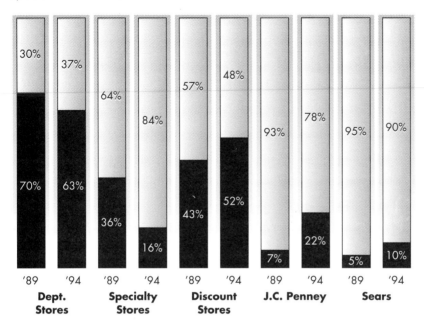

'89	'94	'89	'94	'89	'94	'89	'94	'89	'94
Dept. Stores		Specialty Stores		Discount Stores		J.C. Penney		Sears	

INNERWEAR
By Product

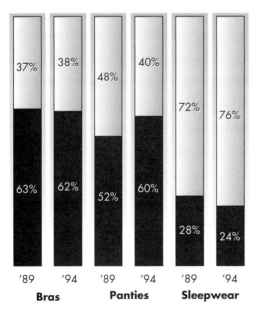

Private Label

National Brand

Figure 7.12

Private-label versus branded purchases of innerwear. *Women's Wear Daily.*

Mervyn's, the 270 store Hayward, California-based division of the Dayton Hudson Corporation, develops its own private label programs internally. By engineering its own products, Mervyn's has cut its product development cycle from one year to six months, and has maintained better control over design, production, and cost. Mervyn's develops more than fifteen private labels, including Sprockets for kids, Cambridge for men, and several women's labels such as Windridge, Life Style, High Sierra, and Cheetah.

MERVYN'S

Developing a Mervyn's private label is a joint effort between buyers, merchandisers, and product managers. Merchandisers are the creative force in the product development triad. With an assimilation of ideas from sources, such as color services and European markets, merchandisers translate current trends into specific product needs. As "creative engineers" they determine silhouette, fabrication, and colorway. Product managers are the technical force in the team. They source the fabric, cost the item, and determine an appropriate producer based on cost and logistical factors such as delivery.

Advanced technology is fundamental to Mervyn's private label success story. A CAD system enables merchandisers to design garments on a computer screen using software with a library of basic fabrics, patterns, and garment styles. Modifications to the fabric, such as changing color brightness or the size of a print, are easily implemented, as are style modifications, such as the fullness of a skirt or the treatment of a sleeve. Pattern makers then sketch patterns on a table while viewing the results on a computer screen. Samples are made and reviewed for fit and drape.

The system computes the total cost for constructing and delivering the garment, itemizing cost factors, such as the number of labor minutes required to perform each construction operation (e.g. "attaching a sleeve"), and the cost of the fabric. The cost is reviewed for consistency with Mervyn's gross margin expectations, and the price expectations of Mervyn's customer. If the cost is too high, the garment or fabric design is modified to lower cost. For instance, fabric can be conserved by reducing the fullness of a skirt or the size of a print on a fabric so that there will be less waste matching the fabric at seams. The final manufacturing specifications are transmitted by electronic mail to technically capable manufacturers worldwide.

Drizen, Ruth. (August 1993). Move over manufacturers! Here comes Mervyn's. Apparel Industry Magazine.

PRIVATE LABELS AS BRANDS

The word *brand* or *branded* is used to refer to goods marketed by their producer. However, Kurt Salmon Associates, an international management consulting organization, defines a *brand* as any recognizable name that adds value to a product because of consumers' perceptions of the name.[49] A name that is meaningful to consumers is a brand. A name that is meaningless, is not a brand.

Some retailers promote their private labels with extensive advertising. JCPenney supports its private label programs with television advertising, newspaper inserts, and direct mail. Macy's advertises its Morgan Taylor and Jennifer Moore labels alongside its branded goods.[50] According to the Kurt Salmon interpretation, these stores "brand" their private label merchandise with heavy advertising. Therefore, *The Gap* is a brand, since consumers associate The Gap's name with quality and value. This explanation justifies the seemingly paradoxical reference to private labels as *store brands* or *private brands*.[51]

SUMMARY POINTS

- Branded merchandise is identified by a name and/or symbol that consumers associate with certain product characteristics such as price, quality, value, fit, styling, and prestige.
- Consumer purchases are brand driven when clear distinctions exist among competing brands and when the distinctive characteristics are important to the consumer.
- Brands are extended by the addition of related products or product lines. Licensing is a form of brand extension requiring no capital investment on the part of the licensor.
- Private label merchandise is exclusive to a retailer's product mix and affords a retailer an opportunity for higher profit margins.

KEY TERMS AND CONCEPTS

better line	bridge line	diverter
brand-driven purchase	budget line	licensing
brand extension	designer brand	moderate line
branded merchandise	designer line	private label

FOR DISCUSSION

1. Obtain the histories of several branded products from the public relations departments of the companies that produce them. Compare the brands' growth relative to innovative product development, brand extension, creative advertising and promotion, and licensing agreements.

2. Determine which products within a category of merchandise at a local department store or full-line discounter are private label and which are branded. Compare the private label goods to the branded in terms of quality, price, fashion level, presentation, and percentage of total product mix. What distinctions, if any, do you observe?

ENDNOTES

1. Staff. (October 1992). 37 brands earn "power" ranking. *Discount Store News.* pp. 1, 60.

2. Light, Larry. (1993). *Building Brand Relationships.* New York: American Association of Advertising Agencies. p. 6.

3. Much of the information on branded products in this chapter was obtained from the October 1993 edition of *The Fairchild 50,* a supplement to *Women's Wear Daily,* edited by Edward Nardoza.

4. Staff. (August 1952). The seamless stocking. *Department Store Economist.* pp. 68–70.

5. Underwood, Elaine. (April 25, 1994). Indiglo watch lights up better times for Timex. *Brandweek.* pp. 30–32.

6. Cuneo, Alice. (January 23, 1995). Levi Strauss sizes the retail scene. *Advertising Age.* p. 4.

7. Cuneo, Alice. (August 14, 1995). Custom-fit clothes system to expand. *Advertising Age.* p. 38.

8. A *push* strategy involves business-to-business advertising by one channel member to the next.

9. Prud'homme, Alex. (September 23, 1991). What's it all about, Calvin? *Time.* p. 44.

10. Therrien, Lois. (December 23, 1991). This marketing effort has L'eggs. *Business Week.* p. 50.

11. Brookman, Faye. (February 19, 1993). Stores seek a bridge between classes. *Women's Wear Daily.* p. 9.

12. Parola, Robert. (May 22, 1992). The designer decades. *Daily News Record.* pp. 81–82.

13. Marlow, Michael. (December 20, 1991). Guess at 10: $550 million and growing. *Women's Wear Daily.* pp. 1, 6–7.

14. Darnton, Nina. (August 1992). The joy of polyester. *Newsweek.* p. 61.

15. Tosh, Mark. (December 14 1994). Wal-Mart's signing of Kathie Lee, Catalina signals branded push. *Women's Wear Daily.* pp. 1, 11.

16. Staff. (June 20, 1994). Private label assortment strengthens as a select alternative to national brands. *Discount Store News.* p. 63.

17. Ozzard, Janet. (June 22, 1994). Lee stakes a new claim. *Women's Wear Daily.* pp. 8–9.

18. Siler, Julia. (July 15, 1991). OshKosh B'Gosh may be risking its upscale image. *Business Week.* p. 140.

19. Born, Pete. (March 4, 1994). May dropping Ultima, cites "diluted cachet". *Women's Wear Daily.* pp. 1, 11.

20. Born, Pete. (April 8, 1994). Federated to drop Revlon's Ultima II. *Women's Wear Daily.* p. 4.

21. Hellman, Mary. (February 7, 1992). Taking a romance stance. *San Diego Union-Tribune.*

22. Friedman, Arthur & Rutberg, Sidney. Chazen see '94 comeback for Claiborne. *Women's Wear Daily.* pp. 1, 11.

23. Born, Pete. (June 23, 1995). Leonard Lauder: On the record. *Women's Wear Daily.* pp. 5–7.

24. Monget, Karen. (March 13, 1995). Innerwear: Big shifts. *Women's Wear Daily.* p. 14.

25. Purchases of denim blue jeans are generally considered brand-driven. However, according to a March 10, 1995, article in *Women's Wear Daily* (pp. 1, 6–8), private labels have been gaining considerable market share in recent years, indicating an erosion of brand loyalty.

26. Rosenberg, Joyce. (February 12, 1995). Toy Fair showcases licensed, new toys. (Springfield, MA) *Sunday Republican.* pp. G1, G2.

27. Staff. (January 13, 1995). Jantzen said near pact to make Nike swimwear, activewear lines. *Women's Wear Daily.* p. 2.

28. Lockwood, Lisa. (February 2, 1994). Hear CK jeans license near. *Women's Wear Daily.* p. 2.

29. D'Innocenzio, Anne. (July 20, 1994). Hot flicks fill supporting role for SA, stores. *Women's Wear Daily.* p. 1, 8–9.

30. Staff. (June 1990). What's up, Doc? Hare-raising bunny is 50! *Stores.* pp. 16–17.

31. Fitzgerald, Sheryl. (June 1, 1986). It's all in the name. (Springfield, MA) *Sunday Republican.* p. D3.

32. Morgenson, Gretchen. (May 10, 1993). Back to basics. *Forbes.* pp. 57–58.

33. Staff. (April 8, 1994). Cygne Designs buys Fenn Wright & Manson. *Women's Wear Daily.* p. 9.

34. Struensee, Chuck. (January 26, 1993). Evergreen sets up NY showroom. *Women's Wear Daily.* p. 10.

35. Friedman, Arthur. (September 28, 1994). Competition in private label mounts . . . and so does demand. *Women's Wear Daily.* pp. 18–19.

36. Ozzard, Janet; Lockwood, Lisa & D'Innocenzio, Anne. (March 30, 1995). Private label powers up. *Women's Wear Daily.* pp. 6–8.

37. Perman, Stacy. (December 8, 1993). Department stores to focus more on own brands. *Women's Wear Daily.* p. 24.

38. Spethmann, Betsy. (July 26, 1993). Private label. *Brandweek.* pp. 30–31.
39. Monget, Karyn. (August 29, 1994). Sleepwear firms target discounters. *Women's Wear Daily.* p. 6.
40. Rudolph, Barbara. (November 21, 1988). Invasion of the cachet snatchers. *Time.* p. 114.
41. Adams, Muriel. (June 1989). Private label programs: Major changes. *Stores.* pp. 10–19.
42. Staff. (May 27, 1993). Dealing with Dillard's. *Women's Wear Daily.* pp. 4–5.
43. Ozzard, Janet; Lockwood, Lisa & D'Innocenzio, Anne. (March 30, 1995). Private label powers up. *Women's Wear Daily.* pp. 6–8.
44. Hoch, Stephen & Banerji, Shumeer. (Summer 1993). When do private labels succeed? *Sloan Management Review.* pp. 57–67.
45. Gill, Penny. (May 1990). Private label: More or less. *Stores.* pp. 71–75.
46. Miller, Cyndee. (November 9, 1992). Better quality, packaging boost popularity of private label goods. *Marketing News.* pp. 1, 14–15.
47. Adams, Muriel. (June 1989). Private label programs: Major changes. *Stores.* pp. 10–19.
48. Morgenson, Gretchen. (May 10, 1993). Back to basics. *Forbes.* pp. 57–58.
49. Staff. (May 1990) Can a private label become a brand? *Stores.* p. 79.
50. Staff. (June 1989). Marketing private label. *Stores.* pp. 20–21.
51. DeNitto, Emily. (September 13, 1993). They aren't private labels anymore—they're brands. *Advertising Age.*

chapter eight

MERCHANDISE RESOURCES

As marketing channel intermediaries, retailers play a critical role in linking producers and consumers. Understanding the role of retailers as channel intermediaries requires knowledge of the interactions that occur between retailers and their customers, as well as knowledge of the interactions that occur between retailers and their suppliers. The terms *vendor, supplier,* and *resource* are commonly used to refer to the sources from which retail buyers obtain merchandise to sell in their stores. Chapter 8 covers the various types of merchandise resources and the ways in which retailers interface with each.

After you have read this chapter, you will be able to discuss:

The resources from which retail buyers obtain merchandise.

The places at which retail buyers and their suppliers transact business.

Imports as part of a merchandise mix.

The functions of a resident buying office.

MANUFACTURERS

A **manufacturer** uses labor and machinery to convert raw materials into finished products. The traditional concept of manufacturing encompasses a comprehensive range of functions, such as product design, materials procurement, and the complete production process. Today, the role of the manufacturer is often less inclusive. Many manufacturing organizations *assemble* finished products with component parts produced by other manufacturers. Other manufacturing organizations are actually design companies that develop product concepts and then contract other manufacturers to make the product according to clearly defined specifications. Many contract foreign producers because of the low labor costs in some foreign countries. Manufacturers sometimes operate their own production facilities in foreign countries to reap this economic advantage.

Some manufacturers employ an internal staff of salespeople to sell their products to retailers. A **direct sales force** is responsible for meeting with prospective retail buyers, explaining the features of the organizational product line, and processing orders. As the liaison between

Figure 8.1

Some manufacturers employ a direct sales force to sell their product lines.

Retail

SALES REPRESENTATIVE

Market leader, prestige fashion jewelry company seeks an enthusiastic, industrious entry level Sales Representative to serve as a liaison between Napier and department stores in the New Jersey, Pennsylvania and Long Island areas.

Responsibilities include training and motivation of sales consultants and implementing promotional activities. Excellent communications, interpersonal and organizational skills required. The ideal candidate will be a dynamic team player who brings excitement to the role in a challenging retail environment. This position requires some travel.

We offer a competitive wage program, excellent medical benefits, 401(K) profit sharing plan and expense reimbursement. Kindly forward resume and salary history to the attention of: Human Resources Department, The Napier Co. Napier Park, Meriden, CT 06450. No. phone calls or fax please. E.O.E. M/F/H/V

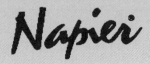

SALES REPS

Leading fashion sunglass manufacturer is seeking strong sales reps to sell specialty stores and chains. **ALL TERRITORIES OPEN.** (Dept. stores not included). Commission plus bonus incentives available. Please fax resume to: Troy Miller (212) 861-8275 or call (212) 861-7421.

Figure 8.2

Some manufacturers contract the services of manufacturers' reps as an alternative to a direct sales force.

the manufacturing organization and its retail accounts, a direct sales force often troubleshoots problems with delivery, damaged goods, and credits for returned merchandise. The members of a direct sales force are regular, permanent employees of the manufacturing organization. Their sales responsibilities are often assigned by geographic territory. They are often paid a commission based on what they sell. Members of a direct sales force are often called *account representatives* or *account executives*.

Some manufacturers contract the services of manufacturers' representatives as an alternative to employing a direct sales force. A **manufacturers' rep** is an independent sales agent whose income is based on commissions earned by selling manufacturers' products within a defined geographic territory. Reps perform a brokerage function in that they bring buyers and sellers together without themselves assuming title, or ownership, of the goods that they sell. Manufacturers provide reps with product training, samples, and leads, as well as marketing communication tools, such as sales literature, catalogs, and other collateral material. Reps often maintain their own offices and showrooms, and absorb their own expenses for travel, support staff, and employee benefits. A rep firm may employ several reps, or a rep can work alone.[1]

Many manufacturers' reps are multiline reps, selling *compatible* but *noncompetitive* lines for more than one manufacturer or principal. Lines of belts, umbrellas, and cold weather accessories (such as gloves, scarves, and hats) are noncompetitive in that a retail buyer's decision to purchase one line is independent of his or her decision to purchase another. The lines are compatible in that the responsibility for buying these lines is typically designated to one buyer in most retail organiza-

KEITH & LINDA	SHOWROOM A-217
STEWART	A-219

A-217 Merchandise Mart 704/377-5556 (sr)
2500 E. Independence Blvd.
Charlotte, NC 28205   704/377-5554 (FAX)

FISHMAN & TOBIN/TFW
   Boys 2-4, 4-7, 8-20 dressy separates, suits, sportswear

FABIL/MEMBERS ONLY
   Boys & girls rainwear, outerwear, accessories, windsuits

ANN MARIE, INC.
   Girls hairbows & hair accessories

FLOMO
   Children's gift sets, stationery, hair accessories, pencil boxes, etc.

OVERBOARD/JIMMY JEAN
   Boys swimwear, shorts, activewear — 2-4, 4-7, 8-20

HORIZON DESIGNS, INC.
   Boys & girls accessories, backpacks, wallets, novelties

FASHIONS BY MONACOE, INC.
   Dancewear, activewear for girls

BOW-RETTES, LTD
   Fashion hairbows & hair accessories

PROTEST FOR BOYS
   Boys silk shirts, also rayons, denims

CHARLES RIVER APPAREL
   Boys & girls rainwear & outerwear — toddler-14, 8-16

Figure 8.3

Manufacturers' reps are often multiline reps who sell compatible but noncompeting lines.

tions. Showing multiple lines on a single sales call spreads the cost of sales over several lines.

Some companies employ both a direct sales force and manufacturers' reps, assigning reps to low volume territories not large enough to warrant the expense of a direct salesperson. Though companies with a direct sales force exercise greater control over their sales function, there are several advantages to hiring manufacturers' reps:

- A rep has a developed sales territory with established retail accounts and can often penetrate a territory more efficiently than a direct salesperson.
- The compatibility of a rep's lines is often the basis for *synergistic sales,* where the sale of one line stimulates the sale of another.
- Unlike a direct sales force, a rep is paid only on what is sold with no additional employment expenses for travel or benefits.

Manufacturers and manufacturers' reps seek each other through the *reps wanted* and *lines wanted* classified sections of trade publications. The Atlanta-based Bureau of Wholesale Sales Representatives is a trade association that offers a search service called *BureauMatch* that matches reps seeking lines with manufacturers seeking reps.

The direct buying policies of many large retailers has threatened the livelihood of manufacturers' reps.[2] Power retailers, such as Wal-Mart, circumvent third-party interactions with reps by dealing directly with producers. By averting manufacturers' reps' commissions, retailers can negotiate lower prices with producers.

MERCHANT WHOLESALER-DISTRIBUTORS

Some manufacturers sell indirectly to retailers through intermediaries called **merchant wholesaler-distributors.** Unlike manufacturers' reps who do not assume title of the goods that they sell, merchant whole-saler-distributors buy manufacturers' products, and then resell them to retailers. These wholesalers facilitate the distribution of goods from producer to retailer. A producer minimizes its sales transactions by selling to a limited number of wholesalers, instead of directly to many retailers. A retailer minimizes its purchase transactions by buying products from a few wholesalers, instead of directly from many producers. Wholesalers also sell products for industrial, commercial, and institutional use. *Distributor* and *jobber* are names commonly used to refer to wholesalers.

A wholesaler's selling price is most often higher than a producer's selling price in that the wholesaler's price must cover the wholesaler's operating costs and profit, though the volume discounts that wholesalers obtain from manufacturers cover a portion of these operating costs. In spite of higher prices, retailers sometimes elect to buy from wholesalers because of shorter lead time, the time lapse between the point at which an order is placed, and the point at which an order is delivered. Small independent retailers buy from wholesalers because wholesalers accept smaller orders than producers who often have minimum order requirements that exceed the inventory needs of many small retailers. Small, frequently delivered orders minimize a retailer's inventory investment, resulting in lower inventory carrying costs.

Many wholesalers offer financial, logistical, and marketing support to their customers. A *rack jobber* performs virtually all of a retailer's inventory management and promotional functions for a product line. Ingram Merchandising Services is the nation's largest rack jobber for home entertainment products, serving full-line discounters, supermarkets, and video, music, book, and computer software stores. IMS's product assortment includes over 6000 audio titles, 6000 video titles, 1000 book titles, and 16,000 computer software products. An IMS merchandising specialist attractively displays an assortment of titles tailored to each store's market on fixturing provided by IMS. A computerized inventory management system replenishes stock as it is sold to ensure the constant availability of even the most popular titles. Selections are periodically adjusted based on rate of sale to maximize sales and minimize inventory and space investments. Ingram also provides an advertising program for key titles and new releases.

With the exception of goods imported from other countries, the typical channel of distribution for the retailers and the product categories discussed in this text does not include wholesalers. However, wholesalers are used extensively in food distribution and by small, independent retailers for certain categories of merchandise such as toys, sporting goods, consumer electronics, hardware, prerecorded music, books, and office supplies.

IMPORTS

Goods imported from other countries add variety and distinction to merchandise assortments with fabrications, designs, and workmanship peculiar to their country of origin, and unavailable in the United States. Italian leathers, hand-loomed Indian rugs, and African Kente cloth are all examples of distinctive imports. Wedgwood china from England, Louis Vuitton luggage and accessories from France, and Bally shoes from Switzerland, have enhanced the exclusivity of the offerings of many U.S. retailers for decades.

Imports are often less expensive than goods of comparable quality made in the United States because of the lower wages paid to workers in less-industrialized countries. Lower prices are especially true of labor-intensive products such as shoes, gloves, and men's shirts.[3] Labor unions are often critical of retailers that sell imports, claiming that importing erodes the U.S. manufacturing base, and exploits the underclasses of underdeveloped countries. Price-conscious consumers are unfazed by organized labor's position, however, and are more likely to make a purchase decision based on product appeal and value than on country of origin.

Importing is conducted by manufacturers, wholesalers, and retailers. As noted earlier in this chapter, many manufacturing organizations

Figure 8.4

Imports can add variety and distinction to merchandise assortments.

import domestically designed products that are produced by foreign contractors. Domestic and foreign wholesalers import goods to sell directly to retailers or through manufacturers' reps. Large retailers bypass importers as channel intermediaries by directly importing goods. Some of these retailers operate foreign buying offices that work in tandem with their domestic buying organization to source goods, place orders, and arrange shipment. May Department Stores own and operate eight such offices in Hong Kong, Taipei, Seoul, Bangkok, Singapore, Manila, New Delhi, and Colombo, Sre Lanka. Retailers that do not maintain foreign buying offices often contract the services of *commissionaires* familiar with a foreign market. A **commissionaire** is paid a commission to act as a retailer's agent in the market by screening resources, facilitating order placement, ensuring quality control, and making payment and shipping arrangements.

Imports are subject to **tariffs,** or *duties,* levied by the U.S. government to restrict foreign competition. Tariffs are based on import penetrations and the competitive price of domestic goods. Imports are restricted by **quotas,** quantitative limitations placed on the amount of merchandise that may be imported from a country within a time period. Quotas are established country by country and by category of

Figure 8.5

Some domestic wholesalers import goods to sell directly to retailers.

Nippers Slippers

Quality Infants' Slippers for ages 3 to 24 months.

NOVELTY DESIGNS

COMFORTABLE

UNIQUE & PLAYFUL

Made in Australia of 80% wool and 20% viscose upper. Trims made of 100% pure Australian lambswool.

Imported and Distributed by:
STERLING IMPORTS
Four Copley Place ▪ P.O. Box 78 ▪ Boston, MA 02116-6504
TEL: (617) 267-1176 ▪ FAX: (617) 421-9530
Contact: Liane Crawford

merchandise. The Generalized System of Preferences (GSP) allows certain products to be imported from developing countries without quotas. Importers often employ the services of **customs brokers,** agents licensed by the U.S. Treasury to represent importers in customs matters. Brokers expedite goods through customs by preparing the necessary customs forms, processing the payment of tariffs, and arranging for inland transportation.

High procurement costs inflate the actual, or **landed cost,** of imports. Overseas buying trips, packing, shipping, insurance and storage expenses, tariffs, and commissionaires' and customs agents' fees increase the cost of imports. There are other factors that may affect a retailer's decision to import:

- Landed costs are sometimes uncertain because of fluctuations in currency rates of exchange.
- Imports require a longer lead time than domestic goods, sometimes as long as a year. Shipping delays can result in costly markdowns when merchandise arrives at the end of, or even after, the selling season for which it was purchased.
- Imports tie up a retailer's capital for considerable time in that imports are paid for prior to being shipped, long before the point at which they will generate sales.
- Retailers that import directly are responsible for compliance with the laws that govern tariffs and quotas, as well as those that govern product safety standards, and labeling for textile fiber identification and care requirements.
- It is often difficult to collect on damaged or unacceptable goods, and costly to return them.[4]

HONG KONG AGENT

OVER 10 yrs — Existing business exp & connections with Chinese National I/E Corp., looking for U.S. Importers of ladies apparel to manufactured in proc. For further info please contact Ms. Mabel Li at fax (852)-25784499 or G.P.O. Box 2930 Hong Kong

---

S O U R C I N G

By Israeli experienced agent in Israel and other countries. No duty or quota from Israel. Top quality. Contact NY office 212-563-4440.

Figure 8.6

A commissionaire is paid a commission to act a retailer's agent in a foreign market.

Company Profile 8.1

Cristalleria Artistica la Piana is Italy's largest domestic producer of lead crystal stemware and giftware, and one of the largest lead crystal producers in the world.

In 1979, CALP created a brand called Royal Crystal Rock to import and market to the United States. Presently, RCR is distributed through fine specialty store and department store conglomerates, such as Dayton Hudson and Federated. In department stores, RCR is positioned as either the opening price point in the crystal department, or an upper-end price point in the housewares department.

RCR has a permanent showroom at Forty One Madison Avenue in New York. The product is also sold via six other major market showrooms operated by manufacturers' reps, and by fifty-eight traveling manufacturers' reps. Though relatively new in a brand-dominated marketplace, RCR's patterns have made it to the *Top Ten* list of registered crystal patterns published annually by *Modern Bride* magazine.

Understanding the urgencies of breaking ads and demanding brides, RCR carefully guards against delivery crises. Though normal transoceanic sailing time from Liverno, Italy to New York is only ten days, RCR allows a thirty-day lead time to allow for the perilous and unanticipated occurrences that plague importers, such as dock workers' strikes. Safe arrival at the port of New York does not guarantee expeditious delivery. Food and Drug Administration inspectors at the pier sometimes delay shipments to check for snails and barnacles attached to surfaces of containers wet by stormy seas.

RCR hires a customs broker to expedite processing at the pier to avoid paying detention fees levied on containers that remain on the dock for too long. The customs broker ascertains that the goods are classified within the guidelines of the law and favorable to the importer. For example, the broker ascertains that the duty on a set of stemware is based on the price as a set and not the price of the units in the set. Since a set is less expensive than its individual components, a lower duty rate will be charged on a set. The broker also arranges transportation of the containers from the pier to the RCR distribution center in Brooklyn or directly to stores.

MARKETS

Retail buyers transact business with suppliers in several types of settings. Large retail organizations have *sample rooms* in which traveling vendors show their lines by appointment. Today, buyers are more likely to view lines in nonretail locations remote from their stores. The current offerings of manufacturers, manufacturers' reps, wholesalers, and importers are often displayed in **showrooms** staffed by a sales force which presents the product line to prospective buyers. Showrooms for a particular merchandise category or group of related categories are often located in a **major showroom building.** In New York, 1407 is a major showroom building for junior apparel; 1411 Broadway is a major showroom building for misses apparel. Forty One Madison Avenue, 225 Fifth Avenue, and 230 Fifth Avenue are New York's major showroom buildings for giftware.

A **market** is a place where buyers and sellers come together to transact business. A market is often identified as a city, or a section of a city, in which a number of showrooms of related product categories are located. New York's fashion accessories market is composed of approximately twenty buildings between Fifth and Eighth Avenues and 35th and 39th Streets. New York's legendary Garment District (now called the Fashion Center) is bordered by Fifth and Ninth Avenues and 35th and 41st Streets. Some markets are also major manufacturing centers. Providence, Rhode Island, is the manufacturing center and major market for fashion jewelry. The offerings of more than 2100 home furnishing manufacturers are permanently displayed in 150 showroom buildings in High Point and Thomasville, North Carolina, the production source of most of the furniture manufactured in the United States.

Though New York is still the nation's leading market for high-fashion apparel, its importance as an apparel market has diminished in recent years because of the growth of Atlanta, Chicago, Dallas, and Los Angeles as major markets. These regional markets sometimes specialize in specific categories of merchandise. Dallas is the ultimate roundup for westernwear including tack lines, western boots, hats, outerwear, and accessories. Smaller secondary markets are located in Boston, Charlotte, Denver, Kansas City, Miami, Minneapolis, Pittsburgh, San Francisco, and Seattle. Their draw is limited to the geographic areas in which they are located. A decline in the number of manufacturers' sales representatives and retail buyers has threatened the viability of many of these small markets.[5,6,7,8,9]

Figure 8.7

A major showroom building facilitates one-stop buying for retail buyers.

Designed for "one-stop shopping" for buyers, a **merchandise mart** houses an entire market under one roof. Chicago's Merchandise Mart is the oldest mart in the United States, built by the preeminent merchant Marshall Field in 1930. The Atlanta Apparel Mart, the Denver Merchandise Mart, and The Fashion Center in San Francisco are other examples of merchandise marts. A **market center** is a cluster of marts, such as the Dallas Market Center, a six-building complex of 6.9 million square feet housing more than 2400 showrooms including:

- The International Menswear Mart for men's and boys' apparel and accessories, housing more than 3000 lines of mens and boys western apparel and accessories.
- The International Apparel Mart for women's and children's apparel and accessories, housing more than 12,000 lines of women's and children's apparel and accessories.
- Market Hall for temporary exhibits.
- The Trade Mart and the World Trade Center for hardlines, housing more than 17,000 lines of toys, stationery, residential furnishings, and decorative accessories.

Figure 8.8

The growth of major regional markets in Atlanta (photo), Chicago, Dallas, and Los Angeles has diminished the importance of New York as a market.

TRADE SHOWS

A **trade show** is a group of temporary exhibits in a convention center, merchandise mart, or hotel, at which vendors of a single category of merchandise, or group of related categories, present goods to retail buyers. The duration of a trade show ranges from a few days to a week. A trade show and related events are often referred to as a **market,** or *market week.* Some markets are annual events, others occur more frequently. Apparel markets are held as often as five times a year to coincide with the seasonal release of lines. The annual schedules for most apparel markets include:

- Fall I or Transition—March
- Fall II—late May
- Resort/Holiday—August
- Spring—October/November
- Summer—January

Markets are sponsored by trade associations, market centers, and/or management firms that specialize in trade show production such as George Little Management, the largest producer of trade shows for consumer goods. The International Toy Fair is sponsored by the Toy Manufactures of America, a trade group of 235 toy manufacturers and importers.[10] The Fashion Footwear Association of New York (FFANY), and the School and Home Office Products Association (SHOPA) also sponsor trade shows. The International Western Market and Western Lifestyle Show is sponsored by the American Equestrian Marketing Trade Association and the International Menswear Mart in Dallas. WWD/MAGIC International is a men's and women's apparel show held in Las Vegas cosponsored by *Women's Wear Daily* and the Men's Apparel Group In California (MAGIC). ENK Productions is a company that specializes in exclusive fashion apparel and accessories shows, such as *Accessorie Circuit,* Designers' Collective, and *Fashion Coterie.* Exhibitors for ENK shows are selected by a jury to ensure design and quality integrity.

A trade show sponsor secures the trade show facility and then rents space to exhibitors for a fee based on the size of the exhibit booth. The fee covers drayage (the movement of goods from the facility's loading dock to the booth), booth furniture (such as tables, chairs, risers), a listing in the trade show directory (a list of exhibitors by product

HOW TO WORK A TRADE SHOW

1. Allocate enough time for the show. Buyers complain that one of their biggest frustrations during Market Week is simply running out of time. To avoid this problem, it's best to schedule at least one full day for the show.
2. Schedule appointments with key vendors. It's a common perception that appointments are not needed at a trade show; but the fact is, appointments help you schedule your time better and ensure that you address your top priorities.
3. Hold onto your show directory. With its detailed listing of exhibitor names, addresses, phone numbers, and executives in attendance, as well as a showroom guide, the show directory is a valuable resource—both during the show and back at the office.
4. Take advantage of seminar programs. Presentations are geared toward providing you with practical information you can use to gain a competitive edge.
5. Shop with an open mind. Of course, when you attend a trade show it's important to be focused on what you want to achieve—but it's also worthwhile to visit new resources, meet new people, and plan time to just browse. It's these kinds of activities that can help inspire creative, fresh ideas when you return to the office.
6. Watch for the "big picture". Buyers prefer to identify an overall theme or direction for the show, which can be useful when it comes time to make final buying or merchandising decisions.

category compiled for the convenience of the buyers), and publicity efforts designed to draw attendees to the event (such as advertisements in trade publications subscribed to by buyers).[11] To facilitate coverage of the large shows, exhibitors are often grouped together by product category or price level. Exhibits at the National Association of Men's Sportswear Buyers (NAMSB) show are grouped as contemporary, jean-swear, leather/outerwear, young men's and activewear, accessories, or footwear.

At markets, buyers meet major design and manufacturing executives and exchange ideas with other buyers of the same merchandise category from other retail organizations. Trade shows often feature seminars by industry experts on timely topics such as *Vendor/Buyer*

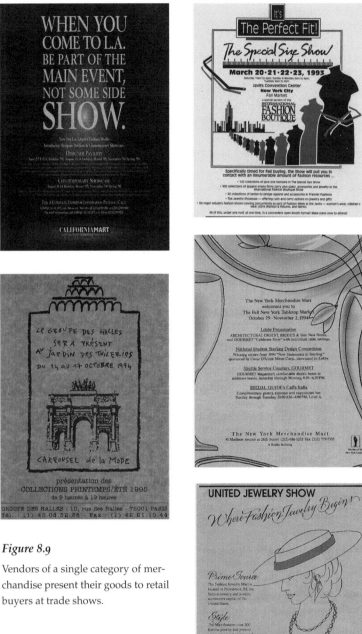

Figure 8.9

Vendors of a single category of merchandise present their goods to retail buyers at trade shows.

Relationships, How to Stop Advertising and Start Marketing, Negotiating the Deal, Competing in the '90s, Spring Trend Update and *Buying the "Hottest" Merchandise Without Getting Burned.* A market's lure is enhanced by fashion shows, cocktail parties, and big-name entertainment. Some markets are major publicity events and media extravaganzas. Fashion Week is sponsored by the Council of Fashion Designers of America. The highlight of Fashion Week is *7th on Sixth*, a production of fifty designer runway shows held under a tent in New York's Bryant Park showcasing the premier collections of major American designers, such as Donna Karan, Adrienne Vittadini, and Bill Blass.[12,13]

With 2800 exhibitors and more than 100,000 attendees, *The Super Show* is the world's largest sports products and sports apparel and athletic footwear trade show. Sponsored by the Sporting Goods Manufacturers Association, the annual event at the Georgia World Congress Center and The Atlanta Apparel Mart attracts over 100,000 buyers. Sports celebrities, robots, bungee jumping, and dirigible-like inflated sports products are typical of the show. Nike has spent as much as $4 million on exhibits of high-tech sensory extravaganzas of music, videos, light, sound effects and interactive videos.[14,15] Some trade shows have an international flavor, including the semi-annual JA International Jewelry Show, a watch and fine jewelry show also held in New York. The Blenheim Group of London produces large international shows that attract buyers worldwide, including *Salon International de la Mode Enfantine*, a semi-annual show held in Paris. Trade shows sometimes showcase a certain country. Israeli Fashion Week, known as *Isar Moda*, is held in New York and London and showcases Israeli designers and manufacturers. The Irish Trade Board sponsors trade shows of Irish giftware, jewelry, and fashion accessories in major U.S. cities.[16]

RESIDENT BUYING OFFICES

A **resident buying office,** or *buying office,* is a marketing and research consulting firm that serves as an adviser to a group of member, or client, stores. Located in major market centers, buying offices provide market information, merchandising guidance, and other services to their membership. The largest number of buying offices are located in New York City. Some offices have branches in other cities in the United

Company Profile 8.2

In 1957, The Portman Companies converted a parking garage in downtown Atlanta into showroom space for the home furnishings industry. The success of this initial venture spawned the construction of the Atlanta Merchandise Mart, the Atlanta Decorative Arts Center, and the Atlanta Apparel Mart, all of which compose the Atlanta Market Center. Today, the Atlanta Market Center is the major market of the southeast. The Apparel Mart also includes the International Sports Plaza, a center for the sporting goods industry.

AMC is the trade show division of The Portman Companies, ranking fourth nationally in the number of trade shows produced annually with shows held not only at the Atlanta Market Center, but at other market and convention centers across the country. AMC conducts shows in a broad spectrum of industries, including men's, women's, and children's apparel, gifts, and furniture. The shows range in size from 50 to 3000 booths, and 1500 to 45,000 attendees.

As trade show professionals, AMC offers a comprehensive range of services to trade show sponsors, including site selection, production of brochures, media relations, and the coordination of functions and entertainment for the shows. The Surf Expo, the premier trade show of the active and beach lifestyle industry, is among AMC's unique productions. Held twice annually in Orlando, Florida, the show attracts sporting goods and active apparel retailers from throughout the country. Exhibitors of apparel lines, such as accessories and casual footwear, represent about 75 percent of the product mix. Exhibitors of hardlines, such as surf boards and sailboats, represent the remaining 25 percent. Highlights of the show include an industry golf tournament, a surfboard shaping demonstration, and lots of "schmonding" (schmoozing and bonding) among industry majors.

Reflecting a growing interest in the outdoor lifestyle, the Great Outdoors Expo is a relatively new AMC show held annually in Boston. Exhibitors include manufacturers and wholesalers of outdoor sporting goods, such as camping, skiing, and fishing equipment, as well as manufacturers of footwear and outdoor apparel. Attendees include mass merchandisers, catalogers, department stores, and sporting goods retailers.

Lee, Georgia. (October 17, 1994). Atlanta mart challenges the nineties with a new lineup, new look. Women's Wear Daily. *pp. 22–24.*

States and around the world. Many buying offices specialize in certain categories of merchandise and/or types of stores, limiting their services to areas such as bridal, furs, or large sizes. The members of a buying office are often similar in terms of merchandise mix, size, and retailing format.

The original buying offices were buying services for the owners of apparel stores too distant to make frequent trips to New York, the major fashion market. For a fee, an office assumed the responsibility of selecting and ordering all or part of a client store's inventory. This allowed member stores to devote full-time attention to the task of operating their stores without the interruption of time-consuming and costly market trips.

The primary role of the present-day buying office is that of adviser, product developer, and importer for member stores. Buying offices forecast future market conditions by studying consumer behavior, demographics, and emerging trends. The information is channeled to client stores through a communication network of bulletins, surveys, and reports. Buying offices facilitate buyers' market trips by arranging travel and hotel accommodations, compiling lists of recommended resources to visit, and providing office space. Offices host buyers' meetings during major markets as a forum for exchanging ideas. Some offices respond to the needs of individual members by store visits and by researching solutions to problems peculiar to a store.

Market coverage responsibility in a buying office is assigned by merchandise category to *market specialists* sometimes called *market reps* or *resident buyers*. Market specialists communicate market conditions to client stores, such as fashion trends, new resources, hot items, opportunistic buys, and promotional opportunities. Their market expertise is based on daily market contact and information from various sources, such as vendors, member stores, mills, research firms, designers, and the trade media.

The wholesaling of private label merchandise has become an important buying office function. Buying offices source large quantities of goods for the collective needs of many member stores, and then resell the goods to their clients enabling even the smallest independent to participate in private-label programs. Another buying office function is **group buying,** the pooling of orders for branded merchandise, store fixtures, and services from many members to meet minimum order requirements, or to negotiate quantity discounts.

The development of catalogs as regular-price or promotional

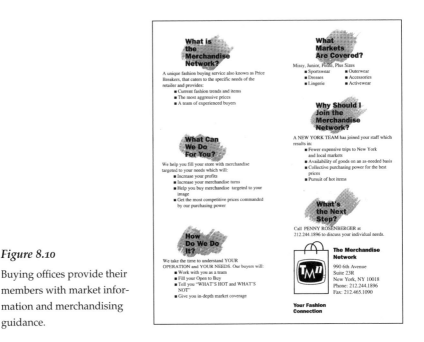

Figure 8.10

Buying offices provide their members with market information and merchandising guidance.

direct-mail pieces is another important function of the buying office. The office produces a single catalog featuring goods common to the assortments of member stores at a fraction of the cost of each store producing its own piece. Production costs are minimized by negotiating cooperative advertising from the vendors whose merchandise is featured in the catalogs.[17]

There are five major types of buying offices:

1. Salaried or fee office
2. Associated or cooperative office
3. Syndicated office
4. Private office
5. Commission office or merchandise broker

Salaried or Fee Office A **salaried** or **fee office** is the most common type of buying office. A salaried office is owned and operated independently of its member stores, most of which are privately owned specialty stores that pay the buying office an annual fee for services. Collectively, salaried offices have more members than other types of buying offices. Martin Bayer Associates is a better men's wear and women's wear office. Price Breakers is an off-price women's wear specialist. Dianne Cohan Associates specializes in female apparel in misses, junior and large sizes. The Doneger Group has grown to be the largest independent office through the acquisition of several other independents, such as Burns Winkler, Jack Braustein, and Young Innovators. All are located in New York City.

Associated or Cooperative Office An **associated** or **cooperative office** is a nonprofit organization jointly owned by a group of independently owned member stores. The stores are shareholder owners of the office that participate in its governance through a board of directors. Because of the commitment of shareholder ownership, associated buying offices are not as common as other types of offices. A hallmark of the associated buying office is the *figure exchange* whereby the buying office compiles various performance data from member stores to create industry standards to which individual stores can compare their performance.

The Associated Merchandise Corporation (AMC), and Frederick Atkins are two cooperative buying offices. A continuing decrease in the number of independent department stores has resulted in reduced memberships for these offices. The membership of Frederick Atkins once exceeded forty stores. Today its membership includes fewer than thirty stores. Several Atkins members including Ivey's and Pizitz, were acquired by another Atkins member, Dillard's. Other members such as McCurdy's of Rochester, New York, Miller & Rhoads of Richmond, Virginia, and Steiger's of Springfield, Massachusetts, have ceased operation.

Syndicated Office A **syndicated office** is owned and operated by a retail conglomerate. May Merchandising is responsible for product development, imports, and domestic market coverage for the eight operating divisions of the May Department Stores Company. Federated Merchandising is a division of Federated Department Stores that is responsible for developing merchandising strategies for more than 400 Federated stores. FM coordinates Federated's innovative buying team process whereby groups of buyers representing Federated's six department store divisions collectively determine the mix of suppliers for Federated stores. The buyers at division level then make assortment decisions on the offerings of each vendor. Federated's commitment to each of these key vendors is used as leverage to negotiate price, promotional support, delivery, and other concessions. FM was responsible for

> ### MAY MERCHANDISING
>
> - MDSI is May Company's private label import program. All May Company divisions give input to our May Company market representatives and Steering Committees in St. Louis for items that we want developed or duplicated at a better price than that of our competition.
>
> - MDSI is often used as our primary label for basic items which we sell year after year, although items are often slightly altered each year via the use of different color palettes or a change in structural details.
>
> - MDSI is profitable for use because although we pay less, we are able to sell similar merchandise at the same price as our competitors.
>
> - All import purchases are bought through May Company. The MDSI order is placed through your MDSI Coordinator and then the order is downloaded to our POM system. For each order that is placed, Filene's receives and MDSI contract, which is then distributed to the appropriate buying office. MDSI purchases are often received several months in advance of their open-to-buy date.
>
> - MDSI purchases and receipts are excluded until the open-to-buy date of the purchase order. All MDSI purchases appear in the on-order until the open-to-buy month of the purchase order.
>
> *Examples of May Company Private Labels:*
>
>   Men's — John Ashford
>
>   Better Sportswear — Valerie Stevens
>
>   Young Attitudes — Pacer, Amanda Smith
>
>   Moderate Sportswear — Karen Scott

Figure 8.11

May Merchandising is a syndicated buying office responsible for developing private-label programs for the operating divisions of May Department Stores.

developing Federated Accelerated Sales & Stock Turnover (FASST), an inventory-management system designed to increase sales and inventory turnover by expediting the movement of goods from suppliers to the selling floor. FM's recent focus has been to cultivate the home business with in-store interior design studios and the rollout of free-standing

Company Profile 8.3

Located in the heart of the Fashion Center, The Doneger Group is an independent buying office that was founded in 1946 by Henry Doneger. Originally serving specialty retailers of women's apparel, The Doneger Group has expanded its client base and the merchandise categories in which it specializes through the acquisition of other offices, such as Estelle Shomer Associates, Atlas Buying Corporation, and Independent Retailers Syndicate. Presently, The Doneger Group's client list includes more than 850 department and specialty stores and discounters, representing more than 7000 store locations and $25 billion in sales.

The Doneger Group is organized into several divisions, each specializing in a particular product category, including Doneger Mens-wear, Doneger Kids, and Doneger Home Connection. Other divisions include Henry Doneger Associates, specializing in women's apparel and accessories; Doneger Buying Connection, specializing in women's large sizes; Doneger Tall Buying, specializing in women's tall sizes; and Price Point Buying, specializing in off-price opportunistic buying. Other Doneger Group divisions include D3-Doneger Design, a color and trend forecast service; and HDA International, an import/export division serving domestic and international retailers. The Doneger Group offers a range of services to its clients including favorably priced group buys of hangers, packaging, mannequins and store fixtures, and participation in various promotional and fashion catalogs.

home galleries. Some syndicated buying offices have moved from New York to their corporate office location. May moved its buying office to St. Louis.[18] Mercantile moved its buying office to Fairfield, Ohio.[19]

Private Office A **private office** is owned and operated by a single large retail organization as an extension of its corporate merchandising function. Through a private office, a retailer maintains market presence even when its merchandising function is executed at a corporate office remote from a major market. Stein Mart, a Jacksonville, Florida-based chain of off-price better female apparel stores, and Hill's Department Stores, a Canton, Massachusetts-based regional discounter have private offices in New York. Neiman Marcus operates a private New York office in that the store's merchandising uniqueness renders it incompatible with the membership of other offices.

Commission Office or Merchandise Broker   A **commission office** or *merchandise broker* is an independent representative of a group of manufacturers. The office derives its income from commissions paid by manufacturers for merchandise sold to its member stores. Commission offices were once popular among small independent retailers unable to afford membership in other types of offices. The commission office is nearly extinct, though a few remain in business as of this writing: Jack J. Greenman Associates is a commission office for ethnic men's wear and boys' wear; Tall Associates is a commission office for tall sizes for women.

SUMMARY POINTS

- A manufacturer uses labor and machinery to convert raw materials into finished products. Manufacturers use either a direct sales force or manufacturers' reps to sell their products to retailers.
- Merchant wholesaler-distributors buy manufacturers' products and then resell them to retailers. Wholesale-distributors facilitate the distribution of goods between a producer and a retailer.
- Imports add variety and distinction to a retailer's product mix and often afford a retailer an opportunity for higher profit margins.
- Showrooms, marts, markets, and trade shows are nonretail settings in which sellers and retail buyers come together to transact business.
- A buying office is a marketing and research consultant that serves as an adviser to its member or client stores by providing market information, merchandising guidance, and other services.

KEY TERMS AND CONCEPTS

associated office	manufacturer	resident buying office
commissionaire	manufacturers' rep	salaried office
commission office	market	showroom
customs broker	market center	syndicated office
direct sales force	merchandise mart	tariff
group buying	merchant wholesale-	trade show
landed cost	distributor	
major showroom	private office	
building	quota	

FOR DISCUSSION

1. Request a trade show calendar from a market center that lists each show's sponsor. Call several sponsors to request media kits for their shows. Compare the shows in terms of size, attendees, and entertainment fanfare.
2. Compare several imported and domestic items at a local retailer. Do you think that price or distinctiveness motivated the buyer's purchase? Explain.
3. Obtain information from a salaried buying office concerning its fee schedule and the services that it provides. Do you feel that the membership fee is a worthwhile investment for a retailer, relative to the benefits of membership? Explain.

SUGGESTED READINGS

Staff. *Facing the Forces of Change 2000: The New Realities in Wholesale Distribution.* Washington, DC: Distribution Research & Education Foundation.

Dickerson, Kitty. (1994). *Textiles and Apparel in the Global Economy.* Englewood Cliffs, NJ: Prentice Hall.

Stone, Elaine. (1994). *Exporting and Importing Fashion.* New York: Delmar.

ENDNOTES

1. Marshall, Michael & Siegler, Frank. (January 1993). Selecting the right rep firm. *Sales & Marketing Management.* pp. 46–49, 83.
2. Robben, John. (Summer 1993). Have toys, will travel: My father's journey. *Family Business.* p. 63.
3. Dickerson, Kitty. (1995). *Textiles and Apparel in the Global Economy.* Englewood Cliffs, NJ: Prentice Hall. p. 461.
4. Staff. (1983). *Apparel Ready Reference: Buyers Guide to Meeting Product Safety & Quality Standards.* United States Testing Co. p. 6.
5. Feitelberg, Rosemary. (December 31, 1994). NY gripe: Regional schedules. *Women's Wear Daily.* pp. 21–22.
6. Friedman, Arthur. (January 25, 1994). Buyers want cheaper, safer SA. *Women's Wear Daily.* p. 8.
7. Friedman, Arthur. (June 15, 1993). The missing buyers. *Women's Wear Daily.* pp. 6–7.
8. Haber, Holly. (June 20, 1994). Dresses, casual spark Dallas market. *Women's Wear Daily.* p. 15.
9. Lee, Georgia. (January 22, 1992). Small markets trying harder. *Women's Wear Daily.* p. 23.
10. Collins, Glenn. (February 13, 1995). Toy fair is facing challenges. *New York Times.* pp. D1, D4.

11. Carley, Carole. (1993). *Trade Shows/Market Trips.* Atlanta: AMC Trade Shows.

12. Friedman, Arthur. (October 25, 1993). SA gets it together. *Women's Wear Daily.* p. 4.

13. Weber, Bruce. (April 9, 1995). Fashion in the park with tents. *New York Times.* pp. B1, B7.

14. Lee, Georgia. (February 7, 1994). Women's apparel in spotlight at Atlanta Super Show. *Women's Wear Daily.* p. 12.

15. Lloyd, Brenda. (January 26, 1995). *Women's Wear Daily.* pp. 20, 21.

16. Staff. (March 20, 1995). Irish Groups set major trade show. *Home Furnishings Daily.* p. 49.

17. Bivins, Jacquelyn. (May 1989). Buying office status report. *Stores.* pp. 54–61.

18. Moin, David. (January 23, 1993). May Dept. Stores will move merchandising unit to St. Louis. *Women's Wear Daily.* p. 2.

19. Monget, Karyn. (July 25, 1994). May Co. buyers say meet us in St. Louis. *Women's Wear Daily.* pp. 1, 10.

20. Robben, John. (Summer 1993). Have toys, will travel: My father's journey. *Family Business.* p. 63.

chapter nine

MEASURES OF PRODUCTIVITY

Maximizing the return on investments of assets is a universal objective for both businesses and individuals. In a retail organization, generating sales from two important assets: inventory and selling space is a critical merchandising objective. In general, retailers want to maximize sales while minimizing investments of inventory and space. Chapter 9 deals with some of the measures that are used to monitor the performance of inventory and selling space as assets.

After you have read this chapter, you will be able to discuss:

Productivity as a measure of performance.

The relationship between turnover and stock-to-sales ratios.

Sales-per-square-foot as a measure of productivity.

PRODUCTIVITY

Productivity is a measure of the number of units of output produced per unit of input. Stated in mathematical terms:

$$productivity = \frac{output}{input}$$

Productivity measures performance. High productivity indicates that output has been maximized with a minimum investment of input. Low productivity is unsatisfactory and an indication that productivity should be increased by increasing output, decreasing input, or both increasing output and decreasing input.

Measures of productivity are common in the manufacturing sector where input and output are often quantitatively defined. In an apparel manufacturing operation, the productivity of a pressing function can be measured by dividing the number of garments pressed by the amount of time it takes to press them.

$$productivity = \frac{units\ pressed\ (output)}{number\ of\ hours\ worked\ by\ the\ presser\ (input)}$$

$$productivity = \frac{2400\ garments}{8\ hours}$$

$$productivity = 300\ garments\ per\ hour$$

The concept of productivity is not as easily applied within service industries because of the difficulty in quantitatively defining output and input. Though sales are a numerically measured retail output, intangible outputs, such as customer satisfaction, are difficult to quantify. In spite of these limitations, retailers apply productivity measures whenever a relationship between input and output can be defined numerically.

TURNOVER

Turnover, or *stockturn,* is the number of times that an average inventory is sold within a time period. Turnover describes the movement of merchandise, or the velocity at which goods come in and out of a unit of business, such as a department or store. Turnover reflects the amount of sales generated per dollar of inventory invested. Turnover is computed by dividing sales for a period by the average inventory for the same period:

$$turnover = \frac{sales}{average\ inventory}$$

Turnover is generally stated as a whole number carried to one decimal place.

An **average inventory** is the average amount of inventory on hand within a time period. An average inventory can be computed by dividing the sum of the beginning and ending inventories of a period by two. The average inventory for a month is computed by dividing the sum of the inventory on hand at the beginning of the month, called the **beginning-of-month inventory,** or *BOM,* and the inventory on hand at the end of the month, called the **end-of-month inventory** or *EOM,* by two.

$$average\ inventory = \frac{BOM + EOM}{2}$$

The EOM of one month is equal to the BOM of the succeeding month. It is logical to assume that if a store closes with a $2 million inventory on the last day of a month, it will open the next day with a $2 million inventory. Maintaining recorded values of BOM and EOM inventories is a common inventory control practice in retail organizations.

The average inventory for periods longer than a month are based on the average inventories of the months within the period.[1] The average inventory for a year can be computed by dividing the sum of the average inventories of each month in the year by twelve.

$$average\ inventory = \\ \frac{\frac{(BOM + EOM)_1}{2} + \frac{(BOM + EOM)_2}{2} \ ... \ + \frac{(BOM + EOM)_{12}}{2}}{12}$$

The formula can be simplified. Since each EOM is equal to the BOM of the succeeding month, the EOMs can be eliminated from the formula without affecting the value of the average. However, the EOM of the last month must be retained in the computation, since it is not repeated as a succeeding BOM.

average inventory =

$$\frac{BOM_1 + BOM_2 + BOM_3 \cdots + BOM_{12} + EOM_{12}}{13}$$

The number *13* is used as the denominator since thirteen figures are used in the computation of the numerator: twelve BOMs and one EOM. The formula can be adapted for other periods. The average inventory for a six-month season beginning in February and ending in July is computed as follows:

average inventory =

$$\frac{BOM_{FEB} + BOM_{MAR} + BOM_{APR} + BOM_{MAY} + BOM_{JUN} + BOM_{JUL} + EOM_{JUL}}{7}$$

The Computation of Turnover

The following example demonstrates the computation of turnover: The men's sweater department at Dolan's Department Store generated

Table 9.1   **BOM AND EOM FOR MEN'S SWEATER DEPARTMENT, DOLAN'S DEPARTMENT STORE**

Month	BOM	EOM
1	$ 2,500	$ 2,500
2	$ 2,500	$ 2,500
3	$ 2,500	$ 5,000
4	$ 5,000	$ 2,500
5	$ 2,500	$ 7,500
6	$ 7,500	$ 2,500
7	$ 2,500	$ 5,000
8	$ 5,000	$ 5,000
9	$ 5,000	$ 5,000
10	$ 5,000	$ 7,500
11	$ 7,500	$12,500
12	$12,500	$ 5,000

Each BOM is equal to the EOM of the preceding month.

sales of \$30,000 last year. The BOMs and EOMs for each month are listed in Table 9.1. Average inventory is computed as follows:

$$average\ inventory = \frac{BOM_1 + BOM_2 \cdots + BOM_{12} + EOM_{12}}{13}$$

$$average\ inventory =$$
$$\frac{\$2500+2500+2500+5000+2500+7500+2500+5000+5000+5000+7500+12500+5000}{13}$$

$$average\ inventory = \frac{\$65,000}{13} = \$5,000$$

Turnover is computed as follows:

$$turnover = \frac{sales}{average\ inventory}$$

$$turnover = \frac{\$30,000}{\$5,000} = 6.0$$

The turnover of the men's sweater department at Dolan's Department Store for last year was 6.0. In other words, an average inventory of \$5000 was sold six times.

The components of the turnover formula must agree in terms of time. To compute turnover for a *year*, sales for the *year* are divided by the average inventory for the same *year*. To compute turnover for a *month*, sales for the *month* are divided by the average inventory for the same *month*. Turnover can be computed for any period, however, annual turnover is the most common computation. The remaining discussion of turnover presumes the period of a year, unless otherwise specified. Though retail sales and inventory values are typically used to calculate turnover, turnover can be calculated based on units of inventory or its wholesale cost.

High Versus Low Turnover

As a measure of inventory productivity, high turnover is more desirable than low turnover. The mathematical relationship between sales and average inventory in the turnover formula indicates that turnover can be increased by increasing sales, decreasing average inventory, or both increasing sales and decreasing average inventory. The latter strategy

TURNOVER REPORT

Period Ending 07/31/95

CL.	TOTAL	SPFLD	PLAZA	LONG	WEST	EAST	BERK	ENFLD	HAMP	INGLE	MANCH
1 AV IN	35,267	4,382	1,724	2,962	2,655	5,271	3,118	4,853	2,753	3,306	4,265
SALES	44,603	3,475	1,527	2,390	2,979	7.332	4,766	5,416	3,339	7,908	5,467
TRNOVR	1.3	.8	.9	.8	1.1	1.4	1.5	1.1	1.2	2.4	1.3
2 AV IN	4,851	413	71	55	229	896	214	581	198	929	1,038
SALES	4,587	918	103	45	302	1,345	323	376	328	589	252
TRNOVR	.9	2.2	1.5	.8	1.3	1.5	1.5	.6	1.7	.6	.2
3 AV IN	16,015	1,964	52	1,010	—	2,738	3,276	1,338	64	2,888	2,588
SALES	10,309	1,232	22	890	—	1,607	1,194	539	10	3,150	1,661
TRNOVR	.6	.6	.4	.9	—	.6	.4	.4	.2	1.1	.6
4 AV IN	63,151	4,623	3,626	4,005	5,248	8,312	5,880	6,239	7,460	9,702	5,600
SALES	84,458	5,436	5,071	2,904	6,057	12,938	8,121	8,470	10,162	20,675	4,618
TRNOVR	1.3	1.2	1.4	.7	1.2	1.6	1.4	1.4	1.4	2.1	.8
5 AV IN	45,861	4,363	3,432	2,652	3,306	7,601	3,478	5,096	2,798	7,698	5,535
SALES	23,979	1,632	1,315	1,002	2,014	3,917	2,326	2,656	2,597	5,216	1,298
TRNOVR	.5	.4	.4	.4	.6	.5	.7	.5	.9	.7	.2

Figure 9.1

A turnover report for five classifications of merchandise in a ten-unit chain.

has become an important merchandising objective for most retailers: to generate more sales on less inventory.

To demonstrate the impact of average inventory on turnover, consider the following: A jeweler consistently sells 600 gold chains each year. Sales are highly predictable in that the jeweler sells exactly fifty chains each month. To prepare for the 1995 selling period, the jeweler wrote orders for 600 chains and arranged for their delivery just prior to the beginning of the year. As anticipated, the jeweler sold fifty chains during each month of 1995. The turnover (based on units) of the gold chains is calculated as follows:

$$average\ inventory = \frac{BOM_1 + BOM_2 \cdots + BOM_{12} + EOM_{12}}{13}$$

$average\ inventory\ 1995 =$
$$\frac{600 + 550 + 500 + 450 + 400 + 350 + 300 + 250 + 200 + 150 + 100 + 50 + 0}{13}$$

$$average\ inventory\ 1995 = \frac{3900}{13} = 300$$

$$turnover = \frac{sales}{average\ inventory}$$

$$turnover\ 1995 = \frac{600}{300} = 2.0$$

Prior to the beginning of 1996, the jeweler sought advice from a retail consultant relative to improving turnover. The consultant suggested that the jeweler turn the gold chains faster by carrying less inventory throughout the year. The jeweler accomplished this objective by ordering fifty chains each month instead of 600 chains at the beginning of the year, thereby carrying an inventory of no more than a month's supply of chains at any point during the year. The turnover of the gold chains for 1996 is computed as follows:

$$average\ inventory = \frac{BOM_1 + BOM_2 \cdots + BOM_{12} + EOM_{12}}{13}$$

$average\ inventory =$
$$\frac{50 + 50 + 50 + 50 + 50 + 50 + 50 + 50 + 50 + 50 + 50 + 50 + 0}{13}$$

$$average\ inventory = \frac{600}{13} = 46$$

TURNOVER

When two components of the turnover formula are known, the third can be computed by cross multiplying. Sales can be computed by multiplying the equation by average inventory when turnover and average inventory are known:

$$turnover = \frac{x}{average\ inventory}$$

$$x = turnover \times average\ inventory$$

When sales and turnover are known, average inventory can be computed by multiplying the equation by x and dividing by turnover:

$$turnover = \frac{sales}{x}$$

$$x = \frac{sales}{turnover}$$

$$turnover = \frac{sales}{average\ inventory}$$

$$turnover = \frac{600}{46} = 13.0$$

Note that the sales for 1995 and 1996 are equal, but that the 1996 average inventory turned more than six times faster than the inventory of 1995. The consultant's suggestion to maintain smaller inventories was prudent advice that resulted in improved turnover.[2]

There are several reasons why high turnover is more desirable than low turnover. When inventories turn slowly, customers see the "same old thing" upon each return store visit. Customers who faithfully shopped the jeweler each month in 1995 saw the same selection of chains for an entire year. In 1996, customers saw a new selection each month. Also slow moving goods often become *shopworn*, soiled or damaged because of exposure or customer handling. Finally, the money and space tied up in stagnant, slow turning inventories inhibits investments in fresh salable goods.

Though high turnover is generally a desirable goal, there are disadvantages associated with excessively high turnover. Just as *low* turnover can be indicative of *too much inventory, high* turnover can be

---

SPECIAL ORDERS

Retailers sell goods by "special order" when style, color, size, or fabric specifications are unique to each customer. Custom draperies and monogrammed stationery are examples of special order goods. Goods for which there is infrequent demand, such as extra-long men's suits, are often special ordered, as are big ticket items, such as furniture. Special orders minimize a retailer's inventory investment, since samples are often the only inventory carried in stock. Special order goods turn quickly, since special order sales are transacted as soon as the goods are received.

In spite of these inventory management advantages, special order sales are labor intensive in that each customer's purchase requires processing an order and arranging for subsequent pick-up or delivery. Problems occur when special order specifications are incorrect or incorrectly followed. The retailer must absorb the cost of errors attributable to the store. Perhaps the greatest difficulty with special orders is that customers have become accustomed to the immediate gratification of taking their purchases home with them, an opportunity that special orders do not afford them.

---

indicative of *too little inventory.* Again consider the jeweler's scenario: Customers who shopped at the beginning of 1995 saw an extensive selection of 600 chains. The same customers who shopped at the beginning of 1996 saw a meager selection of only fifty chains. Imagine how disappointed customers were on their 1996 visit recalling the previous year's extensive assortment. Thus, high turnover may be indicative of limited assortments of styles, colors, or sizes, an inventory condition that will result in lost sales.

There are also disadvantages associated with maintaining low inventories and placing small orders.

- It is more costly to process many small orders than a few large orders. Again consider the jeweler: A single order was placed and processed for 1995. Twelve orders were placed and processed for 1996. This increased by twelvefold the amount of time spent processing orders, tracking them, paying invoices, and so on.
- Buyers who purchase small quantities may forego quantity discounts, price incentives based on quantities purchased. A buyer must decide whether these price concessions are worth carrying higher inventories.

	Department Stores		Specialty Stores	
Category	Median	Superior	Median	Superior
Female Apparel	3.1	3.4	2.6	3.1
Female Accessories	2.1	2.3	1.8	3.5
Men's and Boys' Apparel	2.3	2.7	2.3	2.9
Infants' and Children's Apparel	2.9	3.3	2.7	2.9
Footwear	1.4	1.7	2.0	2.2
Cosmetics	2.3	2.7	1.4	1.6
Leisure and Home Electronics	1.9	2.6	1.7	2.2
Home Furnishings	1.7	2.0	1.5	2.1
Other Hardlines	3.2	6.8	3.1	10.1
Other Merchandise	4.9	6.9	2.2	4.1
TOTAL	2.5	3.1	—	—

Figure 9.2a

Annual turnover for department and specialty stores by category of merchandise.

Category	Turnover
Apparel	3.1
Ladies'	4.2
Men's	4.0
Shoes	2.7
Girls'	2.7
Accessories	3.0
Infants'	3.4
Boys'	3.2
Housewares	3.1
Consumer Electronics	2.9
Domestic	2.6
Food (including Pet Food)	6.2
Health and Beauty Care	3.9
Toys	2.5
Pharmacy	9.9
Sporting Goods	2.4
Automotives	3.1
Stationery	2.8
Lawn and Garden	3.8
Paint/Hardware	2.7
Household Cleaners	5.7
Jewelry/Watches	1.9
Photography	4.6
RTA/Furniture	2.8
Cosmetics	2.0
Crafts	1.8

Figure 9.2b

Annual turnover for full-line discounters by category of merchandise.

Category	Turnover
Men's Clothing	
Men's Suits	1.4
Men's Coats	1.3
Sport Coats	1.5
Dress Slacks	1.6
Total Men's Clothing	1.4
Men's Sportswear	
Sport Shirts	2.3
Sweaters	2.0
Activewear	1.8
Casual Slacks	1.7
Jeans	2.0
Jackets & Heavy Outerwear	2.1
Coordinated Leisurewear	2.2
Total Men's Sportswear	1.9
Men's Furnishings	
Dress Shirts	1.5
Neckwear	2.0
Hosiery	2.0
Men's Belts	1.6
Men's Accessories	1.1
Underwear	1.2
Sleepwear	1.4
Men's Headwear	1.3
Total Men's Furnishings	1.6

Figure 9.2c

Annual turnover for men's specialty stores by category of merchandise.

A buyer's job involves making critical decisions relative to how much inventory to order or to carry. These decisions are driven by multiple factors, including turnover, the availability of goods, the availability of cash, and the amount of inventory needed to maintain adequate selections. Increasing turnover is an objective to which buyers dedicate considerable attention. In its college recruitment material, Parisian, a specialty department store group based in Birmingham, Alabama, boasts of changing its inventory every 3.5 months. To increase turnover, Goody's invested in an automatic reordering system that reordered basic goods every week instead of every month.[3]

Turnover by Category of Merchandise

There is no universally *good* turnover rate. Acceptable turnover rates vary by category of merchandise relative to the characteristics of the goods. To illustrate this point, assume that the following three items in a department store sell and turn at the same rate as the gold chains:

Toasters/Housewares Department: Purchasing an inventory of 600 toasters for an entire year is an acceptable (though not ideal) buying decision. Changes in toaster styles are minimal over time, and toasters do not deteriorate by sitting on a stockroom shelf for an extended period. The last fifty toasters in inventory at the end of the year are as salable as the first fifty toasters sold at the beginning of the year.

Robes/Intimate Apparel Department: Purchasing an inventory of 600 robes for an entire year is not an acceptable buying decision. Seasonal changes in styles and fabrications necessitate frequent inventory changes throughout the year. The lightweight spring robes that are in stock at the beginning of the year are not salable at the end of the year when longer styles in flannels and velours are in demand.

Muffins/Coffee Bar: Purchasing an inventory of 600 muffins for an entire year is an unquestionably unacceptable buying decision. The limited shelf life of the muffins renders them unsalable the day after delivery, not to mention twelve months later.

The examples serve to demonstrate a fundamental principle related to turnover: that **perishable goods** need to turn more quickly than nonperishables. Perishable merchandise has a limited shelf life or selling period. In a broad interpretation, fashion goods are *perishable*. Fashion goods are less salable over time because of seasonal changes in color, style, and fabrication. The turnover of nonperishable goods should also be monitored. Nonperishables that remain on racks or shelves for extended periods can become shopworn while tying up valuable space and inventory dollars.

STOCK-TO-SALES RATIOS

A **stock-to-sales** ratio is the proportionate relationship between a BOM and sales for the corresponding month. The formula for the stock-to-sales ratio is:

$$stock\text{-}to\text{-}sales\ ratio = \frac{BOM}{sales}$$

When sales are $10,000 and BOM is $30,000, the stock-to-sales ratio is computed as follows:

$$stock\text{-}to\text{-}sales\ ratio = \frac{\$30{,}000}{\$10{,}000}$$

$$stock\text{-}to\text{-}sales\ ratio = 3.0$$

A 3.0 stock-to-sales ratio indicates that the BOM is three times sales. Stock-to-sales ratios are most often expressed as whole numbers carried to one decimal place.

The breadth of an assortment is a determinant of its stock-to-sales ratio: the broader the assortment, the higher the stock-to-sales ratio. Consider the stock-to-sales ratios of men's dress shirts and men's sport shirts: Because dress shirts are buttoned at the neck, collar sizing must be very exact. To accommodate this close fit, dress shirts are manufactured in collar sizes that range from 14 to $17\frac{1}{2}$ inches, with half-inch increments between sizes. Because the sleeve length of a dress shirt must correspond to the sleeve length of a jacket, dress shirt sleeves are cut in lengths that range from 32 to 35 inches, with one inch increments between sizes. A complete size assortment of one dress shirt style in one color is thirty-two shirts, eight neck sizes times four sleeve lengths.

Men's sport shirts, on the other hand, are worn unbuttoned at the neck, and their fit is unrelated to any other garment. Thus, neither the collar nor the sleeve of a sport shirt must be as exact a fit as the collar or sleeve of a dress shirt. Consequently, sport shirts are cut in four general sizes: small, medium, large, and extra large, each size with average collar and sleeve length combinations. A complete size assortment of *one* sport shirt style in one color is four shirts.

A retailer that plans to sell an equal number of dress shirts and sport shirts will need more dress shirts than sport shirts. The amount of stock needed to sell a *single* style/color dress shirt is thirty-two shirts, while the amount of stock needed to sell a *single* style/color sport shirt is only four shirts. Thus, dress shirts will require a higher stock-to-sales ratio than sport shirts.[4]

In general, assortments with a broad range of sizes or styles require high stock-to-sales ratios. Women's shoes have a high stock-to-sales ratio because of an extensive assortment of numeric sizes and corresponding widths. Many department stores and full-line discounters abandoned ready-made curtains and draperies as businesses because of high inventory requirements. Each style/color requires an assortment of lengths, and several pairs of each to accommodate multipair purchases.

A stock-to-sales ratio is an inverse expression of turnover. A stock-to-sales ratio is computed by dividing an inventory figure (BOM) by

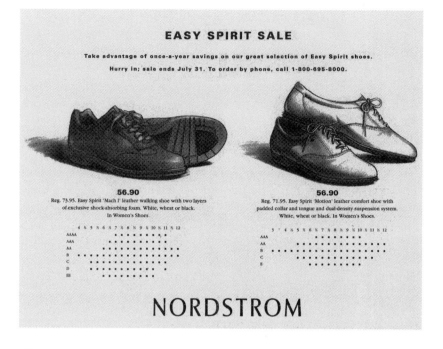

Figure 9.3

Goods with an extensive assortment of sizes have a high stock-to-sales ratio.

sales. Turnover is computed by dividing sales by an inventory figure (average inventory). Thus, turnover and stock-to-sales ratios have an inverse relationship; that is, as one increases the other decreases. Consequently, a *high* turnover is indicative of a *low* stock-to-sales ratio, and low turnover is indicative of a high stock-to-sales ratio.

As merchandising concepts, turnover and stock-to-sales ratio are often uttered in the same breath. Consider a slow-turning women's hosiery department. The buyer determines that the low turnover is a result of the high stock-to-sales ratios that each brand of hosiery requires to ensure complete color and size assortments. To increase turnover, the buyer must choose between two strategies to reduce average inventory: carrying the same number of brands with reduced assortments of size and color or, carrying fewer brands with full assortments of size and color.

The latter is the preferable alternative. Carrying the same number of brands with reduced assortments of sizes and colors will frustrate customers looking for a particular size or color within a brand. It is less frustrating to a customer to find a brand unavailable, than to find many brands represented by poor assortments. A shrewd buyer would edit the number of brands carried, eliminating those that closely duplicate each other in terms of price, quality, color, and style assortment.

In theory, a stock-to-sales ratio cannot be less than 1.0. A stock-to-sales ratio is 1.0 when BOM and sales are equal, implying that all of the merchandise on hand at the beginning of the month, is sold during the month. This is an infrequent circumstance except in the case of very fast-turning goods continuously replenished throughout the month, or seasonal merchandise, such as Christmas decorations where it is hoped that all of December's BOM will be sold by the end the month.

Stock-to-Sales Ratio Variations

Busy selling periods require higher stock-to-sales ratios than slower periods. To demonstrate this principle, consider an assortment of cotton sweaters available in five colors and four sizes (S/M/L/XL). Assume that the buyer plans to sell only one sweater during the first month of the season. A BOM of twenty sweaters is required, representing a complete assortment of five colors and four sizes. Assume that

Table 9.2   **MONTHLY STOCK-TO-SALES RATIOS**
          FOR A DEPARTMENT

Month	Sales	BOM	Stock-to-Sales Ratio
1	$ 20,000	$ 40,000	2.0
2	$ 20,000	$ 40,000	2.0
3	$ 25,000	$ 45,000	1.8
4	$ 10,000	$ 30,000	3.0
5	$ 10,000	$ 30,000	3.0
6	$ 5,000	$ 25,000	5.0
7	$ 5,000	$ 25,000	5.0
8	$ 5,000	$ 25,000	5.0
9	$ 40,000	$ 60,000	1.5
10	$ 30,000	$ 50,000	1.7
11	$ 40,000	$ 60,000	1.5
12	$ 30,000	$ 50,000	1.7
TOTAL	$240,000	$480,000	2.0

The aggregate stock-to-sales ratio for the year is 2.0 based on total BOMs divided by total sales.

the buyer increases the sales plan to two sweaters. Since planned sales have doubled, should the buyer double the BOM to include two of each size and color? Hardly. A BOM of twenty sweaters is still an adequate assortment to support the sale of two sweaters, since the chance of a second customer wanting the same size and color as the first customer is only one in twenty, assuming that one size/color combination is as desirable as another. Nineteen sweaters is a 95 percent in-stock rate ($19/20 = 0.95 = 95\%$), a very acceptable inventory position for most categories of merchandise.

When planned sales are one sweater, the stock-to-sales ratio is 20.0 (20:1). When planned sales are two sweaters, the stock-to-sales ratio is only 10.0 (20:2), substantiating the claim (though rather simplistically) that "peak" selling months require lower stock-to-sales ratios than "slow" months. At some point during the season, planned sweater sales will reach a point that will necessitate increasing the inventory of each size and color as the chance of two customers wanting the same size and color increases. However, at no point will a full assortment of sweaters be required for each customer.

Table 9.2 lists monthly stock-to-sales ratios for a department. Note that the range of ratios falls between 1.7 and 5.0. The months with the highest sales have the lowest stock-to-sales ratios, while the months with the lowest sales have the highest stock-to-sales ratios. Since periods of high sales require lower stock-to-sales ratios than periods of low sales, it is reasonable to conclude that merchandise turns faster during periods of high sales, than periods of low sales. During peak selling periods, merchandise flows in and out of stores rapidly, while during slow selling periods, goods turn at much slower rates.

Figure 9.4

Beginning-of-month stock-to-sales ratios for men's specialty stores.

Category	Median
February	8.6
March	8.3
April	8.3
May	8.4
June	7.3
July	8.5
August	8.8
September	8.8
October	8.7
November	8.5
December	4.4
January	7.9

SALES-PER-SQUARE-FOOT

Sales-per-square-foot is a measure of productivity that reflects the amount of sales generated relative to the amount of space dedicated to presenting and storing the goods. As an input, square footage represents the capital outlay for constructing the retail space, and the operational expenses associated with renting, heating, lighting, cleaning, and staffing the space. Square footage is based on the physical dimensions of a selling area, and often includes stockrooms, fitting rooms, service areas, and adjacent aisles. The formula for computing sales-per-square-foot is:

$$sales\text{-}per\text{-}square\text{-}foot = \frac{sales}{square\ footage}$$

Sales-per-square-foot can be measured for any period, however, an annual measurement is the most common. Sales-per-square-foot can be computed for any unit of business such as a store, a department, a fixture, or a category or brand of merchandise.

The following demonstrates the calculation of sales-per-square-foot: Assume that a department store allocates 1000 square feet within its misses sportswear area to an Alfred Dunner shop. Last year the shop generated sales of $400,000. Sales-per-square-foot for the shop are computed as follows:

$$sales\text{-}per\text{-}square\text{-}foot = \frac{sales}{square\ footage}$$

$$sales\text{-}per\text{-}square\text{-}foot = \frac{\$400,000}{1000\ square\ feet}$$

$$sales\text{-}per\text{-}square\text{-}foot = \$400$$

For each square foot of space dedicated to the Alfred Dunner line, $400 in sales were generated.

As a measure of productivity, high sales-per-square-foot values are generally more desirable than low values. The mathematical relationship between sales and square footage indicates that sales-per-square-foot productivity can be increased by increasing sales, decreasing square footage, or both increasing sales and decreasing square footage. Generating more sales in less space is a universal objective for every retailer. Though high sales-per-square foot are desirable, excessively high sales-per-square foot can be an indication that a selling area is too

Table 9.3   **LEADERS BY SALES-PER-SQUARE-FOOT**

Company	'94 sales per sq. ft.
Sears, Roebuck	$739.99
Today's Man	479.00
Cosmetic Center	354.32
Wal-Mart	297.60
Office Depot	293.96
T.J. Maxx	252.33
Barnes & Noble	243.16
Ross Stores	215.36
Stein Mart	205.00
Bed Bath & Beyond	202.23
Venture	180.83
Kmart	174.27
ShopKo Stores	164.32
Caldor	162.29
Dress Barn	154.02
Ames	143.75
All For A Dollar	138.04
Goody's	136.90
Burlington Coat Factory	136.29
Warehouse Family Dollar Stores	85.36

crowded. A crowded shopping environment can inhibit sales and prevent the effective presentation of goods.

Space productivity expectations differ by category of merchandise. The physical size of merchandise is a factor. If a department store's fashion jewelry counter and furniture department generate the same annual volume, the sales-per-square-foot of the fashion jewelry department will be higher than the sales-per-square-foot of the furniture department because of the lesser amount of space required to present the jewelry.

Turnover is another factor relevant to sales-per-square-foot expectations. If men's sport shirts and men's dress shirts generate the same annual volume, but sport shirts turn twice as fast as dress shirts, then the average inventory of dress shirts is twice the average inventory of sport shirts. Since sport shirts require only half the space of dress shirts, sport shirts are more productive in terms of sales-per-square-foot.

Though sales-per-square-foot is the most commonly used measure of space productivity, any measure of space can be used. Cubic measures can be used when height or vertical dimension is a factor in presenting goods for sale, as in the case of stacked goods, or goods presented on shelved walls or fixtures. Linear inches can be used to measure the space productivity of linear configurations of space, such as shelving and case lines of jewelry. Numerators other than sales can be used as an output relative to spatial input. Some stores compute gross-margin-per-square-foot. Gross margin is a gross profit figure from which net profit is derived.

Space Allocation

Retail selling space is strategically allocated to maximize sales-per-square-foot. Consider the following: A 10,000 square foot specialty store generates annual sales of $3 million. The space is divided among four categories of merchandise. The square footage, annual sales, and sales-per-square-foot for each category appear in Table 9.4. The figures in the *Industry Standard* column are hypothetical sales-per-square-foot industry standards. Retail trade associations provide statistics such as these as benchmarks by which retailers can compare their performance.

Note that the store's sales-per-square-foot of $300 is behind the industry standard of $339. In other words, the store is not generating enough sales relative to its size. Further analysis reveals the problem areas: Dresses at $100 per foot, and outerwear at $200 per foot, are performing behind the industry standards of $250 per foot and $320 per foot, respectively. Sportswear and accessories pose no apparent problem: The sales-per-square-foot of the sportswear area matches the

Table 9.4 **SALES-PER SQUARE FOOT FOR WOMEN'S SPECIALTY STORE**

Category	Square Footage	Annual Sales	Sales/Square Foot	Industry Standard
Sportswear	4,000	$1,600,000	$400	$400
Dresses	3,000	$ 300,000	$100	$250
Outerwear	2,000	$ 400,000	$200	$320
Accessories	1,000	$ 700,000	$700	$400
TOTAL	10,000	$3,000,000	$300	$339

SALES-PER-SQUARE-FOOT REPORT			
	Sales	Sq. Ft.	Sales/Sq. Ft.
SPRINGFIELD	650,057	8,400	77
PLAZA	380,913	2,400	158
LONGMEADOW	393,760	3,100	127
WESTFIELD	624,037	4,300	145
EASTFIELD	1,326,974	7,500	176
BERKSHIRE	757,365	4,500	168
ENFIELD	680,453	6,000	113
HAMPSHIRE	663,411	2,950	224
INGLESIDE	1,416,906	4,800	295
MANCHESTER	698,635	6,850	101
TOTAL	7,592,516	50,800	149

Figure 9.5a

A sales-per-square-foot report for a department in a ten-unit chain.

	Department Stores		Specialty Stores	
Category	Median	Superior	Median	Superior
Female Apparel	150	171	182	259
Female Accessories	142	184	177	412
Men's and Boys' Apparel	109	160	217	394
Infants' and Children's Apparel	62	99	—	—
Footwear	—	—	247	439
Cosmetics	256	343	225	239
Leisure and Home Electronics	64	129	241	321
Home Furnishings	56	104	123	168
Other Hardlines	—	—	332	778
Other Merchandise	—	—	197	400
TOTAL	132	169	—	—

Figure 9.5b   Sales-per-square-foot for department and specialty stores by category of merchandise.

industry standard; the sales-per-square-foot of the accessories area is $700 per foot, far exceeding the industry standard of $400 per foot.

The retailer has tried to build dress and outerwear sales with direct mail advertising, new merchandising resources, and promotional pricing. However, none of the tactics have been successful. It is apparent that both businesses have plateaued with little promise of future growth.

The owner decides that the best strategy for bringing the store's sales-per-square-foot closer to industry standards is to reallocate space.

Category	Sales (in billions)	% of store sales	Average dept. size (in sq. ft.)	Sales per/sq. ft.
Apparel	$35.6	28.7%	19,000	$174.9
Housewares	8.6	7.0	3,000	240.0
Consumer Electronics	8.6	7.0	2,700	293.3
Domestics	8.5	6.9	3,300	215.2
Food (including Pet Food)	7.7	6.2	2,200	286.0
Health and Beauty Care	7.4	5.9	3,200	191.9
Toys	7.4	6.2	3,500	175.5
Sporting Goods	4.2	3.4	2,200	258.5
Automotives	4.1	3.3	2,000	186.4
Stationery	4.1	3.3	1,400	245.2
Lawn and Garden	3.7	3.0	2,700	115.4
Paint/Hardware	3.5	2.8	N/A	N/A
Household Cleaners	3.2	2.5	1,200	119.8
Jewelry/Watches	3.0	2.4	1,000	251.7
Photography	2.7	2.2	600	373.6
RTA/Furniture	2.7	2.2	1,900	118.4
Cosmetics	2.2	1.8	1,000	189.2
Crafts	1.6	1.3	1,100	135.5

Figure 9.5c
Sales-per-square-foot for full-line discounters by category of merchandise.

The retailer determines that the ideal amount of space for a $300,000 dress area is 1200 square feet ($300,000 divided by the industry standard of $250 = 1200), and that the ideal amount of space for a $400,000 outerwear area is 1250 square feet ($400,000 divided by the industry standard of $320 = 1250). Reducing the dress area by 800 square feet (the present 3000 square feet less 1200 square feet), and the outerwear area by 750 square feet (the present 2000 square feet less 1250 square feet), will permit the expansion of the accessories area by 1550 square feet (800 square feet plus 750 square feet). This will more than double the size of the accessories area (1550 square feet plus 1000 square feet is 2550 square feet.

The wisdom of expanding the accessories area so dramatically may be questioned. At the current annual volume of $700,000, the addition of 1550 square feet will drop the area's productivity from $700 per foot to $274 per foot ($700,000 divided by 2550 square feet), $126 below the industry standard. However, at $700 per foot, the area's productivity was nearly twice the industry standard, an indication of overcrowding and unrealized sales potential. Expanding the area will create a more comfortable shopping environment, facilitate more attractive presentations of goods, and allow for expanding selections of the popular items and resources. The retailer can expect to generate considerably higher sales that will bring the resulting sales-per-square-foot productivity for the store closer to industry standards.

SPACE MANAGEMENT

Space management is the strategic arrangement of products to maximize sales with a minimum investment of space and fixtures. Space management involves the development of visual models of product

SPACE PRODUCTIVITY REPORT					
Style #	% Movemt	% Space	Style #	% Movemt	% Space
3305	0.8	1.5	4147	3.4	1.8
3113	0.7	1.6	3853	1.6	1.5
6616	0.7	1.7	4918	3.5	1.6
1808	0.5	1.6	6921	2.5	1.5
2000	1.9	1.7	2426	2.4	1.7
4343	1.7	1.6	5783	2.1	1.4
9015	0.8	1.6	9687	3.7	1.8
3864	2.0	1.6	4688	3.4	1.6
7401	3.9	1.7	2498	3.0	1.5
3673	1.7	1.9	6957	3.6	1.6
8848	1.2	1.8	0289	1.9	1.6
7074	1.4	1.6	3278	3.0	1.6
3066	0.7	1.6	4489	1.1	1.4
0089	1.3	1.8	6895	0.6	1.2
7085	0.2	1.7	8980	0.9	1.5
2242	1.0	1.5	4880	1.3	1.6
2757	2.1	1.6	0890	1.2	1.8
7004	0.5	1.7	2134	0.7	3.1
5309	1.6	1.6	2778	0.7	1.4
1016	2.1	1.7	3095	1.4	1.4
1226	0.7	1.5	9800	0.5	1.4
0704	1.3	1.6	7783	0.3	1.4
1004	1.1	1.7	4348	1.8	1.8
3997	1.4	1.5	2390	2.5	1.9
5937	1.2	1.5	0063	1.5	2.8
2618	1.5	1.6	3373	0.7	1.6
9972	1.4	1.7	5218	2.6	1.8
5740	1.1	1.6	1001	2.1	1.7
5611	0.7	1.9	4979	2.5	1.5
1089	3.9	2.2	100.0	100.0	
6668	2.4	1.6			

Figure 9.6

A space management software report that compares percent of turnover to percent of space occupied for items in an assortment.

Figure 9.7

A planogram is an optimum product arrangement. *SMSB Consulting Group, Inc., Melville, NY.*

arrangements called **planograms.** Planograms incorporate an organization's standards for merchandise presentation, product adjacencies, and customer convenience. Planograms ensure the consistent arrangement of goods within stores in multiunit organizations. A planogram can represent an entire store, a store section, or a single fixture or wall section. Planograms can be general, indicating the approximate location of merchandise categories, or specific, indicating the precise location of individual items on fixtures. Planograms are periodically reset to reflect seasonal changes in product assortments. Planograms of fashion goods are reset more often than planograms of basic goods.

Electronic space management software builds predictive models of optimum inventory levels and assortments based on the wholesale cost, retail price, and turnover of each product in an assortment. "What if" capabilities allow the software user to observe the fiscal impact of adding or deleting items from an assortment. Most space management software produces color planograms with product images in scaled dimensions that can be electronically transmitted to stores. The planograms are automatically adjusted by store based on sales data

Company Profile 9.1

The Nielsen Merchandising Solutions Group is a world-wide information organization that caters to the merchandising needs of retailers and their suppliers. A Dun and Bradstreet company, NMSG develops, manufactures, markets, and supports a growing line of predictive modeling space management software with capabilities that reach far beyond conventional space management systems. SPACEMAN is a family of products with a comprehensive set of store fixtures and shelf models applicable to a wide range of retail settings that automates repetitive space management tasks. The end result is an aesthetically pleasing, easy-to-shop product arrangement based on sales and profit objective and the price point and physical characteristics of an assortment.

A.C.Nielsen

SPACEMAN's vast merchandising capabilities can be enhanced by several add on modules that include:

- COMMAND MODULE—Uses historical sales information to adapt basic planogram assortments to special markets or regions.
- ENTERPRISE—Analyzes planograms relative to their adjacency to other product groups and the traffic flow within the store. ENTERPRISE links a planogram to the sales, profit, and inventory movement objectives for an entire store.
- LIVE—A library of product images used to generate full color photographic representations of product arrangements.
- PROMAN—Plans promotional items, strategies, and inventories based on the results of prior promotional events.
- PRICEMAN—Analyzes the competitive position of an assortment relative to competitors' prices and develops a pricing strategy based on price elasticity, competitive activity, and the store's price image and profit objectives.

NMSG offers personalized training and technical support for SPACEMAN users, as well as seminars, publications, and opportunities for user group interactions.

scanned at point of sale. Quantities of slow-turning items are reduced (or deleted) from the assortment, while quantities of fast-turning items are increased. One retailer added three dozen new high-ticket, high-margin items to a 200-item assortment in existing space by freeing space occupied by overstocked items, and dropping slow-moving items.[5] Movement information is also shared with suppliers to ensure timely replenishment of stock.

Electronic space management is closely allied to **category management,** the concept of managing individual categories of merchandise as a business unit, such as a department or a store. Electronic space management was first used in the food industry. However, applications to durable goods and apparel are becoming common. Sears uses electronic space management for home softlines, such as bed and bath linens and ready-made draperies, and for basic apparel, such as jeans, underwear, and hosiery.[6,7,8]

SUMMARY POINTS

- Productivity is a measure of the number of units of output produced per unit of input.
- Turnover is the number of times that an average inventory is sold over a time period. Turnover can be increased by increasing sales, decreasing average inventory, or both. Turnover expectations differ by category of merchandise.
- A stock-to-sales ratio indicates the proportionate relationship between a BOM and the sales for a month. Goods requiring extensive assortments have high stock-to-sales ratios. Goods requiring limited assortments have low stock-to-sales ratios.
- Peak selling periods require lower stock-to-sales ratios than slower selling periods.
- Sales-per-square-foot is a measure of productivity that reflects the amount of sales generated relative to the amount of retail space dedicated to sale of the goods.

KEY TERMS AND CONCEPTS

average inventory	end-of-month inventory	sales-per-square-foot
beginning-of-month inventory	perishable goods	space management
	planograms	stock-to-sales ratio
category management	productivity	turnover (stockturn)

FOR DISCUSSION

1. Compare various categories of merchandise relative to the turnover assumed for each. What characteristics of the goods influence their turnover?

2. Consider several categories or brands of merchandise relative to stock-to-sales ratios assumed for each. What assortment characteristics influence their stock-to-sales ratios?

3. Review a store's assortment of a product line with multiple styles, sizes, or colors. Are there styles, sizes, or colors that have sold out? Are there full assortments, styles, sizes, or colors that have apparently not sold at all? Are there some that are sold out? What inferences can you make about the turnover of the product line? What advice can you give to the person who places replenishment orders?

4. A shoe retailer carries a large assortment of casual, dress, and athletic shoes for men, women, and children in 4000-square-foot locations. The retailer plans to expand to open several new stores, most of which are considerably smaller than existing locations. Based on your knowledge of turnover and stock-to-sales ratios, what advice can you give the retailer relative to determining a merchandise mix for the new stores?

5. Look for a very crowded store. How do the crowded conditions affect shopping ambiance? Your ability to shop?

PROBLEMS

1. Refer to the figures in Table 9.1 to compute the following:
   - average inventory for the last quarter of the year
   - average inventory for the first six months of the year
   - turnover for the last six months of the year assuming sales of $20,000 for the period

   Assume annual sales of $30,000 and that 60 percent of the sales are generated during the last six months of the year.

2. The following list refers to the number of stock-keeping units that need to be carried to maintain a full assortment of sizes, styles, and colors for each of five lines. Assume that the average unit price is $2.50 and that average monthly sales for each line is $100. Compute the stock-to-sales ratio for each.

Line A	100 units
Line B	120 units
Line C	80 units
Line D	200 units
Line E	140 units

What inferences can you make relative to the turnover of each item?

3. The following is a list of sales-per-square-foot figures for the merchandise division of a department store slated for expansion. Corporate sales-per-square-foot standards for each division are also included.

division	sq'	$/sq'	standard
Men's	20,000	600	300
Kids'	10,000	400	250
Ready-to-Wear	50,000	350	300
Accessories	20,000	300	350
Home	30,000	300	250

How many additional square feet are required to match corporate productivity standards? Which divisions need additional space? How much space does each need?

SUGGESTED READINGS

Minichiello, R. (1990). *Retail Merchandising and Control.* Boston: Irwin.
Risch, E. (1991). *Retail Merchandising.* New York: Macmillan.

ENDNOTES

1. If the average inventory for a year were computed by dividing the sum of the year's beginning and ending inventories by two, the resulting figure would not be a representative average. Using the average inventories for each month accounts for the dramatic inventory fluctuations that occur in a year. Ideally, an annual average inventory should be computed by summing each day's inventory and dividing by 365, just as an average daily balance is computed on a savings account or a charge account. However, most retailers do not maintain daily inventory balances, and the cost of generating this information would negate the value of it.

2. The data in this scenario has been manipulated to demonstrate dramatically the effect of average inventory on turnover. In real life, sales are never quite as predictable.

3. Lee, Georgia. (July 22, 1994). Goody's goal: Category killer. *Women's Wear Daily.* p. 14.

4. For pedagogical reasons, assortment considerations other than size were ignored. Sport shirts require a broader range of styles and colors than dress shirts, a selection factor that increases their stock-to-sales ratio.

5. Staff. (September 27, 1993). Category management techniques lead to double-digit sales increases. *Home Furnishings Daily.* p. 6.

6. Robbins, Gary. (April 1993). Softlines, the new frontier for space management systems. *Stores.* pp. 24–26.

7. Stambaugh, Sandie. (February 1, 1993). The basics of planogramming. *Aftermarket Business.* pp. 18–20.

8. Alexander, Stephen & Waldman, Barry. (February 1, 1993). The fourth dimension. *Aftermarket Business.* pp. 18, 20.

MERCHANDISING ACCOUNTING

An understanding of a company's financial statements is important to those
who perform merchandising functions in a
retail organization in that the execution of
merchandising responsibilities impacts several financial statement components and the
organization's fiscal objectives. Chapter 10
covers the analysis and interpretation of some
of the financial statements studied in managerial accounting courses with an emphasis on
merchandising applications and retail inventories.

After you have read this chapter, you will be able to discuss:

Fundamental accounting concepts from a merchandising
perspective.

The interpretation of retail
financial statements.

Gross-margin-return-on-
investment as a measure of
inventory performance.

CASH FLOW

Cash flow is the balance of cash coming into and going out of an organization. A positive cash flow means that more cash is coming into the organization than going out. A negative cash flow means that more cash is going out of the organization than coming in. A positive cash flow is preferable to a negative cash flow, however, even the most successful retailers experience negative cash flow periodically.

Consider the following: A men's shop conducts approximately twenty percent of its business between Thanksgiving and Christmas. The owner arranges for the delivery of goods bought for the holiday season by October 31. The retailer pays most invoices within ten days to take advantage of early payment discounts, and the remaining balances within thirty days. Thus, most holiday merchandise is paid for by mid-November, even though the goods will not begin to yield an appreciable amount of cash from sales until late November. About half of the retailer's customers charge their purchases to a store-sponsored charge account. These sales do not begin to generate cash until about thirty days after the purchases are made.

Figure 10.1 depicts the retailer's cash flow from October through March. A negative cash flow is any point on the graph where the *cash out* line is higher than the *cash in* line. Periods of negative cash flow occur from mid-October through early December, and again through March. The latter negative cash flow is a result of the arrival and payment of spring merchandise in a period of limited cash generation due to low sales volume.

Figure 10.1

Cash flow curve.

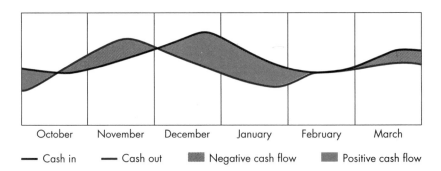

A positive cash flow is any point on the graph where the *cash in* line is higher than the *cash out* line, such as the period between the end of November and early February. A balanced cash flow is represented by points where the *cash in* and *cash out* lines coincide, for example throughout much of February.

Retailers resolve negative cash flows with short-term borrowing from lending institutions. The borrowed funds enable retailers to meet their financial obligations to suppliers, and ensure continued shipment of future orders. Short-term borrowing allows retailers to take advantage of prompt payment discounts that help to offset the interest expense incurred by borrowing. Many retailers have an open line of credit with lending institutions that allows the retailer to borrow and pay back money in a manner similar to that of a revolving charge account with an established limit and regular payments with interest.

Cash flow is a topic that is important to a retail organization's buyers in that payments to suppliers account for significant outlays of money within most retail accounting periods. To enhance positive cash flow, buyers schedule the delivery of goods as close as possible to their point of sale, and negotiate payment terms that delay payments to suppliers as long as possible. Shipments that arrive and are paid for far in advance of their selling season hinder cash flow.

THE BALANCE SHEET

A **balance sheet** is a statement of an organization's assets, liabilities, and owners' equity at a particular point in time. **Assets** are *owned* by an organization. Cash, inventory, and store fixtures are among retailers' assets. Assets are classified according to their **liquidity,** or the likelihood of their conversion to cash. *Short-term,* or *current,* assets will be converted to cash within a year in the normal operation of business. Cash is a retailer's most liquid asset. *Long-term,* or *noncurrent, assets* will not be converted to cash within a year in the normal operation of business. Retailers' long-term assets include store facilities and fixtures.

Inventory is a current asset that receives considerable attention in this text. Inventory is converted to cash as it is sold. The more quickly that inventory is converted to cash, the more quickly the cash can be again invested into new inventory which, in turn, will generate more

11

Nordstrom, Inc. and Subsidiaries

Consolidated Balance Sheets

Dollars in thousands

January 31,	1993	1992
Assets		
Current assets:		
Cash and cash equivalents	$ 29,136	$ 14,651
Accounts receivable, net	603,198	608,227
Merchandise inventories	536,739	506,632
Prepaid expenses	50,771	48,128
Total current assets	1,219,844	1,177,638
Property, buildings and equipment, net	824,142	856,404
Other assets	9,184	7,833
Total assets	$2,053,170	$2,041,875
Liabilities and Shareholders' Equity		
Current liabilities:		
Notes payable	$ 38,319	$ 134,735
Accounts payable	220,176	216,432
Accrued salaries, wages and taxes	158,028	145,792
Accrued expenses	31,141	31,741
Accrued income taxes	22,216	16,402
Current portion of long-term debt	41,316	8,801
Total current liabilities	511,196	553,903
Long-term debt	440,629	502,199
Deferred income taxes	49,314	46,542
Contingent liabilities (Note 11)		
Shareholders' equity	1,052,031	939,231
Total liabilities and shareholders' equity	$2,053,170	$2,041,875

The accompanying Notes to Consolidated Financial Statements are an integral part of these statements.

Figure 10.2

A balance sheet is a statement of assets, liabilities, and shareholders' equity.

sales. Inventory not quickly converted to cash often decreases in value as an asset, especially if it is perishable and becomes unsalable over time.

Liabilities are debts *owed* by an organization. Liabilities are classified according to the time in which they are due to be paid. Payment on *short-term* liabilities is due within one year. Payment on *long-term* liabilities is due in one year or longer. A retailer's short-term liabilities include payables to suppliers, and short-term debts to lending institutions for money borrowed to balance cash flow. Long-term liabilities include mortgages on land and buildings, and long-term financing for extensive expansion and renovation projects.

Owners' equity is the difference between assets and liabilities. Owners' equity is also called *shareowners' equity* and *shareholders' equity*. The relationship between assets, liabilities, and owners' equity is such that:

$$assets = liabilities + owners'\ equity$$

Balance sheet components are in a constant state of flux and subject to momentary change. For instance, whenever a shipment from a supplier is received and paid for, inventory increases and cash decreases. A balance sheet reflects neither sales nor profit performance. Two retailers with similar balance sheets can produce vastly different sales and profit results.

FINANCIAL RATIOS

Financial ratios are analytical tools based on the proportionate relationship between two balance sheet components. Financial ratios are used to assess an organizational level of solvency or financial stability. A **current ratio** is the relationship between current assets and current liabilities. The current ratio measures an organization's short-term debt-paying ability, or ability to pay off current debts with current assets. The formula for the current ratio is:

$$current\ ratio = \frac{current\ assets}{current\ liabilities}$$

A current ratio less than 1.0 indicates that current liabilities are greater than current assets, and that current assets are insufficient to pay off current liabilities, a highly undesirable financial position. A 2.0 current ratio indicates that current assets are twice current liabilities. Generally, 2.0 is considered an acceptable current ratio, though this standard varies by type of industry. Credit rating services use financial ratios to determine an organization's credit worthiness. Compiled by Dun and Bradstreet, the largest credit rating service, the *Business Information Report* compares organizations' financial ratios to industry benchmarks. Suppliers use the *Business Information Report* to determine the risk associated with extending credit to retailers.

Table 10.1   **CURRENT RATIO HISTORIES FOR**
              FIVE MAJOR RETAILERS

	1993	1992	1991	1990	1989
Wal-Mart	1.5	1.7	1.6	1.7	1.8
Merry Go Round	1.6	1.8	1.9	1.9	1.8
Nordstrom	2.4	2.1	2.0	2.1	2.0
The Limited	3.1	2.5	3.1	2.8	2.4
Younkers	3.5	2.7	2.7	2.7	2.1

Financial ratios are also important to factors. A **factor** is a financial intermediary peculiar to the apparel industry that assumes responsibility for collecting manufacturers' receivables from retailers. Factors buy receivables at discounted rates to cover the cost and financial risk associated with collecting them. Factors keep a watchful eye on the fiscal status of retailers and refuse to approve shipments to stores whose financial statements send signals of an inability to pay promptly. The bankruptcies of many major apparel retailers have caused factors to raise their credit approval standards to protect themselves against the possibility of unpaid claims.[1]

INCOME STATEMENTS

An **income statement** is a statement of an organization's profit performance for a specific period of time. The fundamental components of an income statement are revenue, expenses, and net profit. The relationship among the components is expressed by the equation:

$$revenue - expenses = net\ income$$

The income statement is sometimes called a *statement of earnings*, or a *profit and loss statement* (*P&L*). A **profit** results when expenses are less than revenue and net income is positive. A **loss** results when expenses are greater than revenue and net income is negative.

Unlike a balance sheet that represents a particular *point in time*, an income statement represents a specific *span of time*, such as a year, quar-

Figure 10.3

A factor is a financial intermediary that collects manufacturers' receivables from retailers.

ter, six-month season, or month. Income statements can be computed for an entire organization or for a unit of business within an organization, such as an individual store, a group of stores, or a department. Profit or loss is based on the revenue and expenses directly associated with each unit of business.

Income Statement Components

Retail income statements have five major components: revenue, cost-of-goods-sold, gross margin, expenses, and net profit. The relationship among the components is such that:

$$
\begin{array}{r}
\textit{net revenue} \\
-~ \textit{cost-of-goods-sold} \\ \hline
\textit{gross margin} \\
-~ \textit{expenses} \\ \hline
\textit{net profit}
\end{array}
$$

Since a retailer's revenue is generally composed of sales, the term net sales often appears on retailers' income statements. Other sources of revenue may include rent from leasing or renting property or interest on accounts receivable. **Net sales** are **gross sales** minus customer returns:

$$net\ sales = gross\ sales - customer\ returns$$

Though never appearing on an income statement, gross sales are used to determine customer-return rates:

$$customer\ return\ rate = \frac{customer\ returns}{gross\ sales} \times 100$$

Customer returns at $4000 on gross sales of $100,000 represents a return of 4 percent on net sales of $96,000. Return rates are computed for stores, categories of merchandise, and brands. A high customer return rate is often indicative of issues relative to customer service, or the quality or fit of merchandise. Net sales are the "top line" of the income statement from which all other income statement components are derived. High sales attest to the ability of an organization's buyers to select assortments of goods that are appealing to the store's target customers.

The **cost-of-goods-sold,** also called the *cost-of-merchandise-sold* or the *cost-of-sales*, includes the billed cost of merchandise plus workroom and shipping costs, less discounts for early payment, and returns-to-vendors.

$$\begin{array}{l} billed\ cost\ of\ merchandise \\ +\ shipping\ costs \\ +\ workroom\ costs \\ -\ returns\text{-}to\text{-}vendors \\ -\ cash\ discounts \\ \hline cost\ of\ goods\ sold \end{array}$$

Shipping costs are the inbound delivery costs for transporting goods from suppliers. **Workroom** costs represent activities that prepare merchandise for sale, such as steaming and pressing apparel, and refinishing furniture damaged during shipment. Workroom activities change the merchandise in some way. Expenses for ticketing, hanging,

---
10

Nordstrom, Inc. and Subsidiaries

Consolidated Statements of Earnings

Dollars in thousands except per share amounts

Year ended January 31,	1993	% of Sales	1992	% of Sales	1991	% of Sales
Net sales	$3,421,979	100.0	$3,179,820	100.0	$2,893,904	100.0
Costs and expenses:						
Cost of sales and related buying and occupancy costs	2,339,107	68.3	2,169,437	68.2	2,000,250	69.1
Selling, general and administrative	902,083	26.4	831,505	26.2	747,770	25.8
Interest, net	44,810	1.3	49,106	1.5	52,228	1.8
Service charge income and other, net	(86,140)	(2.5)	(87,443)	(2.7)	(84,660)	(2.9)
Total costs and expenses	3,199,860	93.5	2,962,605	93.2	2,715,588	93.8
Earnings before income taxes	222,119	6.5	217,215	6.8	178,316	6.2
Income taxes	85,500	2.5	81,400	2.5	62,500	2.2
Net earnings	$ 136,619	4.0	$ 135,815	4.3	$ 115,816	4.0
Net earnings per share	$ 1.67		$ 1.66		$ 1.42	
Cash dividends paid per share	$ .32		$ .31		$ .30	

The accompanying Notes to Consolidated Financial Statements are an integral part of these statements.

Figure 10.4

An income statement is a statement of revenue, expenses, and net income.

or presenting merchandise on fixtures are not workroom costs. **Returns-to-vendors,** or RTVs, are defective or slow-selling goods returned to suppliers for credit. **Cash discounts** are invoice concessions from suppliers for prompt payment, a topic that will receive considerable attention in Chapter 14.

Expenses are incurred in the day-to-day operation of an organization. Expense categories include payroll, rent, utilities, advertising, and interest on debt. Expenses are classified as either direct or indirect. A **direct expense** is attributable to a specific unit of business; an **indirect expense** is not. Direct expenses cease to exist when the unit of business is eliminated. A store's rent is a direct expense that would no longer exist if the store were closed. Newspaper advertising for a region of stores is an indirect expense for each store that would continue to exist if one of the stores in the region closed.

Category	Department Stores		Specialty Stores	
	Median	Superior	Median	Superior
Female Apparel	39.1	40.9	42.0	46.3
Female Accessories	45.0	46.7	47.2	51.2
Men's and Boys' Apparel	38.2	39.3	44.9	56.1
Infants' and Children's Apparel	38.2	40.9	34.8	43.1
Footwear	38.0	40.7	42.8	45.2
Cosmetics	38.7	38.9	39.8	41.8
Leisure and Home Electronics	37.8	42.8	38.0	47.9
Home Furnishings	36.7	41.3	44.3	48.0
Other Hardlines	27.8	39.5	35.0	48.0
Other Merchandise	32.9	38.8	42.9	48.7
TOTAL	38.4	40.9	—	—

Category	% Gross Margin
Apparel	34.1%
Ladies'	35.0
Men's	33.0
Shoes	38.0
Girls'	31.0
Accessories	46.0
Infants'	28.0
Boys'	35.0
Housewares	29.3
Consumer Electronics	17.3
Domestics	34.0
Food (including Pet Food)	20.6
Health and Beauty Care	16.9
Toys	27.2
Pharmacy	24.9
Sporting Goods	27.2
Automotives	22.9
Stationery	39.4
Lawn and Garden	25.1
.Paint/Hardware	32.1
Household Cleaners	14.5
Jewelry/Watches	38.0
Photography	15.2
RTA/Furniture	32.0
Cosmetics	28.1
Crafts	36.6

Category	% Gross Margin
Men's Clothing	
Men's Suits	46.4%
Men's Coats	45.6
Sport Coats	46.4
Dress Slacks	49.1
Total Men's Clothing	46.0
Men's Sportswear	
Sport Shirts	46.4
Sweaters	44.6
Activewear	45.1
Casual Slacks	45.7
Jeans	47.0
Jackets & Heavy Outerwear	43.1
Coordinated Leisurewear	45.4
Total Men's Sportswear	45.5
Men's Furnishings	
Dress Shirts	49.4
Neckwear	52.3
Hosiery	51.8
Men's Belts	52.1
Men's Accessories	49.6
Underwear	51.1
Sleepwear	50.9
Men's Headwear	46.8
Total Men's Furnishings	50.0

Figure 10.5b

Gross margins for full-line discounters by category of merchandise

Figure 10.5c

Gross margins for men's specialty stores by category of merchandise.

Table 10.2   **A TIME SERIES COMPARISON OF THE NET INCOME PERCENTAGES OF FIVE MAJOR RETAILERS**

	1993	1992	1991	1990	1989
Wal-Mart	3.6	3.7	4.0	4.2	4.1
Merry Go Round	4.3	3.0	6.0	4.6	3.7
Nordstrom	4.0	4.3	4.0	4.3	5.3
The Limited	5.4	6.6	6.6	7.6	7.5
Younkers	3.2	3.7	1.9	2.6	1.2

Table 10.3   **A TIME SERIES COMPARISON OF THE LIMITED'S INCOME STATEMENT COMPONENTS**

	Year 2	% Sales	Year 1	% Sales
Net Sales	$6,160,807	100.0%	$5,523,509	100.0%
Cost-of-Goods-Sold	$4,367,264	70.9%	$3,893,070	70.5%
Gross Margin	$1,793,543	29.1%	$1,630,439	29.5%
Expenses	$1,133,241	18.4%	$ 977,001	17.7%
Net Income	$ 660,302	10.7%	$ 653,438	11.8%

Dollar figures are expressed in thousands

Most retailers minimize indirect expenses by attempting to allocate every expense to some source. For instance, the advertising expense for a region of stores may be allocated among the stores in the region based on the sales volume of each store. Expenses are typically operational in nature, their control falling within the realm of the finance division or store administration.

Gross margin, or *gross profit,* is the difference between sales and the cost-of-goods-sold. Retailers rely on gross margin to cover operating expenses, and ultimately profit. Gross margin expectations vary by retailing format and type of merchandise. Because a "no-frills" strategy results in lower operating expenses for discounters than department stores, discount stores have lower gross margins than department stores. A men's shop expects a higher gross margin from its sportswear category than its suit category in that the gross margin for suits is typically eroded by high alteration workroom costs. Generating gross margin is fundamental to a buyer's mission in a retail organization. Buyers protect gross margin by negotiating favorable prices and terms with vendors, and by managing retail prices so that they yield high sales and generous margins.

Many retailers include buying and occupancy costs in the cost-of-goods-sold that appears in their annual reports. The practice inflates cost-of-goods-sold and reduces gross margin, a tactic that camouflages the *real* cost-of-goods-sold which is a carefully guarded secret in retail organizations. Though buying and occupancy costs are included in the cost-of-goods-sold in public financial statements, most retailers follow the traditional format for internal management reports.

Net income, sometimes called *net earnings,* or *net profit, earnings before taxes,* or *bottom line,* is equal to gross margin minus expenses. Because the generation of net income is the fundamental reason for a company's existence, all of the activities of a retail organization are directly or indirectly pointed to this goal. Net income can be increased by increasing sales, increasing gross margin, decreasing cost-of-goods-sold, decreasing expenses, or any combination of the above.

Component Percentages

A **component percentage** is a ratio of an income statement component, such as gross margin, expenses, or net income, to net sales, expressed as a percentage. The following are formulas for computing four component percentages:

$$\text{cost-of-goods-sold \%} = \frac{\text{cost of goods sold}}{\text{net sales}} \times 100$$

$$\text{gross margin \%} = \frac{\text{gross margin}}{\text{net sales}} \times 100$$

$$\text{expenses \%} = \frac{\text{expenses}}{\text{net sales}} \times 100$$

$$\text{net profit \%} = \frac{\text{net income}}{\text{net sales}} \times 100$$

Component percentages are often used to evaluate performance between two time periods, a comparison called a **time-series comparison.** To demonstrate, refer to the information in Table 10.3, which was derived from two successive annual income statements of The Limited. The figures in the *percent columns* are based on the above formulas. Note that sales increased from year one to year two by $637,298,000, representing a gain of 11.5 percent. However, in spite of this sizable gain in sales, the company's net income slipped by 0.9 percent because

Company Profile 10.1

The Dayton Hudson Corporation is one of the largest department store conglomerates in the United States, boasting sales of more than $21 billion and serving customers in more than one thousand stores in 106 million square feet of retail space in thirty-three states. Dayton Hudson is a diversified conglomerate that operates three groups of stores including:

Target The most upscale of the "*Big Three*" full-line discounters, operating more than 640 stores that feature a broad assortment of fashion and basic hardlines and softlines.

Mervyn's A moderate price department store, operating more than 290 stores in sixteen states and specializing in trendy active and casual apparel and home softlines.

Dayton Hudson Department Stores A division that includes more than sixty full-line department stores operating under the Dayton's, Hudson's, and Marshall Field's banners, offering moderate to better merchandise in nine states and

DAYTON HUDSON CORPORATION

emphasizing superior service and fashion leadership.

A recent Dayton Hudson annual report outlined some of the strategies that enhanced profitability at Dayton Hudson that year. At Target, a new automated merchandise processing system reduced inventory processing costs and improved turnover. A concentration on high-margin, trendy merchandise was also part of the plan. Like Target, Mervyn's increased the efficiency of merchandise processing in distribution centers and stores with technology, and also reduced merchandise processing costs by negotiating with vendors to preticket and hang merchandise. The department store division replaced in-paper newspaper advertising with less expensive Sunday magazine inserts. Like its sibling divisions, the Dayton Hudson Department Store systems were updated to manage the flow of inventory more accurately. The net effect of these efforts was a banner year for Dayton Hudson.

of two factors: lower gross margin (− 0.4%), and an increase in expenses (+0.5%). Though the percentages are seemingly minuscule, the drop in net income amounted to $6,864,000.

Note that the component percentages converted multidigit dollar figures into noncomprehensible three-digit percentages. Component percentages also facilitate comparing stores or organizations of vastly different volume. A meaningful comparison can be made between the performance of a *$6 million* dollar retailer, to The Limited, a *$6 billion* retailer, since percentage ratios cannot conveniently convert income statement components to a scale of 0 to +/ −100 percent, regardless of the dollar magnitude of the components. Naturally, other factors must be considered when comparing the two retailers. As a multibillion dollar organization, The Limited reaps economic advantage unattainable for small retailers.

GROSS-MARGIN-RETURN-ON-INVESTMENT (GMROI)

It is wise to review multiple measures of performance when making merchandising decisions. For instance, assume that space constraints necessitate eliminating one of two categories of merchandise in a store's assortment. Retaining the higher volume producer is an information-poor decision in that it is based only on a single performance measure: sales. Table 10.4 compares two merchandise categories, A and B, on two factors: sales and gross margin. Note that the sales of Category A exceed the sales of category B by $50,000. However, Category B generates $30,000 more gross margin than Category A, and is thus a larger contributor to the store's net income. Therefore, in a decision to eliminate one of the two categories in a store's assortment, Category B should be retained. Naturally, factors other than sales and gross margin should be considered in the decisions. Even high gross margin categories fall under scrutiny if they have high selling expenses or poor space productivity.

Gross-Margin-Return-on-Investment (GMROI) integrates two performance measures, gross margin and turnover, to create a single

Table 10.4   **GROSS MARGIN OF CATEGORY A AND CATEGORY B**

	Category A	Category B
Sales	$300,000	$250,000
Cost-of-Goods-Sold	$180,000	$100,000
Gross Margin $	$120,000	$150,000
Gross Margin %	40%	60%

	Department Stores		Specialty Stores	
Category	Median	Superior	Median	Superior
Female Apparel	2.7	3.0	2.5	3.2
Female Accessories	2.0	2.4	2.3	3.6
Men's and Boys' Apparel	1.9	2.2	2.3	2.7
Infants' and Children's Apparel	2.2	2.8	2.3	2.8
Footwear	1.1	1.4	1.6	2.0
Cosmetics	1.2	1.6	0.9	1.2
Leisure and Home Electronics	1.3	1.7	1.1	2.1
Home Furnishings	1.2	1.5	1.5	2.0
Other Hardlines	1.3	5.4	2.7	5.1
Other Merchandise	2.4	4.4	2.1	2.9
TOTAL	2.0	2.5	—	—

Figure 10.6

GMROI for department and specialty stores by category of merchandise.

measure of performance. The formula for GMROI (pronounced *jim-roy*) is:

$$\text{GMROI} = \frac{gross\ margin\ dollars}{net\ sales} \times \frac{net\ sales}{average\ inventory}$$

Note that *gross margin/net sales* is the component percentage formula for gross margin (without the $\times 100$), while *net sales/average inventory* is the formula for turnover.[2] The formula can be simplified by canceling *net sales*.

$$\text{GMROI} = \frac{gross\ margin\ dollars}{average\ inventory}$$

The derived formula measures the amount of gross margin dollars generated per average dollar of inventory invested.

The following example demonstrates the use of GMROI: As a result of a store renovation, a gourmet cooking shop will gain enough additional selling space to expand a single category of merchandise. The choice has been narrowed to three categories: specialty foods, countertop appliances, and open stock glassware. The shop's annual volume is $2 million. Each category represents about 20 percent of the shop's business. The remaining business is generated by categories, such as cookbooks, cookware, and table and kitchen linens. Countertop appliances yield a 20 percent gross margin ($80,000), specialty foods a

Company Profile 10.2

The *Report of Independent Accountants* is a standard statement that appears in a company's annual reports, indicating that generally accepted accounting principles (GAAP) were used to prepare the financial statements in the report, and that the statements accurately represent the company's financial position. As the recognized leader in retail accounting, Ernst & Young's corporate signature appears on more *Reports of Independent Accountants* of major retailers, than any other *Big Six* accounting firm.

≡Ⅱ ERNST & YOUNG LLP

Ernst & Young's expertise extends beyond the realm of accounting, auditing, and taxation. Providing a comprehensive range of consultative services to retail clients that includes such areas as site selection, long range planning, and employee communications, Ernst & Young also offers professional guidance in inventory management including:

Six largest U.S. public accounting firms: Arthur Andersen, Deloitte & Touche, Coopers Lybrand, Ernst & Young, Price Waterhouse, KPMG Peat Marwick.

- Implementing logistical strategies in distribution centers to cut merchandise processing costs and enhance turnover by reducing the amount of time that inventory is tied up in the distribution pipeline.
- Developing decision support systems for inventory planning.
- Developing analytical tools for measuring merchandise performance and profitability, such as direct product profitability, which measures gross margin at individual product level.

Ernst & Young assimilates the primary information derived from serving its many clients to publish authoritative surveys on key industry issues, such as *Ernst & Young's Survey of Retail Information Technology Expense and Trends*. Ernst & Young also publishes *Retail News*, a quarterly newsletter covering current and emerging issues, such as trends in technology, international expansion, and merchandise quality.

30 percent gross margin ($120,000), and glassware a 50 percent gross margin ($200,000). Specialty foods turn fastest at 10.0 times a year with an average inventory of $3200 at cost. Countertop appliances turn 4.0 times a year with an average inventory of $25,000 at cost. Glassware is the slowest turning category at 1.5 times a year with an average inventory of $50,000 at cost. The GMROI for each category is computed by

Table 10.5   **GMROI FOR THREE MERCHANDISE CATEGORIES**

	Gross Margin	Average Inventory	GMROI
Specialty Foods	$ 80,000	$ 3,200	25.0
Small Electrics	$120,000	$25,000	4.8
Glassware	$200,000	$50,000	4.0

dividing gross margin dollars by average inventory. The results appear in Table 10.5.

Note that specialty foods yield the highest GMROI (25.0), and that glassware yield the lowest GMROI (4.8). If the decision to expand a category of merchandise were based solely on the gross margin, glassware would be the chosen category. However, when turnover is considered, specialty foods fall under a favorable light. Though specialty foods generate fewer gross margin dollars than countertop appliances or glassware, inventory investments for specialty foods are considerably less than inventory investments for the other two categories. In other words, specialty foods yield more gross margin dollar per dollar of inventory carried than countertop appliances or glassware.

In general, high turnover and high gross margin yield high GMROI, and low turnover and low gross margin yield low GMROI. In the example, specialty foods' very high turnover compensates for its low gross margin. Conversely, a very high gross margin can also compensate for low turnover. Because high turnover and high gross margin are very desirable merchandising objectives, maximizing GMROI is an important goal for most buyers.

SUMMARY POINTS

- Cash flow is the balance of cash coming into and going out of an organization.
- A balance sheet is a statement of a retailer's assets, liabilities, and owner's equity. Assets are *owned* by a retailer. Liabilities are *owed*. Net worth is the difference between the two.
- Financial ratios combine two balance sheet components to assess financial stability. The current ratio is a measure of an organization's short-term debt paying ability used by credit rating organizations to

determine credit worthiness.
- An income statement reflects a retailer's profit performance for a specific period. Its components include net sales, cost-of-goods-sold, gross margin, and profit.
- Gross-margin-return-on-investment (GMROI) combines gross margin and turnover in a single measure of performance, measuring the amount of gross margin generated per dollar of average inventory invested.

KEY TERMS AND CONCEPTS

accounts receivable	expense	net loss
assets	factor	net sales
balance sheet	gross-margin-return-on-	return-to-vendor
cash discount	investment (GMROI)	owner's equity
cash flow	gross sales	time-series comparison
component percentage	income statement	workroom cost
cost-of-goods-sold	liability	
current ratio	net income	

FOR DISCUSSION

1. Obtain recent annual reports from several publicly held retail organizations in various retailing formats. Using the consolidated income statements, compute gross margin, expense, and profit percentages. Compare the stores within one retailing format to the stores within another. Explain the reasons for the variances that you find. Compare the percentages for stores within the same format. Explain these variances.
2. GMROI combines two measures of performance to create a single comprehensive measure. Are there other measures of performance that can be combined to create a single measure? Could three measures be combined? What two measures will *not* create a valid measure when combined?
3. The current ratio uses two balance sheet components to create a measure of a retailer's ability to pay its short-term debt. What other balance sheet components can be used to create other ratios? What would the ratios measure?
4. How might the GMROI of an apparel department compare to the GMROI of a furniture department in the same store? Explain.
5. How does the cash flow of a warehouse club compare to the cash flow of a department store? Why?

SUGGESTED READINGS

Eskew, Robert & Jensen, Daniel. (1992). *Financial Accounting.* New York: McGraw-Hill.

Horngren, Charles & Sundem, Gary. (1990). *Introduction to Management Accounting.* Englewood Cliffs, NJ: Prentice Hall.

ENDNOTES

1. Zinn, Laura. (August 26, 1991). Sniffing trouble on Seventh Avenue. *Business Week.* p. 52.
2. It should be noted that the Chapter 9 discussion of turnover advocated using the average inventory at retail to determine turnover; GMROI is based on average inventory at cost. Also there are many variations of the GMROI formula. Some formulas include $\times 100$ in the gross margin portion of the formula, multiplying turnover by gross margin as a percentage of sales instead of as a ratio of gross margin to sales.

chapter eleven

INVENTORY VALUATION

Inventory values have considerable impact on a retail organization's financial statements. On a balance sheet, inventory is an asset that impacts net worth. On an income statement, gross margin and net profit are both derived from the cost-of-goods-sold, a figure based on inventory values. The maintenance of inventory records and the assessment of inventory value are important merchandising functions and the subject of Chapter 11.

After you have read this chapter, you will be able to discuss:

Perpetual inventory systems.

The fiscal impact of shortage.

Last-in, first-out (LIFO) and first-in, first-out (FIFO) as methods of inventory valuation.

PHYSICAL AND BOOK INVENTORY

Retailers periodically determine the value of their inventories to pre-pare financial statements. Cost-of-goods-sold is an income statement component. Computing the cost-of-goods-sold necessitates determining the value of the inventory on hand at the beginning of a fiscal period, adding the inventory purchased during the period, and subtracting the value of the inventory on hand at the end of the period. Retailers also determine inventory values to prepare balance sheets.

The most reliable method of determining the value of an inventory is to count it. A **physical inventory** involves counting and valuating an inventory item by item. Retailers conduct physical inventories at least once a year to determine the cost-of-goods-sold and gross margin for annual financial statements. Most retailers conduct physical inventories twice a year.

To prepare interim monthly and quarterly financial statements, most retailers need to establish the value of their inventory more often than annually or semi-annually. To avoid having to physically count an inventory more than twice a year, retailers maintain a perpetual inventory. A **perpetual inventory system** is an inventory accounting system, whereby the value of an inventory is maintained on a continual basis by adjusting a beginning physical inventory by purchases, sales, and price changes. The resulting figure is called the **book inventory.** The nomenclature dates back to the days when inventory records were maintained in ledgers. Today, the "book" value of an inventory is likely to be maintained electronically by a computer.

In theory, a book inventory should always equal a physical inventory. The balance between a book and physical inventory is maintained by adjusting the book inventory by any changes in inventory status. When new goods are received, the book is adjusted upward by the value of the goods received. When goods are sold, the book is adjusted downward by the value of the goods sold. The book is also adjusted by price changes, such as markdowns, and any other factors that affect the value of a store's inventory, such as RTVs and customer returns.

OVERAGE AND SHORTAGE

In theory a book inventory should always equal a corresponding physical inventory. However, the two seldom match. The discrepancy between the two is called an **overage** when the book inventory is *less* than the physical inventory. The discrepancy is called a **shortage** when the book inventory is *greater* than the physical inventory. A shortage is sometimes called *shrinkage*.

External theft by customers, and **internal theft** by employees are a frequent cause of shortage. Shoplifted items remain on the book, causing the book value to exceed the physical value when a physical inventory is taken. However, shoplifting accounts for only a portion of shortage and does not explain overage. Virtually all overages as well as many shortages are rooted in paper or clerical errors as the following scenarios demonstrate:

- A vase is received into a gift shop inventory and booked at a $28 retail. The item is ticketed at $28, but the 8 looks like a 6. When the vase is sold, the sale is transacted at $26. The book inventory is adjusted downward by $26, resulting in an overstatement of $2, which will emerge as a $2 shortage at the next physical inventory.
- At the end of the selling season, a buyer marks down the remaining pieces of a swimwear group from current clearance prices to 75 percent off the original retails. Fifty pieces of swimwear were each marked down $15 from $44.99 to $29.99. The information was accurately recorded on a change-of-price form, however, the person responsible for entering the price change transactions into the inventory management system entered the digit 5 on the keyboard instead of the digits 5 and 0 when inputing the number of units marked down. The book inventory was adjusted downward by $75 (5 units × $15) instead of $750 (50 units × $15). This resulted in a $675 overstatement of the book inventory that will emerge as a $675 shortage at the next physical inventory.
- A furniture store recorded its physical inventory on optical scanning sheets. A sheet recording a $150 lamp and a $350 table was mislaid and never optically scanned as part of the store's inventory. This resulted in a $500 understatement of the physical inventory, and a $500 shortage.

The examples are just three of the innumerable scenarios that cause paper shortage in retail stores. Though the examples generated shortages, overages would have resulted if circumstances had been changed slightly: if the vase had been sold at a price *higher* than booked; if a figure *greater* than the number of pieces that were marked down were input; or if the lamp and table were recorded twice on inventory sheets.

Category	Department Stores		Specialty Stores	
	Median	Superior	Median	Superior
Female Apparel	2.3	1.9	2.8	1.5
Female Accessories	3.2	2.5	3.7	2.8
Men's and Boys' Apparel	2.3	1.8	2.9	2.0
Infants' and Children's Apparel	1.9	1.4	1.4	1.2
Footwear	1.7	0.9	2.7	1.7
Cosmetics	1.1	0.8	1.3	0.5
Leisure and Home Electronics	2.8	1.9	4.6	2.4
Home Furnishings	2.7	1.6	1.4	1.1
Other Hardlines	2.8	1.7	1.6	0.5
Other Merchandise	2.7	1.3	2.6	1.4
TOTAL	2.3	1.7	—	—

Figure 11.1

Shortage for department and specialty stores by category of merchandise.

Most retailers track shortages and overages by department, store, and category of merchandise. Shortage and overage are expressed as a percentage of net sales of the period between the current and previous physical inventories. Assume that a department has a book inventory of $92,525, a semi-annual physical inventory of $87,375, and net sales of $500,000 for the six-month period. The difference between the book and physical inventories is $5150. Since the book inventory is greater than the physical inventory, the result is a shortage. The shortage percentage is calculated by dividing the shortage by the net sales for the period and multiplying by 100:

$$shortage\ percent = \frac{shortage\ dollars}{net\ sales} \times 100$$

$$shortage\ percent = \frac{\$5150}{\$500,000} \times 100$$

$$shortage\ percent = 0.0103 \times 100$$

$$shortage\ percent = 1\%$$

Shortage varies by category of merchandise relative to factors such as the size and desirability of the merchandise, and the number of units handled in inventory transactions. Fashion jewelry displayed on top of a counter has a high shortage risk because of its pilferable size. Polo/Ralph Lauren men's wear is vulnerable to shoplifting because of its desirability as a product and high street value. Transactional errors are more likely to occur in a greeting card store where *hundreds* of sales transactions are typical of each day, than in a furniture store where *a hundred* sales transactions would represent a very busy day. Shortage also varies by retailing format. The average shortage for department stores is 2.0 percent of net sales.[1]

PHYSICAL INVENTORY

A physical inventory involves identifying each unit of merchandise by price and compiling this information by category and store location. Additional information such as vendor, age, or style number is sometimes required to update management reports that track inventories at these levels. A physical inventory is a tedious function, requiring weeks of preparation that involves tasks such as reticketing merchandise and grouping goods together by price to expedite counting. Rigid controls, such as numbered inventory sheets and detailed floor plans, are used to control the accuracy of a physical inventory.

Stores are often closed during a physical inventory to avoid distraction by the public. Closing stores adds to the cost of taking a physical inventory because of the loss of business during the store's closing. To minimize the loss of business, physical inventories are scheduled on the least productive days of the week, and at the least productive time of day. To minimize counting, physical inventories are conducted at times when inventories are at their lowest point.

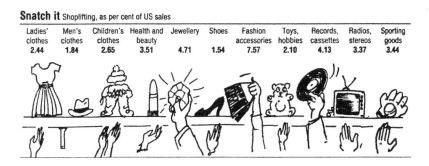

Snatch it Shoplifting, as per cent of US sales

Ladies' clothes	Men's clothes	Children's clothes	Health and beauty	Jewellery	Shoes	Fashion accessories	Toys, hobbies	Records, cassettes	Radios, stereos	Sporting goods
2.44	1.84	2.65	3.51	4.71	1.54	7.57	2.10	4.13	3.37	3.44

Figure 11.2

Shortage as a percentage of sales for all U.S. retailers. *Robert Hunt,* The Economist.

Company Profile 11.1

For more than forty years, RGIS Inventory Specialists have offered professional inventory-taking services to retailers, manufacturers, and wholesalers, relieving them of one of the most burdensome inventory management tasks. As an inventory specialist, RGIS has developed proprietary state-of-the-art equipment that expedites inventory taking. A portable microcomputer is used to scan inventory by bar codes. Non–bar coded inventory data input into an on-site portable computer through a "keying by touch" process that is more expedient than the conventional "call and list" method. The captured inventory information is transmitted from the microcomputer, an on-site portable computer for in-store validation and results, or to a main-frame computer at a RGIS data center where it is compiled at store, department, or sku level. The accuracy of the inventory is ensured by a series of checks that meet the most stringent auditing requirements of certified public accounting firms. Using an impartial external service such as RGIS removes the temptation of store personnel to cover inventory shortage by recording inventory that does not exist. Most stores are inventoried during a six-hour period in which they are normally closed, thus loss of business due to inventory taking is circumvented.

RGIS *INVENTORY SPECIALISTS*

RGIS has more than 260 offices throughout the United States, and a work force of more than 26,000 people who conduct nearly a quarter of a million inventories a year. A recognized leader in inventory management, RGIS has expanded its services to include customer service audits called *mystery shops*, competitive price checking, and replenishment systems for reordering merchandise.

Some retailers inventory selected departments or stores more often than semi-annually. A retailer may inventory a high shortage department, such as fashion jewelry, quarterly; or highly pilferable items, such as camcorders, weekly. A change in department or category structure may necessitate an interim inventory. If Liz Claiborne handbags are transferred from the moderate handbag category to the better handbag category, a physical inventory of the line is taken so that the better category can be charged for the merchandise and the moderate category credited.

Physical inventory data is compiled either internally by the store's finance division, or externally by a contracted service. The results are compared to book inventories to determine shortages and overages. A period of **inventory reconciliation** usually follows a physical inventory during which large discrepancies between book and physical inventories are scrutinized for possible resolution. A shortage of $11,347 in one department in one store, and an overage of the same amount in the same department in another store, may be the result of incorrect (or lack of) processing of the paperwork issued when the goods from one store (the overage store) were transferred to another store (the shortage store). When the reconciliation is complete, the book inventories are adjusted to the reconciled physical inventories. For one brief moment, the book and physical inventories match.

Technological advancements have enhanced the accuracy and speed of physical inventories. Many retailers scan bar codes into computers that compile inventory information down to the stock-keeping unit, or sku level. Some inventory management systems generate lists of booked items identified by sku. The lists can then be compared to the inventory on hand enabling the retailer to identify shortage, not only by a dollar amount within a category or store, but by individual item.

THE FISCAL IMPACT OF SHORTAGE

Inventory shortages and overages affect net profit because of their impact on the cost-of-goods-sold. Shortages *increase* the cost-of-goods-sold and *reduce* gross margin and net income. Overages *decrease* the cost-of-goods-sold and *increase* gross margin and net income. The following scenario demonstrates this principle: Assume that a gift shop's end-of-the-year physical inventory of $50,000 is equal to the book inventory. The cost-of-goods-sold for the period is computed as follows:

beginning-of-year physical inventory	$ 75,000
merchandise receipts during the year	$575,000
merchandise available for sale	$650,000
end-of-the-year physical inventory	− $ 50,000
cost-of-goods-sold	$600,000

The shop's income statement for the period is as follows:

net sales	$1,000,000	
cost-of-goods-sold	600,000	60%
gross margin	400,000	40%
expenses	350,000	35%
net income	$50,000	5%

Assume that the end-of-the-year physical inventory was $30,000, indicating a $20,000 shortage. The cost-of-goods sold would be computed as follows:

beginning-of-year physical inventory	$ 75,000
merchandise receipts during the year	$575,000
merchandise available for sale	$650,000
end-of-year physical inventory	$ 30,000
cost-of-goods-sold	$620,000

The income statement reflecting this change is as follows:

net sales	$1,000,000	
cost-of-goods-sold	620,000	62%
gross margin	380,000	38%
expenses	350,000	35%
net income	$30,000	3%

Note that the cost-of-goods-sold increased from 60 percent to 62 percent of net sales, and that net income decreased from 5 percent of net sales to 3 percent. A $20,000 overage would have the reverse effect on the cost-of-goods-sold and net income. The cost-of-goods-sold would drop to $580,000 and 58 percent of net sales, while net income would increase by $70,000 to 7 percent of net sales.

The example demonstrates the effect of shortage in eroding net income. Though overage produces "paper profit," it is destined to return as a shortage in subsequent accounting periods. Assume that a $1000 gold chain is listed at $1500 by an inventory taker, creating a $500 inventory overage. Since book and physical inventory discrepancies are corrected by adjusting the book inventory to match the physical, the chain will be carried on the book at $1500 until the next physical inventory. If the chain is sold at the correct price of $1000, the book will be adjusted downward by that amount, leaving $500 of unaccounted-for inventory; in other words, a shortage of $500. If the chain is not sold during the subsequent inventory period, a $500 shortage will appear at the next physical inventory if the chain is correctly listed at $1000.

Buyers prefer inventory overages to inventory shortages because of their positive impact on gross margin and net income. However, neither overages nor shortages are desirable in that both reflect inaccurate record keeping and/or poor inventory management. Shortage receives more attention than overage in that shortage is the more likely occurrence. In essence, the type of errors that create shortage are often the same mistakes that create overage.

Shortage Control

Though retailers employ exhaustive efforts to curb theft and the paper errors that cause overage and shortage, inequities between book and physical inventories are inevitable. When retailers open their doors to the public, they become vulnerable to shoplifting. By relying on people to order merchandise, receive and ticket goods, effect price changes, and ring sales on registers, retailers become susceptible to the consequences of human error.

Buyers are accountable for shortage even though many have little control over the stores or distribution centers where many shortages

Figure 11.3

Clover Stores of Philadelphia uses Sensormatic's closed circuit television system to control shoplifting.

Company Profile 11.2

1. Nulty, Peter. (October 7, 1991). Cashing in on security. Fortune. p. 113.
2. Strom, Stephanie. (May 16, 1993). Putting the tag on shoplifters. New York Times. p. 11.

Sensormatic Electronics Corporation helps retailers to curb shortage with microwave technology and electronic article surveillance (EAS) products that currently protect over $100 billion in merchandise throughout the world. EAS systems consist of three basic elements: electronic tags and labels that attach to merchandise, detachers or deactivators that either remove or deactivate the tags, and detecting systems located at exit points of the store. *TellTag* is an intelligent "talking" tag with an embedded computer chip that activates an audio alarm in the tag that is amplified by acoustic tone detectors in the store's ceiling. The tag will beep until a sales associate removes it from the merchandise. Should the merchandise be taken beyond the store perimeter, the tag will beep loudly, enabling store personnel to identify the shoplifter in a crowd.

The Sensormatic product line extends beyond EAS devices. POS/EM is a system designed to reduce theft at the register by monitoring "exceptional" register transactions tied to collusion, such as transaction voids, "no sales", customer returns, and cash refunds. When an exceptional transaction is entered at a register, POS/EM automatically aims a camera at the register, and superimposes the transaction data over a recorded video picture of the sales associate and register.

Potential shop-lifters know that Sensormatic devices increase their risk of being caught. Thus, the intimidating presence of a system deters the would-be shoplifter. Some retailers attribute a 60 percent reduction in shrinkage to Sensormatic.

Sensormatic systems are used to protect all items in a store, or to selectively protect only highly vulnerable items or categories. Though Sensormatic tags are often associated with apparel, the ubiquitous tags can be found on any item or category with a tendency to disappear, including wallpaper sample books, filet mignon, museum pieces, health-club towels, fax machines, newborn babies, and patients with Alzheimer's disease.[1,2]

Sensormatic
WORLD LEADER IN ELECTRONIC SECURITY

originate. Buyers control shortage by monitoring the position and value of inventory through reports of inventory position, price change, and receipts. They foster good inventory management through clear communication regarding ticketing of merchandise, inventory counts, price changes, and RTVs.

POINT-OF-SALE SYSTEMS

Computerized inventory management systems that track thousands of inventory items by store, merchandise category, style number, or brand across hundreds of locations from the point at which they are ordered to the point at which they are sold, have facilitated the maintenance of perpetual inventory systems. A **point-of-sale,** or *POS*, system is a network of computerized cash registers linked to a central processing point, often referred to as a *back office*. A POS system processes sales transactions and related functions, such as credit verification and sales tax computation. As goods are sold, product information, such as style, size, and vendor, is transmitted to the back office by a multidigit number keyed into the register or an electronically scanned bar code. The information is stored in a database and used to adjust book inventories and to compile reports of inventory status that are used to plan assortments, make reorder and markdown decisions, and balance inventories among stores.

At store level, POS information is used to track salespeople's productivity and customer transactions by hour of the day and day of the week for use in scheduling the sales staff. Some POS systems have an electronic mail feature for communicating announcements of promotions and price changes from a central office to stores. As noted in Chapter 5, POS information also has marketing applications. Customers identified by store-issued shoppers' cards or credit cards can be profiled by their purchases and targeted for catalog mailings or other niche marketing strategies. Individual stores can be profiled by their best sellers so that store-specific assortments can be developed. Athlete's Foot, a group of more than 400 athletic footwear stores, can identify a city's favorite sport by the most popular styles of athletic shoes: Detroit prefers basketball, Boston running, and Atlanta tennis. Once appropriate for only large volume, high-transaction retailers, POS systems are now affordable to small retailers.[2,3,4,5]

LIFO and FIFO

Determining the cost-of-goods-sold at the end of a fiscal period is complicated by variations in the cost of merchandise bought during the period. Goods acquired at the beginning of a fiscal period are likely to have been purchased at lower prices than goods acquired at the end of a fiscal period. Two assumptions can be made relative to the cost of goods acquired and sold during the fiscal period:

1. The goods acquired at the end of a fiscal period are sold before the goods purchased earlier in the fiscal period. This describes an inventory concept called last-in, first-out or **LIFO.**
2. The goods acquired at the beginning of a fiscal period are sold before goods purchased later in a fiscal period. This describes an inventory valuation concept called first-in, first-out or **FIFO.**

Consider the Following: A pro shop sells knit shirts in basic colors. The inventory is carried from one season to the next, and periodically replenished with new receipts. The shop began a fiscal year with an opening inventory of 1000 shirts at a unit cost of $25. The shirts retailed at $50. When the shop reordered 2000 units of the same shirt later in the year, the unit cost had increased to $26. These shirts were retailed at $52. The remaining original inventory was marked up $2 per unit to $52 to maintain price consistency. Assume that 2800 shirts were sold throughout the fiscal year: 900 at a $50 retail, and 1900 at a $52 retail.

The following is a computation for the cost-of-goods-available-for-sale during the year:

beginning inventory @ cost (1000 units @ $25)	$25,000
additional receipts (2000 units @ $26)	$52,000
total cost-of-goods-available-for-sale	$77,000

The following is a computation for annual sales:

900 units at $50	$ 45,000
1900 units at $52	$ 98,800
2800 units representing retail sales of	$143,800

LIFO assumes that the receipts that arrived later in the year were sold prior to the beginning inventory. The following is a computation of the cost-of-goods-sold based on LIFO:

2000 shirts at $26 each	$52,000
800 shirts at $25 each	$20,000
2800 shirts at total-cost-of-goods-sold	$72,000

LIFO assumes an ending inventory value of $5000 (200 shirts at $25 each).

FIFO assumes that the beginning inventory was sold prior to the receipts that arrived later in the year. The following is a computation of cost-of-goods sold based on FIFO:

1000 shirts at $25 each	$25,000
1800 shirts at $26 each	$46,800
2800 shirts at total cost-of-goods-sold	$71,800

FIFO assumes an ending inventory value of $5200 (200 shirts at $26 each). The following is a computation of gross margin based on LIFO:

sales	$143,000
cost-of-goods-sold	$ 72,000
gross margin	$ 71,000

The following is a computation of gross margin based on FIFO:

sales	$143,000
cost-of-goods-sold	$ 71,800
gross margin	$ 71,200

Note that FIFO generates a gross margin that is $200 higher than LIFO. The higher FIFO gross margin will ultimately yield higher net income. FIFO will consistently generate higher gross margin and net income than LIFO in periods of inflation when the cost of inventory rises from the beginning of the period to the end. In cases of price decreases, FIFO will yield lower gross margin and net income. Table 11.1 summarizes the effect of LIFO and FIFO during periods of inflation.

The effects of LIFO and FIFO are proportionate to the amount of inflation that occurs during an accounting period. In a period of *very high* inflation, FIFO will yield a *very low* cost-of-goods-sold, and *very high* gross margin and net income. LIFO will yield a *very high* cost-of-goods-sold, and a *very low* gross margin and net income. LIFO and FIFO are not intended to reflect the way in which merchandise is actually sold. Stores typically rotate inventories to ensure that older stock sells before becoming shopworn.

Table 11.1 **COMPARISON OF LIFO AND FIFO**

LIFO	FIFO
yields higher cost-of-goods-sold	yields lower cost-of-goods-sold
yields lower ending inventory values	yields higher ending inventory values
yields lower gross margin	yields higher gross margin
yields lower net income	yields higher net income

LIFO is adopted as an accounting strategy to improve cash flow through the deferral of income tax. Since corporate taxes are paid on net income, a LIFO-induced net income reduction results in the deferral of tax payment, which results in improved cash flow. The domino effect continues: Recall that a negative cash flow is balanced by borrowing money and that the related interest expense reduces net income. By improving cash flow, LIFO results in less borrowing, lower interest payments, and improved earnings. The adoption of LIFO in a period of relatively low inflation will have little impact on net income, however LIFO's impact on net income during a period of high inflation is significant. This is why many retailers adopted LIFO during the early 1970s, a period of double-digit inflation.

Since LIFO is a theoretical accounting assumption contrary to the actual physical flow of merchandise, LIFO retailers often maintain two sets of inventory figures, one for external financial reports, which reflects inventory value using LIFO, and another for nonfinancial internal management reports using FIFO that more accurately reflects the actual movement of goods. Federal tax law revisions have encouraged retailers to adopt LIFO. Previously, the Internal Revenue Service required conformity between the statement of inventory on the balance sheet, the computation of cost-of-goods-sold, and the preparation of tax statements. However, income tax laws have been relaxed to allow LIFO calculations for the preparation of tax statements, and FIFO inventory calculations for financial statements. Thus, a retailer can *minimize* the amount of taxes paid by using LIFO for tax purposes, and *maximize* the statement of earnings on financial statements by using FIFO. Today more than 50 percent of all major retailers use LIFO as an inventory method. Some elect to use a combination of both LIFO and FIFO. Kmart, for instance, uses LIFO for domestic goods, and FIFO for imports.

To assist retailers in determining their cost-of-goods-sold, the U.S. Department of Labor issues a semi-annual (January and July) *Department Store Price Index*, or *BLS*, that reflects price inflation on various categories of merchandise. Many companies develop their own indices to measure inflation within the fiscal year, finding internally derived data more accurate.

SUMMARY POINTS

- A physical inventory is the actual value of inventory determined by a physical count. An inventory's book value is its recorded value. In theory, the book value of inventory should equal the physical value.
- An overage occurs when the book inventory is less than the physical inventory. A shortage occurs when the book inventory is greater than the physical inventory. A physical inventory is conducted periodically to determine overage or shortage.
- Shortages and overages affect net income because of their impact on cost-of-goods-sold.
- A POS system is a network of computerized registers linked to a central processing point.
- LIFO and FIFO are concepts used to determine inventory values for accounting purposes.

KEY TERMS AND CONCEPTS

book inventory	inventory reconciliation	physical inventory
external theft	LIFO	point-of-sale system
FIFO	overage	shortage
internal theft	perpetual inventory	

FOR DISCUSSION

1. Besides the errors described on page 271, what other errors might occur in a retailer's day-to-day operation that would create inventory shortage or overage?
2. Why are some retailers reluctant to use technologically sophisticated shoplifting prevention devices, such as those offered by Sensormatic?

3. Outline the bookkeeping procedures that are necessary in stores without a POS system. Discuss the value of a POS system relative to accuracy and cost effectiveness.

PROBLEMS

1. Determine the overage/shortage in dollars and/or units if:
   - A $100 dress is stolen from a store.
   - A markdown from $20 to $16.99 is recorded as ten units instead of fifty.
   - A sale of $100 is incorrectly transacted as $120.
   - Goods received on the books at $2 per unit are incorrectly ticketed as $3 per unit; there are 100 units.
   - The return of a $50 blouse by a customer is transacted as $60.
   - The return of a $50 blouse by a customer is transacted as a sale of $80.
   - A broken $60 vase is thrown into the trash. No transaction is recorded to remove the vase from the books.
   - A markup is taken on 200 items from $80 to $90; the data entry person enters twenty items.
   - Goods transferred from store #1 to store #2 were miscounted; fifty items at $20 each were recorded as sixty items.
   - A salesperson guessed at a selling price of an $80 item and transacted it at $85.
2. In the LIFO/FIFO example on page 280, assume all of the shirts were sold at $50. What is the effect on cost-of-goods-sold? Gross margin?

ENDNOTES

1. Staff. (January 19, 1991). Krazy Kirk meets Dr Shortage. *Economist.* p. 65.
2. DeLaney, Bob. (February 1994). Information technology: Transforming today's retail enterprise. *Chain Store Age Executive.* p. 52.
3. Lusch, Robert. (January 1990). Retail control systems for the 1990's. *Retailing Issues Letter.*
4. Staff. (December 1991). Electronically linking the front to the back. *American Druggist.* p. 48.
5. Staff. (November 1990). Athletes' Foot steps up inventory control. *Chain Store Age Executive.* pp. 128–130.

chapter twelve

RETAIL PRICING

R etail prices are the source from which gross margin and net profit are derived. In general, high prices yield higher gross margin and profit than low prices. A group of robes priced at $50 each will yield higher gross margin and net profit than if priced at $40. However, high prices can inhibit sales. The robes will not sell at $50 if customers perceive the price as high relative to competitors' prices or the quality of the robe. Customers resist even the most desirable assortments if not correctly priced.

After you have read this chapter, you will be able to discuss:

The intricacies of retail pricing.

The interrelationship of retail pricing components.

Promotional pricing.

The impact of pricing on an organization's sales and profitability.

What constitutes a "correct" retail price? In essence, a correct retail price is high enough to cover an organization's profit objectives, but low enough to stimulate customer purchase. The determination of retail price is an important merchandising function and the topic of Chapter 12.

MARKUP

Retail prices have two components: cost and markup. **Cost** is the portion of a retail price that is paid to the supplier. The terms *wholesale cost* and *wholesale price* are used synonymously with cost to refer to a supplier's price, even when a wholesaler is not involved in the transaction. **Markup,** or *markon,* is the amount added to cost to establish a retail price. The relationship between cost, markup, and retail price is such that:

$$retail\ price = cost + markup$$

When a retailer adds a $2 markup to an item purchased at a wholesale price of $6, the retail price is $8.

$$retail\ price = cost + markup$$
$$\$8 = \$6 + \$2$$

When any two elements of the formula are known, the third can be derived. When retail and cost are known:

$$markup = retail - cost$$
$$markup = \$8 - \$6$$
$$markup = \$2$$

When retail and markup are known:

$$cost = retail - markup$$
$$cost = \$8 - \$2$$
$$cost = \$6$$

Markup can be expressed as a percentage of cost or retail. The formula for expressing markup as a percentage of retail is:

$$markup\ percent = \frac{markup\ dollars}{retail\ price} \times 100$$

$$markup\ percent = \frac{\$2}{\$8} \times 100$$

$$markup\ percent = 25\%$$

The formula for expressing markup as a percentage of cost is:

$$markup\ percent = \frac{markup\ dollars}{cost} \times 100$$

$$markup\ percent = \frac{\$2}{\$6} \times 100$$

$$markup\ percent = 33\%$$

Thus, a $2 markup on an item priced at $8 can be expressed either as 25 percent or 33 percent.

Nonretailers are likely to view markup as a percentage of cost to keystoning, that is doubling an item's cost to establish a retail price, as a 100 percent markup. An item with a $5 cost that is retailed at $10 has a 100 percent markup when markup is expressed as a percentage of cost:

$$markup\ percent = \frac{markup\ dollars}{cost} \times 100$$

$$markup\ percent = \frac{\$5}{\$5} \times 100$$

$$markup\ percent = 100\%$$

Retailers view markup as a percentage of retail. The same item has a 50 percent markup when markup is expressed as a percentage of retail:

$$markup\ percent = \frac{markup\ dollars}{retail\ price} \times 100$$

$$markup\ percent = \frac{\$5}{\$10} \times 100$$

$$markup\ percent = 50\%$$

In retailing vernacular, markup as percentage of retail is always assumed unless otherwise specified. Subsequent references to markup in this textbook will assume markup as a percentage of retail.

WHY RETAILERS EXPRESS MARKUP
AS A PERCENTAGE OF RETAIL

By expressing markup as a percentage of retail, an infinite number of markup percentage possibilities is confined to a range of 0 to 100 percent.

Markup is 100 percent when there is no cost. For instance, when a retailer sells a vendor's sample for $20, the cost is $0 and markup is $20. Markup is 100 percent since

$$markup\ percent = \frac{markup}{retail} \times 100$$

$$markup\ percent = \frac{\$20}{\$20} \times 100$$

$$markup\ percent = 100\%$$

Markup is always 100 percent when cost is $0.

Markup is 0 percent when there is no markup. For instance, when a retailer prices a promotional item at cost, there is no markup. Markup is 0 percent since

$$markup\ percent = \frac{markup}{retail} \times 100$$

$$markup\ percent = \frac{\$0}{\$20} \times 100$$

$$markup\ percent = 0$$

Markup is always 0 when goods are sold at cost.

All other combinations of markup and retail will fall within this 0 to 100 percent range. Regardless of how large a dollar markup is, it can never be greater than 100 percent. Consider the antique dealer who buys a rare piece of Sandwich glass for $1 at a garage sale and resells it for $1000. In spite of the unusually high dollar markup, the markup percentage is still less than 100 percent when expressed as a percentage of retail:

$$markup\ percent = \frac{markup\ \$}{retail\ \$} \times 100$$

$$markup\ percent = \frac{\$999}{\$1000} \times 100$$

$$markup\ percent = 99.9\%$$

continued

Why Retailers Express Markup as a Percentage of Retail *continued*

Had the $999 markup been expressed as a percentage of cost, the resulting figure would be an unwieldy 99,900 percent.

$$markup\ percent = \frac{markup\ \$}{cost} \times 100$$

$$markup\ percent = \frac{\$999}{\$1} \times 100$$

$$markup\ percent = 99900\%$$

Though markup as a percentage of cost has a low end value of 0, its upper end value is limitless. Expressing markup as a percentage of retail confines markup to a manageable 0 to 100 percent range. This makes the concept of markup percentage more comprehensible, and simplifies the comparison of one markup percentage to another.

Another reason for expressing markup as a percentage of retail is that income statement components are stated as percentages of net sales. Since net sales represent retail prices, it makes sense to express markup percent proportionate to a retail value, since markup is frequently discussed in conjunction with income statement components.

When two components of the markup percent formula are known, the third can be derived. When markup percent and retail price are known, the formula can be solved for markup dollars:

$$markup\ percent = \frac{x}{retail\ price} \times 100$$

$$x = \frac{markup\ percent \times retail\ dollars}{100}$$

When markup percent and markup dollars are known, the formula can be solved for retail price:

$$markup\ percent = \frac{markup\ dollars}{x} \times 100$$

$$x = \frac{markup\ dollars}{markup\ percent} \times 100$$

	Department Stores		Specialty Stores	
Category	Median	Superior	Median	Superior
Female Apparel	53.1	54.8	55.1	57.9
Female Accessories	54.9	56.8	58.8	60.6
Men's and Boys' Apparel	52.7	54.8	54.9	59.6
Infants' and Children's Apparel	52.3	55.3	54.1	55.3
Footwear	51.8	53.0	52.4	55.8
Cosmetics	40.0	40.6	40.0	43.6
Leisure and Home Electronics	49.2	51.9	50.8	57.4
Home Furnishings	48.6	51.4	52.0	57.4
Other Hardlines	33.6	44.7	44.4	53.9
Other Merchandise	44.7	48.2	53.7	56.6
TOTAL	50.4	52.3	—	—

Figure 12.1a

Cumulative markup for department and specialty stores by category of merchandise.

Types of Markup

There are several types of markup including:

- initial markup
- cumulative markup
- additional markup

Initial Markup   An **initial markup** is the markup added to cost to establish the first price at which an item will be offered for sale, often called the **original price,** or *regular price.*

Additional Markup   An **additional markup** is added to an existing retail price, often to equate the retail prices of goods purchased at different costs. The following demonstrates a common application of additional markup: A men's store sells Jockey underwear at a 50 percent markup. Presently, packaged T-shirts purchased at a $5 cost are retailing at $10. A new shipment of T-shirts has just arrived at $5.25 per package, reflecting a manufacturer's price increase. To maintain a 50 percent markup, the new shipment will be retailed at $10.50 per package. To equate the retails on both the new and old goods, a $0.50 per unit additional markup is applied to the goods received prior to the manufacturer's price increase.

Category	% Initial Markup
Apparel	46.1%
Ladies'	49.0
Men's	45.0
Shoes	52.0
Girls'	50.0
Accessories	56.0
Infants'	40.0
Boys'	51.0
Housewares	34.3
Consumer Electronics	28.5
Domestics	41.8
Food (including Pet Food)	29.7
Health and Beauty Care	23.2
Toys	36.1
Pharmacy	N/A
Sporting Goods	36.6
Automotives	30.5
Stationery	44.3
Lawn and Garden	36.4
Paint/Hardware	39.8
Household Cleaners	20.9
Jewelry/Watches	58.7
Photography	23.0
RTA/Furniture	41.7
Cosmetics	34.2
Crafts	49.2

Figure 12.1b

Initial markup for full-line discounters by category of merchandise.

Category	% Initial Markup
Men's Clothing	
Men's Suits	55.6%
Men's Coats	55.1
Sport Coats	54.7
Dress Slacks	55.0
Total Men's Clothing	54.8
Men's Sportswear	
Sport Shirts	55.3
Sweaters	55.7
Activewear	55.1
Casual Slacks	54.6
Jeans	50.9
Jackets & Heavy Outerwear	55.5
Coordinated Leisurewear	52.6
Total Men's Sportswear	55.0
Men's Furnishings	
Dress Shirts	55.1
Neckwear	56.1
Hosiery	54.8
Men's Belts	55.0
Men's Accessories	54.0
Underwear	54.3
Sleepwear	55.0
Men's Headwear	54.0
Total Men's Furnishings	55.0

Figure 12.1c

Initial markup for men's specialty stores by category of merchandise.

An additional markup is expressed as a percentage of the retail onto which the markup is added:

$$additional\ markup\ percent = \frac{markup\ dollars}{present\ retail} \times 100$$

In the case of the T-shirts, the $0.50 added to the existing $10.00 retail, represents a 5 percent additional markup.

$$additional\ markup\ percent = \frac{\$\ 0.50}{\$10.00} \times 100$$

$$additional\ markup\ percent = 5\%$$

Cumulative Markup A **cumulative markup** is an aggregate markup on goods with varying markup. The cumulative markup is equal to the total markup dollars on all of the goods, divided by the sum of the retail prices of all of the goods, multiplied by 100.

$$cumulative\ markup = \frac{total\ markup\ dollars}{total\ retail\ dollars} \times 100$$

Assume that a men's wear buyer purchases 500 silk neckties from three vendors at three different wholesale prices: 100 at $9.25; 200 at $9.50; and 200 at $9.75. To facilitate presentation and signing, the buyer retails all of the ties at a single unit price of $20. The cumulative markup for the ties is computed as follows:

$$cumulative\ markup = \frac{total\ markup\ dollars}{total\ retail\ dollars} \times 100$$

$$cumulative\ markup = \frac{100(\$10.75) + 200(\$10.50) + 200(\$10.25)}{500(\$20)}$$

$$cumulative\ markup = \frac{\$5225}{\$10,000} \times 100$$

$$cumulative\ markup = 52.3\%$$

Note that a cumulative markup cannot be calculated by adding the individual markup percentages of each group of ties and dividing by three, since unequal units of each tie are involved. This erroneous calculation would have resulted in a cumulative markup of 52.5 percent, not 52.3 percent.

MARKDOWNS

Markdowns are downward adjustments in retail prices, often called *reductions.* Markdowns can be stated as either *dollars-off* a retail price, or as a *percent-off* a retail price. An ad that reads *"$10 Off Wool Sweaters"* reflects a dollars-off markdown. An ad that reads *"20% off Wool Sweaters"* reflects a percent-off markdown. Additional markups and markdowns are sometimes called *price changes.*

Markdowns are expressed as percentages of retail prices. The formula for computing a markdown percent is:

$$markdown\ percent = \frac{markdown\ dollars}{current\ retail\ price} \times 100$$

A $10 markdown on a $50 sweater is computed as follows:

$$markdown\ percent = \frac{\$10}{\$50} = \times 100$$

$$markdown\ percent = 20\%$$

An additional $10 markdown reducing the sweater to $30 can be stated as a percent-off markdown based on the current price of $40, or the new markdown can be combined with the previous markdown and expressed as a percent-off markdown of the original price:

$$markdown\ percent = \frac{total\ markdown\ dollars}{original\ retail\ price} \times 100$$

$$markdown\ percent = \frac{\$20}{\$50} \times 100$$

$$markdown\ percent = 40\%$$

Markdown dollars can be computed when a markdown percent and retail price are known by multiplying the retail price by the markdown percent.

markdown dollars = retail price × markdown percent (converted to a decimal)

A 30 percent markdown on a dress currently retailing at $80 is computed as follows:

$$markdown\ dollars = \$80 \times .30$$

$$markdown\ dollars = \$24$$

A new retail price is computed by subtracting the markdown dollars from the present retail.

marked down retail price *= present retail price − markdown dollars*

marked down retail price = $80 − $24

marked down retail price = $56

The total markdowns for a period within a unit of business, such as a department or category of merchandise, can be expressed as a percentage of net sales for the same period.

$$markdown\ percent\ for\ a\ period = \frac{total\ markdown\ dollars\ for\ the\ period}{net\ sales\ for\ the\ period} \times 100$$

If the total markdowns taken during August in a junior dress department are $50,000, and net sales for the month are $500,000, the markdown rate for August is computed as follows:

$$markdown\ rate = \frac{\$\ 50,000}{\$100,000} \times 100$$

$$markdown\ rate = 10\%$$

Types of Markdowns

Markdowns are categorized according to their purpose and/or the type of goods to which they are applied. The most common markdown categories are damages, employee discounts, promotional markdowns, and clearance markdowns.

Damages   Goods that are damaged after delivery are neither the vendor's nor the shipper's responsibility and cannot (or at least, should not) be returned for credit. Some retailers sell damaged goods to customers at marked down prices. A $100 dress with broken buttons reduced to an *as is* price of $75 is a good buy for a customer willing to spend a few dollars on a new set of buttons. Absorbing the $25 markdown may be less costly to the retailer in terms of time and effort than sending the garment out for repair. Damaged merchandise that is not salable, such as broken glassware, must be "marked out of stock" by a markdown to a zero retail. When damaged goods are disposed of without being marked out of stock, their retail value remains on the book, resulting in a shortage at the next physical inventory.

As a matter of policy, some retailers refuse to sell damaged goods to customers, feeling that the practice diminishes the store's reputation, and that customers might deliberately damage merchandise to drive down the price. These stores sometimes donate their damages to charity or conduct periodic sales of damaged merchandise for employees.

Figure 12.2

Promotional markdowns are temporary markdowns. Clearance markdowns are permanent.

Employee Discounts Employee discounts are special reductions on employee purchases and an employment benefit characteristic of the retail industry. Employee discounts usually range between 5 percent and 50 percent. Discounts vary relative to markup, which is why department stores typically offer higher employee discounts than discounters. Many retailers vary employee discounts by category or item relative to markup, offering high discounts on high markup goods, and low or no discount on low markup goods, such as sale merchandise. Generous employee discounts are typical of apparel retailers that hope to induce employees to wear their merchandise as a way of promoting it.

Promotional Markdowns Promotional markdowns are price reductions on merchandise featured in promotional events, commonly called *sales*. Promotional markdowns are called **temporary markdowns,** since the promotional goods are marked back up to regular price after the promotional event has ended. The duration of a promotion can range from a few hours, such as a *Midnight Madness Sale,* to several weeks, such as a semi-annual *White Sale* of bed, bath, table, and kitchen linens. To ensure the credibility of an event, it is important that promoted merchandise is not offered at promotional prices during nonpromotional periods.

WEEKLY MARKDOWN REPORT							
DEPT 149	CLASS	WTD POS MKDNS	WTD PERM/TEMP	WTD TOTALS	MTD POS MKDNS	MTD PERM/TEMP	MTD TOTALS
	1	1,177.2	.0	1,177.2	3,577.5	224.3	3,801.8
	2	259.4	.0	259.4	1,241.3	395.2	1,636.5
	3	107.1	.0	107.1	416.9	286.7	703.6
	4	351.7	.0	351.7	968.5	.0	968.5
	5	619.3	60.0	679.3	2,051.4	464.4	2,515.8
	6	306.9	.0	306.9	720.2	36.0	756.2
	7	824.8	.0	824.8	2,001.1	415.1	2,416.1
	8	.0	.0	.0	.0	30.0	30.0
	ALL	3,646.5	60.0	3,706.5	10,976.8	1,851.6	12,828.4

Figure 12.3

A sample of a report of temporary and permanent markdowns.

Clearance Markdowns   **Clearance markdowns** are price reductions that induce the sale of residual or slow-selling merchandise. Clearance markdowns are called **permanent** markdowns in that clearance goods do not return to a regular price, or any higher price, at a later date. Prices on clearance goods are reduced by subsequent additional markdowns until all of the merchandise has sold. A buyer of cold-weather accessories may take a 20 percent clearance markdown on gloves at the end of December. If the gloves do not sell out within a few weeks, the buyer will likely take additional markdowns of 35 percent, 50 percent, and eventually 75 percent off original prices until all of the gloves are sold.

RESIDUAL MERCHANDISE

Residual clearance goods fall into several categories, among them discontinued goods, seasonal merchandise, and broken assortments.

Discontinued Goods **Discontinued goods** can include a category of merchandise, a product line, or a single style, pattern, or color that will not be part of future assortments. A department store may discontinue a slow-selling cosmetics line. A women's specialty store may discontinue dresses to devote more space to sportswear. A manufacturer may

MARKDOWN REPORT

RUN DATE: 05/22/94
WEEK ENDING: 05/21/94
PAGE 89
INTIMATE APPAREL
CCN: 540 SLEEPWEAR

VENDOR NAME	SALES				PUR MU%	STOCK		MARKDOWNS	
	TY	LY	%CHG	%TOTL	STD	$	%TOTL	$	%SLS
PRIVATE LABEL	577.3	285.4	102.3	30.7	51.8	474.1	26.8	75.2	13.0
MISS ELAINE	271.8	133.6	103.5	14.5	53.2	233.3	13.2	54.9	20.2
CAROLE HOCHMAN	116.4	37.3	212.2	6.2	54.4	69.2	3.9	15.7	13.5
DAMEA	129.5	54.9	136.0	6.9	57.3	101.0	5.7	15.8	12.2
KOMAR	145.8	81.6	78.7	7.8	52.3	119.8	6.8	24.5	16.8
VAL MODE	155.8	138.4	12.5	8.3	53.9	223.8	12.6	48.1	30.9
AUGUST SILK	85.8	50.8	69.1	4.6	53.8	100.9	5.7	19.4	22.6
LANZ	74.5	75.3	−1.1	4.0	51.9	97.4	5.5	31.7	42.6
EILEEN WEST	78.6	60.0	31.0	4.2	53.8	74.3	4.2	23.2	29.5
NICOLE	26.3	47.3	−44.4	1.4	54.4	67.4	3.8	5.8	22.2
LORRAINE	19.9	15.2	30.9	1.1	56.1	72.2	4.1	6.1	30.4
NATORI	32.0	35.1	−8.9	1.7	53.9	40.6	2.3	10.9	34.0
CINEMA	48.0	66.5	−27.9	2.6	48.2	24.6	1.4	7.0	14.6
DONNKENNY	32.1	.0	.0	1.7	53.0	25.4	1.4	18.4	57.4
VANITY FAIR	15.9	62.3	−74.4	.9	41.2	8.0	.5	5.5	34.4
SARA BETH	12.3	35.9	−65.8	.7	60.0	15.9	.9	5.9	48.0
RELIABLE MILWAUKEE	1.4	.5	193.9	.1	−1.4	−.1	.1	3.9	
KATHERINE	16.4	9.0	81.4	.9	48.9	16.3	.9	9.8	59.8
BODY DRAMA	10.8	58.6	−81.5	.6		6.6	.4	7.7	71.5
JENNIFER SMITH	1.2	53.5	−97.8	.1		.8	.1	.7	56.6
HOST	7.2	.0	.0	.4		3.1	.2	6.7	92.8
CAL DYNASTY	2.2	60.5	−96.3	.1		2.9	.2	1.4	62.8
EVE STILLMAN	3.3	5.0	−33.5	.2		2.6	.2	1.6	47.7
DIOR	6.8	12.5	−45.6	.4	103.2	7.2	.4	3.7	54.4
ALL BREED & HARTLAN	1.4	15.7	−90.8	.1		2.4	.1	.5	35.9
GILLIGAN	.0	116.8	.0	.0		1.4	.1	.5	.0
UNIDENTIFIED OTHER	.0	3.3	.0	.0		−22.1	−1.3	.4	.0
P.M. STORIES	.0	1.7	.0	.0		.0	.0	.1	.0
EVA DALE	1.9	.0	.0	.1	79.3	3.6	.2	1.9	100.5
N A P	1.9	24.8	−92.4	.1	56.7	.6	.0	2.1	109.8
CHARACTER	.0	3.6	.0	.0		.0	.0	.0	.0
TOSCA	.0	21.5	.0	.0		.2	.0	.1	.0
GROUND CONTROL	.0	3.9	.0	.0		.0	.0	.0	.0
ROBERT LIEN	.0	4.2	.0	.0		.0	.0	.0	.0
L A INTIMATES	.0	7.2	.0	.0		.0	.0	.0	.0
ME AND MY PALS	.0	2.2	.0	.0		.0	.0	.0	.0
VALERIE JONES	.0	16.5	.0	.0		.0	.0	.1	.0
MISS DIOR	.0	13.4	.0	.0		.1	.0	.0	.0
OTHERS	2.3	1.3	73.4	.1		−1.1	−.1	.8	36.6
TOTAL	1878.7	1615.5	16.3	100.0	53.1	1772.4	100.0	406.4	21.6

Figure 12.4

A sample of a markdown report for a sleepwear department.

discontinue unpopular colors in an assortment of bath towels which, in turn, are discontinued by the retailers that carry them.

Seasonal Merchandise **Seasonal merchandise** is salable for a limited time period often defined by a calendar season or a holiday. Seasonal goods are marked down for clearance as their period of salability comes to a close. Velour shirts are marked down as the season for wearing warm clothing passes and customers begin to seek apparel for warmer weather. Examples of seasonal merchandise include swimwear, gloves, and Valentine's Day underwear.

Broken Assortments **Broken assortments** are residual items within groups or sets of related or coordinated merchandise that are sold individually. Items within sets or groups become candidates for clearance markdowns when assortments become "piecy." The remaining pieces of an Alfred Dunner jacket/blouse/skirt coordinate group are marked down when so few pieces of the group remain that it is no longer possible to coordinate an ensemble in any one size or color.

Slow Sellers

Slow sellers are goods that sell at slower rates-of-sale than anticipated. There are innumerable factors that can inhibit the rate at which goods sell. Some of the more common ones include:

Unseasonable Weather Weather that is atypical of a season affects the sale of seasonal goods such as boots, wool sweaters, patio furniture, and shorts. Buyers are often quick to blame poor sales on the weather, since weather is a variable beyond their control.

Wrong Assortments Most buyers are diligent in their efforts to choose assortments that will appeal to their target customers. However, the process is far from foolproof, and even the most carefully chosen assortments of items, brands, price points, sizes, styles, fabrics, and colors become slow sellers when customers determine that the hemlines are too short, the colors are garish, or the prices are too high.

Poor Presentation A sportswear group that is placed on a main aisle in one store may sell out in a week, while the same group remotely placed in the rear of a selling area in another store may not check a single piece in two weeks. Unfortunately, not all of the merchandise in a store can be presented in prime locations. However, the way in which goods are fixtured, faced, folded, hung, sized, or colorized can greatly enhance their rate of sale.

Late Delivery   Seasonal and trend-sensitive goods that arrive after their selling peak become slow sellers. Velvet special occasion dresses are salable for New Year's Eve celebrations. They are useless if they arrive on December 28. To avoid this dilemma, purchase orders include a *do not ship later than* date as an caution to vendors not to ship too late in the selling season.

Clearance markdowns induce the sale of even the slowest selling merchandise. The dress that a customer perceived as a *dog* at $200, becomes ever so attractive at $149.99. Though clearance markdowns are heaviest at the ends of selling seasons, most buyers regularly review inventories to edit slow sellers and broken assortments, which is why clearance racks or clearance sections have become ubiquitous in many retail stores. Clearance prices traditionally have a "9 ending," such as $29.99, indicated in red. It is wise to show the original price of clearance markdowns so that customers can appreciate the value of the markdown.

   In spite of their negative impact on gross margin, clearance markdowns are an important element in a buyer's effort to maintain clean assortments and to free up inventory dollars and fixtures for new goods. Clearance markdowns have a positive impact on turnover in that they decrease the value of inventory and induce sales. A buyer can be subject to as much criticism for taking too few clearance markdowns, as for taking too many.

MAINTAINED MARKUP

Maintained markup is the difference between the cost of merchandise and the actual retail selling price on the net markup that remains after markdowns and additional markups have been subtracted or added to an initial markup. The formula for maintained markup is:

maintained markup = initial markup + additional markups − markdowns

Since reductions are more likely to exceed additional markups, the formula is often stated:

$$maintained\ markup = initial\ markup - net\ markdowns$$

Gross margin can be derived from maintained markup by subtracting transportation and workroom costs, and adding cash discounts:

$$gross\ margin = maintained\ markup - transportation\ costs$$
$$- workroom\ costs + cash\ discounts$$

Therefore maintained markup is equal to gross margin before transportation and workroom costs and cash discounts are netted out or:

$$maintained\ markup = gross\ margin + transportation\ costs$$
$$+ workroom\ costs - cash\ discounts$$

Maintained markup and initial markup are equal when goods are sold at original price. Maintained markup and gross margin are equal when there are no transportation costs, workroom costs, or discounts, or when the net value of all three is zero.

Maintained markup is a convenient tool for evaluating the performance of merchandise in terms of its ability to sustain markup. Consider the following: A sportswear buyer purchased cotton sweaters from two resources. Group A was purchased at $20 per unit and initially retailed at $40. Of the 2000 sweaters in this group, 1500 sold at regular price. At the end of the season, the remaining 500 sweaters were marked down; 300 sold at a first markdown of $30; 150 sold at a further marked down price of $20, and the remaining 50 sold at a final markdown price of $10. Group B was purchased at a $17 per unit cost and initially retailed at $40 also. Of the 3000 sweaters in this group, 1200 sold at regular price. At the end of the season, the remaining 1800 sweaters were marked down; 800 sold at a first markdown of $30, 500 at a further marked down price of $20; the remaining 500 sold at a final markdown price of $10.

After all of the sweaters sold out the buyer computed the maintained markup *dollars* for each group of sweaters as reflected in Table 12.1. Table 12.2 reflects the computation of the maintained markup *percentage* for each group of sweaters.

Note that the initial markup of Group A was 50 percent, and that the initial markup of Group B was 57.5 percent. Subsequent markdowns eroded the initial markup of each group, resulting in an average maintained markup of 44.8 percent for Group A, and 41.4 percent for Group B. Though the initial markup of Group A was *lower* than the ini-

Table 12.1   **MAINTAINED MARKUP DOLLARS FOR TWO GROUPS OF SWEATERS**

Price	Group A				Group B			
	# Sold	Sale $	MU/Unit	Total MU$	# Sold	Sale $	MU/Unit	Total MU$
$40	1500	$60,000	$ 20	$30,000	1200	$48,000	$23	$27,600
$30	300	$ 9,000	$ 10	$ 3,000	800	$24,000	$13	$10,400
$20	150	$ 3,000	0	0	500	$10,000	$ 3	$ 1,500
$10	50	$ 500	–$ 10	–$ 500	500	$ 5,000	–$ 7	–$ 3,500
TOTAL	2,000	$72,500	$16.25	$32,500	3,000	$87,000	$12	$36,000

Table 12.2   **MAINTAINED MARKUP PERCENTAGES FOR TWO GROUPS OF SWEATERS**

	Group A	Group B
Total initial markup dollars	$40,000	$ 69,000
Total original retail dollars	$80,000	$100,000
Initial markup percent	50%	57.5%
Total maintained markup dollars	$32,500	$ 36,000
Total actual retail dollars	$72,500	$ 87,000
Maintained markup percent	44.8%	41.4%

tial markup of Group B, the maintained markup of Group A was *higher* than the maintained markup of Group B. Seventy-five percent of Group A (1500 of 2000 units) sold at the original $40 retail. Only 40 percent of Group B (1200 of 3000 units) sold at the original price of $40. Only 2.5 percent of Group A sold at a retail below cost, whereas over 16 percent of Group B sold below cost.

Though the buyer priced Group B at a higher initial markup than Group A hoping to yield a higher maintained markup, Group A sustained a higher markup over time. Customers resisted Group B's original $40 price point, but perceived the same price for Group A as a good value. Perhaps Group B would have sold better at an original price based on a more modest initial markup.

TACTICAL PRICE CHANGES

Tactical prices changes are strategic markups and markdowns that fall within a retail price zone defined at one end by a price with a standard markup, and at the other end a price with an inflated markup. A

Figure 12.5

A clearance ad for residual merchandise.

markup within the zone is called a **markdown cancellation.** A markdown within the zone is called a **markup cancellation.** The concept of tactical price changes is best explained by an example: A sales representative has offered a retail buyer a closeout price of $15 per pair on a popular pant style. The original wholesale price was $20. The buyer identifies this as a great promotional opportunity in that, at $15 a pair, the pants can be retailed at $29.99 and still yield the department's standard initial markup of 50 percent. The buyer wrote an order for the pants with instructions to the distribution center to book and ticket the goods at a $40 retail. The buyer plans to offer the pants at $40 for a few weeks before reducing them to $29.99 in order to validate the comparative price and to enhance customer perception of the promotional price as a real bargain.

The tactical retail price zone in this scenario is $29.99 at the low end, a point of normal markup, and $40 at the high end, an inflated retail price. Price changes within this zone are called markup cancellations and markdown cancellations. A price reduction from $40 to $29.99 is a markup cancellation, not a markdown, because the new price of $29.99 falls within the tactical price zone. A price increase from

$29.99 to $40 is a markdown cancellation, not a markup. Price changes to points lower than $29.99, are classified as markdowns.

Markup cancellations are unlike typical markdowns in that markdowns taken within the tactical zone are a reflection of a buyer's pricing strategy and not a result of poorly chosen assortments. Tracking markup cancellations and markdowns separately ensures that a buyer's performance isn't tainted by strategic planning. Not all retailers make a distinction between markdowns and markup cancellations, and markup and markdown cancellations, feeling that the effort to track them outweighs its worth. Also, there is difficulty in defining "normal" and "inflated" markup in many retail organizations.

MANAGING MARKDOWNS

Like sales and inventory, markdowns are planned and tracked over time by department and/or category of merchandise and markdown type. Last year's markdowns for the same time are used to project this year's markdowns since, like sales, markdowns fall into cyclical patterns. Markdown projections are also validated against industry standards for comparable markdowns. Markdowns are monitored throughout the season to ensure that actual markdowns do not exceed projections. Excessive markdowns may yield high sales due to the attractive prices of the reduced merchandise, however, gross margin and net income will be negatively affected.

DETERMINING AN INITIAL MARKUP PERCENTAGE

Buyers must price goods at an initial markup that will ensure final selling prices consistent with the organization's profit objectives. In essence, an initial markup must be high enough to cover transportation and workroom costs, less cash discounts, plus expenses and net profit, as well as any markdowns that will reduce the initial price to the final selling price. Like every retail markup, an initial markup is expressed as a percentage of a retail price. An initial markup is based on an initial retail price expressed as a final selling price, or net sales, plus the markdowns that will reduce the initial price to final selling price.

Category	Department Stores		Specialty Stores	
	Median	Superior	Median	Superior
Female Apparel	35.2	28.2	33.9	15.6
Female Accessories	18.2	14.1	26.1	14.3
Men's and Boys Apparel	27.9	20.6	21.4	8.8
Infants' and Children's Apparel	30.0	19.6	33.2	18.8
Footwear	26.8	19.2	20.0	10.9
Cosmetics	1.7	1.1	2.7	1.8
Leisure and Home Electronics	19.7	12.2	16.1	6.8
Home Furnishings	21.2	12.1	10.7	6.9
Other Hardlines	6.8	3.3	7.6	2.9
Other Merchandise	14.2	10.0	24.1	7.9
TOTAL	25.6	17.9	—	—

Figure 12.6a

Markdown percentages for department and specialty stores by category of merchandise.

Category	% Markdown
Men's Clothing	
Men's Suits	18.9%
Men's Coats	24.3
Sport Coats	22.5
Dress Slacks	13.3
Total Men's Clothing	19.2
Men's Sportswear	
Sport Shirts	20.9
Sweaters	24.2
Activewear	25.2
Casual Slacks	19.5
Jeans	8.4
Jackets & Heavy Outerwear	25.6
Coordinated Leisurewear	20.4
Total Men's Sportswear	21.7
Men's Furnishings	
Dress Shirts	12.8
Neckwear	11.9
Hosiery	6.0
Men's Belts	5.4
Men's Accessories	8.7
Underwear	5.3
Sleepwear	8.7
Men's Headwear	15.1
Total Men's Furnishings	10.8

Figure 12.6b

Markdown percentages for men's specialty stores by category of merchandise.

The formula for determining an initial markup percentage is:

initial markup % =

$$\frac{\substack{\textit{transportation costs} + \textit{workroom costs} \\ - \textit{cash discounts} + \textit{expenses} + \textit{profit} + \textit{markdowns}}}{\textit{net sales} + \textit{markdowns}} \times 100$$

Recall from Chapter 10 that *gross margin = expenses + profit.* Thus, the above formula can be simplified by substituting gross margin for expenses and profit:

initial markup % =

$$\frac{\substack{\textit{transportation costs} + \textit{workroom costs} \\ - \textit{cash discounts} + \textit{gross margin} + \textit{markdowns}}}{\textit{net sales} + \textit{reductions}} \times 100$$

Recall that *maintained markup = gross margin + transportation costs + workroom costs − cash discounts.* The formula can be further simplified by substituting maintained markup for transportation costs, workroom costs, cash discounts, and gross margin.

$$\textit{initial markup \%} = \frac{\textit{maintained markup} + \textit{markdowns}}{\textit{net sales} + \textit{reductions}} \times 100$$

In general, high figures in the numerator of the initial markup formula will yield a high initial markup percentage, while low figures will yield a low percentage. For instance, a high initial markup is required for goods with:

- *High markdowns.* An apparel department requires a higher initial markup to achieve the same maintained markup as the cosmetics department because of the apparel department's high clearance markdown rate. Reductions are virtually nonexistent in the cosmetics department where damages and residual merchandise, such as unsold holiday gift sets, are returned to vendors for credit.
- *High freight costs.* Bulky items, such as furniture, necessitate a high initial markup to cover high transportation costs.
- *High workroom costs.* A bridal shop that offers free alterations requires a higher initial markup to achieve the same maintained markup as a dress shop. The workroom costs for turning a hem on very full, multitiered wedding dresses are considerably greater than the workroom costs for turning hems on straight skirts.
- *High direct expenses.* Direct expenses can include commissions or

specialized supplies, such as velvet jewelry boxes. Wal-Mart abandoned its small pet business because of high direct expenses. Though birds, hamsters, and gerbils had the same initial markup as tropical fish, the cost of feeding and caring for a small animal completely erodes its markup if the animal isn't sold within two weeks.[1]

The following demonstrates the calculation of an initial markup percentage:

A shoe buyer's maintained markup objective for a season is 40 percent. The buyer anticipates seasonal markdowns of 20 percent. An initial markup for the season is calculated as follows:

$$initial\ markup\ \% = \frac{maintained\ markup + markdowns}{net\ sales + markdowns} \times 100$$

$$initial\ markup\ \% = \frac{40\% + 20\%}{100\%^2 + 20\%} \times 100$$

$$initial\ markup\ \% = \frac{0.40 + 0.20}{1.00 + 0.20} \times 100$$

$$initial\ markup\ \% = \frac{0.6}{1.2} \times 100$$

$$initial\ markup\ \% = 0.5 \times 100$$

$$initial\ markup\ \% = 50\%$$

Thus, a buyer who anticipates a 20 percent markdown rate for the season must price goods at an initial markup of 50 percent to maintain a 40 percent markup. Though the above formula is preferable because of its simplicity, any of the formulas from which it was derived may be used to calculate an initial markup. Either dollars or percentages can be used in the computation.

Computing a Retail Price Based on a Percentage Markup Objective

A retail price can be computed when an initial markup percentage and cost are known by dividing the cost by the **cost complement,** the difference between the desired initial markup percentage and 100 percent expressed as a decimal.

$$retail\ price = \frac{cost}{100\% - initial\ markup\ \%}$$

Assume that a buyer sees an interesting item at a trade show priced at $12.50. The buyer needs to retail goods at a 55 percent initial markup to achieve a desired maintained markup for the department. The buyer calculates the retail price of the $12.50 item at a 55 percent markup as follows:

$$retail\ price = \frac{cost}{100\% - initial\ markup\ \%}$$

$$retail\ price = \frac{\$12.50}{1.00 - 0.55}$$

$$retail\ price = \frac{\$12.50}{0.45}$$

$$retail\ price = \$27.78$$

The retail price of a $12.50 item at a 55 percent markup is $27.78. For the sake of simplicity and a little extra markup, odd-ending prices are typically rounded up to the nearest 0-ending price ($27.80), or whole dollar price ($28.00).

PROMOTIONAL PRICING

A promotional price is a discounted price that is less than a conventional or regular price. Once the hallmark of discounters, promotional pricing has become an important element in the merchandising strategies of many department and specialty stores. Promotional pricing is often linked to one of the advertised events discussed in Chapter 5.

Retailers conduct price promotions for several reasons:

- To generate customer traffic
- To stimulate sales during a slow selling period
- To induce the sale of related nonpromotional merchandise
- To engage in competitive pricing with other retailers
- To establish an image as a value-oriented retailer

All price changes require book inventory adjustments to maintain the balance between book and physical inventory values. Because promotional prices are temporary, they require two adjustments: markdowns at the beginning of a promotion, and markups at the end of a promotion. Computerized **price lookup** (PLU) technology has facilitated this process. PLU involves maintaining a system file of every

---

PRICE WARS

In the 1940s, there were frequent price wars between New York's historic department stores, Macy's and Gimbels. Both stores sold Modern Library Books with a MSRP of 95 cents for 79 cents. When Gimbels undercut Macy's already low price, Macy's reacted by undercutting Gimbels' price. To meet the demand for the books at these exceptionally low prices, Macy's replenished its inventory by sending employees across the street to buy Gimbels' books. Macy's stamped its newly acquired stock with a red star, and then retailed the books at a price lower than Gimbels'. By the end of the day, the price of Modern Library Books was at an all time low of 45 cents, and every book in Gimbels' inventory had a Macy's star because Gimbels had sent its employees to Macy's to buy back the books.

Kahn, Robert. (January 1992). Toys "R" Us and the Chapter 11 story. Chain Store Age Executive. p. 14.

stock keeping unit in inventory and a corresponding retail price. When the sku is identified at point-of-sale by a number or bar code, the system "looks up" the price and transmits it to a cash register display or monitor while processing the transaction at the looked up price. The prices in the file can be changed to promotional prices for promotional events eliminating the need for a physical count of inventory before or after the promotion. Preparing for an event merely involves identifying promoted merchandise with the appropriate percentage-off or dollar-off signage indicating that the reduction will be taken at the register. This permits retailers to increase the frequency of promotions by reducing the stock-handling costs associated with event preparation and recovery. A PLU system also allows more rigid price control by preventing salespeople from discounting nonpromotional items.[3,4]

Everyday Low Pricing

Though promotional events produce immediate sales results, their long-term effect is questionable. Frequent promotions encourage customers to wait for sales and to buy only at promotional prices. This can be devastating to gross margin and net income since promotional goods carry lower markup. An intense promotional schedule may also cause customers to question the "real" price of goods, assuming that retailers cover promotional markdowns with inflated markups.

Everyday low pricing (EDLP) is a value-oriented pricing strategy involving continuous promotional pricing without the support of advertised events. Everyday low prices are either a retailer's lowest promotional price, or a price between the retailer's highest regular price and lowest promotional price. EDLP facilitates inventory management since product demand is more stable when not driven by sporadic sales. The lower gross margins assisted with EDLP strategy are often offset by reduced advertising expenses, as well as reduced labor expenses since fewer floor moves are required for sale setup and recovery. EDLP is a shopping advantage for customers too busy to chase promotions.

EDLP is fundamental to the warehouse club concept and to the success of discounters such as Wal-Mart and Toys "R" Us, both of which have employed an EDLP strategy since their inception.[5] However, EDLP has not been successful for every retailer. In 1989, Sears closed all of its stores for forty-two hours to retag every piece of merchandise with permanently reduced prices. A year later, Sears abandoned EDLP because sales increases were not significant enough to offset the decreases in gross margin.[6,7] Feeling that their customers enjoy the excitement of promotional events, Target combines its EDLP *Great Buy* program with advertised promotions.[8]

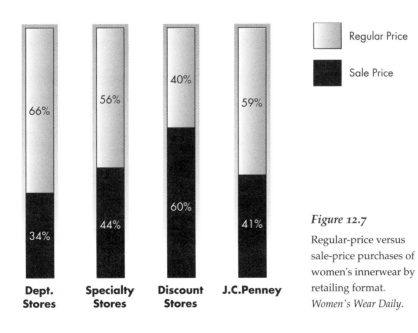

Figure 12.7

Regular-price versus sale-price purchases of women's innerwear by retailing format.
Women's Wear Daily.

DECEPTIVE PRICING

The Federal Trade Commission is a regulatory agency that prevents unfair competition in the marketplace by protecting consumers from abuses such as constraint of trade and deceptive advertising. The FTC issues guidelines that prescribe standards of conduct for various industry segments, including retailers. In addition to FTC guidelines, each state has specific statutes that govern retail trade practices. Because laws vary by state, retailers that conduct business in several states often ensure compliance to the statutes in all states by conforming to the guidelines of the most stringent state. To avoid embarrassment and/or penalty, retailers should be familiar with topics governed by various forms of protective legislation.

Regular Price Comparisons   A stated reduction from an original or regular price is a common form of price promotion. However, the strategy is legitimate only if the promoted items are offered at regular price for a sufficient period of time. That "sufficient period of time" varies by state.[9] One state attorney general's office offers the following guidelines for determining the legitimacy of a regular price comparison:

- That at least 25 percent of the goods were sold at the regular price during the previous six months, or
- That the goods were offered at the regular price for at least 70 percent of the time during the previous six months. This allows approxi-

Figure 12.8

A SLAP ON THE WRIST

The National Advertising Division of the Council of Better Business Bureaus found Montgomery Ward guilty of deceptive pricing practices for advertising a pair of diamond earrings regularly priced at $1199 at a 67 percent markdown price of $399. NAD found that Ward's never sold the jewelry at regular price, even though the earrings were offered at regular price for 186 days out of 365 days. Despite Ward's good faith efforts to sell the jewelry at the regular price, NAD determined that advertising a regular price four times the sale price is unrealistic and has the potential of confusing the customer as to the actual value of the jewelry.

Kahn, Robert. (September 1993). Better business bureau challenges Ward's jewelry ads. Retailing Today.

mately fifty-five promotional days in a six-month period, or ten promotional days a month.

A nonpromotional price should be affected within a reasonable amount of time after a promotion has ended, and should be maintained for a sufficient amount of time thereafter. One state attorney general's office recommends affecting the regular price within sixty days after the end of a promotion, and maintaining the regular price for a minimum of ninety days.

If criteria such as these are not met, it may be determined that a promotional price is, in fact, the regular price, and that promoting the goods as a "sale" is a deceptive practice.

In 1992, a Colorado appeals court upheld the State Attorney General's allegations that advertising by May Department Stores was deceptive and that the company had no intention of selling some of its advertised goods at regular price.

Regular price comparisons should be genuine and not based on exaggerated prices. A retailer should not cushion high promotional markdowns with an excessively high initial markup that exceeds the initial markup customarily taken on the item or merchandise category.

Comparisons to Competitors' Prices Price comparisons to competitors' offerings must be for identical merchandise. Comparing one style or grade of merchandise to another style or grade is deceptive. Champion Reverse Weave sweatshirts are 100 percent cotton and heavier than

Figure 12.9

Retailers sometimes offer customers free merchandise on condition of purchase.

Champion's lower grade 95 percent cotton lightweight *Classic Fleece* sweatshirt. Comparing the price of a *Classic Fleece* sweatshirt to a competitor's *Reverse Weave* sweatshirt is an invalid and deceptive comparison.

Lowest Price A retailer must validate a *lowest price* claim with proof of the customary prices of competitors, a difficult substantiation when competitors have frequent price promotions. Wal-Mart's claim of "Always a low price," avoids the use of the superlative "lowest" for this reason.

Free Merchandise Retailers sometimes offer customers free merchandise, frequently on condition of a purchase. Advertising for this type of promotion often reads:

- "Buy one, get one free"
- "1 cent sale"
- "2 for 1 sale"
- "Gift with purchase"

In general, the offer of free merchandise must be temporary, otherwise the "gift" becomes part of the retailer's everyday offerings. Also, raising the regular price of the required purchase to cover the cost of the free merchandise is a deceptive practice.

Going Out of Business A company should not be established with the intent of going out of business to have a liquidation sale. Many states ensure adherence to this principle by requiring that a business operate for a minimum time period, such as a year, before conducting a going out of business sale (GOB).

GOB must be validated by a planned cessation of business. The sale inventory should not be salted with lower quality goods at higher than normal markup that appears to be part of the regular inventory. States ensure adherence to this guideline by requiring a complete list of inventory on hand at the point at which a going out of business notice is filed.

Bait and Switch Promoting an item as *bait* to lure customers into a store to sell them a higher margin item is illegal. Retailers guilty of **bait and switch** have even penalized salespeople who sold the advertised merchandise instead of a substitute. To avoid bait and switch implications, retailers should have a sufficient quantity of advertised promotional merchandise on hand to meet anticipated demand, unless the advertisement discloses the number of items available, or states "while supply lasts." A key factor in determining the existence of bait and switch is the number of times that an item was advertised, compared to the number of times it was actually sold.

The Raincheck Rule The Federal Trade Commission's *Unavailability Rule* or *Raincheck Rule* is a guide for handling cases of out of stock advertised merchandise. The guide suggests that retailers:

- Issue a **raincheck** that will allow customers to buy the advertised merchandise at a later date at the sale price;
- Offer substitute merchandise of comparable value to the promoted item;
- Offer a compensation that is at least equal in value to the reduction on the promoted merchandise.

Predatory Pricing Some states have anti-trust laws that prohibit **predatory pricing,** a low-pricing strategy designed to put competitors out of business.[10] Small independent retailers claim that large retailers engage in predatory pricing when they sell **loss leaders,** goods priced

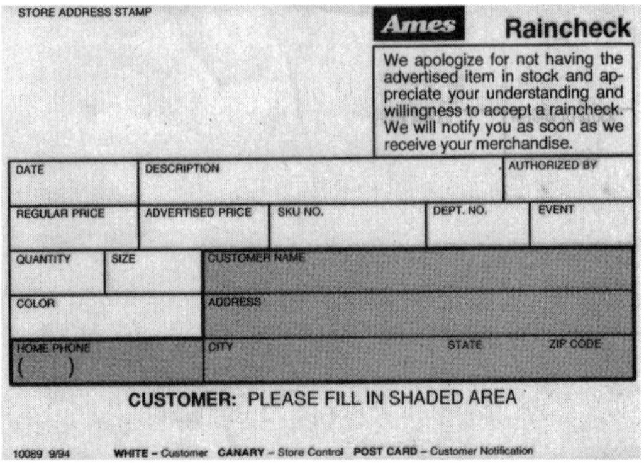
STORE ADDRESS STAMP

Ames Raincheck

We apologize for not having the advertised item in stock and appreciate your understanding and willingness to accept a raincheck. We will notify you as soon as we receive your merchandise.

DATE	DESCRIPTION			AUTHORIZED BY
REGULAR PRICE	ADVERTISED PRICE	SKU NO.	DEPT. NO.	EVENT
QUANTITY	SIZE	CUSTOMER NAME		
COLOR		ADDRESS		
HOME PHONE ( )		CITY	STATE	ZIP CODE

CUSTOMER: PLEASE FILL IN SHADED AREA

10089 9/94 WHITE - Customer CANARY - Store Control POST CARD - Customer Notification

Figure 12.10

A raincheck allows a customer to buy out-of-stock advertised merchandise at sale price at a later date.

below cost. Volume discounts enable large retailers to sell an item at a price that is often lower than the wholesale price charged the small retailer. In 1993, Wal-Mart was found guilty of violating the Arkansas Unfair Practice Act and ordered to pay nearly $300,000 in punitive damages to three Arkansas pharmacies for selling some 200 items ranging from prescription drugs to cosmetics below cost.[11]

RESALE PRICE MAINTENANCE

Resale price maintenance (RPM), or vertical price fixing, is the practice whereby producers enforce the sale of their products at prescribed **manufacturer's suggested retail prices** (MSRP). The Miller Tidings Act (1936) permitted the practice of *fair trade* to insulate small independent retailers from price competition with large chains that paid lower wholesale prices because of quantity discounts. Fair trade allegedly sheltered the image of a product in that a consumer's perception of a product's quality is often tied to its retail price. Fair trade was highly criticized by discounters and consumer advocacy groups as a form of price fixing and a violation of the Sherman Antitrust Act of 1890 which prohibits constraint of trade. In 1975, the Consumer Goods Pricing Act made RPM and fair trade illegal.[12,13]

However, the definition of *price fixing* is ambiguous, leading some to conclude that certain industry practices constitute illegal acts. A manufacturer can choose to channel its products to retailers on the basis of service, training, warranties, and repair and thus refuse to sell to discounters that offer limited service.[14] Upon the complaint of a retailer that a competitor is failing to maintain suggested price levels, a supplier can cut shipment to the price cutter, as long as the supplier does not coerce the discounter to sell at a suggested price. Producers can also structure their cooperative advertisement agreements around a **minimum advertised price** (MAP) to make retailers that sell below the MAP ineligible for cooperative advertising dollars.

The most aggressive opponents of RPM are discount retailers who claim that RPM is contrary to the free market system, and that consumers have the right to buy products at competitive prices through multiple retail channels. Manufacturers of prestige products support RPM because they fear that their products will lose their cachet in consumers' eyes if discounted by mass merchandisers. These suppliers fear that the conventional retail channels will discontinue their product lines sooner than engage in price competition with discounters.

Supreme Court rulings and prevailing political climates have influenced the enforcement of price-fixing legislation by the Justice Department's Antitrust Division and the Federal Trade Commission's Bureau of Competition.[15,16] In 1993, the Stride Rite Corporation paid $7.2 million in damages to settle a price-fixing suit brought by the attorneys general of fifty states and the Federal Trade Commission. Stride Rite had threatened to stop supplying its most popular Keds sneaker styles to retailers that discounted prices. The company was found guilty of price conspiracy when it encouraged retailers to report competitors' price cutting.[17,18] In 1995, Reebok International paid a $9.5 million settlement for threatening to terminate shipment to retailers that violated Reebok's pricing policy.[19]

PRICING: A SCIENCE AND AN ART

Pricing has been called a science and an art. As a science, price is a quantitative decision based on the numeric relationships among various pricing components. As an art, price is a qualitative decision based on intuition and creativity.[20] The following two scenarios demonstrate the nonquantitive considerations that surround pricing decisions.

Right Price, Wrong Customer   A men's wear buyer came across a well-styled and constructed, nicely fabricated dress shirt during a market visit. The buyer perceived the shirt as an exceptionally good value at

SCENES FROM A MALL

"Excuse me, but do you have this sweater in navy?"

"I'll check. Yes, here it is. A medium navy. Do you want to try it on?"

"Ummm...this is $49?"

"No, that bottom price on the tag is what you'd pay in a big department store..."

"Isn't this a big department store?"

"Well, I guess. But it's what you'd pay in another big department store."

"I see. And what's this $39.95?"

"Oh, that was our original price."

"And this $26.50?"

"That's our first markdown."

"So the sweater's $26.50?"

"No, it looks to me...yes, here it is: This scribble up in the corner of the tag—it was marked down again to $19.95."

"Nineteen ninety five? That's not bad. I saw one of these in a catalog for 36 bucks."

"Oh, but it's not $19.95. See the sign? Today only, take another 25 percent off all previously markeddown merchandise."

"So that would come to..."

"Just a sec and I'll grab my calculator. Let's see, that would be $19.95, less $4.98, or $14.97."

"Uh oh, you know I don't think I have that much cash on me and I just thought: I don't have a credit card for this store."

"Do you have American Express?"

"I'm afraid not."

"Well, this would be an excellent time to sign up. If you get a new American Express card and charge something here at the mall this month, they'll take 10 percent off the purchase when your bill comes in. Didn't you see the signs?"

"Uh, no. Say, is that 10 percent off after the 25 percent?"

"Sure is. Oh, and if you have any Bonus Bucks..."

"Bonus Bucks?"

"Yeah, they ran a whole page of coupons in the paper this week— you cut one out and bring it in and you get $5 off any purchase over $10."

Donlon, Barbara. The Boston Herald's Sunday Magazine.

continued

Scenes from a Mall *continued*

"So with the American Express and the Bonus Bucks…"

"Let's see, that would be $14.97, less the 10 percent, or $1.49, so that would come out to $13.48, minus your $5 Bonus Buck—I can run over to CVS and buy a paper and tear one out for you if you want—we're talking $8.48 for the sweater. And listen, I probably shouldn't be telling you this, but if you wait four hours, it'll be even less."

"Less than $8.48?"

"Yeah, well, it's 8 p.m. now, and in four more hours, our Midnite Madness sale starts—20 percent off everything in the store. Everything. Till 6 a.m., that is."

"What happens a 6 a.m.?"

"Our One Day Only PreInventory Sale."

"And that's…"

"My gosh, that would come out to…"

"Eight forty eight, less 50 percent. Let's see, that would give you a total of $4.24."

"But that's only tomorrow."

"That's right. But listen, if you've got a prior engagement, not to worry. Just come back Monday."

"What's Monday?"

"Our Red Tag Sale."

"Don't tell me. Everything with a red tag…"

"Five dollars off anything marked $40 or less. Anything over $40 would be $10 off."

"Uh, let me see if I've got this: $4.24 less $5… the way I figure it, on Monday I get the sweater for nothing and you give me 76 cents change?"

"Two sweaters."

"Two sweaters?"

"Don't you follow our ads? Monday is also Buy One Get One Free Day. Buy a pair of Levi's, get the second one free… buy one sweater, get the second one…"

"I get it, I get it. Look, I've got to admit this sounds like a great deal. But unfortunately I've got a dentist appointment on Monday."

"That's too bad. But listen, if you're free on Tuesday, I'd make it a point to stop by. Doors open at 7 a.m."

"For…"

"Our Going Out of Business Sale."

$20 per unit, but realized that the shirt needed to be priced at a $45 retail to meet the department's maintained markup objective. Because the store's customers have historically resisted shirts priced higher than $35, the buyer is faced with a dilemma. If the shirts are retailed at $40, they are not likely to sell because of price resistance. If the shirts are retailed at $35, they are likely to sell, but the department's maintained markup expectations will not be met.

The decision is clear. The buyer must pass up the shirts and continue the quest for goods at a cost that will allow a retail price consistent with customers' price expectations, and the store's profit objectives.

No Easy Answer   A buyer has computed an initial markup percentage objective for the handbag department, but realizes that the figure is not an immediate answer to every pricing decision. Factors relative to the type of goods, accepted pricing standards, and competition, bear considerable weight on the pricing of individual classes or items as the following considerations for pricing four groups of handbags demonstrates. The four groups are Dooney & Bourke, a seasonal straw and canvas group, a private label group, and an assortment of handcrafted novelty evening bags.

Figure 12.11

Daffy's is positioned as a price leader in the greater New York metropolitan area. *DeVito/Verdi.*

- The pricing of Dooney & Bourke is restricted by the fact that the prestigious line is heavily branded and sold by other stores in the shopping center.
- The prices for the seasonal bags must include a generous provision for seasonal markdowns.
- The private label goods afford considerable pricing flexibility and healthy markup opportunity since customers have no basis for price comparisons.
- Similarly, hand-crafted evening bags afford considerable pricing latitude as **blind items,** goods for which consumers have no frame of reference because of the absence of brand identity and/or infrequent purchase.

SUMMARY POINTS

- Retail prices must be high enough to cover profit objectives, but low enough to stimulate customer purchase.
- A retail price has two components: cost and markup. Markup is expressed as a percentage of the retail price.
- The various types of markup include initial markup, additional markup, and cumulative markup.
- Markdowns are downward adjustments in retail prices. Four categories of reductions include damaged merchandise, employee discounts, clearance markdowns, and promotional markdowns.
- Clearance markdowns are permanent reductions used to liquidate residual merchandise and slow sellers.
- Maintained markup is the difference between the cost of merchandise and the actual selling price.
- Tactical price changes involve a strategy for manipulating markup and markdown within a tactical price zone.
- A retail price can be computed when a desired markup and cost are known.
- Promotional markdowns are temporary reductions for sale events.
- Everyday low pricing is a value-oriented pricing strategy that eliminates the need for extensive promotional advertising.
- Each state has guidelines for valid price referencing to avoid deceptive pricing.
- Resale price maintenance (RPM) is the control of retail prices by a supplier. Under certain circumstances RPM is illegal.

KEY TERMS AND CONCEPTS

additional markup	fair trade	price lookup (PLU)
bait and switch	initial markup	promotional markdown
blind item	loss leader	raincheck
broken assortment	maintained markup	regular price
clearance markdown	manufacturer's	resale price maintenance
cost	suggested retail price	(RPM)
cost complement	markdown	retail price
cumulative markup	markdown cancellation	seasonal merchandise
damaged merchandise	markup	tactical price change
discontinued	markup cancellation	temporary markdown
merchandise	minium advertised price	
employee discount	(MAP)	
everyday low pricing	permanent markdown	

FOR DISCUSSION

1. Give examples of goods that have the potential to become "residual" or "slow-selling" and vulnerable to clearance markdowns. What can be done to minimize the clearance markdowns taken on these goods?

2. A hosiery buyer is writing orders for two groups of cotton socks. One group is an assortment of basic colors. The other group is a holiday assortment with Christmas tree and snowman motifs. The buyer wants to generate the same maintained markup percentage from each group. Which group will require a higher initial markup and why?

3. A furniture retailer operates stores in California, Maine, and Georgia. Most of the retailer's resources ship from High Point, NC. Which stores will require the highest markup if the retailer wants to generate equal maintained markup from all stores? What workroom costs might have to be considered in the computation of initial markup?

4. Compare the promotional pricing strategies of several retailers within different retail formats. What differences/similarities do you note in terms of promotion frequency, advertising vehicles, and the types of merchandise promoted? Compare the promotional pricing strategies of several retailers within the same format. What differences/similarities do you note?

PROBLEMS

1. A sportswear buyer needs to maintain a 50 percent markup. Markdowns are projected at 25 percent. What should initial markup be?

2. What is maintained markup when:
   - gross margin is $50,000
   - workroom costs are $2,000
   - cash discounts are $3,000

4. Cost is $8, retail is $12. What is markup as a percentage of cost? As a percentage of retail?

5. Give an example of a 99 percent markup (as a percentage of retail). Give an example of a 1 percent markup.

6. What is the markdown price of a $20 item that has been marked down 35 percent. What is the price when an additional 20 percent markdown is taken?

ENDNOTES

1. Halverson, Richard. (August 15, 1994). Wal-Mart's live pet biz: Bye-bye birdie. *Discount Store News.* pp. 3, 100.

2. As the denominator upon which income statement percentages are computed, net sales represents 100 percent.

3. Robbins, Gary. (February 1991). New POS power at Talbots. *Stores.* pp. 44–47.

4. Staff. (December 1990). Beyond the challenge: Strawbridge & Clothier builds PLU department. *Chain Store Age Executive.* pp. 86–89.

5. Weiner, Steve. (February 20, 1989). Price is the object. *Forbes.* pp. 123–124.

6. Tyner, Joan. (January 15, 1990). Sears tires return to sales, promotions. *Nashville Banner.*

7. Reda Susan. (October 1994). Is E.D.L.P. coming up S.H.O.R.T.? *Stores.* pp. 22–26.

8. Urbonya, Tim. (December 4, 1989). Target takes aim with "everyday" prices. (Minneapolis/St. Paul) *Citybusiness.*

9. Farhi, Paul. (June 20, 1993). The everlasting sale. *Washington Post.*

10. Ramey, Joanna. (September 11, 1993). Smart strategy or unfair pricing? *Women's Wear Daily.* p. 14.

11. Brookman, Faye. (October 22, 1993). Rivals don't see Wal-Mart easing its price cutting. *Women's Wear Daily.* pp. 1, 7.

12. Rankin, Ken. (May 7, 1990). RPM bill sails through House; Still faces rough seas in Senate. *Discount Store News.* pp. 5, 202.

13. Verdisco, Robert. (March 15, 1993). Enforce the law against retail price-fixing. *Discount Store News.* p. 12.

14. Gannon, Virginia. (May 10, 1991). Price maintenance bill approved by Senate. *Daily News Record.* p. 8.

15. Rankin, Ken. (May 7, 1990). Bush may still veto RPM. *Discount Store News.* p. 10.

16. Rosenberg, Arnie. (May 1, 1991). Retail "price-fixing" is target of proposal. *Aftermarket Business.* pp. 1, 11.

17. Staff. (September 28, 1993). Keds to pay to settle suits. *New York Times.* p. D7.

18. Pereira, Joseph. (September 28, 1993). Stride Rite agrees to settle charges it tried to force pricing by retailers. *Wall Street Journal.* p. A5.

19. Ramey, Joanna. (May 15, 1995). Reebok pays to settle price-fixing lawsuit. *Women's Wear Daily.* p. 9.

20. Verdi, Ellis. (May 15, 1995). Mingling the price message with a quality image. *Discount Store News.* p. 71.

chapter thirteen

PLANNING SALES AND INVENTORY

Planning involves establishing an organization's goals or objectives and strategies
to achieve them. The planning process often
includes **forecasting,** the attempt to predict
trends or outcomes. Planning occurs at all
organizational levels and is critical to a company's success. The absence of planning has
been likened to taking a trip without a road
map. Chapter 13 covers sales planning and
inventory planning, two planning functions
that are germane to the merchandising function of a retail organization.

After you have read this chapter, you will be able to discuss:

The importance of planning in a retail organization.

Sales planning and the relevance of sales plans to other organizational plans.

Inventory planning methods.

Assortment planning.

Resources of information for planning decisions.

TYPES OF PLANS

Plans are categorized by the time period that they cover. A **long-range plan** covers a three-to-five-year period or longer. Developed by top management, long-range plans have significant impact on an organization and include strategies for expansion, market position, and major capital expenditures. A **short-term plan** covers periods shorter than a year. Developed by lower-level managers, short-term plans are narrower in scope than long-range plans. Schedules and budgets are two common forms of short-term plans.

Plans are categorized by their point of origin and the direction that they travel within a table of organization. **Top-down plans** originate at the upper levels of an organization and impact planning at lower levels. When the top management of a retail organization projects a corporate sales objective for the forthcoming year, the plan is then apportioned by merchandise division. Sales plans are then derived for each department. Buyers and planners then determine the categories, vendors, and items that will best support departmental sales plans and ultimately, the organization's sales goal.

Bottom-up plans are developed at lower levels of the organization as building blocks of an organization-wide plan. An organizational sales objective based on the sum total of plans developed at departmental level would reflect bottom-up planning. Most organizations combine top-down and bottom-up planning, recognizing that planning is a two-way street that requires input at every managerial level.[1]

THE 4-5-4 PLANNING CALENDAR

The **4-5-4 calendar** is an accounting calendar used by retailers to structure their fiscal year. The calendar is called *4-5-4* because each month has exactly *four* weeks (28 days), or *five* weeks (35 days) chronologically arranged in a *4-5-4* sequence. Four months have five weeks: March, June, September, and December. The remaining eight months have four weeks. The beginnings and ends of months on the 4-5-4 calendar do not coincide with the beginnings and ends of the same month on a conventional Gregorian calendar. Note that in Figure 13.1, June begins on May 28 and ends on July 1.

The weeks of a month on the 4-5-4 calendar are referred to ordinally. In Figure 13.1, April 2 through April 8 is *the first week of April,* or

MAY   4-5-4 ACCOUNTING CALENDAR   1995

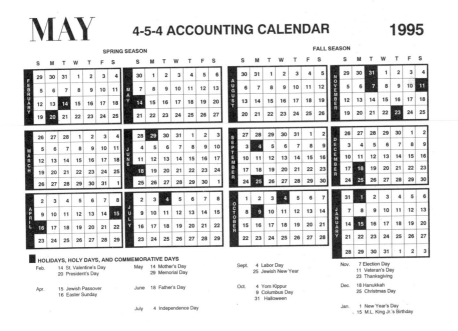

Figure 13.1

The 4-5-4 calendar is an accounting calendar used by retailers to structure their fiscal year.

Week 1 of April. The calendar has two six-month seasons: **spring,** which runs from February through July, and **fall,** which runs from August through January. The year has 364 days and exactly 52 weeks, versus the Gregorian calendar that has 365 days and 52 weeks and a day. An additional week is added to January in the 4-5-4 calendar every five or six years to accrue this extra day and the 366th day of leap years. The nearly universal adoption of the 4-5-4 calendar has enhanced communication within the retailing and related industries.

MERCHANDISING PLANNING STRUCTURES

To facilitate the planning and tracking of sales and inventory, retailers define groups of related merchandise as manageable units of business called **divisions, departments, classifications,** and **subclasses.** These four business units are used to build pyramid-like hierarchies of related merchandise. A division is at the top of a hierarchy and the most broadly defined unit. Subclasses are at the bottom of the hierarchy and the most narrowly defined unit. In Figure 13.2, men's woven shirts are a *subclass* of the men's top *classification* of the men's sportswear *department* in the men's *division* of a department store.

Divisions, departments, classes, and subclasses are identified by product characteristics such as:

- Item (sweater)
- Vendor (Tommy Hilfiger)
- Price range (moderate)
- Size range (junior)
- End use (sportswear)
- Lifestyle (active)
- Selling season (holiday)
- Product composition/fabrication (brass/silk),
- Any product characteristic (basic/fashion, color), or combination of product characteristics (misses better sportswear).

Item and vendor are the two most common ways to identify their business units. Brand-driven products, such as fashion apparel and cosmetics, are typically defined by vendor. A store may define expensive handbag classifications by vendor, such as Gucci, Chanel, Coach, and Dooney & Burke, and less expensive handbag classifications by fabrication, such as leather, vinyl, fabric, and straw, or by style, such as evening/dressy, shoulder, clutch, briefcase, and satchel. Each business unit must represent enough sales volume to warrant being planned and tracked separately.

The diversity of an assortment affects the number of business units in a hierarchy. A department with a few homogeneous products has fewer classifications than a department with many heterogeneous products. Business unit definitions often reflect the wholesale market structure. A housewares buyer buys for a *housewares department* at a *housewares market*.

There are no universal standards for structuring a merchandise hierarchy. Knit shirts may be a *department* in the men's sportswear *division* in one retail organization, and a *subclass* of the men's sportswear *classification* in another retail organization. In general, merchandise hierarchies in large retail organizations have a greater number of precisely defined business units than the merchandise hierarchies of small retail organizations. A large organization's *knit shirt* volume is high enough to stand alone as a department, whereas a small organization's *knit shirt* volume is not.

Some retailers use terms such as *category* or *product group* to define business units. One major retailer groups merchandise into *fine departments* and *major departments*. To further facilitate planning, multistore retailers classify stores as A, B, or C based on physical size and sales volume.

PLANNING SALES

Sales planning is a critically important function in a retail organization in that expense plans, inventory purchases, and profit objectives are all predicated upon planned sales. A store's seasonal selling payroll budget is based on projected sales. Planning sales too low will result in an understaffed store, while planning sales too high will result in an overstaffed store. Sales plans also drive inventory purchases. Sales plans that are too high will yield an overstocked condition and poor turnover; sales plans that are too low will yield an understocked condition and lost sales. Sales plans often include growth strategies for cultivating additional business through new items, vendors, and categories.

Retailers look to the past and present to predict future sales. Last year's sales are often used as a base for planning this year's sales, anticipating that recurring conditions and events that drove sales last year will drive them again this year. Examples include seasonal weather conditions that stimulate the sale of swimwear, lawn furniture, wool coats, and boots, and annual gift-giving occasions, such as Valentine's Day, Fathers' Day, and Christmas that drive sales of chocolates, shirts and ties, and toys.

The past sales upon which future sales are projected must be a **comparable,** or valid, reference point. Easter may fall as early as late March or as late as the end of April. Sales for the week prior to Easter last year are *comparable* to sales for the week prior to Easter this year, even though the weeks may fall in different months. Changes in back-to-school dates (based on when Labor Day falls), a store's promotional calendar, and the number of days between Thanksgiving and Christmas are other factors that must be considered when determining comparable, or *comp,* sales.

Business units must also be comparable. A "12 percent sales increase over last year for comparable stores" implies that a comparison is being made between stores that were open for business this year and last year, and that new stores opened since last year and/or stores closed since last year are not included in the comparison.

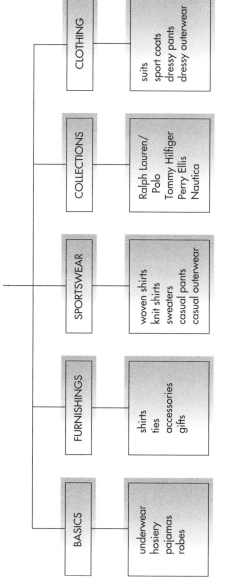

Figure 13.2

A system of departments and classes for a men's division.

Table 13.1   **TRAILING NINE MONTHS SALES REPORT**

Month	Plan	Actual	Percent +/-
February	$ 18,000	$ 18,218	+1%
March	$ 24,000	$ 24,676	+3%
April	$ 28,000	$ 28,795	+3%
May	$ 40,000	$ 41,446	+4%
June	$ 20,000	$ 21,267	+6%
July	$ 15,000	$ 15,311	+2%
August	$ 25,000	$ 27,428	+10%
September	$ 30,000	$ 34,654	+16%
October	$ 35,000	$ 42,659	+21%
TOTAL	$235,000	$204,454	+8%

Historical sales that are used as a planning base should be typical of the period. Last year's cold weather accessories sales for November are an invalid reference for projecting this November's sales if last November was atypically warm. Using last year's sales to project this year's sales will yield an understocked condition if this November's weather is typical of the season. When there is no historical reference point on which to project sales, as in the case of a new store or a new category of merchandise or vendor, the sales history of a similar business unit is often used until a history is developed.

Current trends are valid predictors of future sales in that recent trends are chronologically closer to the future than the distant past. Assume that it is fall and that a planner is using information from a trailing nine months sales report to project sales for a sportswear line for the forthcoming spring season (see Table 13.1). The planner's immediate reaction is to base this spring's plan on last spring's sales with a modest increase to reflect higher wholesale prices. However, the planner notices that last spring's sales were relatively flat, but that impressive gains have been posted since the beginning of the current fall season. The planner decides to plan more aggressively, interpreting the current sales trends as an indicator that the line is garnering a loyal following. Innumerable internal and external factors influence an organization's sales plans. A store's decision to become more upscale will be supported by aggressive sales plans for better goods, and modest sales plans for moderate goods.

"WHILE YOU WERE AWAY FROM YOUR DESK,
THE FOLLOWING TRENDS
HAVE BITTEN THE DUST."

Figure 13.3

Bill Whitehead.

Economic conditions, such as inflation, interest rates, and the general state of the economy, are also evaluated for their potential impact on sales. Slumps in housing construction reduce demand for window treatments. The impact of economic factors varied by type of goods and customer profile. Sales of trendy fashion goods are affected more dramatically by negative economic conditions than sales of functional items, such as refrigerators. The spending patterns of lower income groups are more sensitive to economic shifts than those of upper income groups. Sometimes economic factors have regional impact, such as layoffs in the aerospace industry which have caused a retail slump in Southern California in recent years.

Demographic shifts, fashion trends, and changes in competition impact a retail organization's sales plans. A decline in the teenage population during the 1980s led to downsized junior departments. However, a blossoming teenage population in the 1990s caused many retailers to recapture the junior business with aggressive sales plans and larger inventory commitments. Fashion trends impact sales. A shift from suits to dresses for career dressing will positively impact dress sales and negatively impact suit sales. Changes in the competition affect sales plans. The addition of complementary stores in a shopping area may increase customer traffic and positively impact sales, while new direct competition will have a negative impact on sales.

Unpredictable and uncontrollable factors make sales planning an inexact process. Though objective indicators, such as current sales trends and inflation, are used to project sales, determining the impact of these indicators as well their interaction is often a best guess. Will a manufacturer's price increase induce customers to explore substitute brands? How much will new competition impact sales? For how long? The best plans are the flexible ones that allow for the unforeseen circumstances that might affect them.[2]

PLANNING INVENTORY

Attaining a sales objective is contingent upon having sufficient inventory to support the plan. However, too much inventory also poses problems, such as slow turnover and high clearance markdowns. Inventories must be strategically planned sales objectives are met with minimum inventory investments.

Buyers' purchase and delivery decisions are predicated on inventory projections based on the interaction of two factors: planned sales and desired turnover. To understand the relationship of planned sales and turnover to purchase and delivery decisions, recall the jeweler from Chapter 9 who sold 600 gold chains a year. The jeweler found that a turnover of 2.0 required the purchase of 600 chains at the beginning

Table 13.2 **PLAN SALES FOR A YEAR**

Month	Plan Sales
February	$ 30,000
March	$ 60,000
April	$ 90,000
May	$ 60,000
June	$ 60,000
July	$ 30,000
August	$ 30,000
September	$ 60,000
October	$ 60,000
November	$ 90,000
December	$120,000
January	$ 30,000
TOTAL	$720,000

Table 13.3   **PLAN SALES AND BOMs FOR A YEAR USING THE BASIC STOCK METHOD**

Month	Plan Sales	Plan BOM Inventory
February	$ 30,000	$150,000
March	$ 60,000	$180,000
April	$ 90,000	$210,000
May	$ 60,000	$180,000
June	$ 60,000	$180,000
July	$ 30,000	$150,000
August	$ 30,000	$150,000
September	$ 60,000	$180,000
October	$ 60,000	$180,000
November	$ 90,000	$210,000
December	$120,000	$240,000
January	$ 30,000	$150,000

of the year while a turnover of 13.0 required the purchase of fifty chains each month.

Five methods of planning inventory are presented in this chapter: the basic stock method, the percentage variation method, the stock-to-sales ratio method, the week's supply method, and a formula for replenishing basic stock.

The Basic Stock Method   The **basic stock method** asserts that a BOM should be equal to planned sales plus a basic inventory. The basic stock method formula is:

$$BOM = planned\ monthly\ sales$$
$$+ (average\ inventory - average\ monthly\ sales)$$

The following example demonstrates using the basic stock method to plan the BOMs for a year for a store with planned monthly sales as indicated in Table 13.2, and a desired turnover of 4.0.

Average inventory is computed by dividing annual sales by turnover.

$$turnover = \frac{sales}{average\ inventory}$$

$$4.0 = \frac{\$720,000}{average\ inventory}$$

$$average\ inventory = \$180,000$$

| Buyer | DIV MGR | GEN MGR | DEPT |

6-MONTH MERCHANDISING PLAN FOR PERIOD FROM .... TO .... YEAR ....

STORE NO.			NET SALES		FEB/AUG	MAR/SEP	APR/OCT	MAY/NOV	JUN/DEC	JUL/JAN
ACT LY	PLANNED THIS YEAR	ACT TY	LAST YEAR							
	NET SALES		PLAN							
	AV MO STOCK		THIS YEAR							
	STOCK TURN		EOM STOCK	JAN/JUL	FEB/AUG	MAR/SEP	APR/OCT	MAY/NOV	JUN/DEC	JUL/JAN
	MARK DN %		ACT LY							
	GROSS MARG		PLAN TY							
	MAINT M/U		ACT TY							
			MD LY							
			MD TY							

STORE NO.			NET SALES		FEB/AUG	MAR/SEP	APR/OCT	MAY/NOV	JUN/DEC	JUL/JAN
ACT LY	PLANNED THIS YEAR	ACT TY	LAST YEAR							
	NET SALES		PLAN							
	AV MO STOCK		THIS YEAR							
	STOCK TURN		EOM STOCK	JAN/JUL	FEB/AUG	MAR/SEP	APR/OCT	MAY/NOV	JUN/DEC	JUL/JAN
	MARK DN %		ACT LY							
	GROSS MARG		PLAN TY							
	MAINT M/U		ACT TY							
			MD LY							
			MD TY							

STORE NO.			NET SALES		FEB/AUG	MAR/SEP	APR/OCT	MAY/NOV	JUN/DEC	JUL/JAN
ACT LY	PLANNED THIS YEAR	ACT TY	LAST YEAR							
	NET SALES		PLAN							
	AV MO STOCK		THIS YEAR							
	STOCK TURN		EOM STOCK	JAN/JUL	FEB/AUG	MAR/SEP	APR/OCT	MAY/NOV	JUN/DEC	JUL/JAN
	MARK DN %		ACT LY							
	GROSS MARG		PLAN TY							
	MAINT M/U		ACT TY							
			MD LY							
			MD TY							

STORE NO.			NET SALES		FEB/AUG	MAR/SEP	APR/OCT	MAY/NOV	JUN/DEC	JUL/JAN
ACT LY	PLANNED THIS YEAR	ACT TY	LAST YEAR							
	NET SALES		PLAN							
	AV MO STOCK		THIS YEAR							
	STOCK TURN		EOM STOCK	JAN/JUL	FEB/AUG	MAR/SEP	APR/OCT	MAY/NOV	JUN/DEC	JUL/JAN
	MARK DN %		ACT LY							
	GROSS MARG		PLAN TY							
	MAINT M/U		ACT TY							
			MD LY							
			MD TY							

STORE NO.			NET SALES		FEB/AUG	MAR/SEP	APR/OCT	MAY/NOV	JUN/DEC	JUL/JAN
ACT LY	PLANNED THIS YEAR	ACT TY	LAST YEAR							
	NET SALES		PLAN							
	AV MO STOCK		THIS YEAR							
	STOCK TURN		EOM STOCK	JAN/JUL	FEB/AUG	MAR/SEP	APR/OCT	MAY/NOV	JUN/DEC	JUL/JAN
	MARK DN %		ACT LY							
	GROSS MARG		PLAN TY							
	MAINT M/U		ACT TY							
			MD LY							
			MD TY							

Figure 13.4

A six-month merchandising plan.

Average monthly sales is computed by dividing annual sales by 12:

$$average\ monthly\ sales = \frac{\$720,000}{12}$$

$$average\ monthly\ sales = \$60,000$$

This difference between average inventory and average monthly sales is the basic inventory.

$$basic\ inventory = average\ inventory - average\ monthly\ sales$$
$$basic\ inventory = \$180,000 - \$60,000$$
$$basic\ inventory = \$120,000$$

The basic inventory is added to each month's planned sales to compute BOM. The results are tabulated in Table 13.3.

When turnover is 12.0, the average monthly sales and the average inventory will be equal in the basic stock method. The basic stock will be zero, and BOM will always equal planned sales. When turnover is greater than 12.0, the average monthly sales will be greater than the average inventory. The basic stock will be a negative number and BOM will be less than planned sales. Thus, the basic stock method can only be used when turnover is less than 12.0. The method can be adapted to a six-month or three-month planning period by using the desired turnover for the period and computing average monthly sales based on either three or six months.

The Percentage Variation Method   The **percentage variation method** asserts that a BOM should be a percentage of average inventory. The percentage will vary each month based on planned sales. The percentage variation method formula is:

$$average\ inventory \times 1/2 \left(1 + \frac{plan\ sales\ for\ the\ month}{average\ monthly\ sales}\right)$$

The following applies the percentage variation method to the data in Table 13.2. The calculation of the BOM for February is:

$$BOM = average\ inventory \times 1/2 \left(1 + \frac{plan\ sales\ for\ the\ month}{average\ monthly\ sales}\right)$$

$$BOM = \$180,000 \times 1/2 \left(1 + \frac{\$30,000}{\$60,000}\right)$$

$$BOM = \$180,000 \times 1/2\ (1 + 0.5)$$
$$BOM = \$180,000 \times 1/2\ (1.5)$$
$$BOM = \$180,000 \times 0.75$$
$$BOM = \$135,000$$

Table 13.4 **PLAN SALES AND BOMs FOR A YEAR USING THE PERCENTAGE VARIATION METHOD**

Month	Plan Sales	Plan BOM Inventory
February	$ 30,000	$135,000
March	$ 60,000	$180,000
April	$ 90,000	$225,000
May	$ 60,000	$180,000
June	$ 60,000	$180,000
July	$ 30,000	$135,000
August	$ 30,000	$135,000
September	$ 60,000	$180,000
October	$ 60,000	$180,000
November	$ 90,000	$225,000
December	$120,000	$270,000
January	$ 30,000	$135,000

Table 13.5 **A COMPARISON OF BOMs USING THE BASIC STOCK METHOD AND THE PERCENTAGE VARIATION METHOD**

Month	Plan Sales	BOM-Basic Stock Method	BOM-Percentage Variation Method
February	$ 30,000	$ 150,000	$ 135,000
March	$ 60,000	$ 180,000	$ 180,000
April	$ 90,000	$ 210,000	$ 225,000
May	$ 60,000	$ 180,000	$ 180,000
June	$ 60,000	$ 180,000	$ 180,000
July	$ 30,000	$ 150,000	$ 135,000
August	$ 30,000	$ 150,000	$ 135,000
September	$ 60,000	$ 180,000	$ 180,000
October	$ 60,000	$ 180,000	$ 180,000
November	$ 90,000	$ 210,000	$ 225,000
December	$120,000	$ 240,000	$ 270,000
January	$ 30,000	$ 150,000	$ 135,000
TOTAL	$720,000	$2,160,000	$2,160,000

Table 13.6   **PLAN SALES AND BOMs USING THE STOCK-TO-SALES RATIO METHOD**

Month	Plan Sales	S/S Ratio	BOM
January	$ 30,000	4.5	$ 135,000
February	$ 30,000	4.5	$ 135,000
March	$ 60,000	3.0	$ 180,000
April	$ 90,000	2.5	$ 225,000
May	$ 60,000	3.0	$ 180,000
June	$ 60,000	3.0	$ 180,000
July	$ 30,000	4.5	$ 135,000
August	$ 30,000	4.5	$ 135,000
September	$ 60,000	3.0	$ 180,000
October	$ 60,000	3.0	$ 180,000
November	$ 90,000	2.5	$ 225,000
December	$120,000	2.3	$ 270,000
TOTAL	$720,000	3.0	$2,160,000

Table 13.4 lists BOMs for a year computed by the percentage variation method. Note that when planned sales are *equal* to average monthly sales, the BOM is equal to the average inventory. When planned sales are *less* than average monthly sales, the BOM is *less* than the average inventory. When planned sales are *greater* than average monthly sales, the BOM is *greater* than average inventory. Thus, an *average* sales plan, will require an *average* inventory as a BOM. A *lower* than average sales plan will require a BOM less than average inventory. A *higher* than average sales plan will require a BOM *greater* than average inventory.

Though the basic stock method is simpler than the percentage variation method, the latter is more sensitive to fluctuations in planned sales. Table 13.5 compares the BOMs generated from both methods. Note that the range between the highest and lowest BOM in the percentage variation method ($135,000) is greater than the range between the highest and lowest BOM in the basic stock method ($90,000). The percentage variation method yields higher BOMs than the basic stock method when sales plans are high, and lower BOMs than the basic stock method when sales plans are low.

The Stock-to-Sales Ratio Method The BOMs generated by the **stock-to-sales ratio method** are based on a desired stock-to-sales ratio for a month. The stock-to-sales ratio method formula is:

$$BOM = planned\ sales \times desired\ stock\text{-}to\text{-}sales\ ratio$$

If a desired stock-to-sales ratio is 3.0 and planned sales are $8000, the BOM is computed as follows:

$$BOM = \$8000 \times 3.0$$

$$BOM = \$24,000$$

Recall from Chapter 9 that peak selling periods require lower stock-to-sales ratios than slow selling periods. To demonstrate this principle, the BOMs generated by the percentage variation method were divided by planned sales to calculate the following stock-to-sales ratios for each month. The results are tabulated in Table 13.6.

Note that months with high sales plans have low stock-to-sales ratios, while months with low sales plans have high stock-to-sales ratios. Therefore, the stock-to-sales ratios used in the stock-to-sales ratio method should vary relative to the sales volume each month. The stock-to-sales ratio method is inappropriately applied when an annualized stock-to-sales ratio is used to plan each month's BOM. A range of stock-to-sales ratios should be used unless there is little sales fluctuation from month to month.

The Weeks of Supply Method The three inventory planning methods covered thus far assume that inventories are planned by month. However, some inventories are planned for shorter periods because of higher turnover.[3] The weeks of supply method asserts that the amount of inventory required to support planned sales for a week is based on the number of weeks that an inventory will last relative to a desired turnover and planned sales. The higher the turnover, the lower the number of weeks of supply required. The week's supply formula is:

$$weeks\ of\ supply = \frac{52}{turnover}$$

If the desired turnover is 6.0, then the week's of supply is calculated as follows

$$weeks\ of\ supply = \frac{52}{6.0}$$

$$weeks\ of\ supply = 8.7$$

Annual Turnover	Six Month Turnover	Weeks of Supply	Weekly % Sell
12.0	6.0	4	23
11.0	5.5	5	21
10.0	5.0	5	19
9.0	4.5	6	17
8.0	4.0	7	15
7.0	3.5	8	14
6.0	3.0	9	12
5.5	2.75	10	11
5.0	2.5	11	10
4.5	2.25	12	9
4.0	2.0	13	8
3.5	1.75	15	7
3.0	1.5	17	6
2.5	1.25	21	5
2.0	1.0	26	4

Figure 13.5

Weeks-of-supply and weekly percent sell for various turnover rates.

The resulting figure is multiplied by the weekly planned sales to determine the amount of inventory needed to achieve the sales objective. The amount of inventory required to support a sales plan of $5000 is $43,500 (8.7 × $5000).

The numerator is for determining the weeks of supply is adjusted accordingly when turnover for a period other than a year is used in the computation. The numerator would be 26 if turnover were for a half year. The week's supply method is best applied when sales are relatively stable.

Weeks of supply, or *weeks supply,* is a frequently used measure of inventory that reflects the number of weeks that an inventory will last if sold at a current rate of sale. **Days of supply,** or *days supply,* is the number of days an inventory will last if sold at a current rate of sale. Some stores use a *weekly percent sell* to measure weeks of supply, the percent of the stock on hand that will sell in one week at a current rate of sale.

Formula for the Periodic Replenishment of Staple Merchandise The formula for the periodic replenishment of staple merchandise asserts that staples should be replenished based on the amount of units sold during a typical selling period, the time lapse between the arrival of reorders, and a safety, or reserve, stock. The formula for the periodic replenishment of staples is:

$$M = (RP + DP)S + R$$

- M (maximum) is the amount of inventory needed for the period.
- RP (reorder period) is the time period that defines the frequency with which orders are placed.
- DP (delivery period) is the time period between the point at which an order is placed and the point at which the goods are available for sale. LT (lead time) is the sum of RP and DP.
- S (rate of sale) is the number of units that are typically sold during the reorder period.
- R (reserve stock) is additional stock to avoid stockouts if sales exceed plan. The formula for reserve stock is $2.3\sqrt{(LT)S}$.

The following demonstrates using the formula to replenish goods ordered bi-weekly and delivered in a week, in a store that sells 100 items per week.

$$M = (2 \text{ weeks} + 1 \text{ week}) \times 100 \text{ units per week} + 2.3\sqrt{3 \text{ weeks} (100 \text{ units per week})}$$

$$M = 300 + 2.3\sqrt{300}$$

$$M = 300 + 40$$

$$M = 340$$

OPEN-TO-BUY

Open-to-buy is the amount of merchandise that a buyer needs to order to support planned sales for a period. Open-to-buy is derived from **planned purchases** which are based on:

	(a.) SALES	-SALES	-SALES	-SALES	-SALES	-SALES	-SALES	-SALES	-SALES
					JARROD & YOUNG				
(a1.) APR	PERIOD PLN	13.9	10.6	21.6	27.9	12.2	11.5	17.9	2.7
(a2.) MAR	PTD TY	17.4	13.0	32.3	27.3	18.9	14.6	19.8	3.0
(a3.)	LY	19.4	14.9	25.3	29.0	15.0	14.0	21.6	3.1
(a4.) MAR TY-LY	%CHG	-7.7	-12.8	58.6	-5.9	26.0	4.3	-8.3	-3.2
(a5.) YR TD BOP	MAR TY	12.3	12.0	23.1	19.1	10.2	9.8	13.9	2.3
(a6.)	LY	12.4	9.5	8.5	15.0	8.1	6.5	9.9	1.6
(a7.) YR TY-LY	%CHG	-0.5	26.3	171.8	27.3	25.9	50.8	40.4	43.8
(b.)	STOCK	STK	STK	STK	STK	STK	STK	STK	STK
(b1.) MAR AUDIT	OH BOP	62.6	65.0	74.8	80.2	58.4	47.6	71.0	23.5
(b2.) MAR -MEMO-BNJ	BOP	23.1	5.9	17.0	14.9	4.9	7.2	10.0	1.1
(b3.) MAR NET RCPTS	PTD	37.5	34.2	60.0	76.8	50.1	36.3	53.1	14.3
(b4.) MAR TRANSFERS	IN	0.2	0.8	12.1	2.4	0.3	1.0	3.1	0.2
(b5.)	OUT	-3.2	-5.4	-0.7	-2.4	-5.8	-2.6	-5.6	-0.2
(b6.) LAST WK ON HND	TY	81.8	82.4	105.1	126.3	72.1	64.8	92.4	32.9
(b7.) APR BOP STOCK	PLN	95.3	49.4	86.0	77.0	47.9	59.8	67.8	15.2
(b8.) THIS WK ON HND	TY	88.0	81.6	114.0	129.7	84.1	67.7	101.8	34.8
(b9.)	LY	108.7	57.8	104.3	89.2	54.9	67.5	79.8	17.3
(b10.) TY-LY	%CHG	-20.7	23.8	9.7	40.5	29.2	0.2	22.0	17.5
(b11.) MAY BOP STOCK	PLN	105.5	51.4	91.2	77.2	51.7	56.4	70.0	18.0
(c.) OUTSTANDING	OTB	OUTST	OUTST	OUTST	OUTST	OUTST	OUTST	OUTST	OUTST
MAR	OUTST	1.6	6.3	19.3	12.1	4.8	11.7	15.8	8.6
APR	OUTST	34.9	16.8	22.7	21.3	5.1	17.1	20.0	9.4
MAY	OUTST	14.0	11.5	17.5	17.5	13.0	10.1	14.7	7.0
(c1.) JUN	OUTST								
(c2.) AFTER JUN	OUTST								
(d.) APR OP-TO-BUY	BAL	-3.6	-42.1	-41.5	-54.7	-28.4	-27.4	-43.9	-32.1
(e.)	MARKUP								
(e1.) FEB	ACT %	47.2	47.1	48.4	51.1	47.1	46.9	47.1	47.3
(e2.) FEB	PLAN %								
(e3.) MMU—SEAS TD	TY								
(e4.) BOP MAR	LY								
(f.)	MARKDOWNS	MKD	MKD	MKD	MKD	MKD	MKD	MKD	MKD
(f1.) MAR	PTD								
(f2.) MAR	PLN	0.9	0.8	1.3	1.0	0.9	1.2	1.0	0.4
(f3.) YR TD BOP MAR	TY$	0.2	0.2	1.0	0.4	0.4	0.5	0.4	0.1
	TY%	1.6	1.7	4.3	2.1	3.9	5.1	2.9	4.3
		DEPT	DEPT	DEPT	DEPT	DEPT	DEPT	DEPT	DEPT
		04-02-	04-02-	04-02-	04-02-	04-02-	04-02-	04-02-	04-02-

Figure 13.6

An open-to-buy report.

- The amount of inventory brought forward from the previous period (BOM);
- The planned sales for the period;
- The amount of inventory that must be rolled over to the next period (EOM); and
- The planned markdowns for the period.[4]

The formula for planned purchases is:

planned sales for the month

+ planned markdowns

+ planned EOM

– planned BOM
_____

planned purchases

Open-to-buy is the difference between planned purchases and merchandise on-order. The formula for open-to-buy is:

planned purchases

– on order
_____

open-to-buy

Open-to-buy is comparable to a checkbook balance. Planned purchases are comparable to a beginning checkbook balance. Placing an order is comparable to writing a check. The buyer begins each month with a new balance. A buyer with "no open-to-buy" has a zero open-to-buy balance. A buyer "bought up through March" can place against April's open-to-buy. A buyer is "overbought" when on-order exceeds planned purchases, a condition comparable to an overdrawn checking account. Some buyers overbuy anticipating that some orders will be short shipped or not be shipped at all. Order cancellation is the most common remedy for an overbought condition. Like sales, open-to-buy is planned at various organizational levels such as department and classification.

Discrepancies between planned and actual sales necessitate frequent open-to-buy adjustments. Poor sales for a month will increase the EOM carried into the subsequent month (BOM) necessitating a reduction in open-to-buy. Favorable sales will decrease the EOM carried into the subsequent month necessitating an increase in open-to-buy. Failure to adjust open-to-buy as needed will result in overinventoried or underinventoried conditions. Open-to-buy can be expressed as dollars or units.

An **open-to-ship** is a figure that defines a store's inventory needs. Like open-to-buy, open-to-ship is based on the difference between a store's projected inventory needs and inventory on hand. Merchandise distributors use open-to-ship to determine the type and amount of merchandise to ship to stores from a distribution center.

ASSORTMENT PLANNING

Planned purchases reflect the amount of inventory needed to attain a sales goal. However, determining the *right amount* of inventory is only the first step in determining the *right* inventory. Planned purchases must be translated into assortments of prices, styles, brands, and colors that will meet customers' expectations. Some of the most common merchandise characteristics that buyers use to plan assortments include the following:

Price   Few retail stores are large enough to offer every available price point. Therefore, retailers must limit their assortments to specific price ranges. The price range of an assortment can be defined by its lowest, or opening, price point and highest, or ending, price point. Assortments are also characterized by more general pricing terms, such as moderate or better. Assortments at the various divisions of Federated Department Stores are clearly defined by price. Bloomingdale's assortments are predominantly better; Macy's are upper moderate.

The price points that define the price range of an assortment vary by retail organization. One retailer's lowest priced goods may be another retailer's highest priced goods. One store may consider leather handbags as better, and vinyl handbags as moderate. Another store may include low-end leathers in its moderate assortment, and high-end vinyls in its better assortment.

Defining an assortment by price is closely linked to defining an assortment by quality and fashion level, since higher-priced goods tend to be of better quality and higher fashion than lower-priced goods. The price range of an assortment must be consistent with the store's image and target customer. Thousand dollar dresses at Sears and washable polyester suits at Brooks Brothers are inconsistent with each store's image and customer.

Brand   The brands within an assortment must be consistent with a store's image and its customers' expectations. Buyers choose brands that maximize the store's sales and profit objectives. They replace lackluster brands with brands that show promise of being better investments of inventory and space. The brands that generate the most sales are not necessarily the most productive. Some of the best-selling

BRAND	CLASS.	AVAIL. PRE-PACK	MAKE UP	OPEN STOCK	RETAIL PRICE RANGE	ORDER MINIMUM	U.P.C. CODE	E.D.I. READY	SIZES & WIDTHS Narrow	Medium	Wide	Extra Widths
A'MANO	D	•	•	•	$35-600	12	•	•	4-12	4-12	4-12	
Accessoire Diffusion	D, C, B, HB		•		$145-300	60				4-12		
Accessory Group Inc.,Clip-Ons	AC		•	•	$4-12	4						
Acme	B			•	$80-150	None	•	•	6-9	5-10		
Adirondack Collection	C, S, AC		•		$40-75	12				5-11 full sizes		
Aerosoles - Women	C, B, S	•	•	•	$30-60	None	•	•	7.5-9	5-12		
Alfie's Original Souliers	D, C, B		•		$49-79	12				5-12		
Allure	D, C, B	•	•	•	$60-120	72	•	•	5-10	4-12	6-10	
Amalfi	D, C	•	•	•	$79-150	12	•	•	5-12	4-12	4-10	4A-C
Amante	D, C		•		$60-125	500			4-12	4-12	4-12	
American Eagle	D, C, B	•			$20-70	12	•			5-11		
Amiana (For Women)	D, S		•		$100-200	36		•	5-10	4-11		
Amour By Pepe Jimenez	D	•	•	•	$60-125	None			6-11	3.5-12		S
André Assous	C, B	•	•		$22-200	12			7-9	4-11		
Andrea Cecconi	D, C		•		$115-250	12				5-11		
Andrea Pfister S.R.L.	D, B, AC, HB		•		$200-450	100				36-40		
Ann-Marino	D, C	•			$38-90	12	•	•	7-9	5.5-11		
Anne Jordan	D, C	•			$40-80	12				5-12	7-10	
Anne Klein	D, C, B	•	•		$120-240	108		•	7-10	4-10		
Anne Klein II	D, C, B	•	•	•	$80-145	108		•	7-10	4-10		
Aqua-Talia By Bootlegger	B		•		$80-120	36				5-11		
Arche	C, B, HB		•		$145-210	100				5-12		
Atsco/Private Labels	D, C, B, AC,S	•	•	•	$20-150	None	•		4-12	4-12	4-12	XW
Auditions	D, C, B			•	$40-100	None	•		5-11,12,13	5-12,13	5-12,13	SS-WW

Abbreviations & Symbols: Classifications: **D** - Dress Shoes / **C** - Casuals / **B** - Boots / **AT** - Athletics / **S** - Slippers / **SV** - Service Footwear
AC - Accessories / **HB** - Handbags / **LG** - Leather Goods / **AP** - Apparel / **SC** - Shoe Care Products
• – Available

Figure 13.7

Buyers use vendor profiles such as this to plan shoe assortments by style, price, and size. *Fashion Footwear Association of New York.*

brands sell only at promotional prices. These brands are good volume generators but poor gross margin producers. Determining a brand assortment is closely linked to determining a price assortment.

Private-label decisions are linked to brand decisions. Buyers seek private-label substitutes for basic items with weak brand identity, since private-label goods generate more gross margin than branded goods. However, the mix of private label and branded goods must be carefully balanced. An extensive choice of brands is often an assortment feature that draws many customers to a store, especially for brand-driven purchases.

Size Sized merchandise seldom sells in equal quantities. Thus size assortments based on consumer demand must be strategically

JARROD & YOUNG			
	Sub-Classification	% to Stock	Open-to-Buy in $
A. SUB-CLASSIFICATION	Straight line	20	20,000
	Side pleat	20	20,000
	A-line	15	15,000
	Wrap	15	15,000
	Trouser	15	15,000
	Full	5	5,000
	Dirndl	10	10,000
		100%	$100,000 (OTB share)
	Price Range	**% to Stock**	
B. PRICES	$130.00	5	
	120.00	10	
	100.00	30	
	80.00	30	
	75.00	15	
	65.00	10	
		100%	
	Colors	**% to Stock**	
C. COLORS	Gray heather	10	
	Navy	10	
	Black	25	
	Brown	10	
	Red	10	
	Taupe	15	
	Novelty	20	
		100%	
	Sizes	**% to Stock**	
D. SIZES	4	8	
	6	16	
	8	25	
	10	25	
	12	18	
	14	8	
	16	–	
	18	–	
	20	–	
		100%	
	Fabrics	**% to Stock**	
E. FABRICS	Wool/gabardine and/or crepe	25	
	Wool/flannel	40	
	Wool/silk	10	
	Poly/wool	20	
	Acrylic/rayon	5	
		100%	

Figure 13.8

Assortments can be planned as percentages of total inventory by factors such as price, color, size, and fabric.

planned. An end-of-season clearance rack with a disproportionate number of *smalls* is often indicative of an overabundance of one size, and lost sales to customers seeking other sizes. Suppliers often recommend size distributions based on historical sales records. Shoe manufacturers pack individual shoe styles in case lots, called size runs, that include specific size assortments.

Other product characteristics are used to plan assortments, such as color and style. An innerwear buyer may expand an assortment of black slips when black is a dominant seasonal color for dresses. The anticipation of a strong strapless dress season will encourage an innerwear buyer to maintain a selection of strapless bras. Some assortments are defined by color categories, such as *basic colors* or *fashion colors*. A men's dress shirt assortment may be planned as *solids* and *fancies*, as well as by *cottons* and *blends* (of polyester and cotton).

Assortments are sometimes planned by "look" or lifestyle. A dress assortment may be planned as *career, casual,* and *special occasion.* Some assortments are planned by item. Assortments of small leather goods include key chains, wallets, checkbooks, and change purses. Items are sometimes identified as classifications or subclasses within department/class structures.

Seasonal factors, such as weather and holidays, influence assortments plans. Wool sweaters replace cotton sweaters at the beginning of each fall season. The reverse holds true at the beginning of each spring season. Lacy teddies are an important women's sleepwear item at Valentine's Day. The demand for table linens surges just before Thanksgiving. A full-line discounter reports of planning large inventories of cup hooks in November to respond to a demand by customers who use them to hang holiday lights! Assortment planning is also linked to a store's promotional calendar. A store-wide *Anniversary Sale* requires extensive quantities of goods with broad appeal that can be promotionally priced.

The economic factors that influence sales plans also impact assortment plans. Buyers often slant assortments toward basic practical items at the expense of trendy frivolous items during trying economic times. One fabric mill reports that black velvet special occasion dresses becomes very popular during poor economic times because of their fashion durability. Assortment plans target a store's merchandising objectives. A desire to upgrade a store's image will affect the selection of price and brand. A desire for exclusivity will influence the selection of brands and styles.

Assortments can be planned by units, dollars, and/or percentages. An assortment of small, medium, large, and extra-large knits may be planned in a unit ratio of 2:3:2:1. A misses sportswear assortment may be planned as 40 percent better and 60 percent moderate. The assortment of a men's collections department may be 50 percent Polo, 25 percent Tommy Hilfiger, and 25 percent Claiborne.

Recall from Chapter 2 that assortments are characterized by their depth and breadth. Breadth refers to the number of unique items in an assortment. Depth refers to the selection within the elements of an assortment that define its breadth. There is often a tradeoff between depth and breadth. A department store with a wide assortment of cosmetics brands limits the amount of space that can be dedicated to the selection within each line. By discontinuing brands, the store will free up space for greater depth within the lines that are retained.

In general, narrow and deep assortments are more desirable than broad and shallow assortments. It is better to carry full assortments of a few product lines than piecy assortments of many product lines. A selection is said to be *overassorted* when it has too much breadth and too little depth. Exclusive specialty shops are an exception to this generalization where uniqueness is a fundamental assortment characteristic.

COMPUTERIZED PLANNING SYSTEMS

Computerized planning systems have facilitated the planning of assortments by individual sku and store. "What if" capabilities allow planners to observe instantly the effect of adjusting various planning variables. Because tedious calculations are eliminated, planners devote more time to analytical functions, and less time to computational functions. Computerized planning also integrates plans from various organizational levels to ensure a match between financial and merchandise plans, bottom-up and top-down plans, and unit and dollar plans.[5,6]

Category management involves managing a product category as if it were a separate business entity, such as a store or department. Category management is a customer-driven concept that uses planning technology and historical sales data to develop ideal space allocation and assortments by store. Some observers warn of the dangers of category management in that only the highest turning and highest margin goods are retained in assortments at the expense of core products that may not be profitable, but are popular with consumers. Critics also fear that running a store as a collection of disjointed businesses will disrupt the store's cohesiveness and sales synergy.[7,8,9]

Though computerized planning systems have become common, even in small retail organizations, an understanding of manual systems is fundamental to understanding automated systems, since computerized systems are based on the same theoretical constructs as manual systems.

SOURCES OF PLANNING INFORMATION

Planning involves integrating information from a diverse group of sources. Information on a store's sales history, current sales trends, and inventory status is obtained from internal organizational sources. However, information pertaining to fashion trends, market conditions, and the status of competitors must be obtained from sources external to the organization. The following is a discussion of several external information sources often tapped by retailers, including consumer publications, trade publications, trade associations, forecasting services, and reporting services.

Consumer publications are magazines and newspapers available to the public at newsstands. Targeted to clearly defined market niches, the editorial content of consumer publications provides retailers with insight into the lifestyles, tastes, and needs of specific market segments. Fashion magazines such as *Vogue, Mademoiselle,* and *GQ* are sources of information on current fashion trends for women and men. Newspapers such as the *Wall Street Journal,* and magazines such as *Business Week, Fortune,* and *Forbes,* offer timely information on the general business climate.

Trade publications are targeted to members of a specific industry segment. They feature editorials, business analyses, and information on the current status of major industry players, new products, and governmental legislation relative to the industry. Trade publication advertising provides retailers with information on merchandise resources, trade shows, and trade services. Trade publications often conduct or commission studies of interest to their readership.

Fairchild Publications is the leading source of apparel industry publications including *Women's Wear Daily (WWD),* for the women's apparel industry; *Daily News Record (DNR),* for the textile and men's apparel industries; and *Home Furnishings Network (HFN)* for the home

Figure 13.9

Consumer magazines are sources of information on current fashion trends.

Company Profile 13.1

The Arthur Retail Planning System is a family of products designed to plan and track merchandise across an entire retail organization. A product of Comshare Retail, Arthur is the most widely used merchandise planning and tracking system in the world.

Arthur®

Arthur has the capability of creating unique assortment plans for each unit in a chain based on historical sales information, square footage and fixture capacity, forthcoming sales promotion events, and the sales, gross margin, and turnover objectives for the company and store. The breadth and depth of assortments are based on historical movement of merchandise, reflecting local demands for specific price points, brands, sizes, and styles. Sales and inventory plans are constantly updated based on actual sales. Slow-turning brands, items, colors, styles, and price points are edited from assortments to ensure that only the fastest turning goods remain in stock. The influence of external factors, such as local competition and economic conditions can also be factored into the plan. Arthur maximizes productivity and profitability by identifying growth opportunities and the impact of emerging trends. Each store's plans can be compared to top level sales and profit projections to ensure consistency with overall corporate objectives.

Arthur has the capability of retrieving and synthesizing large amounts of data into detailed reports of sales, inventory, on-order status, average inventory, turnover, and GMROI. These real-time reports are readily accessible in graphic form on high level screens. Currently more than 350 worldwide retailers use Arthur including J. Crew, Linens 'n Things, Hills Department Stores, Kay-Bee Toys, Pier 1 Imports, Tops Appliances, JCPenney, and Barney's.

furnishings and accessories industries. *Buyer's guides* are supplements to *HFN* that cover specific merchandise categories. A typical *buyer's guide* includes sections such as

- *State of the Market:* statistics on a category's growth potential, major resources, and market share by retail channel of distribution.
- *Products Inside and Out:* information on materials and production processes, and glossaries of terms related to the product.
- *Merchandising the Category:* suggestions for pricing, promoting, and presenting the category.

Figure 13.10

Women's Wear Daily is an authoritative apparel industry publication.

Other retail trade publications include *Discount Store News,* a bi-weekly newspaper for discounters published by Lebhar-Freidman, and *Chain Store Age Executive,* a monthly magazine for general retail readership. Trade publications are often targeted to specific product categories. *Gifts & Decorative Accessories* is a monthly publication for gifts, tabletop, gourmet, home accessories, greeting cards, and stationery published by Geyer-McAllister Publications.

Trade associations represent the interests of a particular industry segment. Supported by dues-paying members, trade associations promote goodwill, lobby before legislatures, conduct research, produce trade shows, sponsor conferences, and publish newsletters. The largest trade associations for retailers include the National Retail Federation (NRF), the International Mass Retail Association (IMRA), and the International Council of Shopping Centers (ICSC). Some trade associations represent narrow segments of the retail industry such as the

Figure 13.11

Fashion Watch is a report of new trends, items, and resources published for retailers of female apparel by the Retail Reporting Bureau.

National Association of Menswear Sportswear Buyers (NAMSB) and the Apparel Retailers Association.

Manufacturers' trade associations, such as the Cosmetics, Toiletry, and Fragrance Association and the American Apparel Manufacturers Association, are authoritative sources of information on the product lines produced by their constituents. The research laboratory of the Leather Industries of America at the University of Cincinnati publishes the *Directory of Leather Terminology.* The association also distributes *Leather Facts,* a comprehensive booklet on the qualities and manufacturing of leather published by the New England Tanners Club.

Forecasting services study history and prevailing socioeconomic and market conditions to predict trends in advance of a selling season.

The Color Association of the United States (CAUS) and Intercolor are color forecasting services subscribed to by fiber, textile, and apparel producers, and retailers that develop their own private label merchandise. **Reporting services** survey and analyze specific industry segments, reporting their findings to service subscribers. The *Tobe Report* is a heavily illustrated fashion report that dates back to 1927. The report is a merchandising guide for apparel retailers used to identify the hottest fashion trends and merchandise resources. Johnson's Redbook Service is a reporting service that tracks the sales of leading apparel and textiles producers, chemical companies, and department, specialty, and discount stores.

Other Information Sources

Suppliers often provide retailers product information and market studies designed to support the sale of their product. Though the information is biased, it is free and readily available. **Consultants** are advisers who offer expertise, analyze issues, or resolve problems on a contractual fee basis. A division of Price Waterhouse, Management Horizons is a consulting firm that specializes in strategy development, market positioning, new concept development, merchandising, operations, and retail growth and expansion. Bernard's Consulting Group is a

Figure 13.12

The Center For Retailing Studies at Texas A&M University sponsors symposiums for retailing executives and professors who teach and conduct research in retailing.

Company Profiles 13.2

The Fashion Association began in 1956 as the American Institute of Men's and Boys' Wear as a public relations effort to promote consumer awareness of male fashions. In 1968, the organization became the Men's Fashion Association. In 1992, the group of retailers, apparel manufacturers, mills, and fiber companies expanded their membership to include women's wear and become The Fashion Association.

An authoritative source of consumer fashion information, TFA fosters an on-going relationship between the fashion industry and the media by arranging appearances of corporate executives and designers on local, cable, syndicated, and network radio and TV shows, and producing seasonal video news releases (VNRs) used by more than 100 cable stations on news and talk shows. Other activities of TFA include the production of semi-annual preview fashion shows for the media, the publication of two newsletters, *Faxions* and *Currents,* and the sponsorship of the Aldo Awards for outstanding fashion journalism. TFA also sponsors the American Image Awards to recognize outstanding citizenship in the fashion industry. Honorees have included Dillard's COO, Bill Dillard and Bargert Tygart of Levi Strauss CEO, Robert Hass.

TFA's impressive membership roster includes such names as Burlington, DuPont, Hartmarx, JCPenney, the Kellwood Company, Levi Strauss, Sears, and the VF Corporation.

The National Retail Federation is the world's largest retail trade organization with a membership that includes department, specialty, and discount stores in fifty states and thirty national affiliates. Some of the benefits of NRF membership include access to an in-house staff of experts with a broad base of industry expertise, as well as confer-

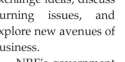

NATIONAL RETAIL FEDERATION

ences, conventions, seminars, and workshops that provide industry leaders the opportunity to exchange ideas, discuss burning issues, and explore new avenues of business.

NRF's government and public affairs division lobbies on behalf of the retail industry on matters of concern to retailers, such as employee benefits,

continued

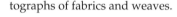

international trade, and business related taxes. The *Washington Retail Weekly* is a NRF publication that apprises members of public policy and legislative issues with potential impact on their business. Other NRF publications include *Stores,* a monthly magazine for retail executives, and *Retail Sales Outlook,* a quarterly publication of economic forecasts. The NRF also publishes the results of commissioned studies and two annual figure exchanges: *Merchandising and Operating Results (MOR),* and *Financial and Operating Results (FOR).*

Promostyl is a Paris-based fashion forecasting service that predicts consumer choices of apparel and accessories twelve to eighteen months in advance of a selling season. Branches in New York, London, and Tokyo serve a diverse group of clients in thirty-five countries. Promostyl communicates its predictions through a series of publications called trend books that cover a range of fashion topics:

- *Influences*—a report of the social and cultural trends that inspire fashion;
- *Color Book*—a color guide with yarn samples;
- *Fabrics, Prints, Patterns and Knit Book*—with print design suggestions, fabric swatches, and photographs of fabrics and weaves.

Trend book information is supplemented by monthly newsletters that include shopping guides, seasonal trend conferences, and trade shows. Other Promostyl services include individual consultation to subscribers to interpret trends by individual markets, and a five-week fashion forecasting and line development course in Paris for students and aspiring apparel professionals. Promostyl also offers the services of designers, graphic artists, and marketing specialists who develop exclusive design concepts for apparel collections, and strategies for positioning, promoting, and distributing them.

retail forecasting and consulting firm that performs market analyses, develops marketing strategies, and conducts seminars for retailers in the United States and Europe. Local, state, and federal governments are reliable sources of information on population, consumer spending, and economic conditions. The *Retail Trade Area Statistics* is a document prepared by the federal government that is very useful to retailers.

Academic institutions are other sources of information. The Center for Retailing Studies (CRS) at Texas A&M University is a corporately sponsored organization, which sponsors an annual symposium for retailing executives and professors who teach and conduct research in retailing. The CRS copublishes the *Retailing Issues Letter* with Arthur Andersen & Co., a bi-monthly essay on critical issues facing retailers. Academic publications available at college and university libraries, such as the *Journal of Retailing* and *Journal of Marketing*, are other sources of helpful information. The American Collegiate Retail Association and the International Textiles and Apparel Association are professional associations of college professors, many of whom conduct and publish scholarly research on merchandising topics.

SUMMARY POINTS

- Planning involves establishing an organization's goals or objectives and the strategies to achieve them.
- The 4-5-4 calendar is an accounting calendar used by retailers to structure their fiscal year.
- Divisions, departments, classifications, and subclasses define related groups of merchandise as manageable units of businesses.
- Sales plans are based on history and the current trends that may impact future sales.
- The attainment of sales objectives is contingent upon having a sufficient amount of inventory to support planned sales. Inventory planning methods are based on planned sales and a desired turnover objective.
- Open-to-buy is the amount of inventory that needs to be purchased for a specific selling period.
- Merchandise assortments are planned by brand, size, price, color, style, lifestyle, and various other factors.
- External information sources include consumer publications, trade publications, trade associations, forecasting services, and reporting services.

KEY TERMS AND CONCEPTS

basic stock method	comparable (stores,	division
bottom-up plan	period, sales, etc.)	fall
category	consumer publication	forecasting
category management	consultant	forecasting service
classification	department	4-5-4 calendar

long-range plans	reporting service	top-down plan
open-to-buy	short-term plan	trade association
open-to-ship	spring	trade publication
percentage variation method	stock-to-sales-ratio method	week of supply method
planned purchases	subclass	

FOR DISCUSSION

1. Develop a structure of departments, classes, and subclasses for the following merchandise divisions. Justify each segmentation as a unit of business:

   intimate apparel
   ready-to-wear
   home division
   accessories
   children's

2. Make a list of cyclical factors that affect the sale of apparel. Classify each relative to their reliability as a predictor. Explain how the impact of these factors will vary by category of merchandise.

3. Make a list of current economic, demographic, lifestyle, and fashion trends that should be considered when planning sales for a forthcoming season for the following departments:

   cosmetics
   activewear
   infants and toddlers
   china and crystal

4. What problems do you perceive in a sales planning method that is exclusively top down? Exclusively bottom up?

PROBLEMS

1. Spring sales for a department have been planned as follows:

February	$4000
March	$8000
April	$9000
May	$7000
June	$5000
July	$3000

   The turnover for the season is 4.0. Plan BOM inventories for each month using the basic stock and percentage variation methods. Compare the results of the two methods.

Compute monthly stock-to-sales ratios using the BOMs from each method. Compare the stock-to-sales ratios that result from each set of BOMs.

2. Assume that markdowns for the season are 15 percent of sales and that markdowns are distributed by month according to the following percentages:

February   20%
March   10%
April   5%
May   15%
June   20%
July   30%

Compute planned purchases for each month. Assume that the EOM for July is the BOM of February.

3. Using the formula for the periodic replenishment of staples, compute M when the rate of sale is 50 units:

DP = 2 weeks
RP = 1 week
S = 50 units per week

4. Develop the following assortments:
   - a vendor assortment of prestige cosmetics lines for a department store by percent.
   - a vendor assortment of mass market cosmetics for a full-line discounter by percent.
   - a size and color assortment for 2500 wool crew-neck sweaters available in S/M/L/XL and in ecru, navy, burgundy, black, and gray.
   - an item assortment for a fine jewelry case featuring onyx.
   - a knit/woven, size, style assortment of 5000 junior tops.
   - a style, color, and size assortment of a major brand of blue jeans.

ENDNOTES

1. Allen, Randy. (1984). *Bottom Line Issues in Retailing.* Chilton Book Company. Radnor, PA: 1984. p. 5.
2. Mahaffie, John. (March 1995). Why forecasts fail. *American Demographics.* pp. 34–40.
3. Faster turning inventories require more frequent ordering.
4. Reductions are included in the computation since reductions reduce the value of the inventory.
5. Robbins, Gary. (July 1989). New planning systems. *Stores.* pp. 61–67.
6. Reda, Susan. (March 1994). Planning systems. *Stores.* pp. 34–37.
7. Hisey, Pete. (May 1, 1995). Category management: Retail's new change-maker. *Discount Store News.* pp. 22, 43.

8. Staff. (December 14, 1992). Category management driven by customer base. *Drug Topics.* pp. 114–116.

9. Staff. (May 1, 1995). Avoid the pitfalls of category management. *Discount Store News.* p. 25.

chapter fourteen

PURCHASE TERMS

A retail buyer's task of seeking quality products at favorable prices is not unlike a consumer's quest for the best values in the retail marketplace. Though consumers have considerable product options, price is rarely negotiable. A greater degree of pricing flexibility exists in the wholesale marketplace where price and other purchase agreements are often negotiable. Retailers who negotiate favorable wholesale prices can pass their savings on to consumers in the form of lower retail prices, and thus compete more effectively with other retailers. Favorable nonprice vendor agreements can increase gross margin, decrease processing expenses, and improve cash flow. Chapter 14 covers the negotiable points of wholesale purchase agreements and their effect on a retailer's pricing and profitability.

After you have read this chapter, you will be able to discuss:

The retail buyer's role as a negotiator.

The impact of vendor payment terms on cash flow and gross margin.

Basic transportation terms.

The importance of strategic partnerships between retailers and their vendors.

DISCOUNTS

Discounts are reductions in the cost of merchandise. A **quantity discount** is a reduction in cost based on the amount of merchandise purchased. *Noncumulative discounts* apply to each order placed. *Cumulative,* or *patronage, discounts* apply to orders placed over time. The discount increases as the accumulated value of the orders increases. Noncumulative discounts encourage large individual orders while cumulative discounts encourage a steady flow of repeat orders. A quantity discount can be stated as a percentage applied to a total invoice. Quantity discounts can also be stated as reductions in unit cost. The unit cost of an item may be $1, however if more than 500 units are purchased, the unit price becomes $0.98; if 1000 units are purchased, the unit price becomes $0.95; and so on.

Vendors offer quantity discounts as sales inducements and to encourage the placement of large orders since it is less costly to pick, pack, ship, and invoice fewer large orders than many small orders. Most vendors have a **minimum order** requirement, a dollar or unit amount that defines the smallest order that the vendor is willing to accept. Levi Strauss' minimum order requirement is $10,000. Quantity discounts give large retailers a significant competitive pricing advantage over small independent retailers. Wal-Mart profitably retails some items at prices lower than the wholesale cost paid by small independents. However, retailers should avoid the temptation to buy excessive amounts of merchandise for the sake of obtaining quantity discounts. Markdowns on excessive inventory can more than negate the advantage of the discounts.

A **seasonal discount** is a reduction in cost for orders placed in advance of the normal ordering period. Seasonal discounts are sometimes stated as price schedules of discounted unit costs for orders placed before specified dates. Pricing programs such as these are often dubbed *Early Bird Specials* or *Pre-season Incentive Program*. Seasonal discounts often involve long-term purchase commitments over time. For instance, a retailer that commits to seasonal orders of $2 million may receive a discount after orders of $1 million have been placed. Long-term purchase commitments allow producers to plan production strategically and to balance the peaks and valleys of the production cycles of seasonal goods. However, retailers assume risk by committing to goods far in advance of a selling season, especially fashion goods. To minimize this risk, some producers offer seasonal discounts based on dollar commitments, allowing buyers to select specific styles closer to the selling season.

Just as the retailer offers slow-selling, end-of-season merchandise at markdown prices to consumers, vendors offer retailers their slow sellers, closeouts, and overruns at off-price at the end of a season. These opportunistic buys are often referred to as end-of-season discounts.

PURCHASE ORDERS

A **purchase order** is a contractual sales agreement between a retailer and a vendor in which items of merchandise, prices, delivery dates, and payment terms are specified. Purchase orders are often categorized by factors such as the type of goods ordered and order status:

Reorder   A **reorder** is for previously ordered goods. Reorders are typically for fast-selling items. Not all merchandise may be reordered. Because fashion goods change so quickly, basic goods are more likely to be reordered than fashion goods.

Fill-In Order   A **fill-in order** replenishes sold-out sizes/styles/colors of a basic inventory assortment.

Special Order   A **special order** is placed for an individual customer. Special orders are often restricted by a vendor's minimum order specifications. Some retailers wait until enough special orders have accrued to satisfy the minimum, however, this practice can lead to customer frustration by delaying the fulfillment of the special order.

Advance Order   An **advance order** is an advance commitment to buy merchandise that may not be available for delivery until the distant future. Producers use advance orders as a barometer to gauge production.

Back Order   A **back order** is for merchandise previously ordered but not received in a partial or *short shipment*. Short shipments are usually the result of vendors having run out of the ordered styles, colors, or sizes. Sometimes vendors substitute out-of-stock goods with other styles, colors, or sizes, much to the dismay of retailers.

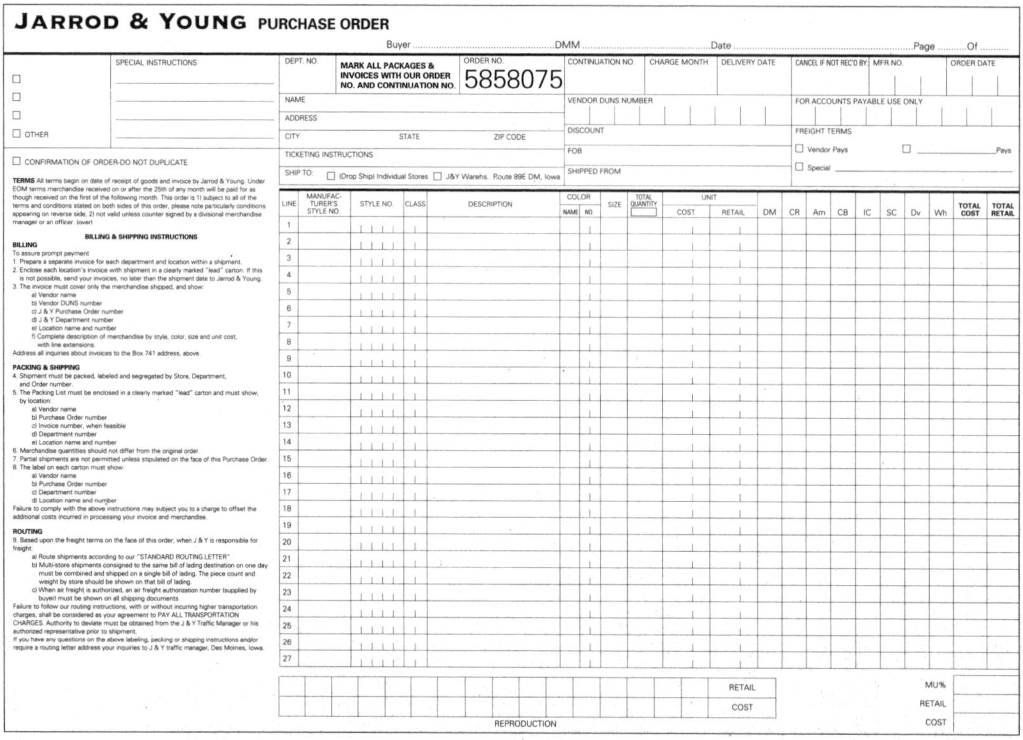

JARROD & YOUNG PURCHASE ORDER

Buyer .... DMM .... Date .... Page .... Of ....

| | SPECIAL INSTRUCTIONS | DEPT. NO. | MARK ALL PACKAGES & INVOICES WITH OUR ORDER NO. AND CONTINUATION NO. | ORDER NO. 5858075 | CONTINUATION NO. | CHARGE MONTH | DELIVERY DATE | CANCEL IF NOT REC'D BY | MFR NO. | | ORDER DATE |

☐
☐
☐
☐ OTHER

NAME

ADDRESS

CITY   STATE   ZIP CODE

VENDOR DUNS NUMBER

DISCOUNT

FOB

FOR ACCOUNTS PAYABLE USE ONLY

FREIGHT TERMS
☐ Vendor Pays   ☐ _____ Pays
☐ Special _____

☐ CONFIRMATION OF ORDER-DO NOT DUPLICATE

TICKETING INSTRUCTIONS

SHIP TO: ☐ (Drop Ship) Individual Stores   ☐ J&Y Warehs. Route 89E DM, Iowa

SHIPPED FROM

TERMS All terms begin on date of receipt of goods and invoice by Jarrod & Young. Under EOM terms merchandise received on or after the 25th of any month will be paid for as though received on the first of the following month. This order is 1) subject to all of the terms and conditions stated on both sides of this order, please note particularly conditions appearing on reverse side, 2) not valid unless counter signed by a divisional merchandise manager or an officer. (over)

BILLING & SHIPPING INSTRUCTIONS

BILLING
To assure prompt payment
1. Prepare a separate invoice for each department and location within a shipment.
2. Enclose each location's invoice with shipment in a clearly marked "lead" carton. If this is not possible, send your invoices, no later than the shipment date to Jarrod & Young.
3. The invoice must cover only the merchandise shipped, and show:
   a) Vendor name
   b) Vendor DUNS number
   c) J & Y Purchase Order number
   d) J & Y Department number
   e) Location name and number
   f) Complete description of merchandise by style, color, size and unit cost, with line extensions.
Address all inquiries about invoices to the Box 741 address, above.

PACKING & SHIPPING
4. Shipment must be packed, labeled and segregated by Store, Department, and Order number.
5. The Packing List must be enclosed in a clearly marked "lead" carton and must show, by location:
   a) Vendor name
   b) Purchase Order number
   c) Invoice number, when feasible
   d) Department number
   e) Location name and number
6. Merchandise quantities should not differ from the original order.
7. Partial shipments are not permitted unless stipulated on the face of this Purchase Order.
8. The label on each carton must show:
   a) Vendor name
   b) Purchase Order number
   c) Department number
   d) Location name and number
Failure to comply with the above instructions may subject you to a charge to offset the additional costs incurred in processing your invoice and merchandise.

ROUTING
9. Based upon the freight terms on the face of this order, when J & Y is responsible for freight:
   a) Route shipments according to our "STANDARD ROUTING LETTER"
   b) Multi-store shipments consigned to the same bill of lading destination on one day must be combined and shipped on a single bill of lading. The piece count and weight by store should be shown on that bill of lading.
   c) When air freight is authorized, an air freight authorization number (supplied by buyer) must be shown on all shipping documents.
Failure to follow our routing instructions, with or without incurring higher transportation charges, shall be considered as your agreement to PAY ALL TRANSPORTATION CHARGES. Authority to deviate must be obtained from the J & Y Traffic Manager or his authorized representative prior to shipment.
If you have any questions on the above labeling, packing or shipping instructions and/or require a routing letter address your inquiries to J & Y traffic manager, Des Moines, Iowa.

LINE	MANUFAC-TURER'S STYLE NO.	STYLE NO.	CLASS	DESCRIPTION	COLOR NAME	NO.	SIZE	TOTAL QUANTITY	UNIT COST	RETAIL	DM	CR	Am	CB	IC	SC	Dv	Wh	TOTAL COST	TOTAL RETAIL
1																				
2																				
3																				
4																				
5																				
6																				
7																				
8																				
9																				
10																				
11																				
12																				
13																				
14																				
15																				
16																				
17																				
18																				
19																				
20																				
21																				
22																				
23																				
24																				
25																				
26																				
27																				

RETAIL   MU%
COST   RETAIL
                      COST

REPRODUCTION

Figure 14.1

A sample purchase order.

Complete Order   A **complete,** or *filled,* **order** has been totally shipped by the vendor.

No Order   A **no order** refers to merchandise that arrives at a retailer's distribution center without a supporting purchase order.

Rush Order   A **rush,** or *priority,* **order** is expedited by the vendor and the retail distribution center, often to replenish a low assortment of fast-selling merchandise, to cover a breaking advertisement, or for the grand opening of a new store.

Past Due Order   A **past due order** has not been received by the purchase order's specified delivery date.

```
PM280 (16.00)                                      02 25 93     15 20 22
              SUMMARY OF OPEN ORDERS BY OPEN-TO-BUY MONTH      USER: T01
DEPT 390.  MFG ....    VENDOR NAME ALL VENDORS
     PO      PO    TOTAL   TOTAL  M U  CUR- MAR   APR  MAY  JUN  FUT-  TOTAL
S  NUMBER  TYPE    COST   RETAIL  PCT  RENT 1993  1993 1993 1993 URE   OPEN
_   1002476 SAM
_   1017326 REG  181137  410226 54.34                 410.2        410226
_   1022375 REG  134429  310220 54.58            310.2            310220
_   1022607 REG   86323  193768 53.93                 193.8        193768
_   1026012 REG  101959  230046 54.17                 230.0        230046
_   1027077 REG    1041    1162  7.35
_   1027671 REG   80398  182748 54.50                 182.7        182748
_  39005809 REG   84332  170458 48.84            170.5            170458
_  39005825 REG  237672  534098 53.98       534.1                 534098
_  39005833 REG   87437  196488 53.36  72.4                        72441
_  39005841 REG   80361  180588 53.36  21.5                        21505
_  39005858 REG   73612  165424 53.36       165.4                 165424
_  39005866 REG   67843  152456 53.36  14.0                        13972
_  39005874 REG   46998  105614 53.36       105.6                 105614

PF1=MENU  PF2=HELP  PF3=RECOVER   PF5=MORE PO'S  PF9=NEW FUNCTION ENTER=CONTINUE
ENTER 'S' TO SELECT A P O
```

```
PM278(16.00)        PO WITHIN VENDOR INQUIRY         02/25/93   15:15:23
 19 - FILENES                       VENDOR DUNS NUMBER:  51318665  USER: T01
  VENDOR NAME: SAHARA
    PO              SHIP                PO              SHIP
  NUMBER  DEPT POM  DATE  PO STATUS   NUMBER  DEPT POM  DATE  PO STATUS
01002476 0390  Y  12/03/92 OPEN ORDER  01017326 0390  Y  03/05/93 OPEN ORDER
01022375 0390  Y  04/01/93 OPEN ORDER  01022607 0390  Y  03/20/93 OPEN ORDER
01025071 0390  Y  04/10/93 PEND W/ERR  01025766 0390  Y  03/20/93 PEND W/ERR
01026012 0390  Y  04/12/93 OPEN ORDER  01026400 0390  Y  04/10/93 CANCELED
09008307 0390  Y  03/25/93 PEND MGMT   39005262 0390  Y  02/01/92 CANCELED
39005353 0390  Y  02/15/92 CANCELED    39005767 0390  Y  10/01/92 CANCELED
39005791 0390  Y  11/20/92 CANCELED    39005809 0390  Y  04/01/93 OPEN ORDER
39005825 0390  Y  02/20/93 OPEN ORDER  39005833 0390  Y  02/10/93 OPEN ORDER
39005841 0390  Y  01/15/93 OPEN ORDER  39005858 0390  Y  03/01/93 OPEN ORDER
39005866 0390  Y  01/25/93 OPEN ORDER  39005874 0390  Y  02/20/93 OPEN ORDER
39005882 0390  Y  12/15/92 OPEN ORDER  39005916 0390  Y  11/13/92 CANCELED
39005932 0390  Y  03/01/93 OPEN ORDER  71025766 0390  Y  03/20/93 CANCELED
76138226 0390  Y  04/01/93 OPEN ORDER  76138234 0390  Y  03/10/93 OPEN ORDER
76138242 0390  Y  02/04/93 OPEN ORDER  76138259 0390  Y  11/25/92 OPEN ORDER
76138267 0390  Y  11/25/92 OPEN ORDER  76138275 0390  Y  01/29/93 OPEN ORDER
76216790 0390  Y  11/25/92 OPEN ORDER  76216808 0390  Y  11/25/92 PEND W/ERR

           PF1=MENU      PF2=HELP    PF3=RECOVER    ENTER=CONTINUE
** 968 ** PRESS ENTER FOR MORE POS
```

Figure 14.2

POM systems track open-to-buy and purchase orders by number, ship date and status.

Standing Order   A **standing,** or *open,* **order** is an outstanding order to which additional items can be added without generating a new order.

Purchase order management (POM) systems have transformed purchase order processing from an inefficient superintensive procedure involving handwritten documents into a computerized system for preparing and transmitting orders electronically. POM systems also track purchase orders by factors such as order number, delivery date, vendor, and category of merchandise.

PAYMENT TERMS

An **invoice** is a vendor's itemized statement of the goods shipped, their unit and extended cost[1], and any additional charges for transportation and/or insurance. **Dating** is the period allowed for the payment of an invoice stipulated in the *terms* section of an invoice. *Net 30* and *net 60* are common expressions of payment terms, meaning that full payment of the invoice is due within thirty or sixty days of the **date of invoice** (DOI), the date that the invoice was issued.

A **cash discount** is a reduction in the amount due on an invoice when payment is made on or before a specified date. Unless otherwise specified, the **cash discount period** begins on the DOI and expires on the designated **cash discount date.** The **net payment period** begins on the cash discount date and ends on the specified **net payment date.** A cash discount is not applied until all other discounts have been deducted. Cash discounts are applied to merchandise charges only. Shipping and insurance charges are not discountable.

A common expression of cash discount terms is *2/10 net 30,* read "two ten net thirty." This means that a 2 percent discount may be deducted from an invoice paid within ten days of the DOI. Once the cash discount period has expired, the full amount of the invoice is due within thirty days of the DOI. The expression *2/10, 1/15, net 30* means that a 2 percent discount may be deducted from an invoice paid within ten days of the DOI, or a one percent discount if paid between eleven and fifteen days. Once both discount periods have expired, the full amount of the invoice is due within thirty days of the date of invoice. The expression *2/10 net 30* may also be written as *2/10, n/30.* When terms are not stated, it is assumed that full payment is due in thirty days. Cash discounts have become standard in many industries. Eight percent is typical of the female apparel industry.

Regular, or *ordinary,* **dating** assumes the DOI as the first day of the payment period. Discount and payment periods can be extended by beginning the period later than the DOI. An **EOM** notation means that the periods begin at the end of the month in which the invoice is dated. If the terms of an August 15 invoice are *2/10 net 30 EOM,* the discount period begins August 31 and a 2 percent discount may be deducted until September 10. Full payment is due through September 30.

Some vendors consider invoices dated the 25th of a month or after as if they were dated the first of the following month. In the case of an August 25 invoice dated *2/10 EOM,* a two percent discount may be deducted through October 10. Full payment is due by October 30. These are highly favorable terms for the retailer who has approximately six weeks to generate cash from the sale of the merchandise and still take advantage of the discount. **Proximo,** or *prox,* **dating** specifies the day of the following month by which the cash discount must be taken; *2% 15th prox. net 30* means that a 2 percent discount may be deducted through the fifteenth of the following month. Full payment is due within thirty days of the DOI.

Advance dating delays the beginning of discount and payment periods until a future date noted "as of." If the terms of an August 15 invoice are *2/10, net 30, as of December 1,* a 2 percent discount may be deducted through December 11. Full payment is due by December 31. Advance dating is also called *post* or *seasonal* dating and is common in the men's wear industry. **Extra dating** adds additional days to the discount and payment periods. If the terms of an August 15 invoice are *2/10, 60X or 2/10, 60 ex.,* a 2 percent discount may be deducted until October 25. Full payment is due November 15. Suppliers use advance and extra dating to induce retailers to accept early shipments of merchandise, preferring to show high receivables on their balance sheets rather than high inventories. A vendor may use these forms of dating to test merchandise in certain stores as early predictors of a season's selling trends.

ROG (*receipt-of-goods*) dating delays the beginning of the discount and payment periods until the goods are received by the retailer. If the terms of a shipment invoiced August 15 are *2/10 ROG,* and the goods arrive on September 1, a 2 percent discount may be deducted through September 11. Full payment is due by October 1. ROG dating compensates for extended shipping time due to slow transportation modes or the transportation of goods over a considerable distance. ROG dating is not used frequently. Dating terms that extend the payment period, such as advance or extra dating, are a more common method of ascertaining that a payment period does not expire before goods are received.

Dating is a frequent point of negotiation between retailers and their vendors. Lengthy payment periods allow a retailer to generate a considerable amount of cash from the sale of goods before having to pay for them, thus enhancing a positive cash flow. Vendors, on the other hand, prefer shorter payment periods, wishing to balance their own cash flow and to meet financial obligations, such as payroll and payments to their suppliers. Some vendors offer incentive programs that combine both discount and dating terms. K-Swiss is a footwear resource that offers multiple discount and extended payment period programs for replenishment orders based on quantities purchased. The *K Campaign Program* qualifies retailers for a 3-percent discount on replenishment orders and thirty-day credit terms with a minimum purchase of 12,500 pair a year; the *S Campaign Program* qualifies retailers for a 2-percent discount on replenishment orders and thirty-day credit terms with a minimum purchase of 3600 pair a year; the *Dealer Advantage Program* qualifies retailers for a 2-percent discount and sixty-days credit terms with a minimum purchase of 9600 pair per year.[2]

COMPUTING A DISCOUNT ON BILLED COST

Cash discounts are computed by multiplying the discount rate by the billed cost on the invoice:

$$cash\ discount = discount\ rate \times billed\ cost$$

A 2 percent discount on a $100,000 shipment is computed as follows:

$$cash\ discount = 2\% \times \$100,000$$
$$cash\ discount = .02 \times \$100,000$$
$$cash\ discount = \$2000$$

The discount is then subtracted from the billed cost to determine the balance due:

$$balance\ due = billed\ cost - cash\ discount$$
$$balance\ due = \$100,000 - \$2000$$
$$balance\ due = \$98,000$$

A balance due can be computed with a single step formula:

$$balance\ due = (100\% - discount\ rate) \times billed\ cost$$
$$balance\ due = (100\% - 2\%) \times \$100,000$$
$$balance\ due = 0.98 \times \$100,000$$
$$balance\ due = \$98,000$$

Anticipation is an additional discount for paying an invoice prior to a cash discount date. The discount is based on the prevailing prime rate of business interest, the number of days that the payment is made prior to the cash discount date, and the balance of the invoice after discount. The formula for computing the additional discount is:

$$additional\ discount = invoice\ balance \times interest\ rate \times time^3$$

Assume that the DOI on the above invoice was August 15 and that payment was made on August 20, five days in advance of the August 25 cash discount date. If the prevailing interest rate is 6 percent, the additional discount is computed as follows:

$$additional\ discount = invoice\ balance \times interest\ rate \times time$$

$$additional\ discount = \$98{,}000 \times 0.06 \times 5/360$$

$$additional\ discount = \$81.66$$

The additional discount is deducted from the $98,000 invoice balance leaving a new balance due of $97,918.34. Anticipation is not a common discounting practice. Many suppliers stipulate "no anticipation" as part of their dating terms.

Cash, or *immediate,* **dating** are payment arrangements with no provision for discount or payment periods. **COD,** or *cash on delivery,* means that cash payment is due upon the delivery of the goods. Suppliers ship COD to new retailers with no established credit, or to retailers with poor credit histories. *Cash in advance* (CBD), and *cash before delivery* (CBD) are other forms of cash dating.

Goods sold **on consignment** are not paid for until they are sold. Consignment arrangements are rare but are sometimes used to sell big ticket items with a slow or unpredictable rate of sale, such as works of art, to minimize the retailers risk:

- A positive cash flow is ensured, since goods are not paid for until *after* they are sold.
- There is no capital tied up in inventory.
- Goods are returned to the vendor if not sold within an agreed upon time period.

Though arrangements are similar, there is a distinction between goods sold on consignment and goods sold **on memorandum.** The title of consignment goods passes from the vendor to the consumer but never passes to the retailer; the title of memorandum goods passes from the vendor to the retailer, usually when the goods are shipped, and then passes to the consumer at the point of sale.

NINE TECHNIQUES OF SUCCESSFUL VENDOR NEGOTIATIONS

1. *Act Collaboratively, Not Competitively.* Negotiation is not "me against you." Recognize that the other party has to come away with a benefit, too. Show them how giving you what you want will help them get what they want.
2. *Prepare.* Do your homework about the other party; gather as much information about them as possible. Even rehearse and outline your remarks.
3. *Know What You Want.* Being able to state specific proposals or plans gives you strength. Don't wait to "see what they offer us." Know in advance what you must have, and what you can afford to give up. Each time you make a concession, get something in return.
4. *Don't Let Your Ego Get in the Way.* When you think of the negotiating process as winning or losing, you have too much ego involved. Don't get sidetracked by personalities or emotions. Stick to the issues.
5. *Learn to Make Time Your Ally.* Time is at the heart of every negotiation. Learn to make it work for you. Try to learn the other party's deadline without giving away yours. Most concessions occur at somebody's deadline.
6. *If You Can't Agree on Point One, Go to Point Two.* Agree even in small increments. Don't get hung up on one issue. It is easier to come back to an issue after you have reached some agreement, and the other person has invested time and energy in working with you.
7. *Be a Creative Risktaker.* If you are known to not take risks, you are predictable and can be easily manipulated. Create your own solutions; there is usually more than one way to get the results you want.
8. *Closing the Negotiation: Wrap it Up.* Don't stay around and chat after you have reached an agreement. If you have what you want, close the negotiation. Don't linger too long, or it may unravel.
9. *Develop Long-term Relationships.* Focusing on long-term goals will keep both parties from being sidetracked by short term frustrations. Knowing you are both in for the long haul means you can solve any problem that arises.

Prepared by Elizabeth Tahir, president of Liz Tahir Consulting, a retail marketing and management consulting and training firm in New Orleans, Louisiana.

THE LONG-TERM IMPACT OF DISCOUNTS

Discounts can dramatically impact a retailer's profitability over time. Consider the retailer who forfeits a $2000 discount on a $100,000 shipment invoiced *2/10 net 30*. The retailer has effectively paid an annual interest rate of 36 percent to use $100,000 for the twenty days between the cash discount date and the net payment date as the following calculation demonstrates:

$$interest = principal \times rate \times time$$
$$\$2000 = \$100,000 \times rate \times 20/360$$
$$\$2000 = \$100,000 \times rate \times 0.056$$
$$\$2000 = \$5600 \times rate$$
$$\frac{\$2000}{\$5600} = rate$$
$$0.357 = rate$$
$$36\% = rate$$

When a negative cash flow prevents a retailer from taking advantage within their cash discount, it is often wise to borrow money. The cash discount savings will exceed the interest paid on the loan, since annual borrowing rates are lower than annualized cash discount rates. Borrowing for short periods to take advantage of cash discounts is a common retailing practice. Favorable dating arrangements yield another important fiscal advantage. Since cash discounts decrease the cost-of-goods-sold, they increase gross margin and ultimately net profit.

TRANSPORTATION TERMS

Transportation terms identify the bearer of the cost of shipping goods from the supplier to the retailer, as well as the point at which the title of the goods passes from one to the other. The cost of transporting goods from a supplier to a retailer is typically absorbed by the retailer. However, transportation terms are sometimes negotiated whereby the supplier absorbs all or part of the transportation costs. Since transportation costs increase the cost-of-goods-sold, favorable transportation terms maximize gross margin and net profit.

FOB stands for *free on board*. Words, such as *origin, factory, destination,* or the name of a city, that follow FOB refer to the point to which a supplier pays transportation charges, and the point at which the title of the goods passes from the supplier to the retailer. *FOB factory* means that the retailer pays the transportation charges from the vendor's *factory* and assumes title to the goods at that point. *FOB destination* means that the vendor pays the transportation charges to the retail *destination* without relinquishing title until that point.

The point at which title transfers from the supplier to the retailer is important when determining the responsibility of lost or damaged goods. When title is transferred to the retailer at the point at which the goods are shipped, the retailer must pay for all of the goods shipped and obtain compensation from the freight carrier for lost or damaged goods. When title is not transferred to the retailer until the goods reach the store, the supplier is responsible for replacing lost or damaged goods, and for recovering the loss from the carrier.

Sometimes suppliers establish an FOB point that equates the cost of transporting their goods to the cost of transporting competitors' goods. A Los Angeles-based supplier competing with a Chicago-based supplier for a Philadelphia retailer's business may ship goods *FOB Chicago*. Shared shipping responsibility can also be expressed as:

FOB factory (or store), charges shared: __ % *factory*, __ % *store*

Figure 14.3

One vendor's purchase terms and conditions.

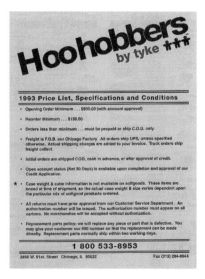

The following is a list of agreements between retailers and that indicate payment responsibility for transportation costs, and the point at which the title of goods is transferred from the vendor to the retailer:

- *FOB origin, freight collect.* The retailer pays the freight charges and owns the goods while in transit.
- *FOB origin, freight prepaid.* The vendor pays the freight charges, but the retailer owns the goods while in transit.
- *FOB origin, freight prepaid and charged back.* The vendor pays the freight charges but is reimbursed for them by invoicing the retailer for the freight charges along with the merchandise. The retailer owns the goods while in transit.
- *FOB destination, freight collect.* The retailer pays the freight charges but the vendor owns the goods while in transit.
- *FOB destination, freight prepaid.* The vendor pays the freight charges and owns the goods while in transit.
- *FOB destination, freight collect and allowed.* The retailer pays the freight charges but is reimbursed for them by a chargeback deducted from the vendor's invoice. The vendor owns the goods while in transit.

Timing the shipment of goods is an important part of a merchandising strategy. Since orders are placed against an open-to-buy planned for a specific period, the timely arrival of merchandise ensures that inventory levels are appropriate to planned sales. Most purchase orders specify two dates to define the delivery parameters: a *do not ship before* date and a *do not ship after* date. Early arrival of goods can be as devastating as late arrival. Unless extra dating has been arranged, early shipments can lead to imbalanced cash flow. Storage is also an issue related to early shipments.

Transportation Arrangements

Transportation *terms* are a function of the retail buyer. Transportation *arrangements* are a function of the retailer's traffic department. Cost-effective transportation arrangements will effectively minimize the cost-of-goods-sold and maximize gross margin and net profit. Transportation costs are a function of the weight and bulk of the merchandise shipped, the distance between the supplier's and the retailer's distribution centers, and the mode of transportation used.

The rates charged by the transportation industry were once regulated by federal agencies, such as the Interstate Commerce Commission and the Civil Aeronautics Board. However, legislation, such as the Motor Carrier Act and the Staggers Rail Act, has significantly deregulated the transportation industry. Deregulation has fostered intense competition among transporters of goods, or *carriers,* who can now tailor rates and services to match the needs of individual shippers. The complexities of a deregulated transportation environment have increased the importance of the traffic function in retail organizations. Traffic managers now have the ability to increase service and decrease costs by favorable negotiations with carriers just as buyers negotiate favorable terms with their vendors.

The four transportation modes used to transport goods from suppliers to retailers include:

1. *Motor carriers,* or truckers, are the most common form of transportation used to transport domestic goods from suppliers to retailers.[4] Motor carriers provide door-to-door service by picking up shipments from a supplier and delivering them directly to a retailer's distribution center. Motor carriers are also used to supplement other forms of transportation that do not offer door-to-door service. Yellow Freight, Consolidated Freightways, and Roadway Express are among the nation's largest motor carriers.
2. *Railroads* are an economical transportation mode used for long hauls of heavy, bulky commodities. Retailers transport goods by rail in conjunction with other transportation modes, such as trucks, reaping the economic advantages of rail and the door-to-door efficiencies of truck. The combination of two or more modes of transportation is called **intermodal transportation.**
3. *Airlines* are the most rapid and most expensive transportation mode. Airlines expose shipments to the least potential for damage, pilferage, or obsolescence. They are only used to transport valuable or highly perishable goods.
4. *Water carriers* are a slow but economic transportation mode used by retailers to import directly goods from foreign sources.

Several services are also available for shipping small packages, including the parcel post service of the U.S. Postal Service and United Parcel Service, a private door-to-door service for transporting packages under seventy pounds. Federal Express and Emery Air Freight also provide

Figure 14.4

Retailers use water carriers to directly import goods from foreign resources.

expedient delivery of very small packages and documents, as do inter-city bus lines such as Greyhound.

Transportation firms are categorized as common, contract, and private. A **common carrier** establishes uniform rates and schedules for all shippers. A **contract carrier** negotiates individual agreements with shippers or small groups of shippers. Some organizations operate as **private carriers** that ship goods with their own transportation equipment and facility. Many large retailers transport outbound shipments of goods from their distribution centers to stores using an internal fleet of trucks.

Retailers sometimes contract the services of transportation intermediaries called **consolidators,** or *freight forwarders.* Consolidators combine less-than-truckload (ltl) shipments from multiple suppliers into truckload (tl) shipments, and then contract carriers to deliver the tl shipments to their retail destinations. Since ltl rates are higher than the tl rates, a consolidator makes a profit by charging shippers rates that are lower than the ltl rates, but higher than tl rates.

Time and cost are the two major factors considered when determining a transportation mode. In general, slower modes of transportation are more economical than more expeditious modes and are appropriate for transporting goods shipped in advance of their selling

1. *Forest, Stephanie & Golby, Ruth. (May 31, 1993). A Pier 1 in every port?* Business Week. *p. 88.*
2. *Brookman, Faye. (January 1991). Re-inventing Pier 1.* Stores. *pp. 76–80.*
3. *Bull, Marion. (April 1994). Pier 1 Imports: Exotic is hip but will it sell in Peoria? You bet!* Port News. *pp. 12–23.*
4. *Gould, Les. (November 1993). Multiple sort systems move 44 million items out on time.* Modern Materials Handling. *pp. 48, 50.*

Company Profile 14.1

Founded in San Francisco in 1962, Pier 1 Imports has become the largest specialty retailer of decorative home furnishings, gifts, and related items in the United States. Pier 1 directly imports from forty-four countries worldwide including China, India, Indonesia, Malaysia, France, Italy, and Germany. More than 7000 containers of merchandise are transported by water carriers to the Ports of Los Angeles, Charleston, Houston, Baltimore, Norfolk, and Savannah each year. Local drayage companies carry goods to Pier 1 distribution centers in Maryland, Texas, California, Illinois, Ohio, and Georgia, while an internal fleet of more than sixty tractors and 200 trailers transports goods to nearly 700 stores located in forty-seven states, Mexico, and Canada. As many as twenty parties are involved in the process of transporting Pier 1 merchandise from point of production to stores, including agents, steamship companies, customs offices, consolidators, and drayage people.

The complexities of direct importing necessitate a close interaction between Pier 1's merchandising and logistical groups. The transportation department fosters informed merchandising decisions by providing buyers with information on special trade agreements to minimize the impact of tariffs on the cost of merchandise. Expedient logistics have reduced the average amount of time that Pier 1 merchandise is tied up on water from ninety days to less than forty days.[1,2,3]

season. However, retailers often pay premium transportation rates to expedite the delivery of perishable goods or goods with immediate consumer demand. A retailer that desperately needs goods for an ad breaking in forty-eight hours will pay premium transportation rates to ensure delivery to cover the ad. Rapid transportation also decreases the amount of time that goods remain in the merchandise pipeline.

THE DISTRIBUTION CENTER

Single-unit retail operations ship goods from suppliers directly to their stores at which point they are unpacked, ticketed, and prepared for the selling floor. Most multiunit retailers ship goods to a central distribution point where they are processed and then distributed to stores. The **distribution center** (DC) performs critical inventory management functions by expediting processing to ensure the timely arrival of goods in stores, and by working closely with buyers to resolve issues related to damaged receipts, short shipments, and supplier substitutions.[5,6] The following is a list of the major functions performed by retail distribution centers:[7]

- *Receiving.* Unloading shipments at the dock.
- *Checking.* Matching the contents of shipments against a packing slip. Quality assurance is often a part of this function.
- *Marking.* Price labeling or ticketing the merchandise.
- *Putaway.* Warehousing basic merchandise for future replenishment of stores or bulk items, such as furniture, for direct shipment to customers.
- *Picking.* The distribution of putaway goods to stores or customers.
- *Distribution.* Allocating shipments to stores.
- *Shipping.* Routing merchandise to stores.
- *Vendor Return.* Processing returns of damaged or slow-selling goods to suppliers for credit.
- *Traffic.* Coordinating the inbound delivery from suppliers and outbound shipments from stores.

VENDOR PARTNERSHIPS

Vendor partnerships are collaborations between retailers and their suppliers to reduce distribution costs, control inventory, increase sales, and improve gross margin and GMROI.[8] These long-term relationships go beyond the traditional interactions between buyers and sellers often including product development, marketing, and merchandise presentation.

Vendor partnerships have many forms. **Floor ready merchandise (FRM)** involves negotiated agreements for packaging, casing, folding, hanging, and ticketing merchandise so that it is ready for selling-floor presentation upon its arrival at the retail distribution center. FRM is shipped as acceptable selling-floor hangers, eliminating *hanger selling*, a labor-intensive process of replacing inexpensive vendor garment hangers with better-quality store hangers. FRM is **preticketed,** or *source-marking* is a function that a vendor can perform more cost effectively than a retailer as part of its own ticketing or packaging process, thus eliminating the need to ticket merchandise with price or other identifying information at retail distribution centers. Though some vendors **case pack,** or *prepack,* shipments with a standard assortment of sizes, colors, and styles, FRM assortments are packed specific to replenishment needs of individual stores. These shipments can be sent directly to designated stores without being sorted at retail distribution centers.

The benefits of FRM are far-reaching. Distribution center operating costs can be reduced by as much as 80 percent, and the average amount of time that goods remain in a DC can decrease from a few days to a few hours. FRM facilitates **cross docking** whereby the distribution center functions like a trucking terminal with merchandise arriving in a truck in one bay, and going out in another truck in another bay with virtually no processing in between. The long-term result is an increase in turnover and GMROI.[9]

Some vendor partnerships involve merchandise presentation. Pacific Coast Feather, a manufacturer of bed pillows and comforters works with retailers to create packaging, fixtures, signage, and sample presentations for their bedding departments.[10] Some vendors offer packaging options. A glassware vendor may offer stemmed glassware as individual units of open stock, or as sets of six or twelve attractively packaged in gift boxes.

MOOTSIES TOOTSIES

Shoes to Die For

SIZE RUN AND BREAKDOWN INFORMATION:

RUN	WIDTH	SIZE RUN	BREAKDOWN
			5 - 6 - 7 - 8 - 9 - 10
D	M	6/10 × 12	1 1 1 2 2 2 2 1
R	M	6/10 × 18	1 2 2 3 3 3 2 2
G	M	5/10 × 18	1 2 5 5 3 2
CD	M	6/10 × 18	2 5 5 4 2
KT	M	6/10 × 12	1 3 3 3 2
AA	N	7/10 × 6	1 1 1 1 1 1

Figure 14.5

Shoe vendors case pack shipments with standard assortments of sizes.

Risk sharing is another type of vendor partnership. Though buyers hope that goods will sell at prices consistent with their gross margin objectives, each order is a gamble in that some of goods may eventually require drastic markdowns. Vendors can share this risk in two ways:

- Return agreements whereby the retailer is allowed to return unsold goods after a specified period.
- Markdown allowances whereby the vendor compensates the retailer for markdowns. The compensation is often based on the difference between a guaranteed gross margin and the actual gross margin with an allowance against future purchases.

Markdown allowances are a sensitive issue between retailers and their vendors. Many vendors resent sharing markdown expenses feeling that markdowns are often attributable to factors controllable by the retailer, such as poor presentation and inadequate selling floor coverage. A shoe company sales representative once responded to a buyer's request for markdown money with the comment that he was in business to sell shoes, not markdowns.[11]

VENDOR-SPONSORED PROMOTIONAL SUPPORT

Many vendors offer retailers promotional opportunities to enhance the recognition and sale of their products in stores.

Cooperative Advertising Cooperative advertising is an agreement between a retailer and a vendor to share advertising expense. The level of a vendor's participation in a cooperative advertising program is based on a retailer's purchases over a specified time period, usually a year. Most cooperative advertising programs place restrictions on the items advertised and the advertising medium and schedule. Some vendors prepare generic advertising for their products that retailers can adapt for their own use with tag lines, such as "Available at all Jacobson's stores," dubbed onto electronic ads or store logos pasted onto print ads. Retailers save considerable advertising production costs by using vendor prepared advertising.

Figure 14.6

Various elements of a cooperative advertising program.

Other forms of promotional support include:

- *Product demonstrations:* Some vendors provide demonstrators to show the effective use of their product or product line in stores. Cosmetic makeovers and countertop appliance demonstrations are common vendor-sponsored demonstrations in department stores.
- *Premiums:* A **premium** is a product offered without charge or at a very low retail price to customers who have made a minimum purchase within a product line. Advertising for premiums often reads: "Yours free with any \$__ purchase of__" or "Yours for \$__ with any \$___ purchase of__". Premiums are common in the prestige cosmetics industry where a free premium is called a **gift-with-purchase,** or *gwp,* and a paid-for premium is called a **purchase-with-purchase,** or *pwp.*
- *Samples:* Samples are small quantities of a product offered without charge to customers independent of a purchase within a line. Samples are common in the prestige fragrance industry.
- *Contest and drawings:* **Contests** are promotional activities that require the demonstration of a skill. **Drawings** or *sweepstakes* are games of chance. Contests are popular for children's products.
- *Displays and exhibits:* Some vendors loan retailers museum-like exhibits for use in displays or in conjunction with a vendor promotion.

Some vendors provide point-of-purchase signage and fixtures to enhance the sale of their product line in stores, a topic of discussion in Chapter 16. Other vendors sponsor training schools for salespeople to highlight new products and provide selling tips. Some vendors pay commissions or other incentives to the retail salespeople who sell their product line.

ELECTRONIC DATA INTERCHANGE (EDI)

Electronic data interchange (EDI) is a partnership between a retailer and a supplier that involves a backward flow of customer purchase information through the distribution pipeline beginning at the retailer's point of sale. The partners use the information to execute their function more efficiently. EDI is sometimes extended to include vendors' suppliers, such as fabric mills.[12]

Company Profile 14.2

Elizabeth Arden

In 1910, Elizabeth Arden developed a group of skin care products to use in her sumptuous New York beauty salon that catered to fashionable women of prominent social position. The creams, lotions, and oils eventually evolved into a complete line of treatment, color, and fragrance products, making Elizabeth Arden a globally recognized name in cosmetics. Along with its two fragrances, *Red* and *Sunflowers*, Elizabeth Arden is a mainstay in most better and moderate department stores, including Bloomingdale's, Burdines, Nordstrom, Saks Fifth Avenue, Dillard's, and Robinson's/May. Since 1990, Elizabeth Arden has been a division of Unilever, the largest worldwide producer of consumer products.

Elizabeth Arden takes an active role in the presentation, promotion, and sale of its product line at the retail level. Realizing the importance of location, the company strategically negotiates with stores for heavily trafficked locations, such as those close to mall entrances, parking lot entrances, and escalators. To ensure a consistent and appealing presentation, Elizabeth Arden develops a schematic for presenting merchandise with standards for facing and stocking products in cases. Tester units and signage are designed to integrate the line's distinctive black and gold packaging to create a strong visual impact.

Elizabeth Arden works closely with retailers to ensure a high level of customer service. The company offers guidance to retailers in selecting beauty consultants consistent with the line's image, and in structuring salary and commission arrangements. Product expertise is assured through on-going training schools that provide beauty consultants with new product information and the latest makeover techniques. *Behind the Red Door*, a corporate training newsletter, offers tips for building sales and information on new product launches. An account coordinator travels from store to store within the retail organization acting as a mentor to the beauty consultant, assisting with promotions, and serving as a link between Elizabeth Arden and the retailer.[1,2]

1. *Zinn, Laura. (June 29, 1992). Beauty and the beastliness.* Business Week. *p. 39.*
2. *Staff. (October 19, 1966). Elizabeth Arden is dead at 81; Made beauty a global business.* New York Times.

EDI involves developing model assortments of product styles, sizes, and colors by store based on sales histories, sales projections, desired turnover, and lead time for delivery. Product information is captured electronically at point of sale and is periodically transmitted to suppliers who then replenish the depleted inventory. EDI is most often used for basic reorderable goods with broad assortments of styles, sizes, or colors, such as cosmetics and hosiery.[13] Dillard's also uses EDI to test fashion goods at the beginning of the season and then reorders the best selling items.[14]

There are several positive outcomes associated with EDI including:[15]

- *Improved in-stock position.* The in-stock position of EDI merchandise is 95 percent or better since assortments are rapidly replenished as merchandise is sold.[16] The in-stock position of non EDI merchandise is often as low as 50 percent. Fewer stockouts result in increased sales, since customers are likely to find their choice of size, color, and style.[17]
- *Better inventory management.* EDI improves turnover since fast-selling goods are re-ordered while slow-turning goods are not. EDI also enhances space productivity since slow sellers are edited from assortments freeing up valuable shelf and floor space for more productive goods in frequent small orders also reduce the amount of inventory carried.
- *Shortened lead time.* Because time-consuming manual ordering tasks are eliminated, some retailers experience as much as a 50 percent reduction in lead time by implementing EDI. JCPenney developed an EDI program with Haggar Apparel that accelerated delivery to the selling floor by ten days. Sales increased by 11 percent with 19 percent less inventory on hand.[18]
- *Greater efficiency.* EDI eliminates errors due to manual counts, data entry, and illegible orders. By reducing administrative tasks, EDI permits buyers to concentrate on selecting merchandise and developing merchandising programs.[19]
- *Increased profitability.* A higher markup is maintained on EDI merchandise since only merchandise that is selling is reordered. Dillard's estimates that the maintained markup on EDI merchandise is 3 to 4 percent higher than non-EDI merchandise, and that every dollar invested in EDI replenished goods is 16.3 percent more profitable than non-EDI goods.[20]

QUICK RESPONSE — PILOT PROGRAM									
Actual Results									
Date	On-hand	On-Order	Sales		Weeks Supply	Inventory Turns	Stock-Outs	Lost Sales	New Order
			Curr.	Avg.					
3/11	1,120	0	50	69.0	16.2	2.7	0	0	33
3/18	799	93	325	94.6	8.4	4.1	1	3	105
3/26	924	138	29	88.6	10.4	4.1	1	2	6
4/3	836	111	95	89.2	9.4	4.3	0	1	36
4/10	857	36	38	85.2	10.0	4.2	0	0	15
4/17	831	51	37	81.8	10.2	4.2	0	0	174
4/24	674	39	193	89.2	7.6	4.7	0	0	174
5/3	816	198	79	88.6	9.2	4.8	0	0	45
5/9	726	207	89	88.6	8.2	4.9	0	0	57

Figure 14.7

EDI increased the turnover of a major retailer's hosiery department from 2.7 to 4.9 while reducing stock-outs and lost sales. *Reprinted by permission from Chain Store Age Executive (Bruce Fox & Andersen Consulting, March 1991, p.5B). Copyright Lebhar-Friedman, Inc. 425 Park Avenue, New York, NY 10022.*

Advance shipping notices (ASN) and shippers container marking (SCM) are two technologically advanced concepts that have enhanced EDI's success. An ASN is a supplier's electronic notification to a retailer that an order has been shipped. SCM involved identifying the contents of cartons by bar codes which are scanned into a retailer's inventory upon receipt. The cartons are then sent directly to stores without further distribution and processing. This paperless transaction speeds up the flow of merchandise while significantly reducing processing expenses.

Suppliers also benefit from EDI. EDI provides them with sales information that can be used to manage inventories and plan production. To complete the trading linkage, some suppliers develop similar partnerships with their own suppliers matching consumer demand at one end of the merchandise pipeline to the availability of raw materials at the other. The standardization of EDI forms and procedures has facilitated the widespread application of EDI. Once the property of large retailers and suppliers, EDI is now technologically and fiscally feasible for small retailers and suppliers.

EDI requires a bond of trust between the retailer and supplier. The retailer must feel confident that a vendor will not share their sales information with competitive retailers, and that the actual contents of cartons matches that which is indicated on the SCM. Some predict that EDI will eventually become a condition of transacting business with many retailers.[21] Dillard's encourages EDI partnerships by charging vendors a handling fee for every purchase order not generated through EDI.[22]

Four companies are experimenting with an EDI concept that could revolutionize the way in which business is transacted between marketing channel members. DuPont (a fiber producer), Springs Industries (a mill), The Warren Featherbone Company (a manufacturer of children's apparel), and Mercantile Stores (a department store conglomerate) are testing a theory that no one in the distribution channel should be paid until goods are sold to consumers. In essence, the retailer acts as a broker. As consumers make retail purchases, the proceeds are split among the four partners according to a predetermined fair share. The system encourages active support of retail sales by all channel members.[23,24]

THE VENDOR MATRIX

A **vendor matrix** is a list of preferred vendors selected at conglomerate level. The decision to include a vendor in a matrix is based on the product line's compatibility with the organization's merchandising objectives, favorable price negotiations, and various forms of vendor support, in exchange for a retailer's commitment to space and estab-

Figure 14.8

Federated Department Stores hosts periodic vendor fairs to recruit new vendors.

lished inventory levels. Some organizations limit their buyers to conducting business only with matrix vendors. Retailers have reduced the number of vendors with whom they conduct business by as much as 50 percent as a result of adopting a matrix.[25,26,27] These streamlined vendor structures are criticized as unholy alliances between *large* retailers and *large* suppliers that limit business opportunities for small suppliers. Some feel that a matrix transforms a buying function into an order-filling function by limiting a buyer's *autonomy*. To negate this criticism, some retailers host periodic vendor fairs to give vendors outside the matrix the opportunity to pitch their goods to buyers for possible inclusion in their assortments.[28,29,30]

VENDOR RELATIONS

Maximizing the amount of merchandise sold to consumers is an objective that is common to both retailers and their suppliers. Though both share common goals, their individual profit objectives are sometimes a source of conflict. A supplier's profit is derived from selling goods to retailers at the *highest* possible prices, while a retailer's profit is derived from purchasing goods from suppliers at the *lowest* possible prices. To circumvent conflict, some retailers publish vendor relations guidelines

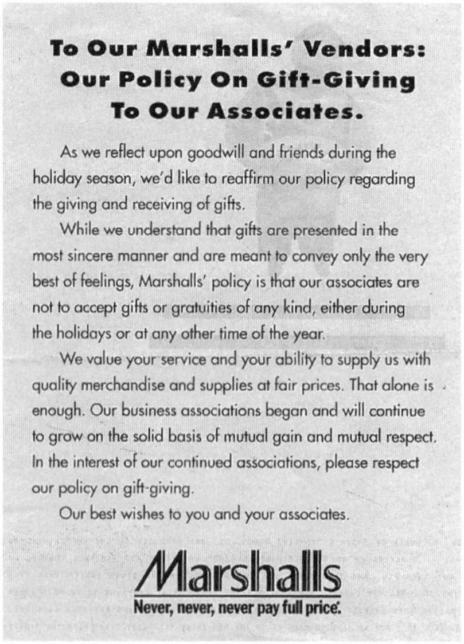
To Our Marshalls' Vendors: Our Policy On Gift-Giving To Our Associates.

As we reflect upon goodwill and friends during the holiday season, we'd like to reaffirm our policy regarding the giving and receiving of gifts.

While we understand that gifts are presented in the most sincere manner and are meant to convey only the very best of feelings, Marshalls' policy is that our associates are not to accept gifts or gratuities of any kind, either during the holidays or at any other time of the year.

We value your service and your ability to supply us with quality merchandise and supplies at fair prices. That alone is enough. Our business associations began and will continue to grow on the solid basis of mutual gain and mutual respect. In the interest of our continued associations, please respect our policy on gift-giving.

Our best wishes to you and your associates.

Marshalls

Never, never, never pay full price.

Figure 14.9

To avoid conflicts of interest, most retailers prohibit buyers from accepting gifts from vendors.

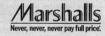

Company Profile 14.3

The VF Corporation of Wyomissing, Pennsylvania is a leading producer of internationally renowned brands of jeanswear, innerwear, children's wear, and casual apparel. VF's popular brands include its namesake line, Vanity Fair, as well as Girbaud, Lee, Wrangler, Riders, Vassarette, Eileen West, and Healthtex. VF's Market Response System, or MRS, links VF to more than 36,000 stores at which VF products are sold, including JCPenney, Wal-Mart, Kmart, and Dillard's. Each day, product information scanned from price tickets is transmitted from stores by satellite or phone line to a VF mainframe. The information is used to restock retailers with full complements of VF assortments based on the styles and sizes that are actually selling.

The results for retailers participating have been overwhelming. Reorder times have shrunk from seventy days to a week. Overall sales have reflected a 17 percent increase while average inventories have decreased by 28.4 percent. The lower average inventory has resulted in an 18.6 percent increase in turnover. VF has also reaped advantages from its investment in MRS. Brand managers use MRS information to develop new styles and identify opportunities for growth. MRS has become a vehicle for efficient production scheduling and for reducing inventories and costs.

Underwood, Elaine. (February 8, 1993). A high-tech marketer in disguise. Brandweek. *pp. 14–17.*

that establish parameters for professional interactions. For instance, to avoid conflicts of interest, many retailers prohibit buyers from accepting gifts or any form of hospitality from vendors, other than an occasional lunch.

In spite of these provisions, interactions between retailers and their suppliers are sometimes adversarial. Vendors provoke retailers by shipping short, shipping late, or making random substitutes for out-of-stock goods. Retailers often retaliate by levying chargeback penalties for incomplete orders or damaged or mislabeled goods. A vendor once reported a $50.50 chargeback on an item with an upside down label: $0.50 was for the error and $50 was for a minimum penalty charge.[31]

Another supplier reported a $10,000 charge back on a $20,000 order for goods that arrived two weeks late. The vendor disputed the charge-back because the goods eventually sold out at regular price, even though they arrived late.[32]

Sometimes transgressions can be traced to the retailer. Common abuses to vendors include taking cash discounts on invoices after cash discount periods have expired, returning as flawed merchandise that was damaged on the selling floor, and canceling ready-to-be-shipped orders with little notice. In 1994, a New York State Supreme Court judge found Wal-Mart's cancellation clause in its purchase order "unconscionable" due to the financial ramifications to the vendor. The clause gave Wal-Mart the right to cancel an order any time prior to shipment, regardless of the stage of production.[33]

SUMMARY POINTS

- Quantity and seasonal discounts are reductions in the cost of merchandise that are mutually advantageous to the vendor and the retailer.
- Dating is the time period allowed for the payment of an invoice. Favorable dating terms reduce the cost-of-goods-sold and improve a retailer's cash flow.
- Transportation terms identify the bearer of the cost of shipping goods from the vendor to the retailer, as well as the point at which the title of the goods passes from one to the other. Time and cost are the two factors that are considered when determining a transportation mode.
- Vendor partnerships are collaborations between retailers and their suppliers to reduce distribution costs, control inventory, increase sales, and improve gross margin and GMROI.
- Electronic data interchange is a trading partnership among marketing channel members whereby each member can access customer purchase information to execute more efficiently their function in the supply pipeline.
- A vendor matrix is a list of a retailer's preferred merchandise resources.
- Retailers and vendors should work together cooperatively to achieve their goals.

KEY TERMS AND CONCEPTS

advance dating	dating	memorandum
anticipation	discount	minimum order
cash dating	distribution center	net payment date
cash discount	drawing	net payment period
cash discount date	EOM dating	past due order
cash discount period	electronic data	premium
cash pack	interchange	pre-ticketing
COD	extra dating	private carrier
common carrier	fill-in order	proximo dating
consignment	floor-ready merchandise	purchase order
consolidator	FOB	purchase with purchase
contest	gift-with-purchase	quantity discount
contract carrier	intermodal	regular dating
cooperative advertising	transportation	ROG dating
cross docking	invoice	seasonal discount
date of invoice	matrix	

FOR DISCUSSION

1. Discuss several categories of merchandise and the characteristics of each that determine how they are transported such as size, value, perishability, and source.
2. Though dating varies significantly by category of merchandise, they are relatively consistent within a category. Can you think of reasons for the discrepancies among product categories?
3. What are the long-term disadvantages of poor vendor relationships?
4. Ask a local retailer to identify some EDI-linked product lines. Compare the retailer's in-stock position of EDI and non-EDI merchandise in the same category relative to color, size, and style assortments. What do you observe?

ENDNOTES

1. Units shipped times unit cost.
2. Staff. (December 9, 1991). K-Swiss offers fill-in terms for volume orders. *Footwear News.* p. 16.
3. Time is expressed in days divided by 360.
4. Staff. (February 1991). Ernst & Young 1990 Survey of Distribution Transportation Warehouse Trends in Retail. *Stores.* p. A14.

5. Staff. (March 6, 1995). Distribution key to survival. *Discount Store News.* pp. 3, 61.

6. Hartnett, Michael. (September 1994). Managing change in retail logistics. Stores. pp. 6–62.

7. *Retail distribution centers: Their function and form.* The Garr Consulting Group. Atlanta.

8. Hisey, Pete. (May 2, 1994). Partnerships paying off. *Discount Store News.* p. 37.

9. Reda, Susan. (April 1994). Floor-ready merchandise. *Stores.* p. 41–44.

10. Blackwood, Francy. (September 27, 1993). Strategic partnerships: *Survival in the '90s. Home Furnishings Daily,* special section. pp. 1–3.

11. Rieger, Nancy & Quinn, Colleen. (June 8, 1992). Markdown money—untold story. *Footwear News.* pp. 2, 12.

12. Cooke, James. (May 1992). Supply-chain management style. *Traffic Management.* pp. 57–59.

13. Ozzard, Janet. (June 2, 1993). Quick Response catches on with Neiman Marcus. *Women's Wear Daily.* p. 19.

14. Fearnley-Whittingstall, Sophy. (April 4, 1994). Saks maps plans for QR, EDI in high fashion. *Women's Wear Daily.* p. 11.

15. Staff. (July 20, 1990). Auto I.D. and EDI Special. *Industry Week.* pp. A1–A26.

16. Staff. (March 1991). Quick response: What it is; what it is not. *Chain Store Age Executive.*

17. An in-stock position of 100 percent, or an availability of *every* item *all* of the time, would require excessive inventory and result in low turnover.

18. Blackwood, Francy. (September 27, 1993). Strategic partnerships: Survival in the '90s. *Home Furnishings Daily,* special section. pp. 1–3.

19. Robins, Gary. (December 1989). New role for the buyer. *Stores.* pp. 34–37.

20. Thronton, Meg. (March 1992). QR's great divide. *Apparel Industry Magazine.* pp. 26–32.

21. Friedman, Arthur. Retailers' advisory to vendors: Get with the program. *Women's Wear Daily.* pp. 1, 8.

22. Struensee, Chuck. Dillard's leans on vendors to get with efficiencies. *Women's Wear Daily.*

23. Schaffner, Karen. (January 1992). New partnership shatters paradigms. *Apparel Industry Magazine.* pp. 6, 7.

24. Kron, Penny. (December 1992). The 1992 all-stars. *Apparel Industry Magazine.* AS 24–28.

25. Gellers, Stan. (March 29, 1993). Converting clothing to the matrix system. *Daily News Record.* pp. 16, 20.

26. Walsh, Peter; Spevack, Rachel; Hart, Elena & Salfino, Catherine. (March 29, 1993). Doing business in the '90s. *Daily News Record.* pp. 14, 24, 26.

27. Reda, Susan. (March 1994). Rx for WSRG: Clean sweep. *Stores.* pp. 20–22.

28. Staff. (August 1, 1994). Impact of the mammoth merger. *Home Furnishings Daily.* p. 59.

29. Hessen, Wendy. (October 3, 1994). Accessories makers: Mass doors getting tougher to unlock. *Women's Wear Daily.* pp. 1, 8.

30. Moin, David. (February 21, 1995). Federated opens doors to new suppliers, says, "No matrix here". *Women's Wear Daily.* pp. 1, 40.

31. Feitelberg, Rosemary. (March 6, 1995). Vendor ire mounts as stores hike chargeback penalties. *Women's Wear Daily.* p. 10.

32. Staff. (November 20, 1989). Should mfrs. run their own depts.? *Daily News Record.* p. 32.

33. Duff, Christina. (August 4, 1993). Nation's retailers ask vendors to help share expenses. *Wall Street Journal.*

34. Staff. (November 30, 1994). Wal-Mart cancel clause "grossly unfair" says court. *Women's Wear Daily.* p. 3.

chapter fifteen

MERCHANDISING CONTROLS AND REPORT ANALYSIS

The word *control* is sometimes associated with negative connotations, often linked to restrictions of autonomy or creativity. However, controls are critical merchandising tools that provide information for future planning and ascertain that retailers do not waver from their charted course. Chapter 15 covers some of the ways that controls are used for effective decision-making and for reacting to emerging problems.

After you have read this chapter, you will be able to discuss:

The control function in a retail organization.

Control standards.

The analysis of control reports and their use as decision-making tools.

CONTROL STANDARDS

Control involves measuring actual performance against goals or standards and reacting to the causes of any deviations for goals or standards. Control is a three-step process that includes:

- Establishing goals or standards
- Measuring deviations of actual performance from standards
- Reacting to deviations

Controls enable decision makers to react to problems before they become critical.

A **control standard** is a reference point or benchmark used to measure performance. Plans are standards. A *$2.0 million sales goal for August,* a *$25,000 open-to-buy for March,* and *projected net income of 4 percent of net sales* are all standards. Like plans, standards are often based on comparable prior performance. *Last year's girls' department sales during the week prior to school opening* is a standard for measuring *this year's girls' department sales during the week prior to school opening.*

The aggregate performance of similar business units is often used as a standard. The percentage sales increase (or decrease) for *all* stores in a chain can be used as a standard to measure the sales performance of *individual* stores. **Penetration** is a measure of the performance of a single business unit as percentage of the aggregate performance of all similar business units. A *4 percent penetration* can refer to the performance of a store that has generated 4 percent of the sales of all stores in a chain, or a category of merchandise that has generated 4 percent of the sales of all categories in a department.

Internal standards are derived from data obtained from within an organization. **Industry standards** are derived outside an organization, often by a trade association. The National Retail Federation annually publishes a *Department and Specialty Store Merchandising and Operating Results,* or *MOR,* a listing of industry standards for maintained markup, markdowns, shortage, gross margin, and turnover, compiled by merchandise category and sales volume.

The validity of a comparison to a standard is based on the similarity of the standard to that which is being measured. To quote a trite but apropos cliche, the comparison must be "apples to apples and oranges to oranges." Comparing this year's *July* better sportswear gross margin to last year's *September* gross margin is an invalid comparison in that

July gross margins are heavily eroded by end-of-season markdowns, while September clearance markdowns are minimal. Comparing the garden shop sales of a full-line discount store to the sales of *all* garden shops in the chain is not as valid as a comparison to stores in the same geographic region. Regional weather conditions dramatically affect horticulture sales, making a comparison outside the region less valid than a comparison within the region.

A standard is sometimes validated by comparing actual performance to multiple standards. Assume that actual sales for a month are 20 percent under plan, and 10 percent over last year. The 30 percent discrepancy between the comparisons to the two standards may be an indication that the plan for this year was unrealistically optimistic.

Multiple standard comparisons sometimes reveal problems veiled by a comparison to a simple standard. Assume that a shoe store's actual December sales exceeded plan by 7 percent, and last year's sales by 9 percent. The store manager was delighted by this commendable performance until comparing the store's performance to the chain's performance. The manager found that the sales for *all* stores exceeded plan by 12 percent, and last year by 14 percent. The store lagged behind the chain's performance to both planned and last year's sales by five percentage points.

Deviations

A **deviation** is a discrepancy between actual performance and a standard. If planned sales for a week are $2000, and actual sales are $2500, then there is a $500 deviation from planned sales. A deviation's direction is expressed by attributing negative values to deviations less than a standard, and positive values to deviations greater than a standard. The direction of a deviation is a performance indicator. A +*$500* deviation from planned sales is favorable, while a −*$500* deviation is not. Not all positive deviations are desirable. A +$500 deviation from planned expenses is not favorable, while a −$500 deviation is.

The degree of a deviation is expressed by dividing the deviation by the standard and multiplying by 100 to convert to a percentage:

$$percent\ of\ deviation = \frac{amount\ of\ deviation}{standard} \times 100$$

MULTIPLE MEASURES

It is often wise to review both dollar and percentage deviations together to determine the significance of the deviations. Consider a comparison of November's plan to actual sales for two outerwear categories in Table A. The *+/- percent* column shows a percentage shortfall in rainwear that is twice the percentage shortfall of wool coats. However, the *+/- $* column indicated that the sales shortfall of wool coats is far more serious in terms of dollars than the sales shortfall of rainwear. Since wool coat sales were planned significantly higher than the rainwear sales, the -10 percent deviation from the wool coat sales plan represents a far greater sales deficit in dollars than the -20 percent deviation from the rainwear sales plan.

The situation is characteristic of a store in a northern climate where November sales projections for wool coats far exceed sales projections for lightweight rainwear. As depicted in Table B, the scenario would reverse itself in April when sales projections for rainwear exceed sales projections for wool coats. In this case, the -20 percent and $10,000 sales shortfall in rainwear would be more distressing than the -40 percent and $2000 sales shortfall in wool coats.

Table A   NOVEMBER

Category	Plan	Actual	+/- $	+/- %
Wool Coats	$100,000	$90,000	-$10,000	-10%
Rainwear	$10,000	$8,000	-$2,000	-20%

Table B   APRIL

Category	Plan	Actual	+/- $	+/- %
Wool Coats	$5,000	$3,000	-$2,000	-40%
Rainwear	$50,000	$40,000	-$10,000	-20%

The +$500 deviation from plan sales represents a +25 percent increase over plan:

$$percent\ of\ deviation = \frac{+\$500}{\$2000} \times 100$$

$$percent\ of\ deviation = +25\%$$

The resulting percentage expresses the degree of the deviation. A $500 increase on a $2500 sales plan (+20 percent) is more impressive than a $500 increase on a $25,000 sales plan (+2 percent).

Control Objectivity

Qualitative controls measure performance descriptively such as a customer satisfaction survey that asks respondents to rate a store's customer service as *excellent, very good, fair,* or *poor.* Qualitative ratings are subjective in that one person's perception of "good" may differ from another person's. Quantitative controls measure performance numerically. Quantitative controls are objective. The calculation of a *5 percent increase over last year's sales* will yield the same figure regardless of who performs the calculation.

Quantitative controls reduce the emotion in the communication between managers. A store manager may complain to a buyer that inventory is *low.* The buyer may argue that the inventory is *not low. Low* and *not low* are biased qualitative assessments. The store manager's assessment is biased by a single-store perspective. The buyer's assessment is biased by a multistore perspective. Each party should quantitatively define *low* and *not low* to resolve the dispute objectively. Comparing the store's stock-to-sales ratio to the chain's, or comparing the percentage of inventory that the store owns to the percentage of the chain's sales that the store generates, is a rational quantitative stance.

Control Intervals

Controls are established at specific time intervals such as hourly, daily, weekly, monthly, quarterly, seasonally, or annually. The frequency of a control is based on the likelihood and/or significance of deviations from standards. Inventory that turns twenty-six times a year requires more frequent monitoring than an inventory that turns only twice a year. Controls of fast-turning inventories must be established at short intervals to ensure that minimum stock levels are maintained and that replenishment orders are placed before stockouts occur. In general, controls should be established at intervals that will allow timely reaction to meaningful deviations from standards.

Some controls encompass multiple time intervals. Sales are often controlled by week, month, season, and year. Multiple time interval comparisons broaden the perspective of an assessment. The trauma of

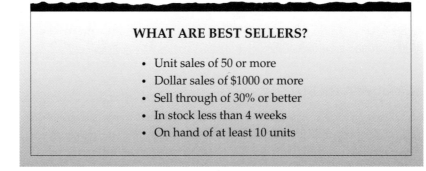

WHAT ARE BEST SELLERS?

- Unit sales of 50 or more
- Dollar sales of $1000 or more
- Sell through of 30% or better
- In stock less than 4 weeks
- On hand of at least 10 units

−50 percent deviation from plan sales for a week is diminished by the fact that sales are +20 percent to plan for the month, and +15 percent to plan for the season.

Control Levels

Controls are established at the same organizational levels as plans. In most retail organizations sales and inventory are controlled by category, department, and division, and also at store, district, and regional levels. Like plans, controls are used by managers relative to the nature and scope of their responsibility. A store manager may monitor a store's sales by category daily. A district manager may monitor total store sales daily. A regional manager may monitor total store sales weekly. The time constraints of the work day make it impossible for a regional manager of 100 stores to monitor daily the sales of every category in every store. Store managers can perform this task more effectively in that they have a narrower scope of responsibility.

REPORTS

Retail organizations compile various types of management reports that reflect the status of sales, inventory, and profitability by comparing actual performance to standards (*last year, plan*) for defined business units (*store, category of merchandise*) for specified periods (*month, year*). Some management report titles that are common to many retail organizations include *Best Seller Report, Inventory Position Report,* and *Monthly Sales Report.*

Compiling reports was once a labor-intensive, error prone process that involved tedious paper chasing. Today, computerized inventory

Company Profile 15.1

Retail Pro is a point-of-sale inventory management system designed for single and multi-unit apparel and accessories retailers. A Product of California-based Retail Technologies International, Retail Pro's point-of-sale features include credit card authorization, price-lookup, and customer profiling.

Profile is a unique feature of Retail Pro that provides instant access to key statistical information about any item or group of items with real time reports of sales in units or at retail, gross margin, inventory balance by store, and inventory received, sold, on-hand, and on-order. The system also provides information about best customers, best sellers, worst sellers, or the items most frequently returned or marked down by vendor, price point.

Retail Pro's focused and easily understandable reports can be displayed on a screen, printed, or stores for later viewing. Bar graphs can be generated to analyze sales by department, vendor, week/month, salesperson, customer, hour, day, size, or store, and arranged alphabetically, or ranked from best to worst by units, gross margin, retail dollars, or cost. Retail Pro's matrix capabilities allow pulling two dimensions, such as size and color, together in a grid. Ralph Lauren, Pendleton Woolen Mills, and Louis Vuitton are among the users of Retail Pro.

management systems compile data into reliable, easily accessible real-time reports that allow store managers to monitor best sellers and salespeople's productivity, and to locate merchandise for customers in other stores in the chain. Buyers rely on their reports to review sales factors such as location, price, and vendor to make strategic merchandising decisions relative to reordering, transferring, or marking down merchandise. Computerization has facilitated inventory tracking at very precise levels. A men's dress shirt inventory that was once manually tracked by units and store can be tracked by price, vendor, color, and sleeve and collar size with less effort.[1,2]

Exception Reports

A wealth of readily accessible information has resulted in report proliferation in some retail organizations. To avoid this, some retailers gener-

---

CHECKLIST FOR REVIEWING PROBLEM DEPARTMENTS

Is the percentage of stock appropriate to the percentage of sales? If not, how much stock must be obtained to reach an adequate level? Where will it come from? What is the on-order status?

Analyze the sales by classification. Are poorly performing classes adequately stocked? Is the stock in well, performing classifications depleted?

Are all classes productive? If not, should the non-productive classes be eliminated so that the productive ones can be further developed through additional floor space and inventory?

Is basic merchandise filled in? *Every* size, color, style?

Are groups broken? Is "piecy" merchandise frustrating customers, inhibiting presentation, tying up inventory dollars, and slowing your turnover?

What are the company's best sellers? Are they your best sellers? If not, why? Location? Stock level?

What are your competitors selling?

If stock levels are adequate, can you trade off slow-moving merchandise for more productive merchandise?

Are markdowns being taken in a timely manner? Have you taken a disproportionately large or small amount of markdowns?

Walk the floor. Has prime floor space been dedicated to your most productive classes, resources, and items? Have presentation standards interfered with moving goods quickly?

Figure 15.1

One retailer's checklist for reviewing sales and inventory reports.

ate **exception reports** that include only major deviations from standards, bypassing minor ones. A sales report may include only deviations that are 10 percent over plan, and 10 percent under plan. Filtering out deviations, within a -10 percent to $+10$ percent range reduces the size of the report and the amount of time required to review it.

Note that even "good" deviations ($+10$ percent to planned sales) should be included in an exception report. Since inventory allocations are predicated on planned sales, a store that is running significantly ahead of plan is likely to be underinventoried.

REPORT FORMATS AND ANALYSIS

Though all reports are used to assess performance and as sources of information on which to effect decisions, report formats vary from one organization to another. Though most retailers generate reports of sales, inventory, and profitability, reports differ relative to the level of information, format, frequency, and application. The following are facsimiles of actual reports obtained from several retail organizations. The company names have been changed to ensure the confidentiality of the information. The reports represent an infinitesimally small sample of the myriad report types and formats used by retail organizations.

Turnover Report

Davidson's Department Store generates an annual turnover for over 500 categories of merchandise at its twelve specialty department stores. Figure 15.2 is a section of the 1996 report for the Junior Department's knit top category.

DAVIDSON'S DEPARTMENT STORE

1996 TURNOVER REPORT

Department: Junior Sportswear
Category: Knit Tops
Division: Sportswear

	Chain	Westfield	Eastfield	Northfield
Average Inventory LY	$110,338	$ 8,933	$ 7,642	$ 9,651
Average Inventory TY	$118,431	$ 9,324	$ 6,371	$10,497
% Change Inventory	+7.3%	+4.4%	− 16.6%	+8.8%
Sales LY	$548,322	$43,165	$39,063	$47,671
Sales TY	$588,871	$28,160	$46,158	$49,880
% Change Sales	+7.4%	− 34.8%	+18.2%	+4.6%
Turnover LY	5.0	4.8	5.1	4.9
Turnover TY	5.0	3.0	7.2	4.8

Figure 15.2

Features of the Report The report includes this year's and last year's sales and average inventory by store and chain and the percentage change to last year for each. Turnover for this year and last year is calculated by store and chain. Sales and turnover performance can be assessed by comparing a store's performance to the chain's. Turnover issues can be traced to sales and/or average inventory.

Observations Assume that a 5.0 turnover is acceptable for the category according to industry standards. This year's Northfield sales increased by 4.6 percent, while inventory increased by 8.8 percent. Turnover decreased from 4.9 to 4.8. Though the 4.6 percent sales increase is a desirable result, the proportionately greater amount of inventory required to generate the increase negates the favorable judgment. The objective is to produce a sales increase with an equally proportionate inventory to yield the same turnover (4.9), or to produce a sales increase with a proportionately lower inventory to yield a higher turnover (greater than 4.9). The decrease in turnover is slight, however, and close to the 5.0 standard. Thus, the matter should receive little attention.

An additional 4.4 percent investment in inventory at Westfield resulted in a 34.8 percent decrease in sales, and a dramatic decrease in turnover from 4.8 to 3.0. Westfield's sales performance (−34.8 percent) is inconsistent with the chain's sales performance (+7.3 percent), a 42.1 percent deviation (7.3 percent minus −34.8 percent). The deviations are significant and worthy of investigation. If the sales decline is due to a permanent factor, such as the entry of new competition in the marketplace, then inventory allocations should be adjusted to reflect diminished sales. Assortments should be carefully edited so that only the best-selling resources and items are retained. If the sales decline is due to a temporary factor, such as a store renovation that disrupted business for a period, allocations should remain the same anticipating that completion of the renovation will alleviate the store's lackluster sales performance.

Eastfield experienced an 18.2 percent sales increase, and a 16.6 percent decrease in inventory, while turnover increased from 5.1 to 7.2. Unlike Westfield, Eastfield's sales and inventory are both headed in the right direction. This year's sales increase was achieved with a proportionately smaller inventory. The only cause for concern is that Eastfield's inventory may be turning *too quickly* at 2.2 turns greater than the chain's 5.0. Remember that an excessively high turnover may be indicative of stockouts and/or broken assortments. Thus, Eastfield's inventory may need to be fortified by a generous infusion of merchandise to support an optimistically upward sales trend (18.2 percent) that far exceeds the chain's average (+7.4 percent).

Note that a $3500 decrease in Westfield's average inventory, and a $3500 increase in Eastfield's average inventory would have yielded turnover figures close to the company's 5.0 standard (4.8 and 4.7 respectively). Balanced inventories among stores can be maintained by regularly monitoring inventory positions and by correcting inequities through the proper allocation of new shipments of merchandise. Some companies resolve inventory inequities among stores by transferring goods from overinventoried stores to underinventoried stores. Many companies avoid interstore transfers however, because of high processing and transportation expense, and the fact that transferred goods are dormant for the several days that they are in process.

Annual Review of Merchandising Statistics

The Acme Buying Office compiles an annual report of merchandising statistics by department for its member stores. Figure 15.3 is the 1995 report for men's basics.

Features of the Report   The report includes comparative percentages for this year's and last year's markdowns and gross margin for each member, as well as this year's employee discounts, shortage, and cash discount percentages. The report also includes turnover and an aged inventory indicator, the percentage of inventory over six months old, as well the par and median for each group of reported figures. In this case, the *median* is the middle number when the statistics are ranked from worst to best. The *par* is the middle number of the best half of the statistics when ranked from worst to best.

Observations   Note that Member 8's gross margin improved greatly (37.2 percent to 43.0 percent) because of a dramatic decrease in markdowns from the second highest store (18.9 percent) to the median store (7.5 percent). Unfortunately, taking fewer markdowns has left Member 8 with a high percentage of aged inventory (23 percent), the fourth highest in the group. Stagnant merchandise has also caused Member 8 to yield the lowest turnover in the buying office (3.2).

	Mark Downs		Emp. Disc.	Short-age	Cash Disc. to Pur.	Gross Margin		Inventory Data	
	This Year	Last Year				This Year	Last Year	Turn-Over	Age of Inventory
1	4.2	3.5	0.5	0.9	8.0	49.3	49.7	4.6	27
2	8.4	7.7	0.7	2.6	—	45.0	45.4	3.7	05
3	10.7	9.3	0.8	3.4	7.9	43.9	45.3	4.3	26
4	10.0	13.6	0.7	5.6	5.2	43.9	45.3	3.5	33
5	6.2	5.5	0.7	2.1	7.9	47.8	48.5	5.4	—
6	8.6	11.6	1.2	2.4	7.7	46.9	46.8	4.9	07
7	6.4	10.3	2.0	0.7	7.8	48.1	44.7	5.5	17
8	7.5	18.9	1.5	2.1	6.0	43.0	37.2	3.2	23
9	12.8	6.6	1.1	2.8	7.6	45.6	48.5	6.6	11
10	3.9	4.3	0.9	0.5	7.8	49.6	48.4	6.4	01
11	4.6	6.1	0.8	5.5	8.2	45.7	46.3	7.7	04
12	4.5	7.5	0.8	1.7	6.8	46.8	44.1	5.6	—
13	14.1	19.2	0.9	2.5	7.7	44.6	42.5	3.3	04
14	3.9	5.5	0.6	3.6	7.6	48.1	45.9	4.3	20
15	7.5	7.3	0.7	0.6	7.4	47.9	47.7	5.4	23
16	9.5	9.0	1.3	2.4	8.3	45.9	46.5	5.7	07
PAR	4.5	5.5	0.7	0.7	7.9	48.1	48.5	5.7	04
MED	7.5	7.5	0.8	2.4	7.7	46.8	46.3	4.9	11

ACME BUYING OFFICE

ANNUAL REVIEW OF MERCHANDISING STATISTICS

Men's Basics

Figure 15.3

Member 10 is the star of the buying office. At 49.6 percent, Member 10's gross margin is the highest in the group because of a low markdown rate (3.9 percent), the lowest for the group. A low markdown rate at Member 10 has not resulted in a high percentage of aged inventory or slow turnover, however. Only 1 percent of Member 10's inventory is more than six months old. A 6.4 turnover exceeds par, and is the second highest in the buying office.

Stock-to-Sales Ratio Report

Tie One On compiles a monthly stock-to-sales ratio report for each of the five categories of merchandise sold by its ten fashion accessories pushcarts of trendy selections of scarves, hairgoods, sunglasses, and small leather goods. Figure 15.4 is April's report for all categories.

Features of the Report The report includes the EOM and sales for each cart, and the resulting stock-to-sales ratio. The report also includes each cart's EOM and sales penetrations. Based on the premise that penetrations of inventory should closely match penetrations of sales, the inventory position of each cart can be evaluated by comparing EOM penetrations to sales penetrations.[3]

Observations Note that the greatest discrepancies between EOM and sales penetrations are at Midway Plaza and Canyon Crest: 6 percent and 13 percent respectively. Midway Plaza is overinventoried (high EOM penetrations relative to its sales penetration), while Canyon Crest is underinventoried (a low EOM penetrations relative to its sales penetration). Midway Plaza owns 11 percent of the EOM, but generated only 5 percent of total sales. Canyon Crest owns only 10 percent of the EOM, but generated nearly a quarter of the company's sales (23 percent). Comparing the problem cart's stock-to-sales ratios to the 6.4 aggregate stock-to-sales ratio further substantiates the inventory

	EOM		Sales		S/S Ratio
TIE ONE ON					
STOCK-TO-SALES RATIO REPORT					
April					
	EOM		**Sales**		**S/S Ratio**
TOTAL CHAIN	$156.7	— %	$24.4	— %	6.4
Midway Plaza	$ 16.3	11.0%	$ 1.3	5.0%	12.5
Hamilton Heights	$ 12.4	8.0%	$ 1.1	5.0%	11.3
Bayshore	$ 15.6	10.0%	$ 2.2	9.0%	7.1
Long Beach	$ 12.4	8.0%	$ 1.4	6.0%	8.9
Town Center	$ 13.1	8.0%	$ 3.2	13.0%	4.1
Canyon Crest	$ 14.7	10.0%	$ 5.6	23.0%	2.6
Riverside	$ 10.3	7.0%	$ 1.3	5.0%	7.9
Eastridge	$ 21.3	14.0%	$ 3.6	15.0%	5.9
Chapel Hill	$ 22.5	15.0%	$ 3.1	13.0%	7.3
Fairfield Commons	$ 16.1	10.0%	$ 1.6	7.0%	10.1

Figure 15.4

inequity. Midway Plaza, with the highest stock-to-sales ratio (12.5), has nearly twice the proportionate amount of inventory to sales for all carts (6.4), while Canyon Crest, with the lowest stock-to-sales ratio (2.6), has less than half of the proportionate amount of inventory to sales for all carts. The inventory should be reallocated to alleviate these inequities.

Inventory Position and Sales

Monkeys and Pumpkins compiles a monthly report of stock-to-sales ratios and sales and inventory penetrations by category of merchandise for ten upscale children's apparel stores. The report also includes month-to-date, season-to-date, and year-to-date sales compared to plan and last year. Figure 15.5 is a segment of the report for May for the infant layette category.

Features of the Report The report lists the BOM, receipts, interstore transfers, markdowns, sales, and EOM for each store and the chain, as well each store's percentage of the chain's BOM, receipts, sales, and EOM. Like the previous report, the report is based on the premise that penetrations of inventory should closely match penetrations of sales. The inclusion of BOM, EOM, receipts, transfers, and markdowns in this report permits a careful analysis of inventory activity within the month. The report also includes plan and actual stock-to-sales ratios for the month, and month-to-date, season-to-date, and year-to-date sales with percentage comparisons to plan and last year. The format facilitates a concurrent review of both inventory position and sales by store.

Observations Broadway is overinventoried. The store owned 14 percent of the chain's BOM, received 11 percent of the chain's new receipts, but generated only 7 percent of the chain's sales. Broadway's EOM was planned at 12 percent of total, but the actual EOM was 17 percent of total. The store's 6.7 actual stock-to-sales ratio was the highest in the chain, considerably higher than the chain's 4.2 stock-to-sales ratio.

Bel Air is underinventoried. The store generated 28 percent of the chain's sales, with only 14 percent of the chain's BOM. Though new receipts were generously distributed to Bel Air (28 percent), the allocations sold as rapidly as they arrived, leaving the store with only 13 per-

MONKEYS & PUMPKINS
May
INVENTORY POSITION AND SALES

	Total	%	Broadway	Crossroads	Village Square	South Gate	Ingleside	Bel Air	Buena Vista
		%	%	%	%	%	%	%	%
BOM	$227,525		14	14	18	14	9	14	16
Receipts	47,163		11	11	22	11	8	28	10
Sales	54,048		7	—	21	9	10	28	13
EOM Act	198,110		17	14	18	14	8	13	15
EOM Plan	159,100		12	12	23	12	9	16	16
S/S Act	4.2		6.7	4.1	3.0	5.1	3.1	1.6	4.2
S/S Plan	4.6		5.2	4.7	2.8	6.5	5.5	1.9	6.0

SALES TO DATE BY DEPARTMENT AND STORE

	Total	%	Broadway	Crossroads	Village Square	South Gate	Ingleside	Bel Air	Buena Vista
		%	%	%	%	%	%	%	%
MTD last yr	$48,902	11	16−		21−	2−	18−	27	—
MTD plan	50,500	7	23−	6	12−	26	71	9	27
MTD this yr	54,048		7	12	21	9	10	28	13
STD last yr	143,151	29	5−	23	12	26	10−	33	—
STD plan	168,200	10	5−	2	8	31	39	12	2
STD this yr	184,854		9	11	25	9	8	28	10
YTD last yr	285,840	26	2−	19	19	6	12−	25	—
YTD plan	341,200	6	4−	9	16	15	2	12	22−
YTD this yr	361,221		9	11	26	6	7	29	10

Figure 15.5

cent of the chain's EOM. The store's 1.6 stock-to-sales ratio was the lowest in the chain, considerably lower than the chain's 4.2 stock-to-sales ratio.

Note Bel Air's sales growth. Month-to-date, season-to-date, and year to-date sales are +27 percent, +33 percent, +25 percent to last year respectively, the highest percentage sales increases of any of the stores. Note also that Bel Air's stock-to-sales ratio was planned at a modest 1.9, while the company's stock-to-sales ratio was planned at 4.6. The meager plan may have been the result of basing the plan on last year's inventory and sales. However, Bel Air's dramatic growth made last year's figures invalid benchmarks.

Sales and Stock-to-Sales Ratios

Allied Specialty Stores generates a monthly report of stock-to-sales ratios for more than fifty categories of merchandise common to most of its twenty-eight women's specialty stores. Figure 15.6 is the sleepwear department report for November.

Features of the Report   The report includes monthly sales for the category by store and total chain, and percentage comparisons to last year. The report also includes the monthly stock-to-sales ratio for the category by store, and last year's comparable ratio. Ranked percentage of sales increases/decreases and stock-to-sales ratios facilitate the assessment of individual store performance. The rankings range from one, the best performer, to twenty-three, the worst performer. Though there are twenty-eight stores in the chain, only twenty-three have reported figures since the other five stores do not carry the category. Pars and medians for percentage sales increases/decreases and this year's and last year's stock-to-sales ratios appear at the bottom of the report.

Observations   Store 15 most typifies the November performance of an Allied store. Last year's 5.1 stock-to-sales ratio defined the median, as did this year's −1 percent sales decrease, while this year's 5.4 stock-to-sales ratio came very close to the 5.1 median.

Store 28 produced the highest percentage sales increase for the month (28.3 percent, rank 1), but unfortunately, the store's monthly stock-to-sale ratio is one of the highest in the group (7.8, rank 23). The positive perception of Store 28's sales increase is negated by the excessive amount of inventory that was carried to generate those sales.

Store 9 is a stellar performer. Monthly sales increased by 17.3 percent (rank 3), while the stock-to-sales ratio ranked second in the group. Though the stock-to-sales ratio increased from 2.9 to 3.8, the increase is consistent with the par increase from 3.4 to 4.4.

Store 6 is one of the poorest monthly sales performers (−17.4 percent, rank 20), but one of the best stock-to-sales ratio performers (4.0, rank 3). The "better than par" ranking is a dubious distinction, however. The poor sales performance may have resulted from inventories that were too low. A higher stock-to-sales ratio may have generated significantly greater sales.

ALLIED SPECIALTY STORES
SALES AND STOCK-TO-SALES RATIOS

Department: 3300 Sleepwear
November

Store	($00) Sales	% Change	Rank	MONTH STOCK-SALES RATIO			
				THIS YEAR		LAST YEAR	
				Ratio	Rank	Ratio	Rank
1	3,474.9	2.0	11	6.8	22	7.1	22
2	1,616.0	19.2	2	5.8	17	8.9	23
3	710.6	−4.7	14	5.4	13	5.1	12
4	265.3	−11.6	18	4.7	8	4.7	8
5	672.5	−20.3	22	4.7	8	3.3	4
6	180.7	−17.4	20	4.0	3	2.5	1
7	401.3	2.2	10	5.1	12	5.0	11
8	174.7	5.7	6	5.4	13	5.1	12
9	532.8	17.3	3	3.8	2	2.9	2
10	485.3	−8.4	17	—	—	—	—
11	373.4	2.4	9	4.6	6	6.2	18
12	371.4	−7.6	15	4.8	10	5.4	15
13	309.3	−17.7	21	5.6	16	3.2	3
14	157.6	5.6	7	3.2	1	3.4	5
15	221.1	−1.0	12	5.4	13	5.1	12
16	—	—	—	—	—	—	—
17	66.2	−23.8	24	4.9	11	4.2	6
18	99.7	−12.8	19	6.2	19	6.2	18
19	154.5	−4.1	13	4.4	5	4.8	9
20	147.3	4.2	8	4.2	4	4.3	7
21	110.6	12.5	4	4.6	6	4.9	10
22	—	—	—	—	—	—	—
23	49.5	−20.5	23	6.5	20	5.8	17
24	—	—	—	—	—	—	—
25	49.2	6.3	5	5.9	18	6.7	20
26	—	—	—	—	—	—	—
27	29.6	−7.8	16	6.6	21	5.6	16
28	22.2	28.3	1	7.8	23	6.8	21
PAR		5.7		4.4		3.4	
MED	10,675.7	−1.0		5.1		5.1	

Figure 15.6

Vendor Sales Report

Dee Klein's compiles a weekly report of sales by major vendor for each of the twenty departments at its two women's specialty stores. Figure 15.7 is the Vendor Sales Report for the cosmetics department for week ending August 15.

Features of the Report The report includes this year's and last year's sales by vendor, the percentage change from last year's sales to this year' sales, and sales penetration by vendor. The report also includes month-to-date, season-to-date, and year-to-date figures.

Observations This week's Estee Lauder sales were 46 percent behind last year's sales for the same week. Though the immediate reaction is one of concern, further exploration reveals that last year's sales were unusually high because of a gift-with-purchase promotion not recurring until next week. Estée Lauder's sales penetration for the week is 32 percent, consistent with the line's month-to-date (33 percent), season-to-date (28 percent), and year-to-date (31 percent) penetrations. Lancome sales are a greater concern to the buyer. The line's sales are 20 percent behind last year with no apparent justification. The line's sales penetration for the week is 14 percent, considerably lower than its month-to-date (17 percent), season-to-date (23 percent), and year-to-date (18 percent) penetrations. Reasons for the sales shortfall, such as low inventory or inadequate staffing, must be investigated.

DEE KLEIN'S
VENDOR SALES REPORT
Week Ending August 15

	WTD				MTD				STD				YTD			
	TY	LY	%	%	TY	LY	%	%	TY	LY	%	%	TY	LY	%	%
Estée Lauder	4.5	8.3	− 46	32	9.6	8.9	+8	33	25.0	24.2	+3	28	150.1	140.5	+6	31
Clinique	4.5	4.2	+7	32	8.5	8.5	+2	29	28.0	27.1	+3	31	160.2	160.1	0	33
Elizabeth Arden	3.0	3.1	− 3	21	6.2	6.2	+5	21	15.5	14.3	+8	17	90.4	88.8	+2	19
Lancome	20.0	2.5	− 20	14	5.0	5.0	+2	17	20.8	19.8	+5	23	85.3	80.2	+6	18
TOTAL	14.0	18.1	− 23	100	29.3	29.3	+5	100	89.3	85.4	+5	100	486.0	469.6	+3	100

Figure 15.7

Sales by Category

Steinert's compiles a monthly report of sales by department, classification, and store for the fifty departments in its ten updated misses apparel stores. Figure 15.8 is the dress department report for March.

	This Year DOL	Plan DOL	PCT	Career		Casual		Special Occasion		Suits		Petites	
	STEINERT'S												
	SALES BY CATEGORY												
	March												
Willow Station	10100	12600	20−	3230		1291		3036		1568		965	
	7%	9%		32%	7%	13%	7%	30%	9%	16%	8%	10%	5%
Amity Plaza	5381	5800	7−	1817		269		2760		282		253	
	4%	4%		34%	4%	5%	2%	51%	8%	5%	1%	5%	1%
Village West	4742	2900	64	1955		592		1642		551			
	3%	2%		41%	4%	12%	3%	35%	5%	12%	3%		
Cherry Creek	10553	10600		4549		101		3417		1146		1337	
	7%	7%		43%	9%	1%	1%	32%	10%	11%	3%	13%	7%
Bishop's Corner	22873	24400	6−	7734		3221		5508		4660		1748	
	16%	17%		34%	16%	14%	18%	24%	16%	20%	23%	8%	9%
University Place	18276	16900	8	7072		2855		2668		2036		3643	
	13%	12%		39%	14%	16%	16%	15%	8%	11%	10%	20%	18%
Hickory Hill	12280	13900	12−	3616		1325		3484		2003		1850	
	9%	10%		29%	7%	11%	8%	28%	10%	16%	10%	15%	9%
Lincoln Park	11939	11300	6	2555		1430		2194		1792		3966	
	8%	8%		21%	5%	12%	8%	18%	6%	15%	9%	33%	20%
Westwood Village	31716	33000	4−	11135		4598		6690		3972		5318	
	22%	23%		35%	22%	14%	26%	21%	20%	13%	20%	17%	26%
Chestnut Park	13268	12600	5	5834		1751		2589		1832		1261	
	9%	9%		44%	12%	13%	10%	20%	8%	14%	9%	10%	6%
TOTAL	141135	144000	2−	49503		17438		33994		19848		20312	
				35%	100%	12%	100%	24%	100%	14%	100%	14%	100%

Figure 15.8

Features of the Report The report includes the department's actual and plan sales by store, a corresponding percentage comparison, and a plan and actual penetration of chain total. Departmental sales are broken out by classification for each store. Penetrations are computed for each classification as a percentage of total departmental sales, and a percentage of total sales for the classification in all stores.

For instance, career dresses at Willow Station represents 32 percent of the total dress department sales in that store. The category represents 7 percent of the total sales for the category in all stores.

Observation Special occasion dresses is an important classification at Amity Plaza, generating about half (51 percent) of Amity Plaza'a total dress business. The category represents only about a quarter (24 percent) of the total dress department sales in all stores. Though special occasion dresses is a significant percentage of Amity Plaza's dress business, the category represents only 8 percent of special occasion dress sales in all stores. The 8 percent penetration ranks at the low end of a range of penetrations that span from 5 percent to 20 percent. The importance of the category is dwarfed by the fact that Amity Plaza is small store that generates only 4 percent of the company's total dress sales. Thus, special occasion dresses are significant to the store manager of Amity Plaza, but Amity Plaza's special occasion dress business is not as significant to the buyer of special occasion dresses who is likely to favor the two stores that generate over a third of the category's sales: Bishop's Corner (16 percent) and Westwood Village (20 percent). The significance of the special occasion category at Amity Plaza should stimulate a review of the assortment. Perhaps the dress department's total inventory is appropriate for a 4 percent dress store, but does the assortment reflect the fact that 51 percent of the store's dress business is special occasion dresses, or that casual dresses, petites, and suits each only represent 5 percent of Amity Plaza's dress business? If inventory is allocated based on the total company's penetration of business by class (24 percent to special occasion, 14 percent to suits, and 14 percent to petites), then Amity Plaza may be overinventoried in petites, suits, and casual dresses, and underinventoried in special occasion.

Likewise, the petite category represents a third (33 percent) of the dress sales at Lincoln Park, but the category only represents 14 percent of total dress sales in all stores. If inventory is allocated based on the total company's penetration of business by class (14 percent to petites), then Lincoln Park may be underinventoried in this classification.

Sales performance for a single month is too narrow a time frame upon which to base decisions regarding a store's classification structure, or allocation of floor space or fixturing. However, if April's category penetrations by store were to remain relatively stable throughout the year, an analytical merchant might contemplate the following: Five percent of sales in a 4 percent dress store is hardly enough business to warrant carrying casual dresses, suits, and petites at Amity Plaza. If Amity Plaza's assortment is based on the sales, imagine how paltry the selections must be in those categories! Why not discontinue all three categories at Amity Plaza and devote the vacated space to special occasion dresses? Though a business plateaus at some point, special occasion dresses seems to have greater potential than casual dresses, suits, or petite dresses, making the expansion of the special occasion dress category at Amity Plaza a prudent investment of space and inventory.

A similar thought process can be used to analyze Cherry Creek's dress business. If only 1 percent of the chain's casual dress business is generated by Cherry Creek, and if only 1 percent of Cherry Creek's dress sales are generated by the casual dress category, then why carry casual dresses at Cherry Creek? It seems wiser to devote the casual dress classification's fixtures and inventory dollars to stronger sales-generating classifications, such as career and special occasion dresses.

Style Status Report

Barry's Basement generates a weekly report of the distribution of specific style numbers among its ten off-price men's stores. Figure 15.9 depicts the report for a cotton turtleneck for the week ending October 8.

Features of the Report   The report includes a twelve-week sell-through, the number of units sold in the past twelve weeks divided by the number of units received in that period. The report also includes rate-of-sale information by store and chain:

- STP is the number of units sold last week
- S2W is the number of units sold during the prior two weeks
- S4W is the number of units sold during the prior four weeks
- S12W is the number of units sold during the prior twelve weeks
- AWS is the average weekly sales computed by dividing the number of S12W by 12.
- OH is the units on hand

	STP	S2W	S4W	S12W	AWS	OH	OO	OP	TWC OW	BAL
Willow Station	86	145	263	492	41.0	1108		697	27W	411–
Amity Plaza	63	121	220	378	31.5	547		536	17W	11–
Village West	42	76	128	226	18.8	429		320	23W	109–
Cherry Creek	74	129	245	438	36.5	722		621	20W	101–
Bishop's Corner	187	313	600	1157	96.4	1256		1639	13W	383
University Place	53	100	248	578	48.2	819		819	17W	0
Hickory Hill	103	182	338	585	48.8	1074		830	22W	244–
Lincoln Park	67	136	254	568	47.3	846		804	18W	42–
Westwood Village	205	350	602	1206	100.5	1093		1709	11W	616
Chestnut Park	74	119	228	536	44.7	1034		760	23W	274–
TOTAL	954	1671	3131	6164	513.7	8928		0	17W	0

Table title:

BARRY'S BASEMENT
STYLE STATUS REPORT
October 8

Figure 15.9

- OO is the units on order
- TWSO is the total weeks supply on hand, computed by dividing AWS by OH.

    The TWSO for the chain is an important reference point for computing OP, or optimum stock, computed by multiplying the chain's TWSO by a store's AWS. OP is the number of units that the store requires to match the chain's TWSO based on the store's AWS.

- BAL is the difference between OH and OP, or the number of units that should be transferred into a store (positive value) or out of a store (negative value) to match the store's TWSO to the chain's TWSO.

Observations Willow Station, Village West, Cherry Creek, Hickory Hill, and Chestnut Park are overstocked: Bishop's Corner and Westwood Village are understocked. The inventory should be reallocated from the generously inventoried stores.

SUMMARY POINTS

- Control is monitoring or measuring actual performance or status relative to goals or standards.
- A control standard is a reference point, benchmark, or guideline used to measure performance.
- A deviation is the discrepancy between actual performance and a standard.
- Qualitative control measures are subjective. Quantitative control measures are objective.
- Controls are established at specific time intervals such as hourly, daily, weekly, monthly, quarterly, seasonally, or annually.
- Control levels parallel planning levels.
- A report is a compilation of timely information synthesized into a meaningful form.
- Most controls are generated by computerized systems that electronically transmit, process, and store timely information reliably and cost-effectively.
- Exception reports include major deviations from standards, bypassing minor ones.

KEY TERMS AND CONCEPTS

control	exception report	penetration
control standard	industry standard	qualitative control
deviation	internal standard	quantitative control

FOR DISCUSSION

1. Discuss the use of internal versus external control standards. What are the advantages/disadvantages of each?
2. Discuss qualitative and quantitative assessments of a buyer's performance. Discuss the strengths and weaknesses of each.
3. Relate the importance of control systems to the success of EDI.
4. Identify a factor that should be controlled
   a. daily
   b. weekly
   c. monthly
   d. seasonally
   e. annually
   Justify the control frequency.

ENDNOTES

1. Robbins, Gary. (February 1991). New POS power at Talbots. *Stores.* pp. 44–47.
2. Staff. (December 1993). Real-time data updates. *Stores.* pp. 40–41.
3. The percentage of total inventory allocated to a store in a multiunit chain should not exactly match the percentage of the chain's total sales that the store generates. High volume stores should own proportionately less inventory than low volume stores, and thus have higher turnover and lower stock-to-sales ratios. Let us assume that in the case of Tie One On, the match between inventory and sales should be close, though not exact.

chapter sixteen

STORE LAYOUT AND MERCHANDISE PRESENTATION

In large retail organizations, the task of creating attractive shopping environments is the responsibility of professionals with expertise in architectural and interior design, the building trades, and visual arts. Though not directly responsible for store planning, buyers and other merchandising incentives play important consultive roles as sources of information on fashion trends, fixture and space requirements, and other merchandise-related topics. To interface with store planners and visual merchandisers, buyers need an understanding of fundamental store layout and merchandise presentation concepts. Chapter 16 covers some of these topics.

After you have read this chapter, you will be able to discuss:

The value of retail selling space.

Strategies for placing goods in a store.

Some basic merchandise presentation concepts.

Fixturing and signage as merchandising tools.

STORE PLANNING AND DESIGN

A store's physical appearance is an image component that conveys messages about offerings, pricing strategy, and market positioning. A **prototype** is a model store that combines elements of decor, lighting, fixturing, and signage to create a shopping ambiance consistent with the store's image and target customers. A prototype is a synthesis of standards for operational efficiency, merchandise presentation, and customer service.[1] Appealing prototypes have enhanced the success of many retail organizations. Customers of The Gap are attracted by a clean well-lighted prototype designed for shopping ease, while round-cornered fixtures at The GapKids ensure the safety of its patrons. Though specialty stores are best known for their distinctive prototypes, model stores are developed within all retailing formats. The development of a prototype facilitates "cookie cutter" expansion whereby a large number of stores are opened in a short time.

Prototypes are often tested in several markets before being implemented, and are periodically reviewed for effectiveness. The cost of constructing a store can range from under $50 to more than $500 a

Figure 16.1

A prototype combines decor, lighting, fixturing, and signage to create a shopping ambiance consistent with a store's image and target customers. *Hanna-Barbara.*

Company Profile 16.1

Formerly known as SDI/HTI, FRCH Design Worldwide is one of the most respected names in retail design and archi-tecture. The firm's roots date back to 1968 when Space Design International (SDI) was founded in Cincinnati. In 1990 SDI acquired another well-known retail design firm, Hambrecht Terrell International, founded in New York in 1980. SDI/HTI was restruc-tured and renamed FRCH in 1995 when Joseph B. Cicio, former CEO of the I. Magnin division of R.H. Macy, joined the firm.

During its nearly thirty-year history, the company has served an impressive roster of clients that includes department stores, spe-cialty stores, shopping centers, restaurants, entertainment facili-ties, and banks in twenty-two coun-tries. FRCH's client list in the United states includes Borders Books & Music, Bloomingdale's, Eddie Bauer, Heitmann Retail Properties, Kenneth Cole, Lazarus, Sears, Liz Claiborne, The Limited, Marshall Field's, JMB/Urban Development, Saks Fifth Avenue, Sears, and Timberland. Among the company's international clients are Selfridges and the House of Fraser (England), Central Depart-ment Stores (Thailand), Hankyu (Japan), Cheung Kong (Hong Kong), Myer/Grace Bros. (Aus-tralia) and Hamashbir (Israel). The second largest retail-focused design firm in the United States, FRCH employs more than 200 professionals in its New York, Cincinnati, and Singapore offices. The company has won more than 150 archi-tectural interior design and graphic design awards.

FRCH views each store as a client's permanent advertising vehicle. A holistic approach to design combines the visual ele-ments of architecture, color, layout, lighting, furnishings, and graphics to create a shopping environment that will entice customers to spend more time and money in a store. The end result is a functional and visually exciting store that distin-guishes the retailer from other com-petitors in the marketplace. FRCH stores are enduring classics that appeal to target customers for many years.

CAD technology enables FRCH to produce renderings, ele-vations, and 3-D presentations accurately and quickly. FRCH's close supervision of the construc-tion ensures that projects stay on schedule and within budget. FRCH also offers a design service for developing environmental graph-ics, in-store signage, and various forms of packaging such as boxes and shopping bags. This compre-hensive approach has resulted in a track record of successful projects and a high repeat rate among FRCH clients.

Staff. (September 1991).
Points of light.
Architectural
Lighting.

square foot.[2] In conjunction with their *no frills* strategy, most discounters execute simple store designs of vinyl tile floors, fluorescent lighting, and highly functional fixturing. The Ralph Lauren museum-like flagship on New York's Madison Avenue, and the high-tech Nike Town on Chicago's Michigan Avenue are both examples of pricey store designs.

Prototype development is a store planning function. Some retailers operate an internal store planning department, while others contract professional design firms to develop prototypes. Many retail organizations combine the services of both an internal function and outside firms. The activities of store planning were once limited to allocating floor space, setting construction timetables, and selecting paint colors and wallcoverings. Today store planning is a far more comprehensive function that involves market research, merchandising strategies, space management, and interior, graphics, and lighting design.

Updating and expanding existing facilities is also a store planning function.[3] Renovations range in scope from replacing carpeting and a few fixtures to gutting and rebuilding entire stores. Store renovations have become more frequent as retailers attempt to keep pace with competition and fast-changing market conditions.[4]

Computer-aided design and drafting (CADD) systems have greatly facilitated store design, reducing the time that it takes to design a 200,000-square-foot store from four months to a week. CADD systems have a database of design shapes, such as wall sections, fixtures, fitting rooms, wrap desks, and even images of folded sweaters, that can be called from storage, thus eliminating the need to create unique images for each new project.[5,6]

VISUAL MERCHANDISING

Visual merchandising is the retail organizational function responsible for enhancing sales by creating visually appealing shopping environments. Storefront window displays were once the major responsibility of visual merchandising. Historically, windows have played an important role in the notoriety of many retailers. Animated Christmas windows at Lord & Taylor's Fifth Avenue store have become a New York tourist attraction. Under the design direction of Gene Moore, the legendary windows of Tiffany & Co. of New York have featured some of the most exquisite jewels in the world using unusual props such as pasta, dirt, and empty spools of thread. Tiffany's Easter windows often have an egg theme. One year the eggs were scrambled.

Visual merchandising responsibilities have expanded beyond window displays to include floor layout, the development of standards for merchandise presentation, and signage. Visual merchandising is also an influential voice in store design.[7]

STORE LAYOUT

A strategically designed store layout combines the effective use of merchandise and aisles to draw customers through a store to maximize their exposure to the store's offerings. A layout can increase the amount of time and money that customers spend in a store. A layout should be flexible, allowing frequent moves as trends change and as poor layout decisions surface.

The value of selling-floor space is an important store layout consideration. Just as the value of a retail site is predicated on customer traffic, the value of space within a store is predicated on the number of customers that pass through or by the space. Consider the following: A four-level department store is connected on the second level to a single-level enclosed shopping center. The mall entrance is the only entrance to the store.[8] An average of 4000 customers enter the store each day. Typically, about 25 percent of the customers are destined for each floor. Centrally positioned escalators are the store's only people movers. Several assumptions can be made relative to the value of each floor as selling space based on the above information:

- The second floor is the most valuable space in that all 4000 customers who enter the store must pass through the second floor.
- The third floor is the next most valuable space in that an average of 2000 customers pass through the third floor on a typical day.
- The first and fourth floors are the least valuable space in that only the customers destined for these floors pass through them.

As traffic carriers, aisles are an important factor in defining the value of selling space. Space that is close to an aisle is more valuable than space remote from an aisle. Aisles are classified according to their size and the amount of customer traffic that they carry. A **major,** or

Company Profile 16.2

Rich's is committed to the belief that customers learn about fashion not by watching television or reading fashion magazines, but by observing the way that merchandise is presented at Rich's. The Visual Merchandising division at Rich's is charged with creating presentations that portray the very latest fashion statements in apparel and home furnishings, preserving Rich's long-standing tradition of fashion leadership in the South. Achieving this ambitious goal requires the coordination of a diverse group of players, among them in-house carpenters, and a design team that creates point-of-sale and informational signage and graphics.

One of the most important visual merchandising functions at Rich's is the development of spring, fall, and holiday prototype stores. The process begins well in advance of each season with meetings of a visual merchandising team and divisional merchandise managers to identify key trends for the forthcoming season. Plans are prepared for presenting merchandise according to these trends in the prototype. Goods are shipped to the prototype store before being shipped to the other stores so that the prototype can be set. The prototype is photographed and a 300-page book is prepared for each store with photographs of each presentation and written instructions for implementation. The book is supplemented with information concerning the amount of merchandise ordered for each store, and a book of *zonegrams*, flow charts showing appropriate adjacencies and the front to back placement of merchandise for each department. Store managers and visual merchandisers meet with the divisional merchandise managers and corporate visual managers for a half-day in the prototype store. Within two weeks, all of the stores are set to the prototype.

Cole, Tom. (October 1993). *Visual Teamwork at Federated.* VM+SD. pp. 22–28.

main, **aisle** is a wide aisle that connects a store's extremes. Discounters sometimes refer to main aisles as *power aisles.* Contrasting colors or floor compositions of wood, marble, carpeting, or tile are often used to define major aisles. A **secondary aisle** is a narrow aisle that interconnects major aisles, often carrying traffic through selling areas. Secondary aisles are often not as clearly defined as major aisles. The alignment of fixtures sometimes define secondary aisles.

A store's points of entrance effect traffic flow. Assume that the mall is expanded with a second level of stores, and that an additional mall entrance is opened to the third level of the four-level store. Assuming that the number of customers who enter the store from each mall entrance is evenly distributed, the value of the second floor will diminish, and the value of the third floor will increase. The redistribution of traffic will effectively equate the value of the two floors. Direct entrances from parking lots and garages also enhance and/or balance store traffic.

Traffic is critical to the sale of certain types of merchandise. Recall from Chapter 6 that fashion goods are often purchased because of their novelty or aesthetic appeal. Fashion goods are best placed in heavily trafficked areas to maximize the exposure of their aesthetic qualities. In general, basic goods require less exposure than fashion goods.

Two terms that classify merchandise according to customer purchase habits are important to store planners. Purchases of **destination goods** are planned. Purchases of **impulse goods** are unplanned. Big-ticket items, such as furniture, are often considered destination goods. Less expensive items, such as candy, are often considered impulse goods. Destination goods are strategically located in remote areas to pull traffic through a store since, as planned purchases, customers will

Figure 16.2

A main aisle is a major traffic carrier. *Myer-Adelaide.*

Figure 16.3

Aisles and strategically placed merchandise will pull traffic through a store to maximize their exposure to the store's offerings.

seek them out. Impulse items are located in high-trafficked areas to maximize their exposure. Some goods are destination/impulse hybrids. Cosmetics purchases are both planned and unplanned.

The terms *basic, fashion, impulse,* and *destination* can be combined to define four types of merchandise, fashion/impulse, basic/destination, basic/impulse, and fashion/destination, each with a strategic location in a store:

- Fashion/impulse goods, such as fashion jewelry, are placed in high traffic locations for visual prominence. Their aesthetic appeal stimulates unplanned purchases.

- Basic/destination goods, such as mattresses, are placed in remote locations. Because customers seek out basic/destination goods, they serve as magnets that pull customers through a store exposing them to other merchandise. Public restrooms and sales support areas, such as giftwrap, are also customer destinations that pull traffic through stores.

- Basic/impulse goods, such as hosiery, are placed in high trafficked areas that are secondary to the more heavily trafficked areas in which fashion/impulse goods are placed.

- Fashion/destination goods, such as outerwear, are placed in locations that are less heavily trafficked than the locations of basic/impulse goods, but not as remote as the areas occupied by basic/destination goods. As destination items, customers will seek out fashion/destination goods. However, as fashion goods, they require semi-prominent locations.

An **adjacency** is merchandise that is located next to other merchandise for customer convenience and to stimulate the sale of the adjacent goods. Handbags are a good adjacency to shoes, and vice versa. Girls' sizes 4–6x are a good adjacency to girls' sizes 7–14 for the convenience of customers who straddle both size ranges. Private label goods are often placed adjacent to branded goods, hoping that customers lured to heavily advertised branded products will select the higher margin private labels. Sometimes goods are exposed in more than one location to reap the advantage of multiple adjacencies, a concept called **cross merchandising.** Cosmetics organizers are the colorful plastic carrying cases with compartments that are popular among teens. Many of the full-line discounters triple expose the item in the three departments: cosmetics, health and beauty care, and jewelry.[9]

Store planners are often posed the dilemma of placing goods that cannot be absolutely categorized as basic, fashion, impulse, destination, or any combination thereof. As a destination item, women's innerwear is often placed in secondary locations in department stores. Some stores experimented with moving hosiery from high-trafficked main aisles to the less-trafficked innerwear areas, feeling that innerwear and hosiery were goods adjacencies. The result was disastrous for many retailers who found that the hosiery sales generated by the innerwear adjacency did not compensate for the loss of impulse sales.

MANNY'S MEN'S SHOPS

To demonstrate these principles of store layout, consider the case of Manny's Men's Shops, a chain of eight men's specialty stores departmentalized as follows:

- Clothing: suits, sport coats, dressy slacks and outerwear.

Manny's Men's Shops

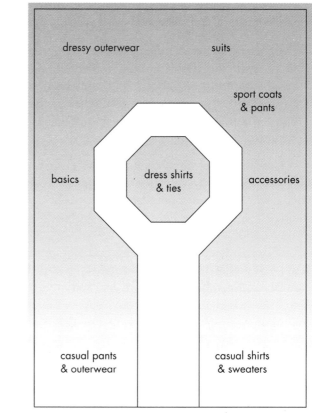

Figure 16.4

A store layout for Manny's Men's Shops.

- Furnishings: dress shirts, ties, accessories (belts, small leather goods, jewelry), and basics (underwear, hosiery, pajamas, and robes).
- Sportswear: casual pants, knit and woven shirts, sweaters, casual outerwear and activewear.

The owner is considering a new location in an enclosed shopping center. The space is rectangular with narrow frontage, necessitating that the departments be aligned in a front, middle, back arrangement. The owner develops the following placement strategy:

- Clothing will be placed in the rear of the store. This is high ticket destination merchandise that customers will seek. Higher fashion sport coats will be placed at the front of the department to maximize their exposure.

- Sportswear will be placed in the front of the store. Visually exciting presentations of the store's most fashionable merchandise in this prominent location will lure customers from the mall and stimulate impulse purchases.
- Furnishings will be placed in the middle of the store. This potpourri of categories is a good bridge between Sportswear and Clothing. Underwear and hosiery are a basic/destination, basic/impulse hybrid. As basic/destination goods they do not warrant a prime location, but as basic/impulse goods, their sales will be enhanced by the customer traffic en route to the Clothing Department. Shirts and ties are a perfect adjacency to suits in that suit sales will stimulate sales of shirts and ties.

FIXTURES

Fixtures are store furnishings used to present or store merchandise. Commonly called *racks* or *counters*, fixtures also include service desks, display props, and customer seating. Fixtures fall into several categories based on their use.

- **Floor fixtures** are free-standing units used to present goods on the selling floor.
- **Top-of-counter fixtures** are units that are placed on top of counter height fixtures (thirty-eight inches) to display goods such as carded earrings.
- **Display fixtures** are used to show goods not available for customer selection.
- **Storage fixtures** are used to store fill-in or backroom inventory.

Some fixtures are multifunctional. A floor fixture may have drawers for storing fill-in merchandise or understock. The storage function in fixturing has significantly diminished in importance as retailers endeavor to improve turnover by carrying lower inventory and less reserve stock.

Most fixtures are designed to maximize capacity, minimize the use of floor space, and attractively show merchandise. **Four-ways** and **T-stands** are four-armed and two-armed fixtures often made of chrome, primarily used to present apparel. Goods hung on four-ways and T-stands face the customer, exposing the most visually appealing

a

b

c

d

e

f

g

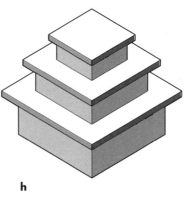

h

Figure 16.5

a-c. Three top-of-counter fixtures.

d. A T-stand.

e. A rounder.

f. A four-way.

g. Cubes.

h. A "Gap" table.

part of most garments. Faced-out goods consume considerably more space than side hung goods that are hung on linear or circular bars with the side of the garment facing out. **Rounders** and other types of rodded fixtures are used when facing out is unimportant, as in the case of basic goods or clearance markdowns.

Nonhanging goods, such as flat, packaged, and folded merchandise, are presented on various types of fixtures:

Tiered tables, commonly called *Gap tables,* are used to present various types of nonhanging goods. Large cartoned goods, such as housewares, are often stacked high on **platforms. Cubes** are typically made of glass and used to present folded goods, such as shirts and sweaters.[10] **Lip tables,** or *dump tables,* are used for haphazard presentations of clearance goods.

Fixtures can be classified as either closed-sell or open-sell. **Closed-sell fixtures** restrict customer access to merchandise, requiring salesperson assistance for making selections. Easily damaged or highly pilferable big ticket items, such as fine jewelry, are housed in closed-sell fixtures. **Open-sell fixtures** permit customer access to merchandise, allowing selection without the salesperson assistance. Open-sell fixtures are far more common than closed-sell fixtures for two reasons:

- Use of open-sell fixtures results in lower selling costs, since fewer salespeople are needed to service customers.
- Customers are more likely to purchase goods that they can readily test, feel, or try on. Rich's, the Atlanta-based division of Federated Department Stores, is experimenting with open-sell fashion jewelry fixtures. The cases open from the front and the jewelry slides forward on a tray. Both the sales associate and the customer stand on the same side of the case. Signs invite customers to open the case and examine the merchandise.

Mobility and flexibility are important fixture characteristics in that fixtures need to be moved and/or adjusted often to accommodate seasonal changes in merchandise assortments. Many department stores annually transform their female outerwear departments into swimwear departments and then back again. Fixtures must also accommodate changes in the merchandise itself, such as changes in the physical dimensions of packaging that require adjusting the shelves on which the goods are presented.

Modular fixtures and slatwall are good examples of flexible fixturing. Modular fixtures are individual units designed to be used separately or configured into larger fixture groupings. Slatwall is a series of horizontal "slats" separated by grooves onto which chrome hardware, plexiglass, or glass fixtures can be mounted with minimal effort to shelve, peg, or hang goods.

VENDOR FIXTURES

Vendor fixtures are supplied by vendors to distinguish their brands from the competition and to enhance consistent presentation of their product in all stores. Vendor fixtures run the gamut from corrugated cardboard top-of-counter units to custom-designed fixtures for in-store shops for upscale brands such as Ralph Lauren, Liz Claiborne, and Nautica. Inexpensive vendor fixtures are often provided without charge with a minimum order. More expensive fixtures are priced to cover the cost of production.

Vendor fixtures are especially desirable for products not easily presented on conventional fixturing because of their shape or packaging. Vendor fixtures often include point-of-purchase (POP) signage or graphics that are linked to national advertising campaigns. Though

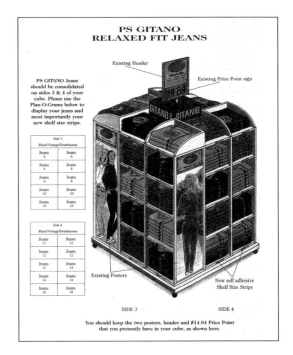

Figure 16.6

Vendor fixtures are specifically designed for a product line.

Company Profile 16.3

Jockey International, Inc. ("Jockey") of Kenosha, Wisconsin, established its preeminence in underwear merchandising in the 1930s when it introduced cellophane packaging for its men's line and the male contour form for displaying the product. Since the 1970s, Jockey has offered retailers a fixture program to enhance the presentation and sale of the JOCKEY product line in stores.

Jockey's understated fixtures are fabricated in neutral laminates that blend well with the design elements of any store. Modular units of various capacities can be adapted to a small store with a limited JOCKEY assortment, or to a large store with a complete JOCKEY shop. The fixture program is supported with logos in dimensional mirror letters, torsos, and other promotional aids, as well as literature depicting detailed floor plans. Jockey also offers the services of a staff of merchandising professionals who will evaluate a retailer's business and develop a merchandising plan. Jockey encourages participation in the fixture program by providing stores with high quality fixturing at a reasonable price.

In 1982, Jockey introduced JOCKEY FOR HER, a line of cotton underwear for women, applying the concept of individual packaging that had been so successful in the men's line. A rotating, acrylic fixture that holds forty dozen packages of underwear, yet only requires 1.5 square feet of floor space was one of the enticements that encouraged retailers to experiment with this revolutionary concept of selling women's underwear. Today, Jockey sells nearly as much women's underwear as men's.

JOCKEY and JOCKEY Figure Design are trademarks of and used with permission of Jockey International, Inc.

vendor fixturing for hardlines is common, an increasing number of soft-lines vendors now offer fixture programs.[11] Retailers must be conscious of the compatibility of vendor fixtures with other fixtures and the store's overall design. A selling area with an assortment of vendor fixtures may give a very disjointed visual impression.

MERCHANDISE PRESENTATION

Merchandise presentation involves the application of standards or techniques to show merchandise to maximize its attractiveness and to facilitate customer selection. Merchandise presentation involves grouping merchandise together on a fixture or within an area in the store based on one or more similarities. Goods may be grouped based on common:

Merchandise Category   A presentation of a complete selection of a category or item utilizes the breadth and depth of an assortment to create a strong visual impression. Presentations by category facilitate customer selection when the item or category is the primary selection factor ("Please show me your selection of socks.") Goods that are often presented by category include shorts, sweaters, and microwave ovens.

Color   Merchandise of the same color is often presented together to create color impact. Color statements are often associated with a seasonal color trend or a holiday theme, such as red for Valentines Day. Likewise, goods are often presented by design or print, such as paisley or stripe, to tie in with a seasonal fashion trend. Color presentations facilitate customer selection when color is a primary selection criterion ("Where are the white blouses?" or "I need a black leather handbag to go with these shoes.").

Colors within a multiple color assortment are arranged in vertical blocks. The visual impact of goods such as bath towels, knit shirts, and socks is maximized when the colors are arranged from left to right, warm to cool, light to dark.

Figure 16.7 is an example of a color spectrum used for color blocking. Note that the spectrum begins with white and ends with black. The warmest color is yellow and the coolest color is blue. Transitional colors (such as peach) bridge the colors from which they are derived (yellow and orange).

Fabrication or Composition   Goods are often grouped by fabric as part of a seasonal fashion statement or to create tactile statements, such as "soft dressing." Silk neckties, satin robes, and woven and knit tops are examples of goods presented by fabrication. Nonapparel goods are also presented by the material of which they are made, such as down pillows, silver hollowware, and leather handbags. Color, fabrication, and composition are sometimes linked, as in the case of straw hats, brass hollowware, and sterling silver jewelry. The presentation of fine jewelry by stone and metal effectively creates a color presentation: red (ruby), green (emerald), black (onyx), sapphire (blue), and sterling (silver).

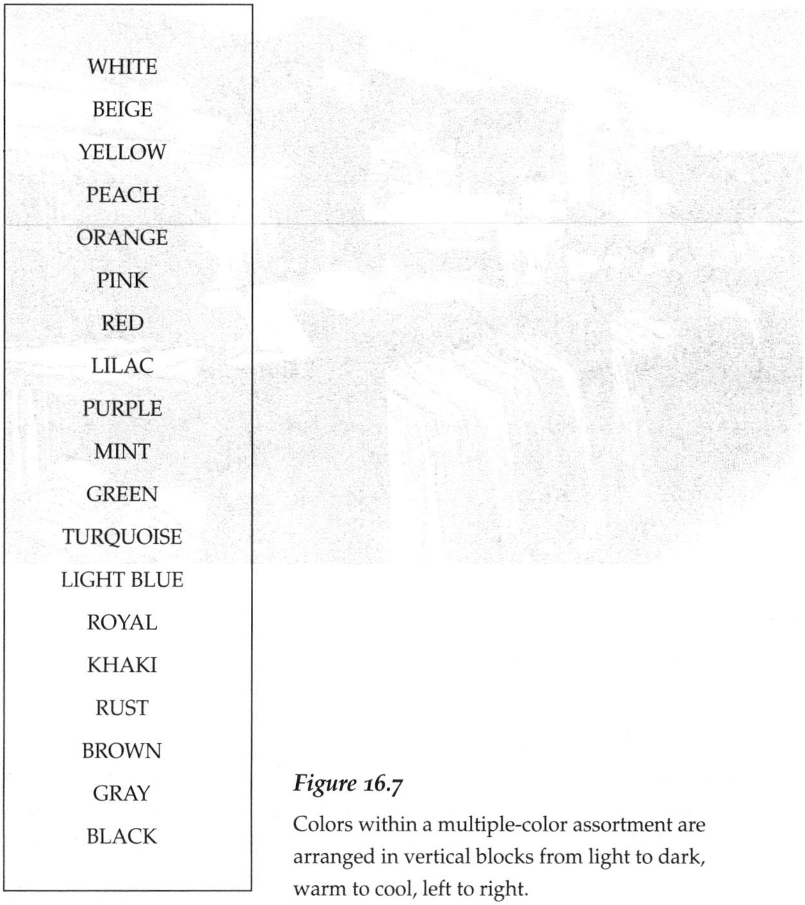

WHITE

BEIGE

YELLOW

PEACH

ORANGE

PINK

RED

LILAC

PURPLE

MINT

GREEN

TURQUOISE

LIGHT BLUE

ROYAL

KHAKI

RUST

BROWN

GRAY

BLACK

Figure 16.7

Colors within a multiple-color assortment are arranged in vertical blocks from light to dark, warm to cool, left to right.

Style   Merchandise is presented by style for customer convenience and visual impact. Goods often grouped by style include men's dress shirts (long sleeve and short sleeve), women's hats, (narrow brim and wide brim), and silk scarves (square and oblong). Vendor styles are also grouped together, such as Levi's 501, 505, and 550 blue jeans.

Price/Quality   Goods are grouped by price and/or quality to facilitate customer selection when an assortment has a wide range of quality or price points. A department store may group handbags as designer (Louis Vuitton, Gucci, and Fendi), bridge (Coach and Dooney & Bourke), better (Liz Claiborne), and moderate (Capezio).

Figure 16.8

A sized presentation of men's suits at Nordstrom.

Size Merchandise is sized to facilitate customer selection. Sized merchandise is typically presented from small to large, left to right, top to bottom, front to back. In a sized presentation of denim jeans on a shelved wall, the pant with smallest waist and shortest leg length is at the upper left of the presentation, and the pant with the largest waist and longest length is at the lower right of the presentation. Sizing is often used to present broken assortments such as markdowns.

Vendor Full-brand assortments are presented together for strong brand identity and to facilitate brand driven purchases of goods, such as cosmetics, hosiery, and innerwear. Vendor presentations are appropriate for presenting coordinated merchandise such as Liz Claiborne and Alfred Dunner sportswear. Vendors encourage the "shop within a shop" by supplying retailers with fixturing, signage, and floor plans.

There are innumerable themes by which goods can be grouped together for presentation, such as end-use presentations that show customers how goods can be coordinated or used together. Examples include table settings of china, crystal, and flatware, room settings of furniture, and layered apparel coordinates of jackets, pants, and tops.

Lifestyle presentations are targeted to customers of similar demographic/psychographic profiles. A department store's junior and young men's departments are examples of lifestyle presentations. Music, color, and lighting distinguish these areas from the rest of the store.

The above criteria for grouping merchandise are often combined in a hierarchy to create a standard for presenting merchandise. Men's knit polo shirts may be presented by:

- vendor (Ralph Lauren),
- fabrication (interlock and mesh),
- color (blocked on a wall left to right, warm to cool, light to dark),
- size within each color (top to bottom, small to extra-large).

Though often associated with presentations of softlines, merchandise presentation standards are developed for accessories and hardlines as well. Crate & Barrel uses product color and style to create exciting presentations of housewares and decorative accessories. The Zale Corporation has developed a unique customer-friendly approach for presenting jewelry. Jewelry stores typically present merchandise by

Figure 16.9

A vendor presentation of goods at Burdines.

PRESENTATION STANDARDS FOR JEWELRY

- Present jewelry in shallow (third vision) showcases. Arrange merchandise from the front to back of the case. Create a balanced symmetrical look with a focal point in the middle of each case. Group sets and coordinating pieces together on ramped pads, encompassing a pair of earrings with a matching necklace. A coordinating bracelet or pin can be presented directly to the side to encourage multiple sales. Do not clutter the cases. Minimize duplication of styles in a case and store duplicates in drawers directly below the presentation. Sales associates should sell from the drawers, not the case, unless the last piece is in the case.
- Use top-of counter fixtures for earring presentations. Earrings should relate to the merchandise in the case below. Group earrings by story, i.e., pierce ears, clip ears, vermeil drops, buttons, hoops, stone, and so on. Top-of-counter fixtures are limited to two per five feet of showcase and must be carefully placed to achieve a balanced look. Sparsely filled fixtures should be removed from the counter.
- Tailored goods such as Monet and Napier are presented by vendor and identified with signage. Never mix vendors in a case. This merchandise is produced by story or look and must be presented in that fashion.
- Present fashion and designer jewelry either by vendor or look, with the exception of Dior, which is always presented by vendor.
- Feature fashion looks of sterling presentations. Use interesting pieces as a focal point.
- Display 14K earrings in boxes or within a case. 14K chains should be displayed on ramped pads according to type and size of chain. Do not angle necklaces. Display vertically or horizontally to the front of the case. Group together matching fashion sets and use display ramps, bangle holders, ring holders, and so on to enhance the presentation.
- Always present clearance jewelry on separate fixtures or promotional lip tables.
- Watches are presented by vendor and identified by signage. Swatch and Gucci should have their own cases. Better watches, such as Seiko and Citizen, can be presented together. Fashion watches, such as Guess and Fossil, can be presented together and should be set up by story and band color. Swatch should be merchandise by color in the suggested patterns. Citizen, Seiko, and Gucci should be presented on their own showcase pads.

Figure 16.10

GARFIELD © 1991 Paws, Inc. Dist. by UNIVERSAL PRESS SYNDICATE. Reprinted with permission. All rights reserved.

metal and stone. Zales presents goods by category, so that rings, watches, necklaces and other items are grouped together regardless of metal or stone. The approach assumes that customers are more likely to shop by category ("I want to see a selection of rings.") than by stone ("I want to see a selection of jade").[12]

Retail organizations ensure consistent presentations within their stores by publishing merchandise presentation guidelines by category of merchandise in manuals distributed throughout the organization. Though the standards are based on a combination of objectives such as visual appeal, customer convenience, and ease of maintenance, balancing these objectives is sometimes a struggle. Most department stores present men's dress shirts in a vendor/color/size hierarchy creating brand and color impact. However, since some men consider size the primary criterion for selecting a shirt and are frustrated that shirt selections are not grouped together by size, regardless of vendor or color.

SIGNS

Signs are a store image component that facilitate shopping by identifying merchandise by characteristics such as category, brand, size, style, and product features. **Permanent signage** is made of durable materials not intended for frequent change, such as exterior lighted signs and in-store signs identifying selling areas. **Temporary signage** is made of disposable material, such as paper or card stock, and is intended for frequent change. The most common forms of temporary signage

Figure 16.11

Examples of temporary in-store signage.

include in-store signage on fixtures. Temporary in-store signs are important sales promotion vehicles that reinforce advertising, stimulate impulse purchase, and enhance customer convenience by calling attention to promotional events and prices. Fact tags, banners, and reprints of newspaper advertising are among the various forms of temporary in-store signage.

The most common uses of temporary and in-store signs are for the identification of a:

- brand—*OshKosh B'gosh*
- category or item—*Men's Crew Neck Sweaters*
- shop-within-a-shop—from our *Signature Room*
- characteristic or feature of merchandise—*medium* or *100% Cotton*
- price—*25% off ticketed price*
- promotion—*Anniversary Sale*
- policy—*All Sales Final*
- service[13]—*Open a charge and receive 10% off your first purchase*

Temporary in-store signs date back to 1929 when Milton Reynolds developed the concept of "talking price tags" to promote the sale of his

Printasign machine. Today, computer signmaking systems transmit sign copy from central locations for printing at multiple store locations.[14]

SUMMARY POINTS

- A prototype is a model store that combines elements of decor, lighting, fixturing, and signage to create a shopping ambiance consistent with the store's image and target customers.
- Visual merchandising is the organizational function responsible for enhancing sales by creating visually appealing shopping environments. The value of retail selling space is a function of customer traffic.
- A strategically designed store layout combines the effective use of merchandise and aisles to draw customers through a store to maximize their exposure to the store's offerings.
- Fixtures are store furnishings used to present or store merchandise.
- Merchandise presentation standards are techniques for displaying goods using the attributes of the merchandise to maximize its attractiveness and convenience of selection.
- Temporary in-store signage reinforces advertising, stimulates impulse purchases, and enhances customer convenience.

KEY TERMS AND CONCEPTS

adjacency	impulse merchandise	storage fixture
closed-sell fixture	lip table	temporary signage
cross merchandising	major ailse	tiered table
cube	open-sell fixture	T-stand
destination merchandise	permanent signage	top-of-counter fixture
display fixture	platform	vendor fixture
floor fixture	prototype	visual merchandising
four-way	rounder	

FOR DISCUSSION

1. Make a list of several categories of merchandise. Characterize each category as basic/impulse, basic/destination, fashion/impulse or fashion/destination. Examine the various items and vendors within the category. Do the categorizations change for various items and vendors?

2. Visit a local department store or general merchandise discounter. Evaluate the configuration of the store's aisles. Evaluate selling area adjacencies and adjacencies within several areas.

3. Visit several specialty stores that are targeted to clearly defined groups of customers. What are the elements of store design that appeal to the target customers? Why do they?

4. Evaluate a store's temporary in-store signage.

5. Assume the role of a fashion buyer for an apparel department and explain how your merchandise should be presented.

ENDNOTES

1. Staff. (February 21, 1994). Store design, merchandising valuable selling tools. *Discount Store News.* p. 26.

2. Ebstein, Barbara. (September/October 1990). Don't suit yourself. *Retail Store Image.* p. 14.

3. Lubben, Ronald. (September/October 1990). Store planners metamorphosing. *Retail Store Image.* p. 58.

4. Frantz, John. (August 1995). Experts: Store renovations pay off. *Shopping Centers Today.* p. 26.

5. Alar, San. (January 1988). CAD: For the good of creation. *V+D.* pp. 60–62.

6. Robbins, Gary. (December 1991). Cadvantages: Computer aided design boosts productivity at Dillard's, Mervyn's. *Stores.* pp. 25–31.

7. Erlick, June. (September 27, 1993). Visual Merchandising: Seeing is believing. *Home Furnishings Daily.* p. 13.

8. A highly unlikely circumstance, but the example will serve to make a point.

9. Staff. (June 19, 1995). Organizing mass merchants. *Discount Store News.* pp. 75, 76.

10. Weishar, Joe. (October 1990). Fixturing uses and abuses. *VM&SD.* pp. 58–63.

11. O'Leary, Sean. (October 1986). Vendor-supplied fixtures. The trend justifies the means. *Visual Merchandising & Store Design.* p. 88.

12. Williamson, Rusty. (November 29, 1993). Zales unveils user-friendly store format. *Women's Wear Daily.* p. 9.

13. Often called institutional signage.

14. Reynolds, Thomas. (August 1989). P-O-P art. *SM+SD.* pp. 90–95.

APPENDIX

Analysis of Annual Retail Sales

Retail Chains and
Thier Corporate Parents

Glossary

Analysis of Retail Performances for Fiscal 1994

DEPARTMENT STORES

($ in thousands)	Sales 1994	Sales 1993	% Change	Profits 1994	Profits 1993	% Change	Profits to sales 1994	1993	Operating profits 1994	1993	% Change	Shareholders equity 1994	1993	% Change	Profit to avg. equity 1994	Debt interest to sales 1994	Yearend inventory 1994	1993	% Change	Sales to inventory 1994	1993
Sears Merchandising	29,451,000	27,171,000	8.39%	890,000	752,000	18.35%	3.02%	2.77%	1,519,000	1,081,000	40.52%	3,781,000	3,423,000	10.46%	16.20%	4.55%	4,044,000	3,518,000	14.95%	7.28	7.72
Dayton Hudson	21,311,000	19,233,000	10.80%	434,000	375,000	15.73%	2.04%	1.95%	1,044,000	894,000	7.92%	2,777,000	2,737,000	11.18%		2.00%	2,777,000	2,497,000	11.21%	7.67	7.70
J.C. Penney	20,380,000	18,983,000	7.36%	1,057,000	940,000	12.45%	5.19%	4.95%	1,627,000	1,478,000	10.09%	5,615,000	5,365,000	4.66%	12.74%	0.46%	3,676,000	3,545,000	9.34%	5.26	5.35
May	11,877,000	10,989,000	8.08%	782,000	711,000	9.99%	6.58%	6.47%	1,184,000	883,000	34.09%	4,135,000	3,639,000	13.63%	13.13%	1.97%	2,207,000	2,020,000	9.26%	5.38	5.44
Federated[1]	8,316,000	7,229,000	15.04%	187,616	193,248	-2.91%	2.26%	2.67%	549,525	531,919	3.31%	3,639,610	2,278,244	59.76%	3.93%	2.62%	2,360,621	1,180,844	101.60%	3.49	6.12
Dillard	5,545,803	5,130,648	8.09%	251,790	241,134	4.42%	4.54%	4.70%	602,822	584,842	3.07%	2,323,567	2,081,647	11.62%	7.48%	2.24%	1,362,756	1,299,944	4.83%	4.07	3.95
Mercantile Stores	2,819,837	2,726,923	3.29%	103,417	89,309	16.24%	3.67%	3.27%	104,917	86,639	20.94%	886,551	1,338,175		5.10%	1.02%	463,162	425,492	10.17%	6.02	6.42
Broadway Stores[2]	2,086,804	2,082,801	0.28%	365,900	337,500	N/A	N/A	N/A	61,894	-11,055	N/A	385,632	413,707	-6.78%	N/A	4.84%	504,522	427,630	17.98%	4.14	4.88
Kohl's Corp.	1,554,100	1,305,746	19.02%	68,512	53,893	27.13%	4.41%	4.13%	112,875	102,400	20.97%	334,249	262,502	27.33%	14.72%	0.41%	242,986	190,469	30.19%	6.27	6.88
Strawbridge & Clothier	1,006,789	987,027	2.00%	20,032	17,727	13.00%	1.99%	1.80%	258,273	250,715	3.01%	262,352	252,202	4.02%	5.16%	1.94%	143,790	143,132	0.46%	7.00	6.90
Younkers	599,135	597,895	0.21%	13,517	12,262	10.23%	2.26%	2.05%	25,203	26,617	-5.31%	178,864	165,294	8.21%	8.17%	0.86%	110,178	108,298	1.74%	5.44	5.52
Bon-Ton Stores[3]	494,908	336,733	46.97%	13,630	8,779	55.26%	2.75%	2.61%	26,668	17,548	51.97%	112,447	98,551	14.10%	8.43%	1.11%	120,052	55,355	116.88%	4.12	6.08
Bottom line	363,803	392,417	-7.28%	1,516	-2,673	N/A	0.42%	0.68%	22,268	13,963	59.46%	83,725	82,716	1.21%	6.19%	2.82%	80,465	80,495	-0.04%	4.51	5.68
Crowley Milner[4]	109,327	106,935	2.60%	1,031	514	100.58%	0.94%	0.48%	2,369	1,609	37.23%	10,584	9,431	12.23%	6.74%	1.47%	17,994	16,893	6.49%	6.11	6.33
TOTAL	105,915,906	97,235,010	8.93%	3,296,703	3,286,703	8.91%	3.58%	3.39%	8,153,214	6,941,200	17.46%	25,305,601	22,142,421	14.29%		10.41%	18,341,339	15,468,528	18.42%	5.77	6.28

1- 1994 includes results from the acquisitions of Joseph Horne Co. in May and R.H. Macy Co. in December. Latest year includes $65.9 million accounting credit. Latest results reflect several acquisitions. 2- 1993 reflects $45 million in special charges. 3- 1993 reflects a $1.5 million consolidation charge. 4- 1993 includes $3.4 million pretax charge.

SPECIALTY STORES

($ in thousands)	Sales 1994	Sales 1993	% Change	Profits 1994	Profits 1993	% Change	Profits to sales 1994	1993	Operating profits 1994	1993	% Change	Shareholders equity 1994	1993	% Change	Profit to avg. equity 1994	Debt interest to sales 1994	Yearend inventory 1994	1993	% Change	Sales to inventory 1994	1993
Melville	11,285,561	10,458,001	6.15%	307,470	331,790	-7.33%	2.72%	3.18%	610,742	623,637	-2.07%	2,361,605	2,246,846	6.60%	8.77%	0.23%	2,138,243	1,856,772	15.04%	5.28	5.61
Woolworth[1]	8,293,000	9,926,000	-43.65%	-495,000	3,209	N/A	0.57%	0.64%	-174,000	853,000	N/A	1,349,000	1,349,000	0.67%	N/A	0.89%	1,622,000	1,579,000	2.72%	5.11	6.1
Limited	7,320,792	6,545,000	11.85%	448,043	390,000	14.57%	5.19%	5.96%	474,000	500,556	19.89%	3,441,293	3,441,293	11.26%		0.69%	1,074,440	1,024,000	4.95%	6.20	6.13
Nordstrom	3,894,478	3,589,938	8.48%	202,953	140,418	44.54%	5.21%	3.91%	271,576	180,055	50.83%	1,343,800	1,166,504	15.20%	10.53%	0.79%	627,930	586,600	7.23%	6.20	6.13
Gap	3,722,940	3,295,679	12.96%	258,424	140,424	83.92%	8.60%	7.84%	518,420	425,697	21.78%	1,375,232	1,126,475	22.08%	16.52%	0.29%	370,638	331,155	11.92%	10.04	9.95
Neiman Marcus[2]	2,092,906	2,016,914	3.77%	15,926	47,374	-66.38%	0.76%	2.35%	59,336	108,836	-45.48%	-78,918	158,175	N/A	N/A	1.52%	345,145	362,567	-4.81%	6.06	5.56
Edison Bros.	1,492,400	1,412,930	0.92%	20,501	79,756	-43.87%	1.39%	6.98%	55,465	104,937	-47.14%	385,500	407,100	3.47%	3.47%	0.18%	315,140	259,527	-0.39%	4.92	4.83
Charming Shoppes	1,272,883	1,254,122	1.48%	44,689	79,756	-43.43%	3.51%	6.35%	59,450	104,937	-47.14%	598,822	522,100	14.52%	5.45%	0.18%	266,552	259,527	-0.39%	4.92	4.83
Talbots	879,685	736,738	19.39%	35,153	35,153	54.91%	6.19%	4.77%	96,995	65,721	43.02%	386,594	336,719	14.82%	9.83%	0.31%	123,389	112,387	9.96%	7.12	6.55
Merry-Go-Round[3]	782,816	959,878	-18.45%	-186,340	-45,624	N/A	N/A	N/A	-84,801	-51,017	N/A	5,699	191,221	-97.02%	0.25%	0.25%	48,088	71,528	-32.77%	16.28	13.42
Ann Taylor[4]	658,800	501,649	31.33%	31,752	3,209	N/A	4.82%	0.64%	77,291	-6,000	57.67%	326,112	259,271	25.78%	6.97%	2.16%	93,705	60,890	53.89%	7.03	8.24
Profitt's[5]	617,963	200,804	207.32%	16,126	6,063	166.01%	2.61%	3.02%	37,497	-5,000	-18.89%	280,676	104,043	45.68%	6.65%	2.54%	162,080	73,102	121.22%	3.81	2.75
Cato	463,737	407,678	13.70%	18,105	24,802	27.00%	3.90%	6.08%	35,733	44,040	-18.89%	141,508	127,533	10.96%	8.62%	0.03%	54,674	55,614	-2.04%	8.48	7.31
United Retail	357,664	344,090	3.95%	2,976	1,568	89.80%	0.83%	0.46%	6,663	6,426	3.64%	90,672	87,300	3.84%	2.22%	0.08%	37,518	37,901	-1.01%	9.53	9.06
Catherines Stores	256,427	244,743	4.77%	5,600	7,325	-23.55%	2.18%	2.99%	10,550	13,339	-20.91%	68,916	66,063	4.32%	5.49%	0.37%	44,969	37,636	19.48%	5.70	6.50
Deb Shops	202,938	221,070	-8.20%	-2,719	5,146	N/A	N/A	2.33%	-1,376	9,932	N/A	104,918	110,387	-4.95%	N/A	0.00%	28,576	32,773	-12.81%	7.10	6.75
American Eagle	197,913	168,075	17.75%	12,198	6,055	101.45%	6.16%	3.60%	12,028	7,538	59.56%	50,124	4,358	N/A	23.32%	0.94%	45,164	24,366	85.36%	4.38	6.90
Gymboree	188,424	129,582	45.41%	22,195	14,106	57.34%	11.78%	10.89%	35,232	23,045	52.88%	92,629	63,305	46.32%	17.66%	0.00%	34,097	20,398	67.16%	5.53	6.35
Jos. A. Bank	176,054	149,578	17.70%	1,347	3,770	-64.27%	0.77%	2.52%	5,822	-102	N/A	43,631	30,390	60.02%	2.11%	1.38%	51,582	42,641	20.82%	3.39	3.40
Buckle	145,038	129,631	11.89%	7,696	7,201	6.87%	5.31%	5.55%	11,772	11,101	6.04%	51,282	34,413	16.22%	0.35%	0.06%	16,988	12,861	31.78%	8.54	10.06
Wet Seal	132,997	140,129	-5.09%	-1,013	-2,378	N/A	N/A	N/A	-2,248	-4,539	N/A	50,724	51,729	-1.94%	N/A	0.00%	8,194	8,287	-1.12%	16.23	16.91
Fredericks of Hllywd.	132,153	128,516	2.83%	-903	4,737	N/A	N/A	3.69%	-1,228	7,928	N/A	34,413	36,615	-6.01%	16.77%	0.11%	18,097	17,368	4.20%	7.30	7.40
Urban Outfitters	110,121	84,486	30.34%	10,817	7,806	38.57%	9.82%	9.24%	17,576	13,302	32.13%	46,751	35,498	31.70%	21.37%	0.98%	10,381	6,947	49.43%	10.61	12.16
Cache[6]	104,714	86,624	20.88%	4,813	4,928	-2.33%	4.60%	5.69%	5,654	4,910	41.00%	16,430	12,175	34.45%		0.13%	14,935	10,222	46.11%	7.01	8.47
Brauns[7]	93,961	89,050	5.51%	-245	2,861	N/A	N/A	3.21%	598	3,342	-82.11%	17,118	17,118	-1.22%	1.06%	1.06%	15,240	14,728	3.49%	6.17	6.11
Evans[8]	75,195	86,477	-13.05%	-12,064	1,950	N/A	N/A	2.27%	-5,813	1,885	N/A	21,544	33,608	-35.99%	N/A	1.50%	16,401	14,162	15.81%	4.58	6.11
Harold's Stores	58,979	60,940	91.04%	1,846	1,612	29.53%	2.75%	2.65%	3,813	2,900	31.48%	22,260	19,996	11.32%	6.47%	0.36%	17,847	12,647	41.12%	4.25	4.82
Mothers Work	55,282	30,872	30.68%	3,291	911	102.63%	3.13%	2.95%	3,437	1,902	80.70%	19,810	17,656	10.94%	16.81%	0.62%	18,527	10,462	76.75%	3.18	2.95
Chicos FAS		42,302	2.86%		6,091	60.46%	5.95%	14.40%	5,685	7,986	-28.81%	14,226	10,713	32.79%		0.22%	18,556	7,016	-6.56%	8.43	6.03
TOTAL	45,124,750	43,869,234	2.86%	1,399,151	871,963	60.46%	3.10%	1.99%	2,082,468	1,774,497	62.44%	11,877,234	10,882,627	9.14%	11.06%		7,418,856	6,689,817	10.90%	6.08	6.56

1- Year-ago period includes $451 million restructuring charge. 2- 1994 includes a $48.4 million restructuring charge for Contempo Casuals. 1993 includes a $11.2 million accounting charge. 3- 1994 includes $8.9 million in reorganization costs. 1993 includes $6.9 million charge related to its January 1994 bankruptcy filing 4- Year-ago includes a $11.1 million debt refinancing charge. 5- 1994 includes results from the McRae's division acquired in March 1994. 6- 1993 includes a $1.1 million accounting credit. 8- Latest year includes $3.2 million restructuring charge.

DISCOUNTERS

($ in thousands)	Sales 1994	Sales 1993	% Change	Profits 1994	Profits 1993	% Change	Profits to sales 1994	1993	Operating profits 1994	1993	% Change	Shareholders equity 1994	1993	% Change	Profit to avg. equity 1994	Debt interest to sales 1994	Yearend inventory 1994	1993	% Change	Sales to inventory 1994	1993
Wal-Mart Stores	82,494,000	67,344,000	22.50%	2,681,000	2,333,000	14.92%	3.25%	3.46%	4,049,000	3,667,000	13.26%	12,726,000	10,753,000	18.35%	14.81%	0.63%	14,064,000	11,483,000	22.48%	5.87	5.90
Kmart	34,025,000	34,694,000	1.77%	296,000	-974,000	N/A	0.87%	N/A	332,000	957,000	-65.31%	6,032,000	6,093,000	2.07%	0.89%	0.47%	7,252,000	7,382,000	-1.79%	4.61	5.08
Fred Meyer [2]	3,128,432	2,970,982	5.01%	3,169	68,316	-89.61%	0.23%	2.29%	118,236	110,662	6.84%	338,620	527,060	2.07%	0.89%	0.47%	514,473	477,569	7.73%	6.04	6.24
Caldor [3]	2,748,634	2,414,124	13.86%	44,359	33,232	33.48%	1.61%	1.38%	118,236	110,662	6.84%	337,116	291,757	15.55%	9.18%	1.27%	550,932	468,069	17.70%	4.99	5.16
Ames [1]	2,142,827	2,123,527	0.91%	17,026	10,823	57.31%	0.79%	0.51%	104,468	98,085	6.51%	84,917	60,410	40.57%	14.79%	1.24%	430,152	442,198	-2.72%	4.98	4.80
Venture Stores [5]	2,017,283	1,862,590	8.31%	26,717	34,565	-47.09%	1.42%	2.91%	40,479	80,313	-29.04%	296,399	247,935	7.70%	7.36%	0.49%	312,027	283,122	10.21%	6.47	6.56
Bradlees [1]	1,916,655	1,880,611	1.92%	6,735	5,321	1.02%	0.35%	0.36%	57,586	57,598	29.46%	163,432	163,680	-0.16%	2.17%	1.27%	306,218	270,827	13.04%	6.26	6.94
Hills Stores	1,872,021	1,765,546	6.03%	40,431	30,041	34.59%	2.16%	1.70%	105,755	92,465	14.37%	196,904	194,000	0.00%	N/A	0.00%	407,237	409,291	-0.24%	4.50	4.13
ShopKo Stores	1,852,929	1,738,746	6.57%	37,790	32,122	17.65%	2.04%	1.85%	132,501	110,133	20.31%	397,257	373,706	6.30%	6.47%	1.57%	400,623	328,854	21.82%	4.63	5.29
Dollar General	1,448,609	1,132,995	27.86%	73,634	48,557	51.64%	5.08%	4.29%	121,087	80,196	50.99%	323,756	240,717	34.50%	16.58%	0.19%	356,111	260,042	36.94%	4.07	4.36
Family Dollar [7]	1,428,440	1,297,430	10.10%	63,099	64,428	-2.06%	4.42%	4.97%	100,117	102,920	-2.72%	370,172	323,281	14.50%	11.86%	0.02%	403,570	379,354	6.38%	3.54	3.42
Consolidated Stores	1,276,844	1,055,931	21.07%	35,220	40,327	-23.34%	4.32%	4.00%	98,739	57,537	30.03%	315,234	258,633	21.83%	12.42%	0.37%	302,132	223,280	30.48%	4.23	4.17
Value City	866,855	842,199	2.63%	28,831	40,252	-3.37%	4.50%	4.78%	62,237	67,061	-7.19%	217,319	177,519	22.45%	7.72%	0.28%	220,506	223,102	-0.48%	3.92	3.81
Rose's Stores	731,926	1,203,233	-39.17%	-66,207	—	N/A	N/A	N/A	16,403	-10,738	N/A	-35,186	16,096	N/A	N/A	0.61%	119,567	203,150	-41.14%	6.12	5.92
TOTAL	**139,712,553**	**126,060,285**	**10.83%**	**3,347,834**	**1,689,085**	**98.20%**	**2.40%**	**1.34%**	**5,367,858**	**5,549,770**	**-3.28%**	**21,735,494**	**19,862,917**	**9.43%**	**10.57%**		**26,118,353**	**23,011,316**	**13.21%**	**5.35**	**5.46**

1- 1994 includes a $16 million loss from discontinued operations. The year-ago period includes $521 million loss from discontinued operations. 2- 1993 includes $15.9 million writedown of assets. 3- Latest year includes $3.8 million facilities relocation expense. The year-ago period includes a charge of $5.4 million for debt retirement. 4- 1993 includes a $12.5 million gain from litigation settlement and a $13 million charge from a distribution center closing. 5- Year-ago period includes $10.3 million accounting gain. 6- 1993 includes $6.7 million in non-recurring charges. 7- 1994 includes $1.1 million tax benefit. 8- The year-ago period includes a $3.1 million charge for debt retirement.

OFF-PRICERS

($ in thousands)	Sales 1994	Sales 1993	% Change	Profits 1994	Profits 1993	% Change	Profits to sales 1994	1993	Operating profits 1994	1993	% Change	Shareholders equity 1994	1993	% Change	Profit to avg. equity 1994	Debt interest to sales 1994	Yearend inventory 1994	1993	% Change	Sales to inventory 1994	1993
TJX Cos [1]	3,842,816	3,626,604	5.96%	82,619	124,379	-33.57%	2.15%	3.43%	167,703	229,723	-27.00%	696,952	590,900	16.50%	9.16%	0.67%	937,729	772,234	21.42%	4.10	4.70
Burlington Coat Factory	1,468,440	1,198,305	22.54%	45,383	42,903	5.78%	3.09%	3.58%	91,576	77,200	18.62%	389,867	323,111	14.47%	8.54%	0.57%	468,921	352,919	32.87%	3.13	3.40
Ross Stores	1,262,844	1,122,033	12.82%	36,821	29,324	25.57%	2.92%	2.61%	78,502	71,730	9.44%	254,551	228,222	11.54%	9.99%	0.28%	275,183	229,929	20.20%	4.59	4.99
Filene's Basement [2]	608,903	578,821	5.09%	-1,241	-3,159	N/A	N/A	N/A	5,756	-1,724	N/A	112,171	112,523	-0.31%	N/A	0.60%	117,504	121,621	-3.39%	5.18	4.76
Dress Barn	457,324	419,585	8.99%	16,153	19,039	-15.16%	3.53%	4.54%	23,913	27,410	-12.76%	159,197	142,002	12.11%	7.02%	0.00%	79,601	73,403	8.44%	5.75	5.72
Stein Mart	419,220	342,730	22.32%	18,419	16,682	10.41%	4.39%	4.87%	26,151	23,928	9.29%	85,277	66,858	27.55%	15.52%	0.18%	94,944	76,186	24.62%	4.42	4.50
Clothestime [3]	349,980	347,569	0.69%	-11,240	8,167	N/A	N/A	2.35%	-15,308	15,308	N/A	50,913	62,466	-18.49%	N/A	2.51%	24,812	31,859	-22.12%	13.74	10.91
Syms	326,651	316,939	2.42%	8,491	10,847	-21.72%	2.60%	3.40%	35,500	35,511	1.73%	197,341	190,605	3.33%	4.30%	0.02%	96,607	99,418	-2.83%	3.37	3.02
Men's Wearhouse	317,127	240,394	31.92%	22,108	8,739	58.55%	3.82%	3.64%	22,375	15,018	41.45%	84,944	57,867	46.96%	10.63%	0.56%	108,198	77,974	38.75%	2.93	3.08
One Price Clothing [4]	263,326	234,698	20.72%	4,389	8,724	-49.69%	1.55%	3.72%	31,142	32,847	-5.19%	53,074	47,826	10.97%	5.70%	0.10%	26,337	23,315	12.96%	10.76	10.07
Today's Man [5]	216,893	167,072	29.82%	4,608	6,020	-23.46%	2.12%	3.60%	9,567	8,260	15.82%	51,675	56511	-8.56%	5.77%	0.50%	44,207	57,146	-22.64%	4.91	2.92
S&K Famous Brands	112,416	98,976	13.58%	2,548	4,016	-36.55%	2.27%	4.06%	6,575	8,427	-21.98%	37,156	34,441	7.88%	4.69%	0.66%	39,746	37,623	5.64%	2.83	2.63
TOTAL	**9,655,862**	**8,695,726**	**11.04%**	**275,588**	**275,681**	**-0.14%**	**2.27%**	**2.27%**	**483,350**	**544,027**	**-11.17%**	**2,063,108**	**1,913,332**	**7.83%**	**7.25%**		**2,313,979**	**1,932,717**	**19.73%**	**4.17**	**4.50**

1- 1994 includes a $2.7 million charge from cumulative effect of accounting changes and income tax gain. 2- 1994 includes a $2.3 million loss on debt repurchase. The year-ago period includes a $14 million store restructuring charge. 3- Latest year includes a $5.4 million income tax gain and $1.9 million gain from sale of land & building assets. 4- Year-ago period includes a $2.7 million income tax gain. 5- Year-ago period includes a $2.7 million charge for purchase of treasury shares.

MISCELLANEOUS

($ in thousands)	Sales 1994	Sales 1993	% Change	Profits 1994	Profits 1993	% Change	Profits to sales 1994	1993	Operating profits 1994	1993	% Change	Shareholders equity 1994	1993	% Change	Profit to avg. equity 1994	Debt interest to sales 1994	Yearend inventory 1994	1993	% Change	Sales to inventory 1994	1993
Spiegel	2,706,791	2,337,235	15.81%	25,100	48,705	-48.47%	0.93%	2.08%	132,626	159,508	-16.85%	573,217	567,485	1.45%	2.01%	3.15%	597,761	438,669	36.11%	4.53	5.33
Home Shopping Network [2]	1,126,514	1,046,580	7.64%	16,777	-22,781	N/A	1.49%	N/A	26,679	-6,949	N/A	206,443	196,554	5.03%	5.51%	0.52%	118,801	110,930	7.10%	9.48	5.81
Lands' End [1]	992,106	869,975	14.04%	36,096	43,729	-17.45%	3.64%	5.03%	63,525	70,410	-10.00%	189,128	177,285	6.68%	12.99%	0.18%	168,652	149,688	12.67%	5.88	9.43
TOTAL	**4,825,411**	**4,253,790**	**13.44%**	**77,973**	**69,653**	**11.94%**	**1.62%**	**1.64%**	**222,830**	**223,049**	**-0.10%**	**974,788**	**941,324**	**3.55%**	**5.39%**		**885,234**	**699,487**	**26.55%**	**5.45**	**6.08**

1- 1994 includes a charge of $35 million reserved for the anticipated sale of a subsidiary. 2- 1993 included a litigation charge of $13 million.

($ in thousands)	Sales 1994	Sales 1993	% Change	Profits 1994	Profits 1993	% Change	Profits to sales 1994	1993	Operating profits 1994	1993	% Change	Shareholders equity 1994	1993	% Change	Profit to avg. equity 1994	Debt interest to sales 1994	Yearend inventory 1994	1993	% Change	Sales to inventory 1994	1993
DEPARTMENT STORES	105,915,905	97,245,913	8.90%	3,786,703	3,296,703	14.85%	3.58%	3.39%	8,153,219	6,941,980	17.46%	26,505,080	22,142,921	11.25%	10.70%		18,341,331	15,463,593	15.42%	5.77	5.23
SPECIALTY STORES	45,124,750	41,869,234	2.85%	1,389,151	871,963	60.46%	3.10%	1.99%	2,082,468	1,774,497	62.44%	11,877,234	10,862,621	9.14%	8.06%		7,418,866	6,689,817	10.90%	6.08	6.56
DISCOUNTERS	139,712,553	126,060,285	10.83%	3,347,834	1,689,085	98.20%	2.40%	1.34%	5,367,858	5,549,770	-3.28%	21,735,494	19,862,917	9.43%	10.57%		26,118,353	23,011,316	13.21%	5.35	5.46
OFF-PRICERS	9,655,862	8,695,726	11.04%	219,058	275,681	-20.54%	2.27%	3.17%	483,252	544,027	-11.17%	2,063,108	1,913,332	7.83%	7.25%		2,313,979	1,932,717	19.73%	4.17	4.50
MISCELLANEOUS	4,825,411	4,253,790	13.44%	77,973	69,653	11.94%	1.62%	1.64%	222,830	223,049	13.82%	974,788	941,324	3.55%	9.83%		885,234	699,487	26.55%	5.54	5.85
TOTAL	**305,234,482**	**280,114,045**	**8.97%**	**8,830,717**	**6,203,085**	**42.36%**	**2.89%**	**2.21%**	**17,109,722**	**15,032,543**	**13.82%**	**61,956,225**	**55,742,621**	**11.15%**			**55,077,761**	**47,881,866**	**15.03%**		

RETAIL CHAINS & THEIR CORPORATE PARENTS

Retail Chains	Corporate Parents
5-7-9 Shops	Edison
Abercrombie & Fitch	Limited
Accessory Lady	Woolworth
After Thoughts	Woolworth
Aeropostale	Federated
Arcadia	Claire's
Art Explosion	Claire's
Ashbrooks	Woolworth
Athletic X-Press	Woolworth
Attivo	Merry-Go-Round
August Max Woman	The Casual Corner Group
A.V.C. Superstore	Tandy
Baby Gap	Gap
Bacons	Mercantile
Bakers	Edison
Banana Republic	Gap
Barnes & Noble	Barnes & Noble
Baskin	Hastings Group
Bath & Body Works	Limited
B. Dalton Bookseller	Barnes & Noble
Bergdorf Goodman	Harcourt General
Bergner's	Carson Pirie Scott
BJ's Wholesale Club	Waban
Bloomingdale's	Federated
Bob's	Melville
Boogies Diner	Merry-Go-Round
Bookstar	Barnes & Noble
Bookstop	Barnes & Noble
Boot Factory	Genesco
Borders	Borders
Boston Store	Carson Pirie Scott
Brentano's	Borders
Bud's Outlets	Wal-Mart
Builders Square	Kmart
Burdines	Federated
Cacique	Limited
Canary Island	Woolworth
Carimar	Woolworth
Carson Pirie Scott	Carson Pirie Scott
Castner Knott	Mercantile
Casual Corner	The Casual Corner Group
Casual Male Big & Tall	J. Baker
CD Superstores	Borders
Champs Sports	Woolworth

RETAIL CHAINS & THEIR CORPORATE PARENTS (continued)

Retail Chains	Corporate Parents
Charter Club	Federated
Chess King	Merry-Go-Round
Cignal	Merry-Go-Round
Claire's Boutiques	Claire's
Clothestime	Clothestime
Cloth World	Fabri-Centers
Coda	Edison
Coles	Borders
Colorado	Woolworth
Computer City	Tandy
Contempo Casuals	Harcourt General
Crossroads	Home Depot
CVS	Melville
Dara Michelle	Claire's
Dave & Buster's	Edison
Dayton's	Dayton
Dejaiz	Merry-Go-Round
Der Schuh	Woolworth
Dillard's	Dillard
D.J.'s Fashion Center for Men	Merry-Go-Round
Doubleday Book Shops	Barnes & Noble
East 57th	Claire's
Easy Spirit	U.S. Shoe
El-Bee Shoe Outlets	Elder
Elder-Beerman	Elder
Electric Avenue & More	Ward
Exhilarama	Edison
Expo Design	Home Depot
Express	Limited
Facconable	Nordstrom
Factory to You	Genesco
Famous-Barr	May
Famous Brand Outlets	Tandy
Famous Footwear	Brown
Farmas	Woolworth
Fayva	J. Baker
Filene's	May
Florsheim Shoe Shops	Florsheim
Foley's	May
Footaction	Melville
Foot Locker	Woolworth
Footquarters	Woolworth
Gallery One	Woolworth
GapKids	Gap

RETAIL CHAINS & THEIR CORPORATE PARENTS (continued)

Retail Chains	Corporate Parents
Gayfers	Mercantile
G.C. Murphy	Riklis
G+G	Petrie
Going to the Game!	Woolworth
Goldsmith's	Federated
Hardy	Genesco
Hartfield's	Petrie
Hecht's	May
Henri Bendel	Limited
Hit or Miss	TJX
HomeBase	Waban
HomeGoods	TJX
Homelife Furniture	Sears
Hudson's	Dayton
Hypermart USA	Wal-Mart
H.L. Green	Riklis
Jarman	Genesco
Jas K. Wilson	Hastings Group
J. Baker	J. Baker
J.B. White	Mercantile
JC Penney	J.C.Penney
Jean Nicole	Petrie
Jeans West	Edison
J.J. Newberry	Riklis
Jo-Ann Fabrics	Fabri-Centers
Johnston & Murphy	Genesco
Jordan Marsh	Federated
Joslins	Mercantile
Journeys	Genesco
J. Riggings	Edison
Karuba	Woolworth
Kaufmann's	May
Kay-Bee	Melville
Kerr Drug Stores	J.C.Penney
Kids Foot Locker	Woolworth
Kids 'R' Us	Toys 'R' Us
Kinney	Woolworth
Kmart	Kmart
Lady Foot Locker	Woolworth
Lady Plus	Woolworth
Lane Bryant	Limited
Lazarus	Federated
L'accessory	Claire's
Lechmere	Ward

RETAIL CHAINS & THEIR CORPORATE PARENTS (continued)

Retail Chains	Corporate Parents
Leeds	Edison
Leopold, Price & Rolle	Hastings Group
Lerner New York	Limited
Limited Too	Limited
Linens 'n Things	Melville
Lingerie Time	Clothestime
Lord & Taylor	May
Macy's	Federated
Margo's	Elder
Marianne	Petrie
Marshall Field's	Dayton
Marshalls	Melville
Mathers	Woolworth
McCrory	Riklis
McDuff Electronics and Appliances	Tandy
McLellan	Riklis
Media Play	Musicland
Meier & Frank	May
Meldisco	Melville
Merry-Go-Round	Merry-Go-Round
Merry-Go-Round Outlet	Merry-Go-Round
Mervyn's	Dayton
M.J. Carroll	Petrie
Moderna	Woolworth
Montgomery Ward	Ward
Musicland	Musicland
Naturalizer	Brown
Neiman Marcus	Harcourt General
N.E.T. Works	Merry-Go-Round
New York Fabrics	Fabri-Centers
Nordstrom	Nordstrom
Nordstrom Rack	Nordstrom
Northern Elements	Woolworth
Northern Getaway	Woolworth
Northern Reflections	Woolworth
Northern Traditions	Woolworth
Oaktree	Edison
OfficeMax	Kmart
Old Navy Clothing Co.	Gap
On Cue	Musicland
Outlet World	Ward
Parade of Shoes	J. Baker
Payless Shoe Source	May
Penhaligon's	Limited

RETAIL CHAINS & THEIR CORPORATE PARENTS (continued)

Retail Chains	Corporate Parents
Petite Sophisticate	U.S. Shoe
Petrie's	Petrie
Planet Music	Borders
Portfolio	J.C. Penney
Precis	Edison
Prior	Kmart
Radio Shack	Tandy
Randy River	Woolworth
Rave	Petrie
Reflexions	Woolworth
Repp Ltd.	Edison
Rich's	Federated
Robinsons-May	May
Rubin	Woolworth
Rx Place Drug Mart	Woolworth
Sacha London	Edison
Sam Goody	Musicland
Sam's Club	Wal-Mart
San Francisco Music Box Company	Woolworth
Scribner's Bookstores	Barnes & Noble
Sears	Sears
S.H. Kress	Riklis
Sight & Save	U.S. Shoe
Silk & Satin	Woolworth
Space Port	Edison
Spirale	Edison
Stern's	Federated
Structure	Limited
Stuarts	Petrie
Suncoast Motion Picture Company	Musicland
Super Kmart Center	Kmart
Target	Dayton
Target Greatland	Dayton
T.G.&Y.	Riklis
Thayer McNeil	Florsheim
The Bargain! Shop	Woolworth
The Best of Times	Woolworth
The Bon Marche	Federated
The Edge in Electronics	Tandy
The Gap	Gap
The Home Depot	Home Depot
The Incredible Universe	Tandy
The Jones Store Co.	Mercantile
The Limited	Limited

RETAIL CHAINS & THEIR CORPORATE PARENTS (continued)

Retail Chains	Corporate Parents
The Sports Authority	Kmart
This End Up	Melville
Thom McAn	Melville
Thrift Drug	J.C. Penney
Time-Out	Edison
T.J. Maxx	TJX
Toofers	Merry-Go-Round
Topkapi	Claire's
Toys 'R' Us	Toys 'R' Us
Vic Jensens	Woolworth
Victoria's Secret	Limited
Waldenbooks	Borders
Walker's	Hastings Group
Wal-Mart	Wal-Mart
Wal-Mart Supercenter	Wal-Mart
Webster	Edison
Weekend Edition	Woolworth
Western Auto Supply Co.	Sears
Wild Pair	Edison
Williams the Shoemen	Woolworth
Wilsons	Melville
Winkelman's	Petrie
Winners Apparel Ltd.	TJX
Woolworth	Woolworth
Work 'n Gear	J. Baker
World Foot Locker	Woolworth
Zeidler & Zeidler	Edison

GLOSSARY

acquisition the purchase of one organization by another, sometimes called a *takeover*.

additional markup a markup added to an existing markup to increase a retail price.

adjacency a product or product category strategically located next to another product or category for customer convenience and to stimulate sales.

advance dating delays the beginning of a payment and/or discount period until a specified future date. Also referred to as *post* or *seasonal dating*.

advertising conveys a message to a large group of people through a mass medium.

anchor a major shopping center tenant.

anticipation an additional discount based on prevailing interest rates for paying an invoice prior to the cash discount date.

assets that which is owned by an organization.

associated buying office a buying office jointly owned by a group of independently owned and operated member stores. Also known as a *cooperative buying office*.

average inventory the amount of inventory on hand within a period computed by dividing the sum of the beginning and ending inventories by two.

bait and switch the illegal practice of luring customers with a low-priced advertised item with the intent of selling them a higher-priced item.

balance sheet a statement of an organization's assets, liabilities, and owners' equity.

bankruptcy occurs when an organiza-

tion becomes insolvent or incapable of paying its debts.

basic goods goods that remain the same from one season to another.

basic stock method an inventory planning method that asserts that a beginning-of-month inventory should equal planned sales for the month plus a basic inventory.

beginning-of-month (BOM) inventory the inventory on hand at the beginning of a month.

better line an apparel line priced at the upper end of a department store's selection.

bidding war a series of counter-offers by two or more parties interested in acquiring the same organization.

billed cost the cost of merchandise that appears on a supplier's invoice.

blind item an item for which consumers have no price reference.

book inventory a recorded perpetual inventory value.

bottom-up plan plans developed at the lower levels of an organization as building blocks of an organization-wide plan.

branch a microcosm of a large urban flagship store offering the same categories of merchandise but in limited selections.

brand a name and/or symbol associated with certain product characteristics, such as price, quality, fit, styling, and prestige.

brand-driven purchase a customer choice based primarily on brand.

brand extension using an existing

449

brand name on a new product or product line to reap the benefits of the brand's reputation.

breadth   the number of unique items, categories, styles, brands, sizes, colors, or prices in a merchandise assortment.

bridge line   an apparel line made with less expensive fabrics and fewer details than a designer's top-of-the-line creations.

buyer   a person who buys and prices merchandise for resale.

cannibalization   results when a retailer spins-off a new merchandising concept too closely related to existing businesses, or when a chain opens new stores too close to existing stores.

case-packed goods   prepacked merchandise with a standard assortment of sizes, colors, and styles.

cash discount   a reduction in the amount due on an invoice when payment is made on or before a specified date.

cash discount date   the expiration date of a cash discount period.

cash discount period   a payment period that begins on the date that an invoice is issued and ends on the cash discount date.

cash dating   cash payment arrangements, often referred to as COD (cash-on-delivery).

cash flow   the balance of cash coming into and going out of an organization.

catalog showroom   a discounter that sells consumer electronics, home accessories, sporting goods, toys and juvenile products, and jewelry by catalog and in a retail showroom. Also called a *hardlines specialty store.*

category   a group of related merchandise, sometimes called a *classification.*

category killer   a discounter that offers a deep selection of branded merchandise in a single merchandise category at discounted prices, thus "killing" the category

of business for other retailers.

category management   managing a category of merchandise as an independent business unit.

central business district (CBD)   an urban hub of commerce and transportation, commonly called *downtown.*

centralization   performing functions for an organization's remote facilities from a single location, usually a corporate office.

chain   two or more stores with the same ownership and identity.

classic   a long-enduring fashion.

clearance markdowns   price reductions that induce the sale of various types of residual or slow-selling merchandise.

closed-sell fixture   a store fixture that restricts customer access to the merchandise, requiring salesperson assistance for making selections.

closeout store   a discount store operated by a retailer to clear slow-selling or end-of-season merchandise from its regular-price stores.

commissionaire   an agent who represents retailers that wish to purchase goods in foreign markets.

commission buying office   an independent representative of a group of manufacturers who earns commissions from selling merchandise to a group of retail clients. Also known as a *merchandise broker.*

common carrier   a trucker whose rates are based on established tariffs and schedules between designated points.

community center   a shopping center with approximately 100,000 to 350,000 square feet of retail space often with a supermarket and a full-line discounter as major tenants.

complementary stores   stores that sell goods that complement each other.

component percentage   a ratio that expresses an income statement component as a percentage of net sales.

conglomerate an organization that unites the ownership of independently operated subsidiaries.

consignment goods goods not paid for by a retailer until they are sold.

consolidator a transportation intermediary that combines less-than-truckload (ltl) shipments from multiple shippers into truckload (tl) shipments.

consultant an adviser that offers expertise in a certain area on a fee basis.

consumer the ultimate user of a product or service.

consumer publication magazines and newspapers available to the public at newsstands.

contest a sales promotion activity that requires participating customers to demonstrate a skill.

contract carrier provides services to individual shippers or groups of shippers based on individually negotiated agreements.

control monitoring or measuring actual performance against goals and reacting to the causes of any deviations from goals.

control standard a reference point or benchmark to measure performance.

cooperative advertising involves shared advertising expense between two marketing channel members.

cost the wholesale price paid to a supplier.

cost complement the difference between markup and 100 percent.

cost-of-goods-sold includes payments to suppliers for merchandise, plus workroom and shipping costs, less discounts and returns-to-vendors.

cotenancy requirement a retailer's requirement of the presence of compatible tenants in a shopping center.

cross-docking a logistical concept whereby a retail distribution center functions like a trucking terminal at which merchandise arrives from suppliers in one bay, and is distributed to stores in another bay without any processing.

cross-merchandising presenting merchandise in two or more locations in a store.

cubes a store fixture used primarily to present folded goods.

cumulative markup an aggregate percentage markup on goods with varying markup percentages.

current ratio the ratio of an organization's current assets to its current debts.

customs broker a licensed independent agent who represents clients in customs matters.

date of invoice the date that an invoice is issued.

dating the period allowed for the payment of an invoice.

demographic segmentation the identification of markets by characteristics such as gender, age, education, and income.

department a group of related merchandise; a functional organizational unit that performs related activities.

department manager a person responsible for the merchandising and operational activities of an area in a store defined by department or division.

department store a retailer that caters to multiple needs of several groups of consumers that is most often an anchor of an enclosed shopping center.

depth the selection within an assortment of goods.

designer brand a designer name used as a brand name, also called a *signature brand*.

designer line the exclusive creations of a reputed apparel designer.

destination merchandise a consumer purchase that is typically planned.

deviation the discrepancy between actual performance and a standard.

direct competition occurs when stores offer the same merchandise to the same customers.

direct marketing a direct relationship between a retailer and a customer without the use of a retail facility.

direct-response marketing uses a nonpersonal print or electronic medium to communicate with consumers.

direct sales force a manufacturer's sales staff that sells products directly to retailers.

direct selling selling one-to-one to customers using explanation or demonstration.

discontinued merchandise goods that will not be part of future assortments.

discounter a retailer that sells goods at prices lower than the conventional prices of other retailers.

display fixture a store fixture used to display goods not available for customer selection.

distribution center the location to which suppliers ship goods at which point they are unpacked, prepared for the selling floor, and redistributed to stores.

distributor allocates arriving shipments of merchandise to individual stores based on a store's capacity, current sales trends, and inventory levels.

district manager responsible for a group of stores located within a defined geographic area.

diversification entering a new line of business that differs from present businesses.

divestiture the sale of an organization's assets.

division a group of related departments; another name for a subsidiary.

divisional merchandise manager a person responsible for a merchandise division in a retail organization.

drawing a sales promotion activity in which participants register to win a prize.

economies of scale savings associated with conducting large-scale business.

edge city a mini-metropolis that evolves along an interstate highway within the shadow of a major urban core.

electronic data interchange an information-trading partnership between a retailer and a producer, sometimes extended to include a producer's suppliers.

electronic retailing a form of direct marketing that includes television shopping channels, infomercials, and online computer shopping services.

employee discount a discount on employee purchases typical of the retail industry.

end-of-month (EOM) dating dating in which the payment and discount periods begin at the end of the month in which the invoice is dated, not the date of invoice.

end-of-month (EOM) inventory the inventory on hand at the end of a month.

ethnic segmentation the identification of ethnic groups as targeted markets.

everyday-low-pricing (EDLP) a value-oriented pricing strategy of offering merchandise at promotional prices on a day-to-day basis without the support of advertised sale events as promotional vehicles.

exception report a report that includes only major deviations from standards, bypassing minor ones.

external standard a benchmark derived from information external to an organization.

external theft shoplifting by people who are not employees of the organization.

extra dating adds additional days to payment and discount periods of an invoice.

factor a financial intermediary who buys manufacturers' receivables at discounted rates and then collects payment from retailers.

fad a fashion with a very short life cycle.

fall on the 4-5-4 calendar, the season that begins in August and ends in January.

family life cycle a sequence of family-life stages based on marital status and the presence or absence of dependent children.

fashion a mode or expression accepted by a group of people over time.

fashion director a person responsible for providing buyers with information on dominant trends so that buyers can strategically select assortments.

fashion follower a trend-setter emulator.

fashion goods goods that change frequently.

fashion laggard a consumer who is either slow to adopt a fashion, or slow to give it up.

fashion life cycle the evolution, culmination, and decline of a fashion.

festival center a shopping center of specialty stores, pushcart peddlers, and walkaway food merchants that is often a tourist attraction within a city's cultural and entertainment center. Also, called an *urban specialty center* or *festival marketplace*.

first-in-first-out (FIFO) an accounting concept that assumes that goods acquired at the beginning of a fiscal period are sold before goods purchased later in the fiscal period.

floor fixture a free-standing store fixture used on the selling floor to present merchandise.

floor-ready merchandise (FRM) merchandise ready for selling-floor presentation upon arrival at a retail distribution center.

forecasting an attempt to predict trends or outcomes.

forecasting service an organization that studies prevailing socioeconomic and market conditions to predict trends as far as two years in advance of a selling season.

4-5-4 calendar an accounting calendar used by most retailers to structure their fiscal year.

four-way a four-armed store fixture used primarily to present apparel.

franchise a contractual agreement giving a franchisee the right to sell a franchisor's product line or service, subject to standards established by the franchisor.

free-on-board (FOB) a transportation term followed by indications of the point to which a supplier pays transportation charges, and the point at which the title of the goods passes from the supplier to the retailer.

full-line discounter a discounter that offers a wide assortment of hardlines and softlines that includes private-label goods and lower-priced brands not offered at department stores. Also called a *general merchandise discounter*.

general manager a person with the ultimate responsibility for the merchandising and operation of a store.

general merchandise manager a person who manages a group of merchandise divisions.

geographic segmentation the identification of markets by geographic region of the country.

gross-margin-return-on-investment (GMROI) a measure of performance that combines gross margin and turnover.

gross sales   net sales plus customer returns.

group buying   pooling orders from many retailers to meet minimum order requirements or to take advantage of quantity discounts.

hardlines   nontextile products.

high fashion   apparel in the early stage of the fashion life cycle available through designers or exclusive stores.

impulse goods   unplanned purchases.

income statement   a statement of revenue, expenses, and profit for a specific period.

indirect competition   when stores offer the same merchandise categories but different prices and brands.

initial markup   the first markup added to the cost of merchandise to determine an original retail price.

initial public offering   the first offering of stock on a public exchange.

institutional advertising   image-oriented advertising that reinforces a store's position as a leader in value, service, fashion, selections, or prestige.

intermodal transportation   combining two or more modes of transportation.

internal buyout   the acquisition of an organization by its employees.

internal standard   a benchmark derived from information within an organization.

internal theft   shoplifting by employees.

inventory reconciliation   an attempt to resolve large discrepancies between book and physical inventories.

invoice   a vendor's itemized statement of the goods shipped, their unit and extended cost, and any additional charges for transportation and/or insurance.

joint venture   a foreign expansion strategy involving a partnership between a retailer and a foreign partner.

junk bonds   high-yield, high-risk commodities issued by retailers to finance acquisitions.

knockoff   a less-expensive imitation or copy of a successful branded product or product line.

landed cost   the actual cost of an import that includes expenses for overseas buying trips, packing, shipping, insurance, storage, duties, and commissionaires' and customs agents fees.

last-in-first-out (LIFO)   an accounting concept that assumes that goods acquired at the end of a fiscal period are sold before goods purchased earlier in the fiscal period.

lease department   a retailer that operates as a department within another retail store.

leveraged buyout   an acquisition financed through debt.

liabilities   debts owed by an organization.

licensing   an agreement that involves the use of a merchandising property in the design of a product or product line.

line function   an organization's mainstream activities.

lip table   a store fixture often used to "dump" clearance goods. Also called a *dump table*.

long-range plan   an organizational plan that covers a three-to-five-year period or longer.

loss leader   an item priced below cost to generate store traffic.

maintained markup   the difference between the cost of merchandise and the actual selling price.

major aisle   a main aisle that connects a store's extremes.

major showroom building   a building with showrooms for a particular merchandise category or group of related categories.

manufacturer uses labor and machinery to convert raw materials into finished products. Also called a *producer*.

manufacturer's outlet a discount store operated by a producer to unload overruns, irregulars, and slow-selling goods returned from department and specialty stores.

manufacturers' rep an independent sales agent who sells manufacturers' products within a defined geographic territory.

manufacturer-sponsored specialty store a store owned and operated by a manufacturer to sell its product line.

manufacturer's suggested retail price (MSRP) a retail price established by a producer.

markdown a downward price adjustment.

markdown cancellation a tactical markup.

market a place where buyers and sellers come together; a group of people with the desire and ability to buy.

market center a cluster of merchandise marts.

marketing channel the flow of goods from point of production to point of consumption. Also called the *distribution channel* or the *distribution pipeline*.

market segmentation the process of identifying niche markets undersatisfied or dissatisfied with current marketplace offerings.

markup the amount added to a wholesale cost to establish a retail price.

markup cancellation a tactical markdown.

mass fashion mass-produced fashions extensively distributed through multiple retail channels.

mass market a large group of customers with similar characteristics and wants.

matrix a corporately derived list of preferred merchandise resources.

megabrand a brand that encompasses several related merchandise categories.

memorandum goods goods not paid for by a retailer until they are sold, however, the title of the goods passes from the vendor to the retailer when the goods are shipped, and then to the consumer at the point of sale.

merchandising in the apparel industry, planning, developing, and presenting a product line suitable for a business's intended consumers; in a retail organization, all of the activities associated with buying, pricing, presenting, and promoting merchandise.

merchandise mart a building that houses an entire market under one roof to facilitate one-stop shopping for retail buyers.

merchant-wholesale distributor a marketing channel intermediary who buys goods from manufacturers and then resells them to retailers.

merger the combination of two or more companies to form a single organization.

minimum advertised price (MAP) the lowest advertised price allowed in a co-operative advertising agreement.

minimum order a dollar or unit amount that defines the smallest order that a vendor is willing to accept.

mixed-use center (MXD) a retail, office, parking, and hotel complex that sometimes includes a convention center and/or high rise condominium or apartment complex in one development.

moderate line an apparel line priced at the low end of a department store's selection.

neighborhood center a shopping center with approximately 30,000 to 150,000 square feet of retail space often with a supermarket or a large drug store as major tenants.

net income   the difference between an organization's revenue and expenses.

net payment date   the last day of the net payment period.

net payment period   the payment period that begins on the cash discount date and ends on the net payment date.

net sales   gross sales minus customer returns.

niche market   a small group of customers with characteristics that differ from the mass market.

off-pricer   a retailer that sells manufacturers' irregulars, seconds, closeouts, cancelled orders, and other retailers' end-of-season merchandise.

open-sell fixture   a store fixture that permits customers to make selections without the assistance of a salesperson.

open-to-buy   the difference between planned purchases and merchandise on-order.

open-to-ship   the number of units needed to meet a store's planned inventory projections.

organizational chart   a diagram that depicts a company's corporate structure and lines of reporting and responsibility. Also called a *table of organization*.

outlet center   a strip or enclosed shopping center with a tenant mix of factory outlet stores and off-pricers. Also called a *value-oriented center*.

out-of-home advertising   billboard and transit advertising.

overage   a discrepancy between a book and physical inventory where book is less than physical.

owners' equity   the difference between an organization's assets and liabilities.

party plan   a direct sales strategy that uses the home of a host/hostess to demonstrate a product line to a group of invited customers.

pedestrian mall   a shopping center with an open-air walkway between stores that is closed to vehicular traffic.

penetration   the measure of a single business unit as a percentage of all similar business units.

percentage-variation method   an inventory planning method that asserts that a beginning-of-month inventory should be a percentage of an average inventory.

perishable goods   merchandise with a limited shelf life or selling period.

permanent markdown   markdown that will not return to a higher price at a later date.

permanent signage   signs made of durable materials not intended for frequent change.

perpetual inventory   an inventory accounting system whereby the value of an inventory is maintained on a continual basis by adjusting a beginning physical inventory by purchases, sales, and price changes.

personal selling   one-to-one interaction with a customer.

physical inventory   counting and valuating inventory item by item.

planned purchases   the amount of goods needed to ensure that inventory levels are appropriate for planned sales.

plan-of-reorganization (POR)   a plan to reorganize a bankrupt organization so that it can become profitable.

planogram   a visual model of product arrangements.

planner   a person who projects sales and inventories based on an analysis of sales history, current market trends and an organization's performance objectives.

platform   a store fixture used for stacking large packaged goods.

point-of-sale (POS) system   a network of computerized cash registers linked to a central processing point called a back-office.

power center a shopping center with a tenant mix composed of big box discounters, such as category killers, warehouse clubs, off-pricers, full-line discounters, and supercenters.

predatory pricing a low-price strategy designed to put competitors out of business.

premium a product offered to customers without charge or at a very low retail price tied to a purchase within a product line.

preticketed merchandise goods ticketed by a supplier.

price-agreement plan a type of decentralized buying whereby a central buyer provides stores with a list of preferred merchandise resources from which stores directly order goods.

price lookup (PLU) a system file of stock-keeping units and prices that "looks up" a price at point-of-sale when a bar code or sku number is entered into a POS terminal.

private buying office a buying office owned and operated by a single retail organization as an extension of its corporate merchandising function.

private carrier refers to an organization's internal fleet of trucks used to transport goods.

private company an organization whose stock is not traded on a public exchange.

private-label merchandise - goods that bear the name of a store, or a name used exclusively by a store, that are produced for the store's exclusive distribution.

product developer a person who establishes specifications for the design, production, and packaging of a retailer's private-label goods and then contacts producers to manufacture the goods according to these specifications.

productivity the number of units of output reduced per unit of imput.

promotional markdown a price reduction on merchandise featured in promotional events, commonly called *sales*.

prototype a model store that incorporates an organization's standards for operational efficiency, merchandise presentation, and customer service.

prox dating specifies the day of the following month by which a cash discount must be taken. Also called *proximo dating*.

psychographic segmentation identifying markets by lifestyles, values, and attitudes.

public company an organization whose stock is available to the general public and is sold or traded on a public stock exchange.

publicity "free advertising" through a mass medium in the form of news coverage.

pull strategy producer-sponsored advertising that stimulates consumer demand for a product.

purchase order a contractual sales agreement between a retailer and a supplier in which items of merchandise, prices, delivery dates, and payment terms are specified.

qualitative control a descriptive measure of performance.

quantitative control a numeric measure of performance.

quantity discount a reduction in cost based on the amount of merchandise purchased.

quota a restriction placed on the amount of merchandise that may be imported from a country within a time period.

raincheck allows a customer to buy advertised promotional merchandise at a later date at the sale price.

receipt-of-goods (ROG) dating delays the beginning of payment and discount periods until the invoiced goods have been received.

regional center a shopping center with approximately 400,000-800,000 square feet of retail space with two or more department stores as major tenants.

regional manager a person who supervises a group of district managers.

regular dating assumes that the date of invoice is the first day of the payment period. Also referred to as *ordinary dating*.

regular price an original price.

relationship marketing the use of customer-purchase histories to anticipate future customer needs and to establish on-going, one-on-one customer relationships.

reporting service an organization that surveys and analyzes specific industry segments, reporting their findings to service subscribers.

resale price maintenance (RPM) a practice whereby a producer enforces the sale of its product line at manufacturer's suggested retail prices (MSRP).

resident buying office a marketing and research consultant that provides market information, merchandise guidance, and other services to a group of member or client stores.

retailer sells products and/or services to final consumers.

retail price wholesale cost plus markup.

return-to-vendor (RTV) a damaged or slow-selling item returned to a supplier.

rounder a circular store fixture for hanging goods.

salaried buying office a buying office owned and operated independently of its member stores, also called a *fee office*.

sales-per-square-foot a measure of productivity that reflects the amount of sales generated relative to the amount of retail space dedicated to sale of the goods.

sales promotion activities that induce customer traffic and sales by communicating information pertaining to a store's assortments, prices, services and other sales incentives.

seasonal discount a reduction in the cost of merchandise for orders placed in advance of the normal ordering period.

seasonal markdowns price reductions on goods remaining in stock at the end of a selling season.

seasonal merchandise goods in demand only at certain times of the year.

secondary business district (SBD) a subshopping district in an outlying area of a city.

shopping center a commercial complex with on-site parking that is developed, owned, and managed as a unit.

shortage a discrepancy between a book and a physical inventory where book is greater than physical.

short-term plan an organizational plan that covers a period shorter than a year.

showroom a setting where manufacturers, manufacturers' reps, wholesalers, or domestic or foreign importers present their product lines to prospective retail buyers.

softlines textile products.

space management the strategic arrangements of products to maximize sales with a minimum investment of space and fixtures.

special events promotional attractions intended to create an exciting shopping atmosphere in a store.

special order an order placed for an individual customer.

specialty store a retailer that caters to the needs of a narrowly defined group of consumers with a single or limited number of product categories.

spring on the 4-5-4 calendar, the season that begins in February and ends in July.

staff function an advisory function that supports an organization's line functions and other staff functions.

stock-keeping unit (sku) a unique item in an assortment distinguished from other items by characteristics such as brand, style, color, or size.

stock-to-sales ratio the proportionate relationship between a BOM and planned sales.

stock-to-sales-ratio method an inventory planning method that uses desired stock-to-sales ratios to plan beginning-of-month inventories.

store image the way that a store is perceived by the public. A store's image positions the store in the marketplace, distinguishing it from its competitors.

store-level merchandise manager a person responsible for the merchandising activities of a store.

store operations the retail organizational function responsible for merchandising and operating stores. Also called *store administration* or *store line*.

strip center a linear arrangement of stores connected by an open-air canopy, with off-street parking in front of the stores.

style refers to an item's distinctive characteristics or design features.

subclass a subdivision of a merchandise classification.

subsidiary an operating division within a conglomerate.

supercenter a combined supermarket and full-line discount store, also called a *combination store*.

superregional center a shopping center with more than 800,000 square feet of retail space and three or more department stores as major tenants.

syndicated buying office a buying office owned and operated by a retail conglomerate.

tactical price change a strategic markup or markdown that falls within a retail price zone defined at one end by a price with a standard markup, and at the other end by a price with an inflated markup.

tariff a duty levied by the U.S. government to restrict foreign competition.

temporary markdown a markdown that will return to a higher retail price at a later date.

temporary signage signs made of disposable materials intended for frequent change.

tiered table a store fixture for stacking nonhanging goods, commonly referred to as a *Gap table*.

time-series comparison a comparison of income statement components of two or more time periods.

top-down plan a plan that originates at the top of an organization.

top management functions that appear at the top of a table of organization.

top-of-counter fixture a store fixture for displaying goods on a countertop.

trade association an organization that represents the interests of a particular segment of industry supported by dues-paying members.

trade publication a publication for members of a specific segment of industry.

trade show a group of temporary exhibits of vendors' offerings for a single merchandise category or group of related categories.

trend implies the direction or movement of a fashion.

trend setter a person who adopts a fashion at its introduction, also called a *fashion leader*.

trickle-across theory   proposes the existence of a horizontal adoption process across all socioeconomic groups. Also called the *diffusion theory*.

trickle-down theory   proposes that the origins of fashion can be traced to upper socioeconomic classes and that lower socioeconomic classes imitate the fashions of the wealthy.

trickle-up theory   proposes that fashions float up from lower socioeconomic groups to higher socioeconomic groups. Also called the *status float phenomenon*.

T-stand   a two-armed store fixture primarily used to present apparel.

turnover   the number of times an average inventory is sold within a time period. Also called *stockturn*.

variety store   a disappearing retail format commonly called a *5&10* or *dime store*.

vendor fixture   a fixture supplied by a vendor to distinguish its products from the competition and to ensure consistent presentation in stores.

vendor partnership   a collaboration between a retailer and a supplier that results in greater channel efficiency and better service to consumers.

vertical integration   when an organization performs more than one marketing channel function.

visual merchandising   a retail organizational function responsible for store decor, signage, display, fixturing, and standards for presenting merchandise.

warehouse and requisition plan   a type of decentralized buying whereby a central buyer determines the assortments carried in stores, however, store-level merchandisers choose specific quantities by size, color, and style.

warehouse club   a discounter that sells a limited number of deep-discounted food and general merchandise items in a warehouse setting.

week's supply method   an inventory planning method that asserts that the amount of inventory required to support planned sales for a week is based on the number of weeks that an inventory will last relative to a desired turnover and planned sales.

workroom cost   a labor cost associated with altering, assembling, or repairing merchandise to make it ready for sale.

COMPANY INDEX

SUBJECT INDEX

In addition to the references below, definitions of specific terms can be found in the glossary, pp. 449-460.

465